This item is due for return on

11 1/96

Introduction to Business Law

P W D Redmond LLM
Barrister, formerly Senior Lecturer
in Commercial Law, City of London Polytechnic

Revised by
R G Lawson PhD
Consultant, formerly Senior Lecturer
in Law, University of Southampton

Seventh Edition

THE M & E HANDBOOK SERIES

*To Pauline, Graham, Kirsty
and Catherine, with thanks*

Pitman Publishing
128 Long Acre, London WC2E 9AN

A Division of Pearson Professional Limited

First published as *Mercantile Law* 1964
Second edition 1968
Third edition 1972
Fourth edition 1974
Fifth edition 1979
Sixth edition published as *Introduction to Business Law* 1990
Seventh edition 1993
Reprinted 1995

© Macdonald & Evans Ltd 1964, 1968, 1972, 1979
© Longman Group UK Ltd 1990, 1993

British Library Cataloguing in Publication Data
A CIP catalogue record for this book can be obtained from the British Library

ISBN 0 7121 1045 3

Founding Editor: P. W. D. Redmond

Typeset by FDS Ltd, Penarth.
Printed and bound in Singapore

Contents

Preface ix
Table of cases x
Table of statutes xxii

Part one: The law of contracts

1 **Nature and classification of contracts** 3
Nature of contracts; Classification of contracts; Void,
voidable, and unenforceable contracts; Quasi-contracts

2 **Formation of contracts** 12
Rules governing offers; Rules governing acceptance;
Standard form contracts; Exemption clauses; Certainty of
terms; Terms of a contract; Conflict of laws

3 **Form, consideration and capacity** 32
Formal requirements; Valuable consideration; Rules
relating to consideration; Contractual capacity; Capacity of
minors

4 **Void, voidable and illegal contracts** 46
Mistake; Misrepresentation and fraud; Duress and undue
influence; Illegality; Contracts subject to a disability;
Contracts illegal at common law; Contracts in restraint of
trade

5 **Discharge of contracts 72**
Discharge by performance; Discharge by agreement;
Discharge by operation of law; Frustration of contracts;
Breach of contract and remedies

6 **Privity, assignment and negotiability 90**
Privity of contract; Transfer and assignment of contracts

Part two: Agency and partnership

7 **Agency 107**
Formation of agency; Termination of agency; Duties of
principal and agent; The authority of the agent; Special
classes of agent

8 **Partnerships 125**
Nature and formation of partnerships; Dealings with
outsiders; Rights and duties of partners; Dissolution of
partnership; Limited partnerships

Part three: Mercantile agreements

9 **Sale of goods, supply of goods and services, hire and
hire-purchase 149**
The contract for the sale of goods; Terms implied by the
Sale of Goods Act 1979; Passing of ownership and risk;
Nemo dat quod non habet; Performance of the contract; Rights
of an unpaid seller against the goods; Actions for breach of
contract; Auction sales; Contracts for the supply of goods
and services; Contracts of hire, hire-purchase and
conditional sale

10 **Carriage of goods 187**
Common carriers; Carriage by land; Carriage by air;
Carriage by sea; Bills of lading; Charterparties

11 **Insurance 203**
Nature of insurance; Life insurance; Fire insurance;
Accident, burglary and other forms of insurance; Marine
insurance; State supervision

12 **Bailment 218**
Nature and kinds of bailment

13 **Arbitration and awards 226**
Arbitration; Conduct of proceedings

Part four: Negotiable instruments

14 **Negotiable instruments 245**
Negotiability; Bills of exchange; Signature, delivery and
indorsement; Liability of parties; Acceptance, payment and
dishonour; Cheques; Promissory notes and miscellaneous
instruments

Part five: Securities

15 **Securities 291**
Summary of property law; Securities generally; Pledges and
mortgages of personalty; Liens

16 **Guarantees and indemnities 302**
Nature of guarantee; Position of the guarantor; Discharge
of guarantor

Part six: Consumer protection and competition law

17 **Consumer protection and fair trading 319**
Trade Descriptions Act 1968; Trading Stamps Act 1964;
Fair Trading Act 1973; Estate Agents Act 1979; Consumer
Credit Act 1974; Consumer Protection Act 1987; Food
Safety Act 1990; Miscellaneous matters

18 Competition law 342
Restrictive Trade Practices Act 1976; Treaty of Rome;
Resale Prices Act 1976; Competition Act 1980; The
Monopolies and Mergers Commission

Part seven: Bankruptcy

19 Bankruptcy 359
Commencement of proceedings; Proceedings after
receiving order; The trustee in bankruptcy; Miscellaneous
matters

Appendix: 374
Examination technique

Index 379

Preface

Since the previous edition of *Introduction to Business Law*, the main thrust for the changes and alterations contained in this seventh edition have come from the courts rather than from Parliament. However, two minor, but still commendable enactments were adopted in the later stages of writing — namely the Cheques Act 1992, and the Timeshare Act 1992 — both of which are dealt with herein. More to the point, the chance has been taken to rewrite and represent the law affecting consumer protection, fair trading and competition. This last, with an eye to the growing importance of EC law, has been written to include the more immediately relevant parts of the Treaty of Rome. I have, I hope, remained true to the ideals of the *Handbooks* and presented the law in a way which is simple, accurate and easy to grasp.

R. G. Lawson
May 1992

Table of cases

Akerheim v. De Mare [1959]
A.C. 789; [1959] 3 All ER 485 56
Al Taha, The, *Financial Times*, 9 March
1990 200
Alexander v. Railway Executive [1951]
2 K.B. 882; [1951] 2 All ER 442
219, 220, 222
Alexander v. Rayson [1936] 1 K.B. 169
22, 62, 66
Allcard v. Skinner [1887] 36 Ch. D. 145
60
Aluminium Industrie BV v. Romalpa
Aluminium Ltd [1976] 1 W.L.R. 676
168
Amalgamated Investment and Property
Co. Ltd v. Walker (John) & Sons Ltd
[1977] 1 W.L.R. 164; [1976] 3 All ER
509 *46, 81*
Amber Size & Chemical Co. v. Menzel
[1913] 2 Ch. 239 *68*
Andrabell, *Re* [1984] 3 All ER 407 *168*
Andrews v. Hopkinson [1957] 1 Q.B.
229; [1956] 3 All ER 422 *29, 180*
Anglia Television v. Reed [1972] 1 Q.B.
60; [1971] 3 All ER 690 *85*
Applegate v. Moss [1971] 1 Q.B. 406
[1971] 1 All ER 747 *78*
Appleson v. Littlewoods Ltd. [1939] 1
All ER 464 *4*
Arenson v. Casson Beckman [1977]
A.C. 405; [1975] 3 All ER 901 *231*
Armstrong v. Jackson [1917] 2 K.B. 822
113
Ascherson v. Tredegar Dry Dock Co.
[1909] 2 Ch. 401; [1908] 2 All ER
510 *307*
Ashbury Carriage Co. v. Riche (1875)
L.R. 7 H.L. 653 *43*

Ashington Piggeries Ltd v. Christopher
Hill Ltd [1972] *154*
Associated Japanese Bank
(International) Ltd v. Credit du
Nord SA [1988] 3 All ER 902 *48*
Astley Industrial Trust v. Miller [1968]
2 All ER 36 *119*
Attorney General of Australia v.
Adelaide SS. Co. (1913) 15 C.L.R. 65
67
Attwood v. Lamont [1920] 3 K.B. 571
70
Attwood v. Maude (1868) 3 Ch. 369
135
Avery v. Bowden (1856) 5 E. & B. 714
79, 80, 83
Avon County Council v. Howlett [1983]
1 All ER 1073 *10*

Bainbridge v. Firmstone (1838) 8 A. &
E. 743 *37*
Balfour v. Balfour [1919] 2 K.B. 571;
[1918–1919] All ER 860 *3, 13*
Ballett v. Mingay [1943] 1 K.B. 281;
[1943] 1 All ER 143 *45*
Banbury v. Bank of Montreal [1917]
1 K.B. 409 *119*
Bank of England v. Vagliano Bros.
[1891] A.C. 107 *250, 261*
Bank of Nova Scotia v. Hellenic Mutual
[1991] 3 All ER 1 *213*
Bank of Scotland v. Wright, *Financial
Times*, 7 August 1990 *308*
Banque Financière v. Westgate
Insurance, *Financial Times*, 12
August 1988 *54, 57*
Barber v. Co-operative Wholesale Shop
[1983] Crim LR 476 *333*

Baytur SA v. Finagro Holdings SA [1991] 4 All ER 129 *229*

Behn v. Burness (1863) 3 B. & S. 751 *25, 200*

Belfast Ropework Co. Ltd v. Bushell [1918] 1 K.B. 210 *188*

Bell v. Lever Bros. [1932] A.C. 161 *48*

Ben Line Steamers v. Pacific Steam Navigation Co. [1989] 2 Lloyd's Rep 51 *200*

Benton v. Campbell, Parker & Co. Ltd [1925] 2 K.B. 410 *174*

Beresford v. Royal Insurance Co. [1938] A.C. 586 *206*

Bernstein v. Pamson Motors [1987] 2 All ER 220 *156, 165*

Berry v. Berry [1929] 2 K.B. 316 *76*

Beswick v. Beswick [1968] A.C. 58; [1967] 2 All ER 1197 *91, 92*

Bettini v. Gye (1876) 1 Q.B.D. 183 *26*

Bigg v. Boyd Gibbons Ltd [1971] 1 W.L.R. 913; [1971] 2 All ER 183 *14*

Birkham v. Drake (1841) 8 M. & W. 846 *129*

Birkmyr v. Darnell (1704) 1 Salk. 27 *305*

Blackpool and Fylde Aero Club Ltd v. Blackpool BC [1990] 3 All ER 25 *18*

Blisset v. Daniels (1853) 10 Hare 493 *132*

Bolton v. Mahadeva [1972] 1 W.L.R. 1009; [1972] 2 All ER 1322 *73*

Bolton Partners v. Lambert (1889) 41 Ch. D. 295 *110*

Bond v. Gibson (1808) 170 ER 923 *128*

Bond Worth, *Re* [1980] Ch. 228 *168*

Boorne v. Wicker [1927] 1 Ch. 667 *138*

Boots v. Garrett, *The Times*, 16 July 1980, *321*

Borden (UK) Ltd v. Scottish Timber Products [1981] Ch 25 *168*

Boulton v. Jones (1857) 2 H. & N. 564 *12*

Bourgeois v. Weddell & Co. [1924] 1 K.B. 539 *228*

Brace v. Calder [1895] 2 Q.B. 253 *84*

Bradbury v. Morgan (1862) 1 H. & C. 249 *14*

Bradford Old Bank v. Sutcliffe [1918] 2 K.B. 833 *312*

Braithwaite v. Thomas Cook Ltd. [1989] 1 All ER 235 *276*

Brandao v. Barnett (1846) 3 C.B. 519 *301*

Brewster v. Drennan [1945] 2 All ER 705 *223*

Brinkibon v. Stahag Stahl & Stahlwarenhandelsgesellschaft [1983] 2 A.C. 34 *17*

British Concrete Co. v. Schelff [1921] 2 Ch. 563; [1921] All ER 696 *71*

British Movietonews Ltd v. London, etc., Cinemas Ltd [1952] A.C. 166; [1951] 2 All ER 617 *81*

British Westinghouse Electric & Manufacturing Co. Ltd v. Underground Electric Rail Co. Ltd [1912] A.C. 673. *84*

Brown v. Raphael [1958] Ch. 636; [1958] 2 All ER 79 *53*

Brown & Davis Ltd v. Galbraith [1972] 1 W.L.R. 997; [1972] 3 All ER 31 *27*

Browne v. Brandt [1902] 1 K.B. 696 *223*

Buckpitt v. Oates [1968] 1 All ER 1145 *5*

Burchell v. Wilde [1900] 1 Ch. 551 *138*

Burge v. Ashley & Smith Ltd. [1900] 1 Q.B. 744 *64*

Burnett v. Westminster Bank Ltd [1966] 1 Q.B. 742; [1965] 3 All ER 81 *274*

Bute (Marquess) v. Barclays Bank [1955] 1 Q.B. 202; [1954] 3 All ER 365 *274*

Byrne v. Van Tienhoven (1880) 5 C.P.D. 344 *15*

Campbell v. Edwards [1976] 1 W.L.R.
403: [1976] 1 All ER 785 *231*
Candler v. Crane Christmas [1951] 2
K.B. 164; [1951] 1 All ER 426 *53*
Car & Universal Finance Co. v. Caldwell
(1965) 1 Q.B. 525; [1964] 1 All ER
290 *162*
Carlill v. Carbolic Smoke Ball Co.
[1893] 1 Q.B. 256 *13, 16, 17*
Carter (John) Ltd v. Hanson (H)
Haulage (Leeds) Ltd [1965] 2 Q.B.
495; [1965] 1 All ER 113 *190*
Cassis de Dijon [1979] 3 CMLR 498
347
Castellain v. Preston (1883) 11 Q.B.D.
380 *209*
Cavalier Insurance Co., *Re, The Times*,
31 May 1989 *203*
Cehave N.V. v. Bremer [1976] Q.B. 44;
[1975] 3 All ER 739 *83, 152*
Central Asbestos Co. Ltd. v. Dodds
[1973] A.C. 578; [1972] 2 All ER
1135 *78*
Central London Property Trust v. High
Trees, etc. [1947] K.B. 130; [1946]
1 All ER 256 *41, 74*
Central Newbury Car Auctions v. Unity
Finance [1957] 1 Q.B. 371; [1956]
3 All ER 905 *163*
Cerium Investments v. Evans, *The
Times*, 14 February 1991 *308*
Chandler v. Webster [1904] 1 K.B. 493
81
Chapelton v. Barry U.D.C. [1940]
1 K.B. 532 *19, 20*
Chapman v. Oakleigh Animal Products
Ltd (1970) 114 S.J. 432 *115*
Chappell v. Poles (1837) 2 M. & W. 867
8, 61
Chapple v. Cooper (1844) 13 M & W
252 *44*
Charge Card Services, *Re* [1988] 3 All
ER 702 *75, 167*
Charnock v. Liverpool Corporation
[1968] 1 W.L.R. 1498; [1968] 3 All
ER 473 *27*
Charrington Fuel Oil v. Parvant, *The
Times*, 28 December 1988 *123*

Chaudhry v. Prabhakar [1988] 3 All
ER 718 *112*
Chelmsford Auctions Ltd. v. Poole
[1973] 1 Q.B. 542; [1973] 1 All ER
810 *107*
Chesworth v. Farrar [1967] 1 Q.B. 407;
[1966] 2 All ER 107 *219*
China and South Sea Bank Ltd v. Tan
[1989] 3 All ER 839 *307*
Chloride Batteries v. Faw Freight
[1989] 3 All ER 86 *193*
Christoforides v. Terry [1924] A.C. 566
114
Churton v. Douglas (1859) Joh. 174
143
Citybank NA v. Brown Shipley [1991] 2
All ER 690 *49*
City Centre Properties Ltd v. Tersons
Ltd [1969] 1 W.L.R. 772; [1969] 2
All ER 1121 *230*
Clayton's Case (1816) 1 Mer. 572
75, 302
Clifford Davis Management v. WEA
Records [1975] 1 All ER 237 *22*
Clough Mill v. Martin [1985] 1 W.L.R
111; [1984] 3 All ER 982 *168*
Clutton v. Attenborough [1897] A.C. 90
261
Cohen v. Roche [1927] 1 K.B. 169 *173*
Coldman v. Hill [1919] 1 K.B. 443 *219*
Coldunell v. Gallon [1986] Q.B. 1184
60
Coliseum (Barrow) Ltd, *Re* [1930] 2 Ch.
44 *78*
Collen v. Wright (1857) 8 E. & B. 647
116, 324
Colley v. Overseas Exporters [1921]
A.ER 596 *166*
Combe v. Combe [1951] 2 K.B. 215;
[1951] 11 All ER 767 *41*
Comdel Commodities Ltd v. Siporex
Trade SA [1990] 2 All ER 552
233
Commissioners of Taxation v. English,
Scottish & Australian Bank Ltd
[1920] A.C. 683 *273*
Consolidated Tea & Lands Co v.Oliver's
Wharf [1910] 2 K.B. 395 *187*

Cooper *v.* Phibbs (1867) L.R. 2 H.L. 149 *47*

Couchman *v.* Hill [1947] K.B. 554; [1947] 1 All ER 103 *323*

Coughlin *v.* Gillison [1899] 1 Q.B. 145 *222*

Courtney *v.* Tolaini [1975] 1 W.L.R. 297; [1975] 1 All ER 716 *23*

Couturier *v.* Hastie (1856) 5 H.L.C. 673 *48, 159*

Cowern & Nield [1912] K.B. 419 *46*

Craddock Bros. *v.* Hunt [1923] 2 Ch. 136 *52*

Craig, *Re* [1971] Ch. 95; [1970] 2 All ER 390 *60*

Craven-Ellis *v.* Canons Ltd [1936] 2 K.B. 403 *86*

Cricklewood Property Co. *v.* Leighton's Investment Trust [1945] A.C. 221 *79*

Cullinane *v.* British 'Rema' Mfg. Co. [1954] 1 Q.B. 292; [1953] 2 All ER 1257 *85*

Cummings *v.* Ince (1847) 11 Q.B. 112 *58*

Currie *v.* Misa (1875) L.R. 10 Ex. 153 *36*

Curtis *v.* Chemical Cleaning & Dyeing Co. Ltd. [1951] 1 K.B. 805; [1951] 1 All ER 631 *19, 221*

Cutter *v.* Powell (1795) 6 Term. Rep. 320 *72*

Czarnikov *v.* Roth, Schmidt & Co. [1922] 2 K.B. 478 *232*

D. & C. Builders Ltd *v.* Rees [1966] 2 Q.B. 617; [1965] 3 All ER 837 *40*

Daily Office Cleaning Contractors Ltd *v.* Shefford [1977] R.T.R. 361 *85*

Dakin *v.* Lee [1916] 1 K.B. 566 *87*

Daulia Ltd *v.* Four Millbank Nominees (1978) 2 W.L.R. 621 *16*

David & Mathews, *Re* [1899] 1 Ch. 378 *137*

Davies *v.* Collins [1945] 1 All ER 247 *221*

Davies & Co. *v.* William Old (1969) 113 S.T. 262 *14*

Davis (Clifford) Management *v.* W.E.A. Records Ltd. [1975] 1 W.L.R. 61; [1975] 1 All ER 237 *22*

Davis Contractors Ltd *v.* Fareham U.D.C. [1956] A.C. 696; [1956] 2 All ER 145 *80*

Davitt *v.* Titcumb [1989] 3 All ER 417 *207*

Debtor, *Re* a. [1991] 3 WLR 578 *303*

De Bussche *v.* Alt (1878) 8 Ch. D. 286 *112*

De Mattos *v.* Benjamin (1894) 63 L.J.Q.B. *65*

Dearle *v.* Hall (1828) 3 Russ 1 *94, 245*

Decouvreur *v.* Jordan, *The Times*, 25 May 1987 *34*

Derry *v.* Peek (1889) 14 App. Cas. 337 *55*

Deutsche Bank *v.* Ibrahim, *Financial Times*, 12 December 1991 *303*

Dickinson *v.* Dodds (1876) 2 Ch. D. 463 *15*

Discount Kitchens *v.* Crawford, *The Times*, 5 December 1988 *116*

Dodson *v.* Downey [1901] 2 Ch. 620 *133*

Donovan *v.* Gwentoys [1990] 1 All ER 1018 *78*

Dore *v.* Wilkinson (1817) 171 ER 648 *128*

Doyle *v.* Olby [1969] 2 QB 158 *56*

Dunlop Pneumatic Tyre Co. *v.* New Garage Co. [1915] A.C. 79 *85*

Dunlop Pneumatic Tyre Co. *v.* Selfridges Ltd. [1915] A.V. 847 *38*

Eaglehill Ltd *v.* Neeham Builders Ltd [1973] A.C. 992; [1972] 1 All ER 895 *267*

East *v.* Maurer [1991] 2 All ER 733 *56*

Eastwood *v.* Kenyon (1840) 11 A. & E. 438 *34*

Eccles *v.* Bryant [1948] Ch. 93; [1947] 2 All ER 865 *16*

Edmunds *v.* Wallingford (1885) 14 Q.B.D. 811 *9*

xiv *Table of cases*

El Awadi v. BCCI [1989] 1 All ER 242 *276*

Elder Dempster v. Zochonis & Co. [1924] A.C. 522 *194*

Eliason v. Henshaw (1819) 1 Wheaton 225 *14, 16*

Elpis Maritime Co. Ltd v. Marti Chartering Co. Inc. [1991] 3 All ER 758 *34, 303*

English v. Dedham Vale Properties Ltd (1978) 1 W.L.R. 93 *113*

Entores v. Miles Far East Corpn. [1955] 2 Q.B. 327; [1955] 2 All ER 493 *17*

Esso Petroleum Co. v. Commissioners of Customs and Excise [1976] 1 W.L.R. 1; [1976] 1 All ER 117 *13*

Evans v. Merzario [1976] 1 W.L.R. 1078; [1976] 2 All ER 930 *19, 29*

Faccenda Chicken Ltd v. Fowler [1986] 3 WLR 288 *68*

Falkingham v. Victoria Rly. Commissioners [1900] A.C. 452 *232*

Felthouse v. Bindley (1862) 6 L.T. 157 *16*

Fibrosa Case [1943] A.C. 32 *81*

First National Bank v. Syed [1991] 2 All ER 250 *183*

Fisher v. Bell [1961] 1 Q.B. 394; [1960] 3 All ER 731 *13*

Fisher & Sons, Re [1912] 2 K.B. 491 *127*

Fitch v. Dewes [1921] 2 A.C. 158 *69, 70*

Foakes v. Beer (1884) 9 App. Cas 605 *74, 76*

Foley v. Classique Coaches Ltd. [1934] 2 K.B. 1 *24*

Footman Bower & Co. Ltd., Re [1961] Ch. 443; [1961] 2 All ER 161 *79*

Foster v. Driscoll [1929] 1 K.B. 470 *66*

Foster v. Mackinnon (1869) L.R. 4 C.P. 704 *19, 50*

Frost v. Aylesbury Dairies Ltd. [1905] 1 K.B. 608; [1904–1907] All ER 132 *157*

Gadd v. Houghton (1876) 1 Ex. D. 357 *117*

Garner v. Murray [1904] 1 Ch. 57 *137*

Garnham, Harris & Elton Ltd. v. Ellis (Alfred W.) Transport Ltd [1967] 1 W.L.R. 940; [1967] 2 All ER 940 *189*

Geier v. Kujawa [1970] 1 Lloyd's Rep. 364 *20*

General Billposting Co. v. Atkinson [1909] A.C. 118 *68*

Geogas SA v. Trammo Gas Ltd [1991] 2 All ER 110; [1991] 3 All ER 554 *232*

Gibson v. Manchester City Council [1979] 1 All ER 972 *12*

Goode v. Harrison [1871] 1861–73 All ER (Reprint) 813 *130*

Goodyear Tyre & Rubber Co. Ltd. v. Lancashire Batteries Ltd. [1958] 1 W.L.R. 857; [1958] 3 All ER 7 *91*

Griffiths v. Arch Engineering [1968] 3 All ER 217 *220*

Grist v. Bailey [1967] Ch. 532; [1966] 2 All ER 875 *52*

Guthing v. Lynn (1831) 2 B. & Ad. 232 *13*

Hadley v. Baxendale (1854) 9 Ex. 341 *83, 84, 189*

Haigh v. Brooks (1839) 10 A. & E. 309 *39*

Halfdan Grieg & Co. AS v. Sterling Coal & Navigation Corp. [1973] Q.B. 843; [1973] 2 All ER 1073 *232*

Hampstead Guardians v. Barclays Bank (1923) 39 T.L.R. 229 *273*

Harbutt's Plasticine Ltd. v. Wayne Tank and Pump Co. Ltd. [1970] 1 Q.B. 447; [1970] 1 All ER 225 *22*

Harlington & Leinster Enterprises Ltd v. Christopher Hull Fine Arts Ltd [1990] 1 All ER 737 *155*

Harris v. Nickerson (1873) L.R. 8 Q.B. 286 *14*

Hartley v. Birmingham City DC [1992] 2 All ER 213 *78*

Harvey *v.* Facey [1893] A.C. 552 *14*

Hayes *v.* Charles Dodd [1990] 2 All ER 815 *85*

Heald *v.* Kenworthy (1855) 10 Ex. 739 *118*

Hedley Byrne & Co. *v.* Heller [1964] A.C. 465; [1963] 2 All ER 575 *53, 56*

Helby *v.* Matthews [1895] A.C. 471 *222*

Helstan Securities Ltd. *v.* Hertfordshire County Council [1978] 3 All ER 262 *92*

Hendon *v.* Adelman, *The Times,* June 16, 1973 *246*

Hendy Lennox (Industrial Engines) Ltd *v.* Puttick Ltd [1984] 2 All ER 152 *168*

Herman *v.* Jeuchner (1885) 15 Q.B.D. 561 *66*

Hermann *v.* Charlesworth [1905] 2 K.B. 123 *66*

Herne Bay S.S. Co. *v.* Hutton [1903] 2 K.B. 603 *80*

Hibernian Bank *v.* Gysin & Hanson [1939] 1 K.B. 483 *253*

Hill *v.* Hill (William) Ltd [1949] A.C. 530; [1949] 2 All ER 452 *64*

Hiscox *v.* Outhwaite (No. 1) [1991] 3 All ER 641 *227*

Hitchman *v.* CBS Services, *The Times,* 10 June 1983 *132*

Hochster *v.* De La Tour (1853) 2 E. & B. 678 *82*

Hodgson *v.* Marks [1971] Ch. 892; [1971] 2 All ER 684 *60*

Hoenig *v.* Isaacs [1952] 2 All ER 176 *73*

Hollingworth *v.* Southern Ferries [1977] 2 Lloyd's Rep. 70 *20*

Holmes *v.* Bangladesh Biman Corp. [1989] 1 All ER 852 *194*

Holwell Securities *v.* Hughes [1974] 1 W.L.R. 155; [1974] 1 All ER 161 *17*

Home Counties Dairies Ltd. *v.* Skilton [1970] 1 W.L.R. 526; [1970] 1 All ER 1227 *70*

Home Insurance *v.* Mentor Insurance [1989] 3 All E 74 *227, 228*

Hong Kong Fir Shipping Co. Ltd. *v.* Kawasaki Kishen Kaisha Ltd [1962] 2 Q.B. 26; [1962] 1 All ER 474 *83*

Horn *v.* Minister of Food [1948] 2 All ER 1036 *160*

Horsfall *v.* Thomas (1862) 1 H. & C. 90 *53*

Houghland *v.* Low (R.R.) (Luxury Coaches) Ltd [1962] 1 Q.B. 694; [1962] 2 All ER 159 *218, 219*

Household Fire Insurance Co. *v.* Grant (1879) 4 Ex. D. 216 *17*

Howard *v.* Shirlstar Container Transport Ltd [1990] 3 All ER 366 *60*

Howard Marine *v.* Ogden (1978) 2 W.L.R. 515 *55*

Howatson *v.* Webb [1907] 1 Ch. 537 *51*

Hudgell Yeates & Co. *v.* Watson (1978) 2 W.L.R. 661 *134*

Hyde *v.* Wrench (1840) 3 Beav. 334 *16*

Imperial Loan Co. *v.* Stone [1892] 1 Q.B. 599 *42*

Inche Noriah *v.* Shaik Allie Bin Omar [1929] A.C. 127 *60*

Ingram *v.* Little [1961] 1 Q.B. 31; [1960] All ER 332 *50*

Interfoto Picture Library *v.* Stiletto Visual Programmes [1988] 1 All ER 348 *20*

Ipswich BC *v.* Fisons plc [1990] 1 All ER 730 *235*

Iqbal *v.* London Transport Executive [1973] 16 KIR 329 *115*

Iron Trade Mutual Insurance Co. Ltd *v.* JK Buckenham [1990] 1 All ER 808 *78*

Jackson *v.* Horizon Holidays [1975] 1 W.L.R. 1468; [1975] 3 All ER 92 *91*

James, *Ex p.* [1874] L.R. 9 Ch. 609 *10*

Joachimsson v. Swiss Bank Corporation [1921] 3 K.B. 110 *119*

Jobson v. Johnson [1989] 1 All ER 621 *86*

Johnson v. Agnew [1980] A.C. 367; [1979] 1 All ER 883 *88*

Jones (R.E.) Ltd v. Waring & Gillow Ltd [1926] A.C. 670 *263*

Karsales Ltd v. Wallis [1956] 1 W.L.R. 936; [1956] 2 All ER 866 *323*

Keever, *Re* [1967] Ch 182; [1966] 3 All ER 631 *275*

Keighley Maxsted v. Durant [1901] A.C. 240 *109*

Kelner v. Baxter (1886) L.R. 2. C.P. 174 *109*

Kemble v. Farren (1829) 6 Bing. 141 *86*

Kendall v. Hamilton (1879) 4 App. Cas. 504 *128, 130, 306*

Kennedy v. Thomassen (1929) 1 Ch. 426 *14*

Keppel v. Wheeler [1927] 1 K.B. 577 *112*

Kier v. Whitehead Iron Co. [1938] 1 All ER 591 *18*

King v. Thomas McKenna Ltd [1991] 1 All ER 653 *253*

Kleinwort Benson Ltd v. Malaysia Mining Corporation [1989] 1 All ER 785 *4*

Kores Ltd. v. Kolok Ltd. [1959] Ch. 108; [1958] 2 All ER 65 *70*

Krell v. Henry [1903] 2 K.B. 740; [1900–1903] All ER 20 *80*

K/S Norjal A/S v. Hyunday Co. Ltd [1991] 3 All ER 211 *231*

Lacey (William) Ltd. v. Davis [1957] 1 W.L.R. 932; [1957] 2 All ER 712 *11*

Lampleigh v. Braithwaite (1615) Hob. 105 *40*

Lancashire Loans Ltd. v. Black [1934] 1 K.B. 380 *59*

Lane v. Williams (1692) 1 Eq. 1100 *129*

Lansing Linde Ltd v. Kerr [1991] 1 All ER 418 *69*

Lazenby Garages v. Wright [1976] 1 W.L.R. 459 *172*

Leaf v. International Galleries [1950] 2 K.B. 86; [1950] 1 All ER 693 *46, 48, 56*

Leesh River Tea Co. Ltd v. British India S.N. Co. Ltd [1967] 2 Q.B. 250; [1966] 3 All ER 593 *198*

Legal and General Assurance Society Ltd v. Drake [1989] 3 All ER 923 *206*

Lener v. L.C.C. (1949) 2 K.B. 683 *10*

Leng v. Andrews (1909) 78 L.J. Ch. 80 *69*

Leslie v. Sheill [1914] 3 K.B. 607; [1914–1915] All ER 511 *44*

L'Estrange v. Graucob [1934] 2 K.B. 394 *19, 50*

Levison v. Patent Steam Carpet Cleaning Co. [1978] Q.B. 69; [1977] 3 All ER 498 *23, 219, 220*

Lewis v. Averay [1973] 1 W.L.R. 510; [1973] 2 All ER 229 *50, 52*

Lilley v. Doubleday (1881) 7 Q.B.D. 510 *23, 221*

Lilly v. Smales [1892] 1 Q.B. 456 *117*

Limbrick v. French & Farley, High Court, 8 June 1991 *211*

Limpus v. London General Omnibus Co. (1862) 1 H. & C. 526 *115*

Lloyd v. Grace, Smith & Co. [1912] A.C. 176 *115*

Lloyds Bank v. Bundy [1975] Q.B. 326; [1974] 3 All ER 757 *22, 59*

Lloyds Bank v. Waterhouse [1991] Fam Law 23 *47, 304*

Lockspeiser Aircraft v. Brooklands Aircraft, *The Times*, 7 March 1990 *219*

Loftus v. Roberts (1902) 18 T.L.R. 532 *23*

Logicrose v. Southend United Football Club [1988] 1 WLR 1256 *113*

Lombard Finance v. Brookplain Trading [1991] 2 All ER 762 *312*

Lombard North Central *v.* Butterworth [1987] QB 527; [1987] 1 All ER 267 *85*

London General Omnibus Co. *v.* Holloway [1912] 2 K.B. 72 *304*

London Joint Stock Bank *v.* Macmillan and Arthur [1918] A.C. 777 *120, 275*

Long *v.* Lloyd [1958] 1 W.L.R. 753; [1958] 2 All ER 402 *165*

Long *v.* Millar (1879) 4 C.P.D. 450 *35*

Lumsden & Co. *v.* London Trustee Savings Bank [1971] 1 Lloyd's Rep 114 *266*

Luxor Ltd *v.* Cooper [1941] A.C. 108 *114*

Macdonald *v.* Green [1951] K.B. 594; [1950] 2 All ER 1240 *65*

Mackenzie Mills *v.* Buono [1986] BTLC 399 *262*

Mark *v.* West Yorkshire Insurance Co., Halifax County Court, 27 June 1989 *205*

Marsh *v.* Joseph [1897] 1 Ch. 213 *110*

Marshall (Thomas) (Exports) Ltd *v.* Guinle [1978] 3 W.L.R. 116 *68*

Martell *v.* Consett Iron Co. Ltd [1955] Ch. 363; [1955] 1 All ER 481 *67*

Maschi *v.* Lep Air Services [1972] 2 W.L.R. 1175 *311*

Mason *v.* Provident Clothing Co. [1913] A.C. 724 *69*

Mendelsohn *v.* Normand Ltd. [1970] 1 Q.B. 177; [1969] 2 All ER 1215 *19*

Merrit *v.* Merrit [1970] 1 W.L.R. 1211; [1970] 2 All ER 760 *4*

Mersey Docks and Harbour Board *v.* Coggins and Griffith (Liverpool) [1947] A.C.1; [1946] 2 All ER 345 *115*

Metropolitan Water Board *v.* Dick, Kerr & Co. Ltd [1918] A.C. 119 *80*

MFI *v.* Nattrass [1973] 1 WLR 307 *321*

Microbeads AC *v.* Vinhurst Road Markings Ltd [1975] 1 All ER 529 *153*

Midland Bank *v.* Shephard [1988] BTLC 395 *60*

Miller (James) & Partners Ltd. *v.* Whitworth Street Estates Ltd. [1970] A.C. 583; [1970] 1 All ER 796 *29*

Mitchell *v.* London Borough of Ealing [1978] 2 W.L.R. 999 *219*

Monickendam *v.* Leanse (1923) 39 T.L.R. 445 *9, 35*

Montage G & H GmbH *v.* Irvani [1990] 2 All ER 225 *267*

Montedipe SpA *v.* JTP-RO Jugotanker [1990] 2 Lloyd's Rep 11 *229*

Montefiore *v.* Menday Motor Components Ltd [1918] 2 K.B. 241 *66*

Moorcock, The (1889) 14 P.D. 64 *24, 27*

Morris *v.* Baron [1918] A.C. 1 *76*

Morris *v.* Martin (C.W.) & Sons Ltd [1966] 1 Q.B. 716; [1965] 2 All ER 725 *220*

Morris *v.* Saxelby [1916] 1 A.C. 688 *67*

Mount *v.* Oldham Corporation [1973] Q.B. 309; [1973] 1 All ER 26 *81*

Napier *v.* National Business Agency [1951] W.N. 392; [1951] 2 All ER 264 *61*

National Bank of Nigeria Ltd *v.* Awolesi [1964] 1 W.L.R. 1311 *309*

National Carriers Ltd *v.* Panalpina (Northern) Ltd [1981] AC 675; [1981] All ER 161 *81*

National Mortgage and Agency Co. of NZ Ltd *v.* Stalker [1933] NZLR 1182 *304*

National Provincial Bank *v.* Glanusk [1913] 3 K.B. 335 *304*

National Westminster Bank *v.* Morgan [1985] 1 All ER 821 *60*

Naughton *v.* O'Callaghan [1990] 3 All ER 191 *55*

New Zealand Shipping Co. *v.*
 Satterthwaite [1975] A.C 154; [1974]
 1 All ER 1015   *91*
Newton London Borough Council *v.*
 Singh [1988] RTR 359   *320*
Nicholson & Venn *v.* Smith, Merriot
 (1947) 177 LT 189   *154*
Nicolene Ltd *v.* Simmonds [1953] 1
 Q.B. 543; [1953] 1 All ER 822   *24*
Nordenfeldt *v.* Maxim-Nordenfeldt Co.
 [1894] A.C. 535   *71*
Norman *v.* Bennett [1974] 1 W.L.R.
 1229; [1974] 3 All ER 351   *319*
Norman *v.* Ricketts (1886) 3 T.L.R. 182
 74
North & South Trust Co. *v.* Berkeley
 [1971] 1 W.L.R. 471; [1971] 1 All ER
 980   *113*
North Ocean Shipping Co. *v.* Hyundai
 Construction Co. [1979] QB 705;
 [1979] 3 WLR 419   *58*
Nowell *v.* Nowell (1869) 7 Eq. 538   *142*

Olley *v.* Marlborough Court Ltd [1949]
 K.B. 532; [1949] 1 All ER 127
 20, 223
Orbit Mining & Trading Co. Ltd *v.*
 Westminster Bank Ltd [1963] 1 Q.B.
 794; [1962] 3 All ER 565   *248*
O'Shea, *Re* [1911] 2 K.B. 981   *65*
O'Sullivan *v.* Williams [1992] 3 All ER
 385   *219*
Owen *v.* Tate [1976] Q.B. 402; [1975]
 2 All ER 129   *308*

Parker *v.* Clarke [1960] 1 W.L.R. 286;
 [1960] 1 All ER 93   *5*
Parker *v.* S.E. Railway (1877) 2 C.P.D.
 416   *19–20, 22*
Parkinson *v.* College of Ambulance Ltd.
 [1925] 2 K.B. 1   *65*
Parsons *v.* Uttley Ingham [1978] Q.B.
 791; [1977] 2 Lloyd's Rep. 522   *84*
Payne *v.* Cave (1789) 3 T.R. 148   *13*
Peachdart, *Re* [1984] Ch 131; [1983] 3
 WLR 878   *168*
Pearce *v.* Brooks (1866) L.R. 1 Ex. 213
 65

Pennington *v.* Crossley & Son (1897) 77
 L.T. 43   *74, 270*
Percival Ltd *v.* L.C.C. (1918) 87
 L.J.K.B. 677   *18*
Perry *v.* Stopher [1959] 1 W.L.R. 415
 229
Petraco (Bermuda) Ltd *v.* Petromed
 International SA [1988] 3 All ER 454
 233
Pharmaceutical Soc. *v.* Boots etc. [1953]
 1 Q.B. 401; [1953] 1 All ER 482
 13
Phillips *v.* Brooks [1919] 2 K.B. 243
 50, 56, 162
Phillips Petroleum Co. *v.* Cabaneli
 Naviera [1990] 1 Lloyd's Rep 52
 195
Phoenix Assurance Co. *v.* Spooner
 [1905] 2 K.B. 753   *209*
Photo Production Ltd *v.* Securicor
 Transport Ltd [1980] AC 827   *25*
Pickard *v.* Sears (1837) 6 A. & E. 469
 161
Pickering *v.* Ilfracombe Rail Co (1868)
 L.R. 3 C.P. 235   *61*
Pinnel's Case (1602) 5 Co. Rep. 117a
 40, 74
Planché *v.* Colburn (1831) 8 Bing. 14
 86
Port Swettenham Authority *v.* Wu
 (T.W.) & Co. [1978] 3 All ER 337
 219
Porter *v.* Freudenberg [1915] 1 K.B.
 857   *41*
Porter *v.* Taylor (1817) 6 M. & S. 156
 128
Prenn *v.* Simmonds [1971] 1 W.L.R.
 1381; [1971] 3 All ER 237   *28*
Price *v.* Easton (1833) 4 B. & Ad. 433
 91
Priest *v.* Last [1903] 2 K.B. 148   *158*
Printing & Numerical Co. *v.* Sampson
 (1875) L.R. 19 Eq. 462   *62*

R. *v.* Kylsant [1932] 1 K.B. 442   *54*
R. *v.* Pentonville Prison Governor, *ex p.*
 Teja [1971] 2 Q.B. 274; [1971] 2 All
 ER 11   *42*

Rae *v.* Yorkshire Bank, *The Times*, 12 October 1987; [1988] BTLC 35 *274*

Raffles *v.* Wichelhaus (1864) 2 H. & C. 906 *3, 49*

Ramsden *v.* Lee [1992] 2 All ER 204 *78*

Ramsgate Hotel *v.* Montefiore (1866) L.R. 1 Exch. 109 *14*

Rann *v.* Hughes (1778) 7 Term. Rep. 350n *32*

Rasnoimport v/o *v.* Guthrie & Co. Ltd [1966] 1 Lloyd's Rep. 1 *198*

Read *v.* Price [1909] 1 K.B. 577 *78*

Reading *v.* Attorney General [1951] A.C. 507; [1951] 1 All ER 617 *10*

Reid *v.* Metropolitan Police Commissioners [1973] 1 Q.B. 551; [1973] 2 All ER 97 *162*

Regent OHG *v.* Francesco of Jermyn Street [1981] 3 All ER 327 *164*

Rhodes *v.* Forwood (1876) 1 App. Cas. 256 *114*

Richco International Ltd *v.* International Industrial Food Co. SARL [1989] 1 All ER 613 *228*

Rickards *v.* Oppenheim [1950] 1 K.B. 616; [1950] All ER 420 *74*

Ricketts *v.* Tilling [1915] 1 K.B. 644 *115*

Robb *v.* Green [1895] 2 Q.B. 315 *68*

Roberts *v.* Plaisted [1989] 2 Lloyd's Rep 341 *205*

Robinson *v.* Cook (1815) 6 Taunt. 336 *73*

Robinson *v.* Davison (1871) L.R. 6 Ex. 269 *80*

Robinson *v.* Graves [1935] 1 K.B. 579 *150*

Rogers *v.* Parish (Scarborough) [1987] Q.B. 933; [1987] 2 All ER 232 *156*

Roscorla *v.* Thomas (1842) 3 Q.B. 234 *39*

Rose *v.* Plenty [1976] 1 W.L.R. 141; [1976] 1 All ER 97 *115*

Rose & Frank *v.* Crompton Bros. [1923] 2 K.B. 261 *4*

Roselodge *v.* Castle [1966] 2 Lloyd's Rep. 105 *204*

Ross *v.* London County Bank [1919] 1 K.B. 678 *273*

Routledge *v.* Grant (1828) 4 Bing. 653 *15*

Rover International *v.* Cannon Film Sales (No. 3) [1989] 3 All ER 423 *10*

Rowland *v.* Divall [1923] 2 KB 500 *153*

Rowlandson *v.* National Westminster Bank Ltd (1978) 1 W.L.R. 798 *275*

Royscott Trust Ltd *v.* Rogerson [1991] 3 All ER 294 *55, 56*

Salford Corporation *v.* Lever [1891] 1 Q.B. 168 *113*

Saunders *v.* Anglia Building Society [1971] A.C. 1004; [1970] 3 All ER 961 *47, 51*

Savills *v.* Scott [1988] 12 E.G. 115 *117*

Scammell *v.* Ouston [1941] A.C. 251 *24*

Scarf *v.* Jardine (1882) 7 App. Cas. 345 *109*

Scholfield *v.* Londesborough [1896] A.C. 514 *274*

Schroeder (A) Music Publishing Co. Ltd *v.* Macaulay [1974] 3 All ER 616 *22*

Scorer *v.* Seymour-Johns [1966] 3 All ER 347 *70*

Scott *v.* Avery (1856) 5 H.L.C. 811 *227*

Scott *v.* Coulson [1903] 2 Ch. 240 *48*

Scriven *v.* Hindley [1913] 2 K.B. 564 *49*

Scruttons Ltd *v.* Midland Silicones Ltd [1962] A.C. 446; [1962] 1 All ER 1 *38, 91*

Seddon *v.* N.E. Salt Co. [1905] 1 Ch. 326 *58*

Seymour v. Bridge (1885) 14 Q.B.D. 460 *111*

Seymour *v.* Pickett [1905] 1 K.B 715 *75*

Shadwell *v.* Shadwell (1860) 30 L.J.C.P. 145 *38*

Shaw & Co. *v.* Symmons & Sons Ltd [1917] 1 K.B. 799 *218*

Shayler *v.* Woolf [1946] Ch. 320; [1946] 2 All ER 54 *229*

Shearson Lehman v. Maclaine Wilson
(No. 2) [1990] 3 All ER 723 *172*
Shelley v. Paddock [1978] 2 W.L.R. 877;
[1978] 3 All ER 129 *63*
Simpkins v. Pays [1955] 3 All ER 10 *3*
Sims v. Midland Rly. [1913] 1 K.B. 103
188
Sky Petroleum Ltd. v. V.I.P. Petroleum
Ltd. [1974] 1 W.L.R. 576; [1974] 1
All ER 954 *87*
Smart v. Saunders [1848] All ER
(Reprint) 758 *111*
Smedleys Ltd v. Breed [1974] AC 839
333
Smith v. Cox [1940] 3 All ER 546 *74*
Smith v. Wood [1929] 1 Ch. 14 *310*
Société Commerciale de Reassurance v.
ERAS (International) [1992] 2 All ER
82 *78*
Solle v. Butcher [1950] 1 K.B. 671;
[1949] 2 All ER 1107 *52*
Sorrell v. Finch [1977] A.C 728; [1976]
2 All ER 371 *121*
Spiro v. Lintern [1973] 1 W.L.R. 1002;
[1973] 3 All ER 319 *109*
Springer v. G.W. Railway [1921] 1 K.B.
257 *110*
State of Norway's Application,
Re [1989] 1 All ER 745 *120*
Steinberg v. Scala Ltd [1923] 2 Ch. 452
43
Stekel v. Ellice [1973] 1 W.L.R. 191;
[1973] 1 All ER 465 *127*
Sterns Ltd v. Vickers Ltd [1923] 1 K.B.
78 *162*
Stewart v. Casey [1892] 1 Ch. 104 *40*
Stilk v. Myrick (1809) 2 Camp. 317
39
Stockton v. Mason [1978] 2 Lloyd's
Rep. 26 C.A. *203*
Strathcona S.S. Case [1926] A.C. 108
92
Suisse Atlantique etc. v. N.V.
Rotterdamsche Kolen Centrale
[1967] 1 A.C. 361; [1966] 2 All ER
61 *22, 25*
Sumpter v. Hedges [1898] 1 Q.B. 673
72, 87

Sutcliffe v. Thackrah [1974] A.C. 727;
[1974] 1 All ER 859 *231*
Sykes (F. & G.) (Wessex) Ltd v. Fine
Fare Ltd. [1967] 1 Lloyd's Rep. 24
53

Tai Hing Cotton Mill Ltd v. Liu Chong
Hing Bank Ltd [1985] 2 All ER 847
275
Taylor v. Caldwell (1863) 32 L.J.Q.B.
164 *80*
Taylor v. Laird (1863) 25 L.J. Ex. 329
13
Teheran-Europe Ltd v. Belton (S.T.)
Ltd [1968] 2 Q.B. 545; [1968] 2 All
ER 886 *118*
Thompson v. L.M.S. Railway [1930] 1
K.B. 41 *20*
Thompson v. Robinson [1955] Ch. 177;
[1955] 1 All ER 154 *172*
Thornton v. Shoe Lane Parking Ltd
[1971] 2 Q.B. 163; [1971] 1 All
ER 686 *20*
Tiney Engineering Ltd v. Amods
Knitting Machinery Ltd [1986]
BTLC 324 *40*
Tomlinson v. Broadsmith [1896] 1 Q.B.
386 *129*
Torkington v. Magee [1903] 1 K.B. 644
93
Trade & Transport Incorporated v. Iino
Kaiun Paisha (The Angelica) [1973] 1
W.L.R. 210; [1973] 2 All ER 144 *25*
Trego v. Hunt [1896] A.C. 7 *137, 138*
Tritonia Shipping Inc. v. South Nelson
Forest Products Corpn. [1966] 1
Lloyd's Rep. 114 *230*
Trollope & Colls v. N.W. Metropolitan
Regional Hospital Board [1973] 1
W.L.R. 601; [1973] 2 All ER 260 *27*
Tweddle v. Atkinson (1861) 1 B. & S.
393 *91*

UDT v. Taylor [1980] S.L.T. 28 *181*
Underwood Ltd v. Martins Bank [1924]
All ER 230 *273*
Unigate v. Bentley (25 November 1986)
310

United Dominions Trust *v*. Western [1976] Q.B. 513; [1975] 3 All ER 1017 *51*

United Overseas Bank *v*. Jiwani [1977] 1 All ER 733 *274*

Unitramp SA *v*. Jenson & Nicholson Pty Ltd [1992] 1 All ER 346 *234*

Universal Cargo Carriers Corpn. *v*. Citati [1958] 2 Q.B. 254; [1958] 2 All ER 563 *232*

Victoria Laundry *v*. Newman Industries [1949] 2 K.B. 528; [1949] 1 All ER 997 *84*

Vinden *v*. Hughes [1905] 1 K.B. 795 *261*

Walford *v*. Miles [1992] 1 All ER 453 *23*

Walker *v*. Hirsch (1884) 27 Ch. D. 460 *127*

Walker *v*. Mottram (1881) 19 Ch. D. 355 *138*

Ward *v*. Bignall [1967] 1 Q.B. 534;[1967] 2 All ER 449 *171*

Ward *v*. Hobbs (1878) 3 Q.B.D. 150 4 App. Cas. 13 *52*

Warner Bros. *v*. Nelson [1937] 1 K.B. 209 *89*

Wathes (Western) Ltd *v*. Austins (Menswear) Ltd [1976] 1 Lloyd's Rep. 14 *22*

Watson *v*. Prager (1991) 3 All ER 487 *70, 228*

Watteau *v*. Fenwick [1893] 1 Q.B. 346 *107, 116*

Watts *v*. Morrow [1991] 4 All ER 937 *85*

Webster *v*. Cecil (1861) 30 Beav. 62 *51, 88*

Wheeler *v*. Young (1897) 13 T.L.R. 486 *269*

White *v*. Bluett (1853) 23 L.J. Ex. 36 *39*

White & Carter Ltd *v*. McGregor [1962] A.C. 413; [1961] 3 All ER 1178 *82*

Williams *v*. Carwardine (1833) 4. B. & Ad. 621 *17, 18*

Williams *v*. Curzon Syndicate Ltd (1919) 35 T.L.R. 475 *219*

Williams *v*. Linnitt (1951) 1 K.B. 565; [1951] 1 All ER 278 *223*

Williams *v*. Roffey Bros. & Nicholls (Contractors) Ltd [1990] 1 All ER 512 *39*

Williams & Thomas, *Re* [1909] 1 Ch. 713; (1877) 7 Ch. D. 138 *210*

Wilson *v*. Brett (1843) 11 M. & W. 113 *219*

Wilson *v*. Carnley [1908] 1 K.B. 729 *65*

Wilson & Meeson *v*. Pickering [1946] K.B. 422; [1946] 1 All ER 394 *271*

With *v*. O'Flanagan [1936] 1 Ch. 575 *54*

Woods *v*. Martins Bank [1959] 1 Q.B. 55; [1958] 3 All ER 166 *120*

Woolcott *v*. Sun Alliance and London Assurance Co. (1978) 1 W.L.R. 493 *204*

Worcester Works Finance *v*. Cooden Engineering Co. Ltd [1972] 1 Q.B. 210; [1971] 3 All ER 708 *161*

Wormell *v*. RHM Agriculture (East) Ltd [1987] 3 All ER 75 *157*

Wythes *v*. Labouchere (1859) 3 De G. & J. 593 *304*

Yenidje Tobacco Co. Ltd., *Re* [1916] 2 Ch. 426 *135*

Yonge *v*. Toynbee [1910] K.B. 215 *111, 117*

Table of statutes

Administration of Justice Act 1970
231
Administration of Justice Act 1982
234
Arbitration Act 1950   *226, 227, 228,
229, 230, 232, 234, 235*
Arbitration Act 1975   *226, 227, 229*
Arbitration Act 1979   *226, 232*
Athens Convention 1974   *197*
Auctioneers Act 1845   *173*
Auctions (Bidding Agreements) Act
1969   *174*

Bail Act 1976   *6*
Banking and Financial Dealings Act
1971   *266*
Bankruptcy Act 1914 (repealed)
359, 367, 370, 372
Betting and Loans (Infants) Act
1892   *46*
Betting, Gaming and Lotteries Act
1963   *64*
Bills of Exchange Act 1882
33, 129, 247–71, 273–4, 276–8, 301
Bills of Exchange Act (1882)
Amendment Act 1932   *278*
Bills of Sale Acts 1878–1882   *151, 297*
Business Names Act 1985   *63, 127*

Carriage by Air and Road Act 1979
193
Carriage of Goods by Road Act
1965   *193*
Carriage of Goods by Sea Act 1971
194, 195, 197, 199
Carriage of Passengers by Road Act
1974   *193*

Carriers Act 1830   *190, 191, 193*
Cheques Act 1957   *74, 268, 270, 272,
273, 278*
Cheques Act 1992   *271*
Civil Liability (Contribution) Act 1978
128, 306
Coinage Act 1971   *73*
Coinage Act 1983   *73*
Companies Act 1985   *15, 33, 43, 58,
109, 125, 127, 139, 170*
Competition Act 1980   *347, 348*
Consumer Arbitration Agreements Act
1988   *236*
Consumer Credit Act 1974   *22, 29,
33, 62, 63, 64, 75, 76, 149, 177–83,
222, 263, 279, 293–5, 298, 303, 305,
326, 327, 336, 371*
Consumer Protection Act 1987   *77,
173, 327, 328, 329, 330. 331, 332*
Contracts (Applicable Law) Act 1990
29
Copyright, Patents and Designs Act
1988   *33*
Corporate Bodies Contracts Act
1960   *32*
Criminal Law Act 1967   *66*
Currency and Bank Notes Act 1954
73

Diplomatic Privileges Act 1964   *41*

Employment Protection
(Consolidation) Act 1978   *33*
Enduring Powers of Attorney Act 1985
108, 111, 112
Estate Agents Act 1979   *324–6, 328,
331*

Factors Act 1889 *118, 119*
Fair Trading Act 1973 *323, 324, 348*
Family Law Reform Act 1969 *43*
Financial Services Act 1986 *63, 213*
Fire Prevention (Metropolis) Act 1774
  209
Food Safety Act 1990 *328, 333, 334,
  335*
Forgery and Counterfeiting Act 1981
  255

Gaming Act 1835 *64*
Gaming Act 1892 *64*
Gaming Act 1968 *64*
Gaming and Wagering Acts 1835–1960
  64

Honours (Prevention of Abuses) Act
  1925 *65*
Hotel Proprietors Act 1956 *223, 224*

Infants Relief Act 1874 *44, 46*
Innkeepers Act 1878 *221, 224*
Innkeepers Liability Act 1878 *300*
Insolvency Act 1986 *311, 359, 367,
  371*
Insurance Brokers (Registration)
  Act 1975 *216*
Insurance Companies Act 1982 *215,
  216*

Judgments Act 1838 *234*
Judicature Acts 1873–1875 *51*

Latent Damage Act 1986 *78*
Land Charges Act 1972 *91*
Law of Property Act 1925 *9, 31, 32,
  34, 91, 92, 93, 94, 245, 279, 291, 296*
Law of Property Act (Miscellaneous
  Provisions) 1981 *6–7, 9, 32, 33, 36*
Law Reform (Contributory
  Negligence) Act 1945 *274*
Law Reform (Enforcement of
  Contracts) Act 1954 *33*
Law Reform (Frustrated Contracts)
  Act 1943 *82*
Law Reform (Married Women and
  Tortfeasors) Act 1935 *42*

Law Reform (Miscellaneous
  Provisions) Act 1934 *84*
Law Reform (Miscellaneous
  Provisions) Act 1970 *66*
Life Assurance Act 1774 *206, 209*
Limitation Act 1980 *7, 33, 39,
  77, 79, 235, 269, 270, 312*
Limited Partnership Act 1907 *138–40*
Lloyd's Acts 1871–1982 *215*

Marine Insurance Act 1906 *33,
  211–15*
Married Women's Property Act 1882
  206
Matrimonial Homes Act 1983 *370*
Matrimonial Proceedings and
  Property Act 1970 *42*
Medicines Act 1968 *335*
Mental Health Act 1983 *134*
Mercantile Law Amendment Act 1856
  35, 303
Merchant Shipping Acts 1894–1988
  41, 195
Merchant Shipping Act 1979 *197*
Minors' Contracts Act 1987 *43–5, 307*
Misrepresentation Act 1967 *28, 53,
  54, 55, 136, 153*
Mock Auctions Act 1961 *175*
Monopolies Act 1948 *97*
Monopolies and Mergers Act 1965 *95*

Partnership Act 1890 *125, 128, 129,
  130–6, 306, 311*
Pawnbrokers Acts 1872–1960 *298*
Perjury Act 1911 *232*
Policies of Assurance Act 1867 *207,
  208*
Policyholders' Protection Act 1975
  216
Powers of Attorney Act 1971 *108,
  111*
Powers of Criminal Courts Act 1973
  362
Prevention of Corruption Act 1916
  113

Rehabilitation of Offenders Act 1974
  205

Resale Prices Act 1976   *68 91, 92, 345, 346*
Restrictive Trade Practices Act 1976   *68, 342, 343, 344*
Road Traffic Act 1960   *193*
Road Traffic Act 1988   *91, 92, 211*

Sale of Goods Act 1979   *24, 25, 26, 27, 42, 43, 48, 74, 149–65, 168–74, 179, 300, 323*
Shops Act 1950   *63*
State Immunity Act 1978   *41–2*
Statute Law (Repeals) Act 1969   *63*
Statute of Frauds 1677   *33, 302, 303*
Statute of Frauds Amendment Act 1828   *303*
Suicide Act 1961   *206*
Sunday Observance Act 1677   *62–3*
Supply of Goods and Services Act 1982   *151, 175–6, 179, 220*
Supply of Goods (Implied Terms) Act 1973   *22, 27, 152, 180*
Supreme Court Act 1981   *162*

Third Parties (Rights against Insurers) Act 1930   *211*

Timeshare Act 1992   *336*
Torts (Interference with Goods) Act 1977   *161, 173, 221, 300*
Trade Descriptions Act 1968   *319, 321, 326, 327, 336*
Trading Stamps Act 1964   *321, 322*
Trading with the Enemy Act 1939   *66*
Transport Act 1962   *187, 190, 191, 193*
Transport Act 1968   *187, 190*
Transport Act (London) 1969   *187*
Transport Act 1978   *5*
Transport Act 1985   *190*
Treaty of Rome   *344, 346, 347, 349*

Unfair Contract Terms Act 1977   *5, 21, 22, 23, 33, 55, 154, 155, 156, 157, 175, 176–7*
Uniform Laws on International Sales Act 1967   *17*
Unsolicited Goods and Services Act 1971   *17, 33, 218, 219*
Unsolicited Goods and Services Act 1975   *17, 33, 218, 219*

Part one

The law of contracts

1
Nature and classification of contracts

Nature of contracts

1. Definition of contract

A contract is a legally binding agreement: that is, an agreement which will be enforced by the courts. Sir William Anson, in his *Principles of the Law of Contract*, defined a contract as 'a legally binding agreement made between two or more persons, by which rights are acquired by one or more acts or forbearances on the part of the other or others.'

2. *Consensus ad idem*

An agreement occurs when two minds meet upon a common purpose. This meeting of minds is called *consensus ad idem*, i.e. consent to the matter.

Absence of consensus may make a contract null and void, e.g. where the parties are fundamentally mistaken as to each other's intentions: *Raffles* v. *Wichelhaus* (1864), *see* 4: 5.

3. Agreements which are not contracts

Mere domestic or social agreements are not usually intended to be binding, and therefore are not contracts.

Examples _____

(1) Three friends joined to enter a newspaper competition and agreed to share any winnings. HELD: They intended to create legal relations and their agreement was therefore a binding contract: *Simpkins* v. *Pays* (1955).
(2) A husband promised to pay a housekeeping allowance to his wife. HELD: A mere domestic arrangement, with no intention to create legally binding relations, therefore no contract: *Balfour* v. *Balfour* (1919). (However,

where the spouses are legally separated it will be presumed that they did intend to create a legally binding contract: *Merrit* v. *Merrit* (1970).)

4.   Intention to create legal relations
A binding contract is usually in the nature of a commercial bargain, involving some exchange of goods or services for a price (called the consideration).

But even such bargains will not be legally binding if the parties intend otherwise, i.e. do not intend to create legal relations.

In considering whether sufficient intention to create a binding contract is present, two situations are possible.

(a) Where the parties expressly deny the intention. Here the courts will almost invariably hold that there is no contract:

Examples
(1) A written commercial agreement described itself merely as an 'honourable pledge' and stated expressly that it was not 'to be subject to the jurisdiction of any court.' HELD: The parties did not intend to create legal relations, and the agreement was not a contract: *Rose & Frank Co.* v. *Crompton Bros.* (1923).
(2) A condition imposed by a football pool laid down that the relationship should not be legally binding. HELD: No intention to create legal relations: *Appleson v. Littlewoods Ltd* (1939). (This is a common condition of entrance in football pools etc.)
(3) In *Kleinwort Benson Ltd* v. *Malaysia Mining Corporation* (1989), the plaintiff bank agreed with the defendants to make a loan facility of up to £10m available to the defendants' wholly owned subsidiary which traded in tin. The defendants provided the plaintiffs with two 'letters of comfort' which stated that 'it is our policy to ensure that the business of [the subsidiary] is at all times in a position to meet its liabilities to you' under the loan facility arrangement. The subsidiary later went into liquidation and the plaintiffs sought the whole amount owing from the defendants. When the defendants refused to pay, the plaintiffs brought an action against them to recover the amount owing. The Court of Appeal ruled that a 'letter of comfort' stating that it was the policy of a company to ensure that its subsidiary was 'at all times in a position to meet its liabilities' in respect of a loan made by the lender to the subsidiary did not have contractual effect if it was merely a statement of present fact regarding the parent company's future conduct. On the facts, the comfort letters were in terms a statement of present fact and not a promise as to future conduct, and in the context in which the letters were written were not

meant to be anything other than a representation of fact giving rise to no more than a moral responsibility on the part of the defendants to meet the subsidiary's debt.

(b) Where the parties do not expressly deny intention to create legal relations. Here there is in each case a question of construction for the Court to decide as to whether a contract is intended. Thus:
- (*i*) in commercial agreements there is a rebuttable presumption that a contract is intended; *but*
- (*ii*) in social and domestic or family agreements there is a rebuttable presumption that no contract is intended. (But note that in each case the presumption is rebuttable by evidence to the contrary.)

Examples
---
(1) C persuaded her niece, P, to sell her own house and come and live in C's on condition that C would leave her house to P by will. After some time, C ejected P from the house, and refused to leave it to her by will. P claimed damages for breach of contract. HELD: Although a family agreement, there was consideration for C's promise and evidence of intention to create legal relations. P was therefore entitled to damages: *Parker* v. *Clarke* (1960).
(2) B and O habitually rode in each other's cars. Neither had insurance to cover injury to passengers. While in O's car, B was injured through O's negligence and sued for damages in contract or in tort. B had contributed to petrol costs and claimed this gave rise to a contract. O claimed: (*i*) there was no intention to create a binding contract; and (*ii*) B had consented to the risk of injury, since there was a notice in the car disclaiming liability to passengers. HELD: There was no contract, and B could not get damages (either in contract or in tort): *Buckpitt* v. *Oates* (1968).

If the car owner had advertised for someone to share petrol costs, as he can do under the Transport Act 1978, it is more likely to be presumed that a contract exists. Note that under the Unfair Contract Terms Act 1977, liability for negligence causing death or personal injury cannot be excluded: *see* 2: **18**.

Classification of contracts

5.   Contracts of record
These are obligations whose terms are recorded by a court of record, e.g. the Supreme Court or a county court.

They are not true contracts, since the obligations of the parties arise independently of any agreement and solely by reason of entry upon the court records. Two types are as follows.

(a) *Judgments*: by which a court imposes on some person a legal obligation, e.g. to pay damages. This judgment, when enrolled on the court records, constitutes a contract of record between the parties to the action in which the judgment was pronounced.
(b) *Recognisances:* written acknowledgment of a debt due to the Crown, made before a judge or authorised officer, and enrolled on the court records, e.g. a promise to 'keep the peace' or to attend court when called (an accused person in a criminal case was sometimes released on bail pending trial, on his own recognisance, i.e. a promise to attend when called or to forfeit a stated sum of money); but *see* the Bail Act 1976, s. 8(3).

6.   Contracts by deed
The old law on contracts by deed (specialty contracts) has been drastically amended by the provisions of the Law of Property (Miscellaneous Provisions) Act 1989.

(a) *Deeds and their execution.* The Act abolishes three rules of law. Firstly, it abolishes the rule that deeds have to be written on paper or parchment, although the requirement of writing remains. Secondly, the requirement of sealing for the valid execution of a deed by an individual is abolished, but execution by a corporation remains unaffected. It was held by the Court of Appeal in *First National Securities Ltd* v. *Jones* (1978) that, as a matter of law, it was not necessary for the due execution of a deed that there should be any physical seal attached to, or impressed on, the paper. A document purporting to be a deed was capable in law of being such, even though it bore nothing more than an indication of where the seal should be. This particular document had a circle in which there were letters showing that this was where the seal should go. The signature had been placed across the circle and a witness had signed a clause saying that the document had been signed, sealed and delivered in his presence. The court ruled that this was evidence enough that the document had been executed by the party as his deed. Finally, the Act abolishes the rule that authority by a party to a deed, given to another person to deliver the deed on the party's behalf, must itself be given by deed.

The Act contains new requirements for the execution of deeds, and applies to both individuals and corporations. The instrument must make it clear on its face that it is intended to be a deed, and it must be validly executed. The first requirement would normally be satisfied by the instrument describing itself as a deed. To satisfy the requirement of valid execution, a deed is validly executed by an individual if it is signed by him in the presence of a witness who attests his signature or is signed at his direction, in his presence and the presence of two witnesses who attest the signature, and it is delivered as a deed by him or a person authorised to do so on his behalf. Signing is defined to include making one's mark.

7. Characteristics of contracts by deed

(a) *Consideration:* a deed does not require to be supported by valuable consideration, like simple contracts: *see* below.

(b) *Merger:* a special contract absorbs, or merges into itself, any earlier simple contract made between the same parties and on the same terms.

(c) *Limitation of actions:* an action for breach of a specialty contract can be commenced at any time within twelve years of the breach occurring; but an action for breach of a simple contract must generally be commenced within six years: Limitation Act 1980 and *see* 5: **15**.

> NOTE: Formerly a person who had signed a deed could not thereafter deny the accuracy of statements made therein, i.e he was estopped from denying the accuracy of the deed. This was called *estoppel by deed.* The rule is now obsolete and evidence is admissible to show that the deed is inaccurate, like any other contract.

8. Simple contracts

Simple or 'parol' contracts are by far the most common and important variety. They are informal contracts and may be made in any way — orally, in writing, or by implication from conduct. A person who takes a seat in a bus is entering into an implied contract to pay his fare.

A simple contract must possess the following essentials.

(a) An offer and unqualified acceptance thereof: *see* 2: **1–15**.
(b) Intention to create legal relations: *see* **4** above.
(c) Valuable consideration: *see* 3: **10–12**.
(d) Genuineness of consent (*consensus ad idem*), e.g. the agreement must not have been induced by fraud or coercion: *see* Chapter 4.
(e) Capacity of parties: *see* 3: **20–29**.
(f) Legality of objects: *see* 4: **25**.
(g) Possibility of performance: *see* Chapter 4.
(h) Certainty of terms: *see* 2: **21–23**.

Void, voidable and unenforceable contracts

9. Void contracts

A void contract is one which is destitute of legal effect, i.e. of which the court will take no notice, for example, contracts void on the grounds of fundamental mistake: *see* 4: **1–7**.

Property transferred under a void contract can usually be recovered as the transferee can have no legal right to it: *Chappell v. Poles* (1837). But if the contract is void on the grounds that its object is illegal or contrary to public policy, property transferred is generally irrecoverable: *see* Chapter 4.

10. Voidable contracts

A voidable contract is one which can be made void by one party, at his option. Thus a contract induced by fraud can be avoided by the party misled whenever he chooses: *see* Chapter 4.

11. Unenforceable contracts

An unenforceable contract is one which, though perfectly valid in all other respects, lacks some technical requirement needed to make it enforceable, e.g. some necessary written evidence. Such a contract will not be enforced by the courts unless and until the defect is rectified.

Thus contracts for the sale of land or other disposition of an interest in land can only be made in writing and only by incorporating all the terms which the parties have expressly agreed in one document or, where contracts are exchanged, in each. Where this is not the case, they cannot be sued upon. These provisions are contained in the Law of Property (Miscellaneous Provisions) Act 1989, replacing s. 40 of the Law of Property Act 1925.

But such unenforceable contracts are not void, and therefore if they have been performed and property has been transferred, the court will not intervene to set the agreement aside. Thus if A orally agrees to buy B's house and pays a deposit to B, then later changes his mind and refuses to sign a written contract to purchase the house, B will be unable to sue A for damages or performance of the contract but will be able to keep A's deposit, and the court will not assist A to recover it: *Monickendam* v. *Leanse* (1923).

Quasi-contracts

Sometimes the law imposes obligations of a contractual nature even where no true agreement exists between the parties. The object of such imposition is to prevent a person obtaining 'unjust enrichment' merely because there is no contract between himself and the person seeking the court's aid. The chief examples of such artificial or *quasi-contracts* are given below.

12. Money paid to the use of another
If A, at the express or implied request of B, pays to X a sum of money legally owed by B to X, the law implies a quasi-contract between A and B under which B must compensate A for the sum paid, e.g. where A pays rent owed by B to prevent the landlord seizing A's goods, which are stored at B's premises: *Edmunds* v. *Wallingford* (1885).

13. Accounts stated
Where there has been a series of transactions between A and B and they agree a balance, showing a sum payable by A to B, the agreed balance constitutes an 'account stated.' If B now has occasion to sue A for the amount so stated, he does not need to prove the details of the transactions between them but can rely entirely on the account stated as an admission of indebtedness.

14. Total failure of consideration

Where a valid contract has been made between A and B (supported by consideration) but subsequently B fails to provide any of the promised consideration, there is said to be a total failure of consideration and A can sue for the recovery of any money he has paid.

(Contrast the situation where the consideration has only partially failed, e.g. where A pays money for goods to B, who later delivers some but not all the goods ordered. If A decides to accept this partial delivery, which he is not obliged to do, A can sue for damages for breach of contract, and the damages will be measured as the amount needed to compensate him for his loss, i.e. he is unlikely to recover all the money he has paid. If A decided that he will not accept partial delivery, which he is entitled to do, he can recover all the money paid.)

15. Money had and received

If A wrongfully obtains money to which B is legally entitled, B can sue A for recovery of the money in a quasi-contractual action for money had and received, e.g. where an employee receives money on behalf of his master and refuses to pass it on to the proper recipient.

Thus where B used the authority of his army uniform to assist him in smuggling activities, it was held that the army, as his employer, was entitled to the profits he had made out of the smuggling: *Reading* v. *Attorney-General* (1951).

16. Money paid under mistake of fact

Where money is paid under a mistake of fact it is generally recoverable by the payer, e.g. where an employer overpays wages under a mistake as to the employee's entitlement: *Lener* v. *LCC* (1949). Where a local authority had overpaid an employee it was estopped from recovering amounts where the employee had, in good faith and without notice of the claim and also in reliance on the representation, so changed his position that it would be inequitable to ask him to repay the money: *Avon County Council* v. *Howlett* (1981). *See also Rover International* v. *Cannon Film Sales (No. 3)* (1989).

NOTE: Money paid under mistake of law is generally irrecoverable, since ignorance of the law is no excuse (*ignorantia juris neminem excusat*). But to this rule there are the following exceptions: (1) where the payee knew of or induced the payer's mistake; (2) where the money was paid to an officer of the court, e.g. a trustee in bankruptcy: *Ex parte James* (1874); (3) where money was paid under unjustified threat of legal proceedings against the payer; (4) where the payee was under a fiduciary duty to the payer, e.g. where paid by a client to his solicitor; (5) where the mistake of law is treated as one of fact, e.g. (*i*) mistake of foreign law; (*ii*) mistake as to private proprietary rights.

17. *Quantum meruit*

Where there is a breach of an essential condition in a contract, the injured party may either seek to enforce the contract and sue for damages by way of compensation or treat the contract as discharged, in which case he cannot sue for damages for its breach.

However, where he treats the contract as discharged, and has incurred expenses under it, he is entitled to bring a quasi-contractual action for compensation for work done. This is called a *quantum meruit* action (literally 'how much is it worth?'): *see* 5: **30**.

In addition to providing a remedy in certain cases of breach of contract like those above, *quantum meruit* may also be used by the court to impose quasi-contractual liability where there is no contract between the parties but justice requires that some remuneration should be paid for work done.

Example

L, a builder, did certain work for D on the understanding that D would give him a contract later for some major building work. D did not give L the expected contract and L sued for either (*i*) damages for breach of contract or (*ii*) *quantum meruit* relief. HELD: There was no contract between L and D and therefore L could not get damages, but he was entitled to reasonable remuneration on a quasi-contract: *William Lacey Ltd* v. *Davis* (1957).

2

Formation of contracts

In order to constitute a contract there must be an offer, express or implied by one person (the 'offeror'), and unqualified acceptance, express or implied, by the person to whom the offer is made (the 'offeree'). The House of Lords has emphasised that save in exceptional circumstances, a binding contract requires an offer and an acceptance: *Gibson* v. *Manchester City Council* (1979).

Rules governing offers

1. How made

An offer may be oral, written, or implied from conduct. Thus an implied offer is made by a bus company when it sends its buses along the street and stops them at fixed places to let people get on (the people who then get on a bus are thus accepting the offer by implication).

2. To whom

An offer may be specific, i.e. to a particular person or group of persons, or general, i.e. to the world at large.

(a) *A specific offer* can usually be accepted only by the person or persons to whom it was made: *Boulton* v. *Jones* (1857).
(b) *A general offer* can be accepted by anyone (and usually without prior notification of intention to accept).

Thus a newspaper advertisement offering £100 to anyone who contracted influenza despite using a patent medicine in a specified way was held to be (*i*) a general offer, (*ii*) which could be accepted by conduct, (*iii*) without previously notifying the offeror of the acceptance: *Carlill* v. *Carbolic Smoke Ball Co.* (1893).

3. Communication to offeree

The offer must be communicated to the offeree before it can be accepted.

Example _____

A seaman helped to navigate a ship home, and before sailing wrote to the owners telling them of his intention and asking a particular wage for his services. The owners did not receive the letter of offer until the ship was nearly home. HELD: The owners had no reasonable opportunity to accept or reject the offer, therefore the seaman could not compel them to pay him wages for navigating the ship: *Taylor* v. *Laird* (1856).

4. Certainty of offer

The offer must be definite, not vague or illusory. Thus a promise to pay an increased price for a horse 'if it proves lucky to me' is too vague: *Guthing* v. *Lynn* (1831).

5. Intention to create legal relations

The offeror must intend the creation of legal relations, i.e. must intend that if his offer is accepted a legally binding agreement shall result: *see Balfour* v. *Balfour*; 1: **3**. The House of Lords had indicated that there is an intention to create legal relations where 'free' medallions are given away with so many gallons of petrol purchased: *Esso* v. *Commissioners of Customs and Excise* (1976).

6. An offer must be distinguished from the following

(a) *An invitation to treat* (invitation to make offers), e.g. an auctioneer's request for bids (which will themselves be offers): *Payne* v. *Cave* (1789); or the display of goods in a shop window with prices marked upon them: *Fisher* v. *Bell* (1961); or the display of priced goods in a self-service store: *Pharmaceutical Soc.* v. *Boots, etc.* (1953). But indicating that medallions are given away with the purchase of petrol is probably not an invitation to treat, but is an offer: *Esso* v. *Commissioners of Customs and Excise* (1976).

(b) *A mere statement of intention*, e.g. an announcement of a forthcoming auction sale. Thus a person who attends the advertised place of auction could not sue for breach of contract if the sale were cancelled: *Harris* v. *Nickerson* (1873).

(c) *A mere communication of information* in the course of negotiations, e.g. a statement of the price at which one is prepared to consider negotiating the sale of a piece of land: *Harvey* v. *Facey* (1893).

Example _____

In discussing a possible sale of land, A wrote offering £20,000 and B replied: 'As you are aware that I paid £25,000 for this property, your offer of £20,000 would appear to be at least a little optimistic. For a quick sale I would accept £26,000 . . .' A replied accepting this offer. HELD: B's letter was an offer which A had accepted, so making a contract: *Bigg* v. *Boyd Gibbins Ltd* (1971) C.A.

_____

7.   An offer lapses under the following circumstances

(a) *If either offeror or offeree dies before acceptance: Kennedy* v. *Thomassen* (1929). But the death of the offeror may not invalidate subsequent acceptance provided: (*i*) the offeree did not know of the death when he accepted, and (*ii*) the personalty of the offeror is not vital to the contract: *Bradbury* v. *Morgan* (1862).

(b) *If it is not accepted within* (*i*) the specified time (if any), or (*ii*) a reasonable time, if none is specified. What is a reasonable time depends on the circumstances. Five months has been held to be an unreasonable delay in accepting an offer to take shares in a company: *Ramsgate Hotel* v. *Montefiore* (1866).

(c) *If the offeree does not make a valid acceptance*, e.g. makes a counter-offer or conditional acceptance; or, if a particular manner of acceptance has been requested, he accepts in some other manner, e.g. by sending a letter by mail when a reply by hand was requested: *Eliason* v. *Henshaw* (1819), US case.

> NOTE: Where a counter-offer is accepted the terms of the counter-offer then form the basis of the resulting contract (and not the terms of the original offer): *Davies & Co.* v. *William Old* (1969).

8.   An offer may be revoked any time before acceptance

(a) *Revocation must be communicated.* Until the offeree actually received the revocation, he is entitled to accept and so create a binding contract.

Example

A sent an offer by cable to B on the 1st October requesting acceptance by the same method. B received the offer on 11th October and immediately cabled acceptance. On 8th October A had posted a letter revoking the offer, which did not reach B till after he had cabled his acceptance. HELD: B had accepted before receiving the revocation therefore a contract was made and the revocation was ineffective: *Byrne* v. *Van Tienhoven* (1880).

(b) *Indirect communication.* If the offeree learns of the revocation, he cannot later accept, even though he learns indirectly, e.g. where a prospective purchaser of land learns through a reliable third party that the offeror has sold the land to someone else. He cannot then accept the offer and sue the offeror for damages: *Dickinson* v. *Dodds* (1876).

> NOTE: An offer for shares or debentures in a public company made as a result of an advertisement or prospectus cannot be revoked until the third day after the opening of the subscription lists: Companies Act 1985, ss. 82, 86.

9. Options

An offer to keep an offer open for a specified time (an option) is not binding unless (*a*) made under seal, or (*b*) supported by valuable consideration, like any other simple contract: *Routledge* v. *Grant* (1828).

Problems

(1) A wrote offering to sell a car to B and to keep the offer open 'till Wednesday noon.' On Tuesday B learned through overhearing a conversation that A had sold the car to C on Monday. Can B now accept A's offer and sue A for damages for breach of contract? (*See* **8** above.) Would it make any difference to your answer if B had paid A 25p to keep the offer open till Wednesday? (*See* **9** above.)

(2) A published an advert saying that he would pay £100 to the first person to swim a particular lake on 1st April. B swims the lake and claims the reward. A now says the advert was a joke. Can B compel payment of the reward? (*See* **2** and **5** above.)

> NOTE: In a unilateral contract, which is where A promises to give B something if B first does something for A (see the example in (2) above), it has been said that 'although the offeror [A in our example] is entitled to require full performance of the condition which he has

imposed and although short of that he is not bound, once the offeree [B in our example] has embarked on performance of the condition [as by starting to swim across the lake] there is an implied obligation on the part of the offeror not to prevent performance and he cannot revoke his offer': *Daulia Ltd* v. *Four Millbank Nominees Ltd* (1978).

Rules governing acceptance

10. How made
Acceptance may be oral, written or implied from conduct: *Carlill* v. *Carbolic Smoke Ball Co.* (1893).

But if a particular method of acceptance is required the offeree must accept in the prescribed manner: *Eliason* v. *Henshaw* (1819).

11. Unqualified acceptance
Acceptance must be unqualified and must correspond with all the terms of the offer.

A counter-offer or conditional acceptance operates as a rejection of the offer, and causes it to lapse. Thus where a house is offered for sale at £1000 and the offeree counter-offers £950, the offer lapses: *Hyde* v. *Wrench* (1840).

Similarly, a conditional acceptance 'subject to a proper contract being drawn up' causes lapse of offer: *Eccles* v. *Bryant* (1948) (but an agreement 'subject to contract' would be binding if the phrase simply meant the agreement was to be subject to the terms of a contract already existing).

12. Positive conduct
There must be active acceptance: mere passive intention to accept is ineffective.

Thus an offer by letter containing the words, 'If I hear no more, I shall consider the horse is mine,' is incapable on its own of constituting its own acceptance. There must be some positive communication of acceptance by the offeree; it would not be enough to show that the offeree intended to accept but died before writing a letter of acceptance: *Felthouse* v. *Bindley* (1862). Furthermore, where goods are sent unrequested to a private individual, they can become his after six months without him having to do anything: Unsolicited Goods and Services Acts 1971 and 1975.

13. Communication of acceptance

Normally an acceptance is ineffective unless and until communicated to the offeror.

> EXCEPTIONS: (1) Where the offeror expressly or impliedly waives communication, e.g. where a general offer requires merely conduct as its acceptance: *Carlill* v. *Carbolic Smoke Ball Co.* (1893). Similarly an offer of a reward is accepted by doing what is required, without any previous communication: *Williams* v. *Carwardine* (1833). (2) Where the contract is made by post, or the post is envisaged as the means of communication, e.g. in most commercial contracts today. Here acceptance is complete as soon as it is posted, provided it is properly stamped and addressed: *Household Fire Insurance Co.* v. *Grant* (1879).

In postal cases therefore it does not matter if the letter of acceptance is lost in the post and never reaches the offeror: the contract is complete as soon as the letter of acceptance is posted. As a matter of commercial expediency the Post Office is treated as agent for the offeror, and communication to the agent is treated as communication to the principal.

The same rule applies to telegrams (but where the method of communication is instantaneous, e.g. telex, telephone or fax, acceptance is not complete until it actually reaches its destination. *Entores* v. *Miles Far East Corpn* (1955)). This point was confirmed by the House of Lords in *Brinkibon* v. *Stahag Stahl und Stahlwaren-handelsgesellschaft* (1983) where an offer was made by telex in Vienna and accepted by a telex message from London to Vienna. The House of Lords held that the contract was made in Vienna. The telex machines were in the offices of the respective parties, and the telexes were sent during business hours. The House of Lords left open the position where telexes are transmitted through agencies or outside office hours.

Where acceptance is to be by notice in writing to the offeree, mere posting of acceptance does not constitute notice — actual delivery must be proved: *Holwell Securities* v. *Hughes* (1974).

> NOTE: Mere posting is not sufficient in contracts governed by the Uniform Laws on International Sales Act 1967.

14. Motive for acceptance

No one can accept an offer in ignorance of its existence, but provided he knows of the offer his motive for accepting is usually irrelevant.

Example

C offered a reward for information leading to the arrest of a criminal. W provided the information (knowing of the offer) but saying that she did so simply 'to ease her conscience.' Therefore C refused to pay the reward. HELD: Since W knew of the offer and accepted it, her motive for doing so was irrelevant and she was entitled to the money: *Williams* v. *Carwardine* (1833).

15. Tenders

A tender is a form of offer for the supply of goods or services, usually made in response to a request for tenders. Tenders take the following forms.

(a) *Single offer*, e.g. a tender to build a factory. Acceptance of such a tender constitutes a contract.

(b) *Standing offer*, e.g. a tender to supply goods as and when required. Here the tenderer must supply as and when agreed, whenever an order is made. But he cannot insist on any orders being made at all.

Example

P tendered to supply goods up to a certain amount to the LCC over a certain period. The LCC's orders did not come up to the amount expected and P sued for breach of contract. HELD: Each order made a separate contract and P was bound to fulfil the orders made, but there was no obligation to make any orders at all: *Percival Ltd* v. *LCC* (1918).

(c) *Sole supplier*. The person seeking the tender may agree to take all his requirements for certain goods from the tenderer. This agreement does not oblige him to make any orders at all but if he does require goods within the category agreed he must take them from the tenderer: *Kier* v. *Whitehead Iron Co.* (1938).

NOTE: Where a tender is made before the deadline for the receipt of tenders, a binding contract can arise to consider tenders conforming to the conditions of tender: *Blackpool and Fylde Aero Club Ltd* v. *Blackpool BC* (1990).

Standard form contracts

There is an increasing tendency for an offeror to write out the contract entirely himself, and then demand that the offeree shall accept the detailed terms of the offer without modification.

The offeror may state all his terms in one document or, as in the case of railway tickets, may simply incorporate by reference certain standard conditions contained in another document. These 'offers with terms annexed' are subject to special rules. They include most forms of transport ticket, by air, sea, or rail, many printed leases, and most contracts for the supply of gas, electricity, etc.

16. If the contract is signed by the offeree, he is bound by all the conditions contained in the document signed even if he has not read them: *L'Estrange* v. *Graucob* (1934).

> EXCEPTIONS: (1) Where the offeree can prove he signed the document under a fundamental mistake as to its nature (not merely as to its contents). This is the Common Law defence of *non est factum*. It covers, for example, cases where a person is induced to sign a cheque on the mistaken assumption that it is merely a guarantee: *Foster* v. *Mackinnon* (1869), and *see* 4: **7.** (2) Where he can prove that he was induced to sign as a result of a misrepresentation by the offeror, or the offeror's agent, whether innocent or fraudulent: *Curtis* v. *Chemical Cleaning & Dyeing Co. Ltd* (1951); *Mendelsohn* v. *Normand Ltd* (1970); *Evans & Son* v. *Merzario* (1976). (3) In the case of certain credit and hire agreements, there is in some cases a right of cancellation: *see* 9: **81.**

17. If the contract is unsigned, e.g. railway tickets, the offeree is bound by all the terms in the document or annexed to it if:

(a) a reasonable man would assume the document to be contractual, e.g. not merely a receipt for money: *Chapelton* v. *Barry UDC* (1940);

(b) reasonable care was taken by the offeror to bring the terms of the offer to his attention, e.g. by a notice 'for conditions see Company's rules and regulations' clearly displayed on the face of the ticket. If the notice given is reasonable, the contract is binding whether the offeree reads the conditions or not: *Parker* v. *S.E.*

Railway (1877), or even whether the offeree is illiterate and unable to read them: *Thompson* v. *L.M.S. Railway* (1930); but if it is known that the person cannot read the clause because he is not English he is not bound by it: *Geier* v. *Kujawa* (1970);

(c) notice of annexed conditions must be contemporaneous with the making of the contract: *Olley* v. *Marlborough Court Ltd* (1949) and *Thornton* v. *Shoe Lane Parking Ltd* (1971).

> NOTE: An oral contract could also contain exemption clauses, but they would clearly be harder to prove.

Examples

(1) C took a deck chair from a pile under a notice 'Hire of chairs – 3d.' Later an attendant came round to collect the money and C paid him, receiving in return a ticket which said on it, 'The Council will not be liable for any accident or damage arising from hire of chair.' C put the ticket in his pocket without reading it, thinking it was merely a receipt. The chair collapsed and he was injured and sued the Council. HELD: The Council could not rely on the exclusionary notice since none of rules (*a*), (*b*), or (*c*) above was satisfied: *Chapelton* v. *Barry U.D.C.* (1940).

(2) O registered at a hotel by signing the visitors' book, and then went to his room where a notice was displayed excluding the hotel's liability for articles lost. HELD: He made his contract when he signed the book, and the hotel could not rely on the exclusionary notice since it was not brought to his attention contemporaneously with the making of the contract: *Olley* v. *Marlborough Court Ltd* (1949).

(3) B booked a passage for P and himself on D's vessel. He later received tickets containing an exclusion clause. It was held that the contract was made before the tickets were received, so the exclusion clause had no effect: *Hollingworth* v. *Southern Ferries* (1977).

(d) in *Interfoto Picture Library Ltd* v. *Stiletto Visual Programmes Ltd* (1988) a photographic library provided transparencies to an advertising agency on terms which specified that, if the transparencies were held for longer than 14 days, then a charge of £7.50 per day would be made until their return. The transparencies were held for more than 14 days and the library sought to rely on the above term. The Court of Appeal ruled that this term was particularly onerous since the usual rate at the time was £3.50 per week. Where a clause was unreasonable and extortionate in this way, then it would not be held to be part of the contract unless the party seeking to enforce it could show that it had been fairly and reasonably brought to the attention of the other party. This had not been done in this case, and so the term was not part of the contract.

Exemption clauses

18. Nature of exemption clauses

Annexed conditions are usually aimed at exempting the offeror from some legal liability to which he would otherwise be subject, e.g. liability for negligence in carrying out the contract. Exemption clauses are viewed with increasing disfavour by the courts, and both statutory and judicial restrictions have been imposed on their employment.

Statutory restrictions
Examples are as follows.

(a) The Unfair Contract Terms Act 1977 limits the effectiveness of exclusion clauses in contracts of sale and hire-purchase. In contracts made by businesses with consumers, clauses excluding the implied terms as to description, quality and fitness for purpose are void. The use of such clauses is also unlawful by virtue of the Consumer Transactions (Restrictions on Statements) Orders 1976 No. 1813 and 1978 No. 127. In contracts made between businesses, clauses excluding these terms are valid if they can be shown to be reasonable.

(b) The 1977 Act also imposes restrictions on some exclusion clauses in contracts made on written standard terms or between a business and a consumer (i.e. whether or not on written standard terms). Clauses covered by this part of the Act, s. 3, are only valid if proved to be reasonable. The clauses which are covered by the Act are the following: (*i*) those which seek to exclude or restrict liability for breach of contract; (*ii*) those which claim to allow a contractual performance 'substantially different' from that expected; (*iii*) those which claim to allow no performance at all.

(c) The Act states that no exclusion clause can restrict or exclude liability for negligence resulting in death or personal injury. Where negligence results in any other type of loss, such as damage to property, the clause is valid if it can be proved to be reasonable.

(d) The Unfair Contract Terms Act, s. 8 makes void any term in a contract seeking to exempt a party from legal liability for any misrepresentation made by him before the contract was entered into (unless it is shown that the clause was reasonable).

(e) The Consumer Credit Act 1974, s.173, makes void a term in a contract which excludes the protection afforded by the Act.

(f) The Supply of Goods (Implied Terms) Act 1973 makes void clauses seeking to avoid the warranties as to title and merchantable quality implied into redemptions of trading stamps for goods.

Judicial restrictions

The attitude of the courts can be summarised as follows.

(a) An exclusion clause will never be enforced unless adequate advance notice of it has been given to the other party: *Parker* v. *S.E. Railway* (1877).

(b) Under the *contra proferentem* rule exclusion clauses are narrowly construed against the person who inserted them.

(c) Where the parties are on unequal footing, the court will more readily reject an exclusion clause designed to protect the stronger party. In one case, a young songwriter made an agreement with a publishing company for a five-year period. It was a particularly stringent standard form contract; for example, there was no obligation on the publishers to publish any of the songs produced. It was said, in finding that the contract could not be enforced, that the courts intervene to protect those 'whose power is weak against being forced by those whose bargaining power is stronger to enter into bargains which are unconscionable': *Schroeder (A) Music Publishing Co. Ltd* v. *Macaulay* (1974). *See also Clifford Davis Management* v. *W.E.A. Records Ltd* (1975) and *Lloyds Bank* v. *Bundy* (1975).

(d) Where the exclusion clause seeks to evade liability for breach of a fundamental term of the contract the courts will be particularly reluctant to enforce it: *Suisse Atlantique etc.* v. *N.V. Rotterdamsche Kolen Centrale* (1966); *Harbutt's Plasticine Ltd* v. *Wayne Tank and Pump Co. Ltd* (1970) and *Wathes (Western) Ltd* v. *Austins (Menswear) Ltd* (1976).

Examples

Exemption clauses were thus held void where (1) a bailee for safe custody handed the goods deposited to a stranger instead of returning them to the bailor: *Alexander* v. *Railway Executive* (1951); (2) a bailee stored goods in a warehouse other than that agreed with the bailor and the goods were destroyed by fire: *Lilley* v. *Doubleday* (1881). Where a bailee loses goods, the onus is on him to show he was not in fundamental breach: *Levison* v. *Patent Steam Carpet Cleaning Co.* (1977).

19. Indemnity clauses

The Unfair Contract Terms Act 1977, s. 4, controls clauses which require a consumer to indemnify another party for liability which the latter might incur through negligence or breach of contract. Such clauses are now only valid if they are proved to be reasonable.

20. Guarantees

Where a guarantee is provided by a manufacturer that he will make good loss arising from negligence in the distribution or manufacture of the goods, this guarantee cannot exclude liability for the loss or damage: s. 5 of the 1977 Act.

NOTE: The Consumer Transactions (Restrictions on Statements) Order 1976 requires all guarantees (whether given by the manufacturer or the retailer) to be accompanied by a statement to the effect that the consumer's rights against the retailer are unaffected.

Certainty of terms

21. Terms must be certain

It is for the parties to make their intentions clear in their contract. The court will not enforce a contract the terms of which are uncertain.

Thus an agreement to agree in the future ('a contract to make a contract') will not constitute a binding contract, e.g. a promise to pay an actress 'a West End salary to be mutually agreed between us' is not a contract, since the salary is not yet agreed: *Loftus* v. *Roberts* (1902). Similarly, an agreement providing that the price will be subject to later negotiations is not a contract, since contracts to negotiate are not known to the law: *Courtney* v. *Tolaini* (1975); *Walford* v. *Miles* (1992)

Similarly, where the terms of a final agreement are too vague, the contract will fail for uncertainty, e.g. sale of a van 'on hire-purchase terms' is too vague, since there are several types of hire-purchase agreement: *Scammell* v. *Ouston* (1941).

22. *Id certum est quod certum reddi potest* (that is certain which can be reduced to certainty)

An agreement which at first sight appears to be too vague may be enforced under the following conditions.

(a) If the parties themselves have provided machinery in the contract for resolving the uncertainty, e.g. where no price was fixed for the sale of petrol, but the agreement stated that all disputes should be referred to arbitration, it was held that the arbitrator could fix the prices and so resolve the uncertainty: *Foley* v. *Classique Coaches Ltd* (1934). Also where a five-year contract for the supply of chickens failed to state the number of chickens, but contained an arbitration clause, it was held that the numbers could be fixed by arbitration: *F. & G. Sykes (Wessex) Ltd* v. *Fine Fare Ltd* (1966).

(b) The deficiency can be remedied by the court implying a term, either (*i*) from the course of dealing between the parties in the past (if any), or (*ii*) from trade usages in the particular trade (if any), or (*iii*) where certain terms are implied by statute in similar contracts, e.g. the Sale of Goods Act 1979. The court may always imply a term into a contract to save it from collapse, but will do so only where it is clearly necessary and equitable: *The Moorcock* (1889).

23. Meaningless clauses

An agreement which is definite on the whole will be enforced, notwithstanding the presence of some meaningless or unnecessary words or phrases. The court in such a case will ignore the meaningless words and enforce the contract without them (unless the parties have given such a phrase a common meaning): *Nicolene Ltd* v. *Simmonds* (1953).

Terms of a contract

24. Express or implied terms

The parties may expressly state every term of their contract with varying degrees of precision; or they may simply agree the basic purpose of the contract and leave the detailed terms to be deduced from the surrounding circumstances.

Contractual terms are of two kinds: (*a*) conditions (main terms); or (*b*) warranties (subordinate terms). Whether a term is a condition or a warranty is a question of intention to be deduced by the court in the light of the surrounding circumstances. Mistaken use of the words 'condition' or 'warranty' by the parties will not be regarded as conclusive. And *see* 5: **25**.

25. Conditions

A condition is an essential term which goes to the root of the contract, i.e. it may constitute the main purpose of the agreement, or one of several main purposes.

Breach of condition entitles the injured party to treat the contract as at an end: *Behn* v. *Burness* (1863), and *see* 5: **23–29**. (Alternatively he may treat the breach as a mere breach of warranty, claim damages and insist on the contract being performed.) The Sale of Goods Act 1979, ss.13 and 14, declares that the implied terms as to description, quality and fitness for purpose are conditions, as is the sellers's duty to have a right to sell: s. 12(1).

> NOTE: Fundamental term. This is a condition so important that it constitutes the fundamental purpose of the contract, in the view of the court. Where there is breach of such a term (fundamental breach) the courts will not allow the contract-breaker to escape liability by relying on even an express exemption clause unless the clause clearly covers the particular breach: *Suisse Atlantique etc.* v. *N.V. Rotterdamsche Kolen Centrale* (1966) H.L. (*The Suisse Atlantique* case); *Photo Production Ltd* v. *Securicor Transport Ltd* (1980).
>
> There is no fundamental breach where breach is caused by circumstances beyond the control of the non-performing party and an exemption covers the situation: *Trade & Transport Incorporated* v. *Iino Kaiun Paisha (The Angelica)* (1973).

26. Kinds of condition

(a) *Condition precedent*: a condition that the contract shall not bind one or both of the parties until such condition is fulfilled, e.g. 'this contract is not to be binding until the war ends.'

(b) *Condition subsequent:* a condition under which the contract shall cease to be binding at the option of one party on the happening of a certain event, e.g. 'this contract shall cease to be binding if war breaks out.' This is called a determinable contract and remains binding until the condition subsequent is fulfilled; contrast a voidable contract, which can be made completely void at the option of one party.

(c) *Condition concurrent*: a condition under which performance by one party is made dependent on performance by the others at the same time, e.g. payment of price upon delivery of goods ordered.

27. Warranties

A warranty is a subordinate term, subsidiary to the main purpose of the contract: Sale of Goods Act 1979, s. 61(1).

Breach of warranty entitles the injured party to sue for damages, but he cannot regard the contract as at an end and must perform his part of it.

Example

B promised to attend rehearsals for six days before a concert, but arrived in London only in time for two days' rehearsals, whereat G claimed the contract was discharged by breach of condition. HELD: Attendance at rehearsals was a warranty only and therefore the contract was not discharged, though G was entitled to damages: *Bettini* v. *Gye* (1876). The obligation on the seller that the goods are free from any encumbrance and that the buyer will enjoy quiet possession are *warranties:* Sale of Goods Act 1979, s. 12(2)

28. *Ex post facto* warranties

Where a breach of condition occurs the injured party can (*a*) treat the contract as discharged, or (*b*) if he prefers he may treat the breach as breach of a warranty, go on with the contract and sue for damages.

In some cases he must adopt the second alternative, e.g. where in a contract for sale of goods the purchaser has accepted a substantial part of the goods, before discovering a breach of condition, he must treat the breach as a breach of warranty: Sale of Goods Act 1979, s.11(1).

This treating a breach of condition after it has occurred as though it were a breach of warranty is called treating it as breach of an *ex post facto* warranty, i.e. a warranty after the event.

29. Implied terms

The general rule is that the parties are presumed to have expressed their intentions fully.

The courts will only imply additional terms where it is strictly necessary to give effect to the clear intentions of the parties, or where custom or statute requires the implication: *The Moorcock* (1889), and *see* **22** *above*.

When express terms are clear and unambiguous, the court will only imply a term if it is clear that the parties must have intended it to form part of the contract: *Trollope & Colls* v. *N.W. Metropolitan Regional Hospital Board* (1973).

Example _____

C's insurance company employed the X garage to repair C's car, damaged in an accident. The court found that there was an implied contract between C and X (contrary to X's claim that its only contract was with the insurance company). There was no term in this implied contract fixing the time to be taken for the repairs: X took eight weeks and C claimed damages for unreasonable delay. HELD: In the interests of business efficacy the court implied that repairs must be completed in a reasonable time (in this case five weeks) and awarded damages to C: *Charnock* v. *Liverpool Corporation* (1968); *see also Brown & Davis Ltd* v. *Galbraith* (1972).

_____

Occasionally, terms are implied by statute: e.g. Sale of Goods Act (contracts of sale); Supply of Goods (Implied Terms) Act (hire-purchase): *see* **25** and **27** above.

30. Terms and representations

Frequently during preliminary negotiations one of the parties (e.g. the seller of goods) may make a series of statements, or representations, to help persuade the other party to enter the contract. Whether such representations become terms in the contract (and so binding the maker) depends on the construction which the court puts upon them.

The test is: Did the plaintiff accept the representations as mere inducements, or did he insist that he would not enter into the contract unless the representations could be regarded as binding conditions or warranties?

The following rules apply.

(a) A representation will not be regarded as a term of the contract unless the parties so agree, expressly or by implication.

(b) If a representation is treated as a mere inducement, the plaintiff cannot sue for breach of contract if it proves untrue. (Though he may be able to avoid the contract and obtain damages on the grounds of misrepresentation: Misrepresentation Act 1967, *see* 4: **11**).

(c) If a representation is agreed by the parties to be a term of the contract, the plaintiff's remedies will depend on whether it is regarded by the court as a condition or as a warranty: *see* **25** and **27** above and 5: **25**.

31. Construction of terms

In construing the terms of a contract the courts apply the following rules.

(a) Language used must be construed as far as possible in such a way as to give effect to the intentions of the parties.

(b) Words used must be presumed to have their normal literal meaning, unless the contrary is proved.

(c) Where there are two possible meanings, one legal and the other illegal, the legal meaning is to be preferred so as to render the contract enforceable (illegal contracts are void: *see* 4: **25**).

(d) The contract is to be construed most strongly against the party who drew it up (the *contra proferentem* rule: *see* **18**).

(e) Contracts are to be construed according to their proper law, i.e. usually the law of the country in which they were made: *see* **33**.

(f) If the contract fails to express the undoubted intentions of the parties, the court will rectify it so as to make such intentions express: *see* 4: **9** below.

> NOTE: In construing the terms of a written contract the court cannot admit evidence of (*i*) the negotiations preceding contract, or (*ii*) the parties' intentions during negotiations: *Prenn* v. *Simmonds* (1971) H.L.

32. Collateral contracts

Where A and B enter into a contract the rights and duties arising will normally affect only A and B: *see* Privity of Contract, 6: **1–4**. But sometimes if A was induced to enter into this contract by the representations of X, the court may imply a collateral contract between X and A, the consideration for which is A's agreement to enter into the contract with B.

Example _____

X induced A to buy a car from B on hire-purchase. The hire-purchase contract was between A and B and X was not a party to it. The car was defective and injured A. X's statements as to the condition of the car were found to be false. HELD: A had no remedy against B, by reason of an exemption clause. But there was an implied collateral contract between X and A, under which A promised to buy the car from B; X was liable in damages for his false statements: *Andrews* v. *Hopkinson* (1956). *See also Evans* v. *Merzario* (1976).

NOTE: Under the Consumer Credit Act 1974, B would now be liable in contract for misrepresentations by his agent, X: *see* 9: **84.**

Conflict of laws

33. Conflict of laws

There is an increasing tendency for mercantile contracts to be made between people in different countries and the question may then arise: which of several possible systems of law should the English court apply to resolve a dispute upon the contract?

The position has been affected by the Contracts (Applicable Law) Act 1990, as follows. The major provisions of the Act, which implements the provisions of the Rome Convention, are as follows.

Free to choose

The convention, which is set out in full in a Schedule to the Act, allows the parties to make an express choice as to the proper law, or by implication. This latter will apply where the implication can be 'demonstrated with reasonable certainty by the terms of the contract or the circumstances of the case'. If, at its most basic, a contract is made between parties based in England, with the goods coming from one part of the country to another, then the contract will of course be subject to English law. Again, if a contract does involve a party in this country buying goods from overseas, or from Scotland, and the contract specifies that English courts shall resolve any disputes arising between the parties, then the Act will operate to create the presumption that the English courts will apply English law.

Limitations on choice

This right to choose the proper law of the contract, though, is not unfettered. Thus, if a court is satisfied that, on a proper analysis, the contract really 'belongs' to a particular country, then the 'mandatory' rules (a term which awaits judicial explanation) of that country will prevail, regardless of what the contract might have said. Parties to a contract which had no connection with any country other than England, for instance, could not state that the contract was subject to the laws of France, at least so far as the 'mandatory' rules are concerned.

Then again, the law of the legal system chosen by the parties can be displaced by the law of the country in which the court deciding the matter is situated. This can occur if public policy in that country is in conflict with that of the chosen regime; or is in conflict with that country's mandatory rules.

Where no choice is made

Here the Act states that the contract will be governed by the law of the country 'with which it is most closely connected'. This, in fact, is in essence the test which has long been used in this country to determine the proper law of a contract. The presumption is that the contract is most closely connected 'with the country where the party who is to effect the performance which is characteristic of the contract has, at the time of the conclusion of the contract, his habitual residence or, in the case of a body corporate or unincorporated, its central administration. However, if the contract is entered into in the course of that party's trade or profession, that country shall be the country in which the principal place of business is situated or, where under the terms of the contract the performance is to be effected through a place of business other than the principal place of business, the country in which that other place of business is situated'.

The key phrase here is 'performance which is characteristic'. To give some guidance on its meaning, we can refer to the Report on the Rome Convention reproduced in the *Official Journal* of the EC. It contains an extensive commentary on the convention and may, as the Act itself states, be considered by the UK courts when ascertaining the meaning or effect of any Convention provision. This is what the Report says: 'Identifying the characteristic performance of a contract obviously presents no difficulty in the case of unilateral contracts. By contrast, in bilateral (reciprocal) contracts whereby the parties undertake mutual reciprocal performance, the counter-performance by one of the parties in a modern economy usually takes the form of money. This is not, of course, the characteristic performance of the contract. It is the perfomance for which payment is due, i.e. depending on the type of contract, the delivery of the goods, the granting of the right to make use of an item of property, the provision of a service, transport, insurance, banking operations, security, etc. which usually constitutes the centre of gravity and the socio-economic function of the contractual obligation'. This would seem to suggest that a payment obligation can never be a performance which is 'characteristic' of the contract, a view with which some may differ. In any event, the Report is not binding, rather it is something to be taken into account when considering the meaning of the Convention.

3
Form, consideration and capacity

Generally a contract can be made in any form, but in exceptional cases the law lays down a particular requirement, e.g. that the contract shall be by deed.

All simple contracts must be supported by consideration, that is by some element of exchange which is measurable in money or money's worth, e.g. goods in return for cash, or services in return for wages or goods.

Generally, any person can make any sort of contract, i.e. has full capacity to contract. But certain special classes of person suffer from contractual incapacities of various kinds, e.g. minors.

Formal requirements

1. Generally no formality

Most contracts can be made in any form, i.e. orally, by writing, by telephone, by fax, telegram, or by deed.

But in the following special cases the law requires that a particular form shall be adopted, usually to provide better evidence of the terms and so prevent disputes.

2. Contracts void unless made by deed

(a) Promises of gifts: *Rann* v. *Hughes* (1778).
(b) Transfers of British ships or shares therein.
(c) Conditional bills of sale: *see* 15: **13**.
(d) Certain documents creating or transferring estates or interests in land, e.g. conveyances of land, legal mortgages, and leases for more than three years: Law of Property (Miscellaneous Provisions) Act 1989.

3. Contracts requiring written form

(a) Bill of exchange: Bill of Exchange Act 1882, s. 3(1).

(b) Assignment of copyright: Copyright, Designs and Patents Act 1988, s. 90(3).

(c) Contracts of marine insurance: Marine Insurance Act 1906, ss. 21–23. All policies of life insurance are in practice in writing, but there is no requirement that they should be.

(d) Transfers of shares in registered companies: Companies Act 1985, s.183.

(e) Acknowledgement of statute-barred debts: Limitation Act 1980, s. 30.

(f) Articles of association of registered companies: Companies Act 1985, s. 7.

(g) Regulated consumer credit agreements: Consumer Credit Act 1974, s. 60.

(h) Contracts of employment: Employment Protection (Consolidation) Act 1978, s. 1.

(i) Contracts for directory entries: Unsolicited Goods and Services Acts 1971–1975, s. 3.

(j) Contracts for the sale or other disposition of an interest in land: Law of Property (Miscellaneous Provisions) Act 1989, s. 2.

Company contracts

The rule that a company contract had to be by deed was abolished by the Corporate Bodies Contracts Act 1960. Companies can now make their contracts in whatever form is appropriate to private individuals. The Companies Act 1985 provides that a company contract can be made by a company in writing, under its common seal, or on behalf of the company by any person acting under its authority. A document is executed by a company affixing its common seal, but this is not essential: indeed a company may not have a seal. A document signed by the director and secretary, or by two directors, and expressed to be executed by the company, has the same effect as if executed under the common seal. A document executed by a company which makes it clear that it is intended to be a deed has effect, on delivery, as a deed.

4. Contracts of guarantee

Section 4 of the Statute of Frauds Act 1677 requires contracts of guarantee to be evidenced in writing. A guarantee is a contract to 'answer for the debt, default or miscarriage of another', that is, a contract to discharge another's obligations if that other fails to do so himself, sometimes called a contract of secondary liability. These are to be contrasted with contracts of indemnity, which are promises to discharge another's obligation or to ensure that it is discharged, i.e. a contract in which the indemnifier accepts primary liability (indemnities do not need to be evidenced in writing).

A contract of guarantee can be made enforceable under s. 4 of the Statute of Frauds Act either by having a written agreement signed by the guarantor or his agent, or by having a note or memorandum of the agreement, which can itself be oral, signed by the guarantor or his agent. In the latter case, the intention or capacity of the person signing the memorandum is irrelevant since all that is necessary under s. 4 is the existence of a note or memorandum of a promise to answer for the debt, default or miscarriage of another person signed by the party to be charged: *Elpis Maritime Co. Ltd* v. *Marti Chartering Co. Inc.* (1991).

> NOTE: Guarantees do not need to be evidenced in writing if they are merely part of larger transactions, e.g. where, on his appointment, an agent guarantees to make good losses incurred by his employer if any of the clients introduced by the agent fail to pay their debts. Here, the guarantee is merely part of the contract of agency and therefore the whole contract can be oral if so desired: *Eastwood* v. *Kenyon* (1840).

5. Meaning of 'evidenced in writing'

The minimum of necessary written evidence suffices provided it contains all the material terms of the contract, i.e. any signed note or memorandum of material terms on any scrap of paper. The note or memorandum must contain the following.

(a) *The signature of the 'party to be charged'* or of his agent, i.e. the signature of the defendant in any action brought upon the contract. It need not be signed by the plaintiff in the action. Any writing by which the guarantor of a debt can be identified in a memorandum of the guarantee, and which shows an intention to adopt the guarantee, suffices as a signature for the purposes of s. 4 of the Statute of Frauds: *Decouvreur* v. *Jordan* (1987).

(b) *All material terms* of the contract, i.e. (*i*) names of the parties or sufficient identification; (*ii*) description of the subject matter, e.g. the address of a house being sold; (*iii*) the price or other consideration.

> NOTE: Although, like other simple contracts, guarantees must be supported by consideration, the consideration does not need to be expressly stated in the memorandum of guarantee: Mercantile Law Amendment Act 1856.

6. When and how made

The note or memorandum can be made at any time after the contract is agreed, providing it is made (and signed by the defendant) before the contract is disputed in court.

It may consist of several documents, provided there is sufficient evidence to connect them beyond reasonable doubt, e.g. a letter headed 'Dear Sir' might be linked to the envelope which contained it, so identifying the recipient: *Long* v. *Millar* (1879).

Problem

A contracted to buy a house from B, vacant possession to be given on completion. A paid a 10 per cent deposit and B gave him a signed receipt which identified the parties, stated the purpose of the deposit, but contained no mention of vacant possession. Would this receipt be a sufficient memorandum? Would it be sufficient if it mentioned the requirement as to vacant possession?

7. Effect of non-compliance

If a contract required to be evidenced in writing is not so evidenced, it is unenforceable. Therefore, although it may be perfectly lawful, if one party breaks the contract, the other cannot sue him for damages for breach of contract in the normal way (but he would be entitled to keep any deposit he had obtained: *see* 1: 11).

> NOTE: (1) The parties retain all other rights, except action in the courts. Thus, in an oral contract for the sale of land which fails through the fault of the purchaser, the vendor would be entitled to retain a deposit the purchaser had put down (normally 10 per cent) and the court would not assist the purchaser to recover it: *Monickendam* v. *Leanse* (1923) and *see* 1: 11. (2) If one party has fully performed his part of the contract, the court may give him an order for specific performance, commanding the defendant to perform his

side of the bargain despite the absence of written evidence (this is the equitable doctrine of part performance, and it applies only to contracts for the transfer of some interest in land).

8. The doctrine of part performance

An oral contract for the transfer of any estate or interest in land is invalid: Law of Property (Miscellaneous Provisions) Act, s. 2. Under the old law, the doctrine of part performance was available where the contract was oral, if A had performed his part of the contract, but B then refused to perform his part. The provisions of the 1989 Act now preclude the use of the doctrine.

Valuable consideration

9. Importance of consideration

The courts will not enforce a simple contract unless it is supported by valuable consideration, which is therefore an essential element in most contracts. (Consideration is not necessary in specialty contracts or contracts of record: *see* 1: **5–6.**)

10. Meaning of 'valuable consideration'

It has been defined as 'the price for which a promise is bought' (Sir Frederick Pollock).

Consideration itself means 'some right, interest, profit, or benefit accruing to one party or some forbearance, detriment, loss of responsibility given, suffered or undertaken by the other': *per* Lush J., *Currie* v. *Misa* (1875).

Consideration therefore means the element of exchange in a bargain, and in order to satisfy the requirements of English law it must be valuable consideration, i.e. something which is capable of being valued in terms of money or money's worth, however slight. It may take the form of money, goods, services, a promise to marry, a promise to forbear from suing the promisee, etc.

11. Kinds of consideration

(a) *Executory consideration,* i.e. where the consideration consists of a promise to do something in the future (such as to render a service at a future date).

(b) *Executed consideration,* i.e. where the act constituting the consideration is wholly performed.

Thus if X pays a shopkeeper now for goods which are promised to be delivered later, X has executed his consideration, but the shopkeeper is giving executory consideration, i.e. a promise to be executed in the future.

Rules relating to consideration

These require to be fully learned and understood, and are set out in detail below.

12. Necessity for consideration

Every simple contract must be supported by valuable consideration, otherwise it is normally void.

> EXCEPTIONS: (1) *Gratuitous bailments.* A bailment is the delivery of a chattel to a hirer or borrower for some limited purpose or period. Most bailments are for reward, i.e. are supported by some payment, but even where the bailment is gratuitous it is still recognised as an enforceable contract: *Bainbridge* v. *Firmstone* (1838). (In such cases the courts tend to regard the owner's parting with possession of his chattel as sufficient notional consideration, so that this is not a real exception to the doctrine of consideration.) (2) *Gratuitous services when performance commenced.* If A gratuitously promises to dig B's garden, and fails to do so, B cannot sue A for breach of contract since there is no consideration for A's promise. But it has been suggested that if A once commenced the digging, he would be under an obligation to exercise reasonable care in the work and could be sued for damages if he were negligent.

13. Legality of consideration

The consideration must be legal, e.g. not some illegal act, such as paying someone to commit a crime. If the consideration is illegal, the contract is void: *see* 4: **25–29.**

14. Consideration must move from the promisee

That is, a person seeking to enforce a simple contract in court must prove that he himself has given consideration in return for the promise he is seeking to enforce.

Example _____

D had supplied goods to a wholesaler, X, on condition that any retailer
to whom X resupplied the goods should promise X not to sell them to
the public without fulfilling stated conditions. X supplied goods to S upon
this condition, nevertheless S sold them in breach of stated conditions.
HELD: There was a contract between D and X, and a contract between X
and S, but none between D and S. Therefore D could not obtain damages
from S. The main reason for this decision was the fact that D could not
show that he himself had given any consideration for S's promise to X:
Dunlop Pneumatic Tyre Co. v. *Selfridges Ltd* (1915) (affirmed in *Scruttons Ltd*
v. *Midland Silicones Ltd* (1962), H.L.).

NOTE: Compare this rule with the doctrine of privity of contract,
see 6: 1. In effect, in any contractual action, the court asks two implied
questions which must be satisfied before the plaintiff can succeed in
his action: (*i*) Is the plaintiff a party to the contract he seeks to
enforce? (privity of contract) and (*ii*) if so, has he given consideration
for the promise he seeks to enforce? In *Dunlop Pneumatic Tyre Co.* v.
Selfridges Ltd (1915) the plaintiff failed to supply satisfactory answers
to both questions.

**15. It must be something more than the promisee is already
bound to do for the promisor**

That is, the person seeking to enforce the promise must show
that he himself has undertaken some obligation to the promisor
beyond what he is already bound to do either (*a*) as part of his legal
duty as a citizen, or (*b*) as part of a private contractual duty owed
to the promisor.

Example _____

If a seaman deserts his ship — so breaking his contract — and is induced
to return to his duty by the promise of extra wages, he cannot later sue
for the extra wages since he has only done what he was already contracted
for: *Stilk* v. *Myrick* (1809).

NOTE: Performance by A of an existing duty owed to B will suffice
to support a promise by C to A. Thus where A was engaged to marry
B, and C promised A a sum of money to carry out this promise to B,
it was held that A could sue C for the money as soon as he had
performed his promise and married B: *Shadwell* v. *Shadwell* (1860).
In contrast, where one party to a contract agreed, in the absence of

economic duress or fraud, to make a payment to the other party to the contract over and above the contract price in order to secure completion of the contract by the other party on time, and thereby obtained a benefit in that a penalty clause was avoided, it was held that the obtaining of that benefit could amount to consideration for payment of the additional sum: *Williams* v. *Roffey Bros & Nicholls (Contractors) Ltd* (1990).

16. Consideration must be real

That is, it must not be vague, indefinite, or illusory, e.g. a son's vague promise to 'stop being a nuisance' to his father: *White* v. *Bluett* (1853).

Although the consideration must be real, it need not be adequate, i.e. it is up to the parties to fix their own prices, and providing there is some definite valuable consideration, the court will not set a contract aside merely because the price is inadequate: *Haigh* v. *Brooks* (1839).

But a ridiculously inadequate consideration may be prima facie evidence of misrepresentation or coercion: *see* Chapter 4.

Example _____

A bought a guarantee contract from B which later turned out to be unenforceable. HELD: A had got what he wanted and could not later rescind the contract merely because it turned out to be worth less than he thought: *Haigh* v. *Brooks* (1839).

_____

17. Consideration must not be past

That is, a promise made in return for some past service is unenforceable, e.g. where, having bought a horse, the purchaser promised to give the seller an extra sum because of his satisfaction with the purchase, it was held that the promise was unenforceable since it related to a past sale, and the purchaser was therefore receiving no new benefit as consideration for his new promise: *Roscorla* v. *Thomas* (1842).

EXCEPTIONS: Past consideration is sufficient in the following cases: (1) *To revive a statute-barred claim,* a mere written acknowledgment is enough without any fresh consideration: Limitation Act 1980 (for limitation of actions, *see* 5: **15**). (2) *A bill of exchange can be supported* by any antecedent debt or liability: Bill of Exchange Act 1882, s. 27. (3) Where the past consideration was rendered in response to an

earlier request by the person who subsequently promises to pay for
the service rendered: the rule in *Lampleigh* v. *Braithwait* (1615). Here
the promisor's request is held to imply a promise to pay a reasonable
sum later and the subsequent promise to pay merely fixes the sum:
Stewart v. *Casey* (1892).

Example _____

A asked B to use his influence to obtain a royal pardon for A, who had
committed a crime. B did as he was asked, and later (in consideration of
this past service) A promised to pay B £100. HELD: B could enforce
payment: *Lampleigh* v. *Braithwait* (1615).

18. Payment of a smaller sum will not discharge a liability to pay a larger

The rule in *Foakes* v. *Beer* (1884). Thus if A owes B £100 and
B agrees to accept £50 in complete discharge of the debt, there is
nothing to stop B later changing his mind and suing for the
remaining £50. In *Tiney Engineering Ltd* v. *Amods Knitting Machinery
Ltd* (1986) the plaintiff and defendant were engaged in a
transaction involving the sale of a knitting machine. The parties
met and agreed that a commission should be paid. They later
disagreed whether the commission should be 10 per cent as the
plaintiff claimed, or 5 per cent as the defendant claimed. The
parties met again, and the plaintiff accepted 5 per cent in 'full and
final settlement'. The court of appeal ruled that, since there was
no consideration for the plaintiff's agreement to accept only 5 per
cent commission, and since there was no accord between the
parties when the reduced commission was negotiated, it would not
be inequitable to allow the plaintiff to receive the remaining 5 per
cent.

EXCEPTIONS: (1) *Where the smaller sum is paid in a form or manner
different* from that originally intended, e.g. where the smaller sum is
paid earlier than the debt was due, or where a money debt is settled
in goods, or is paid by handing over 'a horse, hawk, or robe': *Pinnel's
Case* (1602). But it is important to note that the creditor's acceptance
of the smaller sum must be voluntary. Thus where a debtor put
pressure on his creditor to accept a smaller sum, it was held that the
acceptance was not binding: *D. & C. Builders Ltd* v. *Rees* (1966). (2)
Where (*i*) the creditor promises to accept a smaller sum (*ii*) intending
his position to be relied upon and (*iii*) the debtor alters his financial

position in reliance on the promise, the creditor may be estopped from going back on his promise, even though it was unsupported by consideration.

Example ——————————————————————————————

A leased property to B at a rent of £2500 p.a. but promised to accept half this sum during the war years, and B relied on this promise, making no attempt to earn the money necessary to pay the full rent. If later A went back on his promise and sued for the full rental, the court would exercise its equitable discretion and estop A from retracting his promise: *The High Trees* case (*Central London Property Trust* v. *High Trees House* (1947)).

This is an application of the principle of equitable estoppel, whereby a man may be prevented from denying any promise unconscionably even though it was unsupported by consideration. But the *High Trees* rule can only be raised as a defence, and not as a cause of action by the debtor, e.g. where a creditor has retracted his promise to accept a smaller sum and has forced the debtor to pay him the full amount, the debtor could not use the *High Trees* rule as the basis of an action to recover the extra money paid: *Combe* v. *Combe* (1951).

Contractual capacity

The general rule is that all persons have full capacity to make binding contracts, but the following exceptional cases exist: *see also* Minors, **24**, below.

19. Aliens

They have full capacity, save there are limitations as to the ownership of British ships: Merchant Shipping Acts 1894–1988.

Aliens residing in countries at war with Britain are classed as enemy aliens (whatever their nationality). They cannot sue in British courts during war-time, but can be sued; and if sued they can defend the action, appeal, and lodge counter-claims in the normal way, either personally or through agents: *Porter* v. *Freudenberg* (1915).

20. Foreign sovereigns and diplomats

They have diplomatic immunity and cannot be sued in British courts, unless they voluntarily submit to the jurisdiction: Diplomatic Privileges Act 1964. *See also* the State Immunity Act

1978 (no immunity in respect of commercial contracts; or contracts to be performed wholly or partly in the UK).

> NOTE: Diplomatic immunity does not arise until the diplomat's appointment is accepted by the British Government: *R*. v. *Pentonville Prison Governor, ex parte Teja* (1971).

21. Married women

They now have full contractual capacity, can sue or be sued in their own names, can be bankrupted for their debts, etc.: Law Reform (Married Women and Tortfeasors) Act 1935.

The common law doctrine of a wife's agency of necessity was abolished under s. 41 of the Matrimonial Proceedings and Property Act 1970.

22. Mental patients and drunkards

Their contracts are voidable, if (*a*) they were so drunk or mentally unbalanced as not to understand what the contract was about, and (*b*) the other party was aware of this: *Imperial Loan Co.* v. *Stone* (1892). Such voidable contracts can be ratified during lucid or sober intervals.

The Sale of Goods Act 1979, s. 2, lays down that lunatics, drunkards, and minors are bound to pay a reasonable price for necessaries (*see* Minors, **24**, below).

23. Corporations

A corporation is an artificial personalty recognised by the law. Consequently it can only contract through human agents.

Under the *ultra vires* doctrine a statutory or registered corporation can only contract validly within the powers conferred upon it. Any contract which is *ultra vires* ('beyond the powers') is void. (Corporations created by royal charter are not subject to the doctrine, though if they exceed their authority their charter may be revoked.)

> NOTE: (1) *Statutory companies,* i.e. those created by special Act of Parliament: the statute will define the company's powers, and any contract beyond those powers is void absolutely. (2) *Registered companies,* i.e. those incorporated by registration under the Companies Acts: their powers are not usually expressly stated, but such companies must register a memorandum of association in which the objects of the company must be stated. The powers of the

company will then be such powers as are necessary to the achievement of its objects. Any contract which exceeds such powers is void and cannot be ratified even by the unanimous vote of all the members: *Ashbury Carriage Co.* v. *Riche* (1875).

Registered companies must also have articles of association which govern the internal regulations of the company, e.g. the rights of members and the powers of directors. If the directors exceed the powers delegated to them by the articles, the contract is voidable by the company and is said to be '*ultra vires* the directors' (but if the contract in question is within the powers of the company itself, it can ratify such contract if it wishes). However, by the Companies Act 1985, s. 36(4), in favour of any person dealing in good faith with a company, any contract made by directors on behalf of the company is deemed to be *intra vires* ('within the powers') and valid.

Capacity of minors

24. Definition of a minor
The Family Law Reform Act 1969 defines a minor as one who has not reached the age of 18. Much of the old law on the binding nature of contracts by minors was considerably affected by the Minors Contracts Act 1987.

25. Contracts not generally binding on minors
The basic principle is that contracts made by a minor with an adult are binding on the latter only. The contract will bind the minor only if, after reaching his majority, he ratifies the contract. Although a contract may not bind a minor, this does not mean that it is void. Money paid or property transferred under the contract can be recovered by the minor only if he can show that there has been a total failure of consideration. A minor's action to have her name removed from a register of shareholders succeeded but she was not allowed to recover money already paid since she had got the thing bargained for: *Steinberg* v. *Scala Ltd* (1923).

26. Contracts for necessaries
The principal exception to the common law rule that a contract does not bind a minor is where that contract is for 'necessaries'. Section 3 of the Sale of Goods Act 1979 states that '. . . where necessaries are sold and delivered to a minor . . . he

must pay a reasonable price for them'. The section defines 'necessaries' as goods suitable to the condition in life of the minor ... and to his actual requirements at the time of sale and delivery'.

A widow who was a minor was held liable to an undertaker for work in connection with the funeral of her late husband: *Chapple* v. *Cooper* (1844). However, if the minor has more than enough of the articles in question, then more cannot be necessary. An undergraduate was not liable to pay for clothing, including eleven fancy waistcoats, when his father gave evidence that his son was already amply supplied with clothes: *Nash* v. *Inman* (1908). It is to be noted that the minor is liable to pay for necessaries, not at the agreed price, but whatever amounts to a 'reasonable' price.

27. Beneficial contracts of service

If a service contract entered into by a minor is to his benefit, then it is binding. Where a minor entered into a contract of employment as a railway porter, he was required to forgo claims under current legislation in return for joining an insurance scheme. Although that particular scheme might not have been to his benefit, the contract as a whole was, and so it was binding: *Clements* v. *L&NWR* (1894).

Other examples of contracts held to be binding are (*a*) a contract by a professional boxer, a minor, to observe the rules of the sport: *Doyle* v. *White City Stadium* (1929); and (*b*) a contract to write a book and assign the copyright: *Chaplin* v. *Leslie Frewin* (1966).

28. Restitution

The Minors Contracts Act 1987 affords a limited measure of redress to the adult who may otherwise find that the minor may obtain property without having to pay. The Act provides that where a contract is unenforceable against a defendant because he was a minor when it was made, the court may 'if it is just and equitable to do so, require the defendant to transfer to the plaintiff any property acquired by the defendant under the contract, or any property representing it'. There is in addition the equitable doctrine of restitution to allow recovery of property from a minor in relation to property obtained by deception: *Leslie* v. *Sheill* (1914).

29. Guarantees of minors' contracts

Section 2 of the 1987 Act provides that a guarantee of a minor's contract is not unenforceable merely because he is a minor. Before the Act, the guarantee would be a nullity since there was in effect nothing to guarantee.

4

Void, voidable and illegal contracts

These include contracts invalidated because they rest upon some fundamental mistake of fact (void), contracts induced by misrepresentation or coercion (voidable), and contracts which are contrary to some statute or to common law (void and illegal).

Mistake

1. Effect of mistake

The general common law rule is that mistake made by one or both parties in making a contract has no effect on the validity of the contract, e.g. where a person pays an excessive price for goods under a mistake as to their true value: *Leaf* v. *International Galleries* (1950).

However, where the parties contracted under a fundamental mistake of fact, the contract may be void if:

(a) the mistake is one of fact, and not of law or opinion; *and*
(b) the mistake is so fundamental as to negative the agreement.

For a mistake to be 'operative', it must exist at or before the time when the contract was made. Thus, there is no mistake where parties to a contract for the sale of a building believe it is not listed, if the listing occurs after they have made their contract: *Amalgamated Investment and Property Co. Ltd* v. *John Walker & Sons Ltd* (1976).

Mistake which thus renders a contract void is called 'operative mistake.'

A mistaken party will escape liability on a document he has signed if he can satisfy the court that the signed instrument is radically different from the one he intended to sign and that his mistake in signing it was not due to carelessness: *Saunders* v. *Anglia Building Society* (1971); *Lloyds Bank* v. *Waterhouse* (1991).

2. Mistakes of law and of fact

Mistakes of law generally have no effect, since 'ignorance of the law is no excuse' (*ignorantia juris neminem excusat*).

In two exceptional cases, however, mistakes of law are treated as though they were mistakes of fact.

(a) *Mistake of foreign law*, since the laws of a foreign country require to be proved in British courts as ordinary facts.
(b) *Mistake as to private rights*, e.g. a right of property, as where a purchaser buys property which already belongs to him: *Cooper* v. *Phibbs* (1867) (*see* NOTE, 1: **16**).

3. Operative mistakes of fact

It is difficult to deduce consistent principles from the numerous cases on the subject, but it is fairly well established that in the following cases a fundamental mistake of fact will avoid a contract.

(a) Common mistake as to the existence of the subject-matter of the contract.
(b) Mutual mistake as to the terms of an offer, or the identity of the subject-matter.
(c) Unilateral mistake as to the identity of the person contracted with.
(d) Unilateral mistake as to the nature of a contract signed.

> NOTE: *Common mistake* is where both parties make the same mistake. *Mutual mistake* is where each makes a different mistake, i.e. they misunderstand one another. *Unilateral mistake* is where only one party is mistaken. Unilateral mistake is generally of no effect, unless (*i*) it concerns some fundamental fact, and (*ii*) the other party is aware of the mistake. Thus unilateral mistake has no effect where it relates merely to an error of judgement by one of the parties.

4. Common mistake as to existence of subject-matter

This applies when, unknown to both parties, the subject-matter has been destroyed before the contract is made.

Examples

(1) The sale of a life insurance policy on the life of a person who, unknown to purchaser or seller, is already dead: *Scott* v. *Coulson* (1903).
(2) The sale of goods which, unknown to the contractors, have already been destroyed: *Couturier* v. *Hastie* (1856), and Sale of Goods Act 1979, s. 6 (*see* 9: **28**).

> NOTE: Mistakes as to the quality of the subject-matter generally have no effect. The general maxim of English law is *caveat emptor* ('let the buyer beware') and if a man mistakenly pays an unduly high price for something, he has only himself to blame for the bad bargain.

Examples

(1) L paid a senior employee £50,000 compensation for loss of office when dismissing him before his contract had expired. Later L discovered that the employee had committed breaches of duty which would have entitled L to dismiss him without compensation. HELD: L could not recover the money on discovering the truth, since the House of Lords considered that the mistake related only to the quality of what was purchased, namely release from the contract of employment: *Bell* v. *Lever Bros.*(1932).
(2) L bought from G a painting which both mistakenly believed to be by Constable and of great value. Later L discovered it was by an unknown artist and comparatively worthless. HELD: L could not avoid the contract, as his mistake related only to the quality of the subject-matter: *Leaf* v. *International Galleries* (1950).
(3) In *Associated Japanese Bank (International) Ltd* v. *Crédit du Nord SA* (1988), a party concluded a sale and leaseback transaction with the plaintiff in respect of four machines which were described by serial numbers. The obligations assumed by him as lessee of the machines were subsequently guaranteed by the defendant bank. The lessee paid the first quarterly rental but subsequently defaulted. It was then discovered that the machines did not exist. The plaintiff then sued on the contract of guarantee. The defendant contended that it was not liable on the guarantee, either because it was an express or implied condition precedent to the guarantee that the machines existed, or because the guarantee was void because of common mistake. The Commercial Court held that, given that the terms of the guarantee referred to the leasing of four identified machines and stipulated that any substitution of those machines could only be done with the consent of the guarantor, the only sensible construction was that the guarantee was subject to an express condition precedent that there was a lease in respect of existing machines. Alternatively, there was an implied condition precedent to the guarantee that the machines existed, having regard both to the fact that both parties

were informed that the machines existed and to the express terms of the guarantee. The plaintiff's claim was dismissed. The court said that, except where a party seeking to rely on a mistake has no reasonable ground for his belief, a contract will be void for common mistake where both parties share the same mistake as to facts existing at the time the contract is made and the mistake renders the subject-matter of the contract essentially and radically different from the subject-matter which the parties believed to exist. *See also Citibank NA* v. *Brown Shipley* (1991).

5. Mutual mistake

(a) *As to the terms of the offer.* Where the parties misunderstand each other as to the terms of the offer, the contract will be void if the mistake is sufficiently fundamental.

Here there is no real concurrence of offer and acceptance, since the offeree is accepting on a mistaken understanding of what the offeror intended.

Example

A and B contracted to ship a cargo on *The Peerless* from Bombay. Unknown to either party there were two ships of the same name, and both were at Bombay and were due to sail on different dates. A had in mind one of the two ships, and B had in mind the other. HELD: The contract was void: *Raffles* v. *Wichelhaus* (1864).

(b) *As to the identity of the subject-matter*, i.e. the parties misunderstand each other as to what is to constitute the subject-matter of the contract.

Example

At an auction X, misled by the catalogue, bid an absurdly high price for some tow (thinking it was hemp) and the auctioneer accepted the bid thinking that X was merely mistaken as to the value of tow. HELD: Contract void: *Scriven* v. *Hindley* (1913).

6. Unilateral mistake as to the identity of the person contracted with

Such mistake will only operate to void the contract where:

(a) the identity of the person contracted with is of fundamental importance; *and*

(b) this is made clear by the party mistaken before or at the time of contracting (so that the other party knows of the mistake).

> NOTE: Where the parties contracted 'face to face' the presumption is that there can be no mistake as to identity: *Lewis* v. *Averay* (1973). (But this presumption may be rebutted by clear evidence to the contrary: *Ingram* v. *Little* (1960).)

Examples

(1) X, a rogue, entered a jeweller's and offered to buy goods. His offer was accepted, and he then offered to pay by cheque. The jeweller accepted the cheque, but said delivery would be delayed until the cheque was cleared. The rogue then said he was a well-known person and asked to take some of the jewels immediately. Deceived as to his identity, the jeweller let him take some of the jewels. X took the goods and sold them to a pawnbroker, and the cheque proved worthless. HELD: The contract was made before the identity became important, therefore it was not void on the ground of mistake: *Phillips* v. *Brooks* (1919) (the contract was probably voidable on the ground of misrepresentation).

(2) L advertised his car for sale and B, a rogue, answered, describing himself as a well-known film-star. L was impressed and accepted B's cheque after B had produced a film-studio admission card as proof of identity. B then took the car and sold it to A, a *bona fide* purchaser. When L discovered the fraud he sued A to recover the car. HELD: L intended to contract with the man he met 'face to face' and the contract was therefore not void for mistake, but merely voidable for misrepresentation: *Lewis* v. *Averay* (1973) C.A.

7.   Unilateral mistake as to nature of a contract signed

Generally a person who signs a contract is bound by it, even if he has not read it: *L'Estrange* v. *Graucob, see* 2: **16**.

But a person who signs a document under a fundamental mistake as to its nature may have it avoided, e.g. where A is induced to sign a negotiable instrument believing it is merely a guarantee: *Foster* v. *Mackinnon* (1869). Notice that the mistake must be as to the fundamental legal nature of the document — not merely as to its contents.

Examples

(1) A, who was senile, was persuaded to sign a bill of exchange under the misapprehension that it was a guarantee. HELD: The bill was void for mistake: *Foster* v. *Mackinnon* (1869).

(2) A executed a transfer of land under a misapprehension as to its contents and effect. HELD: Contract not void. The mistake was not sufficiently fundamental: *Howatson* v. *Webb* (1907).

(3) G, an elderly lady, signed without reading a document which L informed her was a gift transferring her house to her nephew P. In fact it was a transfer on sale to L (for £3000). G. sought to have the sale annulled. HELD: She failed on the facts of the case because: (*a*) the document was not radically different in type from what she thought she was signing; (*b*) she was careless; and (*c*) she had failed in her evidence to show that she would not have signed had she known the true facts: *Saunders* v. *Anglia Building Society* (1971) H.L.

(4) In another case, a person signed a form in blank addressed to a finance house, believing it to be a hire-purchase agreement. It was, in fact, a loan agreement. It was held that a binding contract existed between the signatory and the finance house. The signatory was under a duty of care to ensure that the completed document represented his true intention. He had not shown he had acted carefully, so he was bound by his signature: *U.D.T.* v. *Western* (1975).

---

8. Mistake in equity

The common law rules relating to mistake stated above render the contract either completely void or completely valid, even though neither conclusion may be completely just.

But since the Judicature Acts (1873–75) allow equity to be administered in all courts to modify the common law in the interests of justice, the courts have used equitable principles to achieve a compromise result where it would be unjust to one or both of the parties to apply the common law doctrine rigidly in cases of mistake.

Equity will thus intervene for the following purposes.

(a) *To rectify* (amend) a written instrument containing patent errors of expression.

(b) *To refuse to order specific performance* of a contract against a defendant who is labouring under a mistake such that it would be grossly unjust to compel him to perform his contract, e.g. where A, by a slip of the pen, writes offering to sell land to B for '£1250' when he meant to write '2250'. Here if B tries to enforce a contract at the lower price equity will refuse to help him and will protect A against the consequence of his mistake: *Webster* v. *Cecil* (1861).

(c) *To set aside an agreement on terms* fair to all parties, where

common law will not declare it void: *Solle* v. *Butcher* (1950). *See also
Grist* v. *Bailey* (1966) where a sale of a house was held voidable on
grounds of common mistake as to value, which was not sufficient
to render the contract void at law. This discretionary power to
rescind the contract operates only if:

- (*i*) the contract is not void at common law (but merely
  voidable in equity): *see Lewis* v. *Averay* (1973);
- (*ii*) there is a fundamental mistake common to both parties;
  and
- (*iii*) the party seeking rescission is not at fault. (The maxim is:
  'He who comes to Equity must come with clean hands.')

9. Rectification

Where a written contract does not accurately express the
intentions of the parties, the court will amend (rectify) the contract
to make it express the true intentions. The party seeking
rectification must prove the following.

(a) The mistake to be rectified lies only in the words used.

(b) There is a complete and final contract between the parties.

(c) There is clear oral or written evidence of the true intention of
the parties.

(d) The mistake is common to both parties: *Craddock Bros* v. *Hunt*
(1923).

Misrepresentation and fraud

10. *Caveat emptor*

In English law a person is generally under no duty to disclose
all facts in his possession to the other contracting party. Each must
protect his own interests unaided. The rule is 'let the buyer beware'
(*caveat emptor*). Keeping silent therefore is generally not
actionable, even though it causes damage to the other party.

Example
H sold pigs 'with all faults' to W, knowing that they had swine fever and
that W was unaware of this. HELD: W could not have the contract set aside:
Ward v. *Hobbs* (1878).

11. Misrepresentation

But where one party makes a positive false statement which deceives the other, this may amount to misrepresentation rendering the contract voidable at the option of the party misled.

The deceived party may also be entitled to damages: (*a*) for deceit, if he can prove fraud, or (*b*) for negligent misrepresentation, unless the defendant can show that he had reasonable grounds for believing that what he said was true: Misrepresentation Act 1967, s. 2(1).

12. What is misrepresentation?

A misrepresentation is (*a*) a false statement (*b*) of material fact, (*c*) made by a party to the contract or his agent, (*d*) which induces the other party to enter into the contract.

Misleading conduct may also amount to misrepresentation, if it presents a misleading picture about material facts and satisfies (*c*) and (*d*) above.

NOTE: (1) *The statement must be of fact*, not of law or opinion (but an opinion expressed by a person who might be expected to know the facts, e.g. by a technical expert on his own subject, may amount to a statement of fact: *Brown* v. *Raphael* (1958)). (2) *It must be of material importance* in the transaction, e.g. in the sale of a car a statement that the car is in good working order. But representations relating to trivial matters, such as the condition of the windscreen wipers, would not amount to actionable misrepresentation. (3) *It must be made by a party to the contract* or his agent, i.e. not by a mere bystander. Thus where A invests money in a company in reliance on a false statement by the company's auditor in the company's balance sheet, A cannot sue the company for misrepresentation because the contract is between him and the company, and the auditor is not an agent for the company for the purpose of making statements to lure investors: *Candler* v. *Crane Christmas* (1951) (but an action might be possible against the auditor for the tort of negligence: *Hedley Byrne & Co.* v. *Hellers, etc.* (1964), H.L.). (4) *It must be relied upon*, i.e. it must succeed in inducing the offeree to enter into the contract. Thus, A sold a broken gun to B and patched the barrel with clay to conceal the crack. B did not examine the gun and therefore was not deceived by the patch. HELD: The misrepresentation was not actionable, since it had no effect on B: *Horsfall* v. *Thomas* (1862). (5) *It must be by positive words or conduct*, not by mere silence unless the silence amounts to active concealment of facts, or silence about some facts puts those revealed into a false and deceptive light. Thus where a company's prospectus showed that it had paid dividends for several years, without disclosing that these had been paid out of reserves as the company was trading at a loss, it was held that the omission was deceptive and amounted to misrepresentation: *R.* v. *Kylsant* (1932). (6) *Statements true when made but becoming false before the contract is made must be corrected.* Thus R arranged to sell a business to Y and estimated profits at £2000 p.a. By the time the sale was completed the profits had fallen considerably. HELD: A's failure to disclose the change amounted to misrepresentation: *With* v. *O'Flanagan* (1936).

Thus an exceptional duty of disclosure is imposed in (5) above where silence is actually deceptive, and in (6) where facts true when stated subsequently become untrue before negotiations are completed. A further duty of disclosure is imposed in *uberrimae fidei* contracts: *see* **19** below.

13. Innocent misrepresentation

If a person makes a misrepresentation believing what he says is true he commits innocent misrepresentation, providing he had reasonable grounds for his belief. The party misled may:

(a) affirm the contract and treat it as binding or may rescind the contract by notifying the other party and — where necessary — obtaining the court's assistance to secure restitution;

(b) sue for damages under the Misrepresentation Act 1967, s. 2. If he obtains damages, he cannot also rescind the agreement. *See also* **14**(*b*).

14. Damages for innocent misrepresentation

Formerly a plaintiff could not secure damages for innocent misrepresentation, but the Misrepresentation Act 1967 gives a right to damages in certain cases.

(a) Where the misrepresentation was made negligently. Note that negligence is presumed; the defendant can only escape liability for damages if he can show that he had reasonable grounds for believing what he said was true at the time the contract was made: s. 2(1). In *Banque Financière* v. *Westgate Insurance* (1989), the Court of Appeal pointed out that s. 2(1) uses the words 'where a misrepresentation has been made . . .'. It therefore held that where a failure to disclose had been made in breach of the rule of *uberrimae fidei* (*see* **19** below), no action could lie under the Misrepresentation Act 1967 since no representation had been 'made': if it had been the intention of the legislature that a mere failure to discharge the duty in the case of a contract *uberrimae fidei* would fall to be treated as the 'making' of a representation within the meaning of the 1967 Act, we are of the opinion that the legislature would have said so. Damages are to be assessed on the basis of the measure of damages in tort for fraudulent misrepresentation (*see* **16**), with the result that the innocent party is entitled to recover any loss which flowed from the misrepresentation, even if the loss could not have been foreseen: *Royscott Trust Ltd* v. *Rogerson* (1991). It has been held that, where an article bought as a result of a misrepresentation could have been sold immediately after the sale for the price paid, but, by the time the misrepresentation has been discovered, its value had fallen by reason of a defect which by then had become apparent, the appropriate measure of damages could be the difference between the purchase price and its value at the time the misrepresentation was discovered, and not the difference between the purchase price and its value at the time of purchase, provided that the article purchased was altogether different from that which had been expected. The case itself concerned a horse whose pedigree had been misrepresented, and this was held to be the purchase of something 'altogether different': *Naughton* v. *O'Callaghan* (1990).

(b) Where the plaintiff has sought rescission, the court has power to award damages in lieu of rescission: s. 2(2)

> NOTE: Any exemption clause seeking to exclude liability for misrepresentation is void unless it satisfies the requirement of reasonableness: s. 3, as substituted by the Unfair Contract Terms Act 1977: *Howard Marine* v. *Ogden* (1978).

Damages are also obtainable against the makers of an innocent misrepresentation made in a company prospectus: Companies Act 1985, s. 67.

15. Fraudulent misrepresentation

'An untrue statement made knowingly, or without belief in its truth, or recklessly, careless whether it be true or false': *per* Lord Herschel, *Derry* v. *Peek* (1889).

Thus if the maker believes that his representation is true, he cannot be guilty of fraud, even if he was negligent or unreasonable in saying what he did: *Akerheim* v. *De Mare* (1959). (But in such cases he may be liable for damages for the tort of negligence: *Hedley Byrne & Co.* v. *Heller, etc.* (1964) and for negligent misrepresentation: *see* **14.**)

16. Remedies for fraudulent misrepresentation

(a) The plaintiff may sue for damages for the tort of deceit (fraud). Damages for deceit or fraudulent misrepresentation are awarded on the basis that the plaintiff is to be compensated for all the loss he has suffered, so far as money can do it: *Doyle* v. *Olby* (1969); *Royscott Trust* v. *Rogerson* (1991); *East* v. *Maurer* (1991).

(b) The plaintiff may repudiate the contract or have it rescinded by the court (with or without claiming damages for deceit).

(c) The plaintiff may affirm the contract and still claim damages for deceit.

17. Limits to the right of rescission

Although the misled party can generally get the contract rescinded (set aside by the court) this right is lost in the following cases.

(a) *Affirmation*: where the injured party has expressly or impliedly affirmed the contract after learning of the misrepresentation.

(b) *Restitution impossible:* where the parties cannot be restored to their original position, i.e. *restitutio in integrum* (total restitution) is impossible.

(c) *Prejudice of third parties*: where an innocent third party has obtained an interest in the subject-matter of the contract in good faith and for value: *see Phillips* v. *Brooks* at **6**, above. (In that case the innocent purchaser of the jewels from the rogue was held entitled to them since he had bought them from a person with a voidable title to them before that title was avoided and without notice of the fraud: *see* 9: **35**).

(d) *Undue delay:* where in a case of innocent misrepresentation the plaintiff delays unreasonably in seeking rescission, the court may refuse to grant him the discretionary remedy of rescission: *Leaf* v. *International Galleries* (1950).

NOTE: Formerly rescission was unobtainable where a contract had been performed under the rule in *Seddon* v. *N.E. Salt Co.* (1905). This rule was abrogated by the Misrepresentation Act 1967, s.1.

18. Representation as a term of a contract

If a representation is made during negotiations and is later incorporated as a term of the contract, the remedies of the injured party will be basically those for breach of contract. The remedies available will then depend on whether the term concerned is a condition or a warranty: *see* 2: **24.**

NOTE: Formerly rescission was unobtainable in such circumstances. But the injured party may now rescind for misrepresentation: 1967 Act, s.1. If, however, the innocent party would have been entitled to rescind the contract without alleging fraud, he will still be entitled to do so even though the misrepresentation has become a term of the contract: Misrepresentation Act 1967, s.1(*b*).

19. Contracts *uberrimae fidei* ('of the utmost good faith')

Although there is no general duty of disclosure, in some exceptional contracts the law imposes a special duty to act with the utmost good faith, i.e. to disclose all material information. In *Banque Financière* v. *Westgate Insurance Co.* (1988), the Court of Appeal ruled that the duty of full disclosure was neither contractual, tortious, fiduciary nor statutory in character, but was founded on the jurisdiction originally exercised by the courts of equity to prevent imposition and did not give rise to a claim in damages.

Failure to disclose renders the contract voidable at the option of the other party (and note the duty of disclosure imposed in ordinary contracts in certain circumstances: *see* **12**(5) and (6) above).

Examples _____

(1) *Contracts of insurance.* The insured must disclose all facts which might influence the judgement of a prudent insurer, whether to decline the risk or increase the premium. In the *Banque Financière* case, the court stated that the obligation to disclose material facts was a mutual and absolute obligation imposing reciprocal duties on both insurer and insured, and in the case of the insurer required him to disclose all facts known to him which were material either to the nature of the risk sought to be covered or the recoverability of a claim under the policy which a prudent insured

party would take into account when deciding whether to place with that insurer the risk for which he was seeking cover.

(2) *Contracts of family arrangement,* for the settlement of family property etc. Each member of the family must disclose any portions he or she has already received without the knowledge of other members of the family.

(3) *Company prospectuses.* Directors, promoters, etc. must make full disclosure of material facts in any prospectus inviting the public to subscribe for shares in the company: Companies Act 1985, ss. 67–69. Failure to do so renders the contract voidable and makes the directors etc. liable for damages.

(4) *Contracts for sale of land.* The vendor must disclose any defects in his title to the land, of which he knows. The duty does not extend to other matters, e.g. there is no obligation to disclose physical defects in the property sold.

(5) *Suretyship and partnership contracts.* These contracts are not *uberrimae fidei* at their formation, but since made they impose a duty of utmost good faith on the parties to disclose to each other all material facts coming to light after the making of the contract (*see* 8: **13** and 16: **4**).

Duress and undue influence

20. Duress

This means actual or threatened violence to the person (not the property) of the party coerced or to his wife, children, or parents, and its effect is to render the contract voidable at the option of the party coerced.

Threats of imprisonment are included under this head, e.g. where A was induced to part with valuable documents by threats of continued confinement: *Cummings* v. *Ince* (1847).

Contracts made under economic duress may also be void: *North Ocean Shipping Co.* v. *Hyundai Construction Co.* (1978).

21. Undue influence

This means any pressure or coercion not amounting to duress that prevents the party coerced from exercising free judgement, and it makes the contract voidable by him at the discretion of the court. (Thus a plaintiff who proves duress is entitled to rescission, while one who can only prove undue influence is dependent on the discretion of the court).

Undue influence covers all types of pressure not amounting to duress, e.g. moral pressure, threats of violence to property, playing on victim's superstitions, etc.

To be actionable the undue influence need not have been exercised by a party to the contract (cf. misrepresentation).

Example _____

A mother coerced her daughter into making a money-lending contract with X, a moneylender, who knew of the mother's actions. HELD: The contract was voidable by the daughter: *Lancashire Loans Ltd* v. *Black* (1934).

22. Undue influence may be presumed

The court presumes that undue influence has been available to one party (and exerted) in contracts between persons in a fiduciary relationship, i.e. where one party is in a position to influence the other unfairly. Wherever undue influence is thus presumed, the burden of proof will lie on the defendant to disprove its exercise if he wishes to preserve the contract.

Undue influence is presumed in contracts between parent and child, trustee and beneficiary, solicitor and client, doctor and patient, priest and communicant, teacher and pupil, etc.

The defendant can disprove undue influence by showing that:

(a) full disclosure of all material facts was made;
(b) the consideration was adequate; *and*
(c) the weaker party was in receipt of independent legal advice.

Example _____

The age and health of the person influenced may be relevant. Thus undue influence was presumed between a woman secretary of strong personality and an aged and infirm employer who had been persuaded to make valuable gifts to her: *Re Craig* (1970). Where an elderly farmer mortgages his property to help a company run by his son, the bank must ensure that he has independent advice: *Lloyds Bank* v. *Bundy* (1975).

23. Other cases of undue influence

Even where it is not presumed, undue influence may still be alleged. In such cases the burden of proof lies on the plaintiff to show that such influence existed and was exerted.

Example _____

A nephew managing the affairs of an elderly aunt persuaded her to give him some shares, for the purpose of getting control of the company. HELD: The contract was voidable, despite the fact that she had received independent legal advice, since the lawyer who advised her to make the contract was not informed that the shares were virtually all the property the woman possessed: *Inche Noriah* v. *Shaik Allie Bin Omar* (1929); *see also Hodgson* v. *Marks* (1971); *National Westminster Bank plc* v. *Morgan* (1985); *Coldunell Ltd* v. *Gallon* (1986) and *Midland Bank* v. *Shephard* (1988).

24. Right to relief lost

Since remedies for undue influence are discretionary, they will only be awarded where the plaintiff's own conduct is equitable. A claim for relief may be disallowed where:

(a) the plaintiff's conduct has been tricky or unfair; *or*
(b) the plaintiff has delayed unreasonably in seeking rescission of the contract: *Allcard* v. *Skinner* (1887).

Illegality

25. Meaning of 'illegality'

An illegal contract is one which is void because (*a*) it is for an illegal purpose, or (*b*) it is contrary to some rule of public policy. In one case, a pilot was engaged to recover certain aircraft in Nigeria, He was advised in Nigeria that his life, and that of his wireless operator, were in danger, and that the Nigerian Government could not protect them. Accordingly, he flew from the country without obtaining air traffic control clearance, in breach of Nigerian law. The court said that contracts would not normally be enforced if this would mean someone benefiting from his criminal conduct. However, the public conscience would not be affronted if the criminal conduct was designed to free the pilot and his wireless operator from pressing danger: *Howard* v. *Shirlstar Container Transport Ltd* (1990).

The courts will generally give the parties to such contracts no protection at all, even to prevent hardship (except as stated in **29** below). Contrast contracts which are void for some other reason than illegality, e.g. mistake, *see* **2** above; in these cases the court will assist the parties to the extent of ordering the return of property transferred under the contract: *Chappell* v. *Poles* (1837).

26. The doctrine of severance

Where a contract is for several independent purposes, some of which are legal and others illegal, the court may sever the illegal terms from the contract and enforce the remaining legal terms: *Pickering* v. *Ilfracombe Rail Co.* (1868), and *see* **49** below.

But this is only possible where the legal and illegal terms are clearly independent. The court will not rewrite the main terms of the contract so as to make it legal: *Napier* v. *National Business Agency* (1951).

27. Presumption in favour of validity

The courts are reluctant to declare any contract void on the grounds of illegality and will do so only where:

(a) a statute clearly prohibits the contract; *or*
(b) a well-established rule of common law makes such contract illegal on grounds of public policy. Otherwise the general attitude of the courts has been stated thus: 'You have this paramount policy to consider — that you are not lightly to interfere with the freedom of contract': *per* Sir George Jessel, in *Printing & Numerical Co.* v. *Sampson* (1875).

28. Consequences of illegality

(a) The contract is entirely void, unless the doctrine of severance can be applied to save part of it.
(b) Money paid or property transferred under an illegal contract cannot be recovered (subject to the exceptions in **29** below). The maxim is *in pari delicto potior est conditio defendentis* ('in cases of equal guilt, more powerful is the condition of the defendant'). Thus where the parties are equally guilty, if the plaintiff is suing for the return of money paid under the illegal contract, the court will usually allow the defendant to keep it. (For the rules applicable where the parties are not equally guilty *see* **29** below.)
(c) Negotiable securities, such as cheques and other bills of exchange, transferred between the parties to the contract are void as between them. But an innocent third party who acquires such securities in good faith and for value can usually enforce them: *see*

14: 2. Thus where A pays a gambling debt to B by cheque, B cannot enforce payment against A; but if B sells the cheque to C, who buys in good faith and without notice of any irregularity, C will be able to enforce the cheque. *See also* Consumer Credit Act 1974, ss. 123–125.

(d) *Ex turpi causa non oritur actio* ('from an evil cause, no action arises'). Where a plaintiff seeking the court's assistance has to base his claim on his own illegal or immoral act, his claim will fail.

Example
_____

A rented a flat to R at £1200 p.a. To avoid tax they agreed to describe the money as £450 for rent and £750 for 'services.' Later R attempted to bilk A by refusing to pay the £750 on the grounds that he had received no services, and A sued for the money. HELD: The contract was illegal as an attempt to defraud the Revenue, and A could not recover the money since he could only get it by admitting that it was really rent and this involved admitting his own guilt. But to prevent R benefiting from this situation the court terminated his tenancy on the grounds that it was illegal, and offfered him a new one at the full rent: *Alexander* v. *Rayson* (1936).
_____

29. Recovery of property transferred
Money paid or property transferred under an illegal contract is normally irrecoverable.

EXCEPTIONS: (1) Where the transferor repents of making the contract before any part of the illegal purpose is carried out, or (2) where: (*i*) He is not *in pari delicto* (equally guilty) with the defendant, e.g. where he was induced to make the contract by the fraud of the defendant (*Shelley* v. *Paddock* (1978)); or (*ii*) The transferee was under a fiduciary duty to protect the plaintiff's interest, and has abused this duty by making the illegal contract, e.g. where he is the plaintiff's solicitor or trustee; or (*iii*) The contract is made illegal by a statute intended to protect a class of which the plaintiff is a member, e.g. a borrower suing to recover excessive interest from a moneylender under a contract illegal under the Consumer Credit Act (which is intended to protect borrowers).

Contracts subject to a disability

30. Contracts for trading or selling on a Sunday
Such contracts were formerly prohibited under the Sunday

Observance Act 1677, but this was repealed by the Statute Law (Repeals) Act 1969. In many cases, the Shops Act 1950 makes it a criminal offence for a shop to be open on Sunday but this does not appear to affect the validity of any contract, though it will probably be the case that the courts would refuse to enforce an action on the contract by either party.

31. Registration of business names

Under the Business Names Act 1985, all orders, invoices, business letters, etc. must disclose the true surnames of all owners of the business (whether individuals or companies) and also the addresses within Great Britain at which they can be contacted. In addition, such information must be displayed on a notice in a prominent position at the business premises. A customer is entitled to ask for a written list of the required information which must be supplied to him immediately. These requirements are relaxed in the case of a partnership of more than 20 persons provided the following conditions are satisfied: the document must not contain the names of any partners except as signatories; and it must state an address at which a full list of partners can be inspected. Actions in contract by a person who has failed to comply with the requirements of the 1985 Act can be dismissed if the defendant can show that he has a claim against that person because of his failure to comply, or if he has suffered financial loss because of such failure. The court can, however, allow the action if it considers it to be just and equitable.

32. Consumer Credit Act 1974

Under the Act, all those who extend credit or hire out goods in the course of a business must be licensed by the Office of Fair Trading. An unlicensed business cannot enforce contracts except with the consent of the Director General of Fair Trading. The Act also requires contracts to be in a specific form; if they are not, they can only be enforced on a court order.

33. Financial Services Act 1986

Investment businesses can only carry on business if they are authorised under the Act or are exempt from the need for authorisation. A contract made in breach of this requirement can be enforced only on a court order. The Act also provides for restrictions on the issue of investment advertisements. Investment contracts made following an unlawful advertisement can be enforced only on a court order.

34. Gaming and wagering contracts

A wager is a promise to give or pay something on the ascertainment of an uncertain future event, e.g. a horse race. A bet is a wager on the result of a game.

Such contracts are void under the Gaming and Wagering Acts 1835–1960. The position is complex, but the following basic rules apply.

(a) Money earned as commission on bets and wagers is irrecoverable: Gaming Act 1892. An agent cannot therefore recover his commission from his principal. But the principal can recover any winnings received on his behalf by the agent: *De Mattos* v. *Benjamin* (1894).

(b) Negotiable instruments given for a bet are given for an illegal consideration and are void as between the parties: Gaming Act 1835. But an innocent third party who becomes a holder in due course of such an instrument may be able to enforce it fully: *see* 14: **38**.

(c) Money lent to a loser to pay his bets is recoverable: *Re O'Shea* (1911); but not if the lender himself pays the winner, since he is then participating in the forbidden transaction: *Macdonald* v. *Green* (1951).

(d) The winner of a wager cannot sue the loser for his winnings even though the loser later makes a fresh promise to pay supported by fresh consideration: *Hill* v. *William Hill Ltd* (1949). This rule still applies, even though the Betting, Gaming and Lotteries Act 1963 legalised gambling in certain circumstances, i.e. the contracts resulting from such legalised gambling were void. *See* now the Gaming Act 1968.

(e) Money paid to a stakeholder to retain pending the result of a wager can be recovered from the stakeholder by the payer at any time before he has handed it over to the other party to the wager: *Burge* v. *Ashley & Smith Ltd* (1900).

(f) The essence of a wager is that neither party has any legitimate interest in the uncertain event wagered upon, except the money staked. Where a party has something to gain or lose apart from the money staked, the agreement is not a wager, e.g. insurance contracts. Thus if A insures his life, his ship, or his house against death, loss or damage, he stands to lose the value of his ship or house (or his life) quite apart from the wager. Although an insurance contract is similar in its other characteristics to a wager, it is valid and enforceable: *see* Chapter 12.

Contracts illegal at common law

35. Contracts tainted with sexual immorality
A contract superficially lawful will be void if, to the knowledge of the parties, its ultimate purpose was immoral, e.g. an ordinary lease of a house would be void if the house was to be used as a brothel.

Example _____
A hired a carriage to a woman knowing that she was a prostitute and would use the carriage for the purpose of soliciting. HELD: The contract was void and he could not recover unpaid hiring charges: *Pearce* v. *Brooks* (1866). This is an example of the working of the maxim *in pari delicto potior est conditio defendentis: see* **28** above.

_____

36. Contracts tending to interfere with the sanctity of marriage
For example, a promise by a married man to marry another woman as soon as his wife is dead: *Wilson* v. *Carnley* (1908).

Were a married man to promise to marry another woman, the other woman could not sue him for breach of promise if she knew he was married when he made the promise. The right to sue for breach of promise to marry has, however, been abolished by the Law Reform (Miscellaneous Provisions) Act 1970, s. 1.

37. Contracts for the sale of public offices or titles of honour
For example, a promise to use influence to obtain a title or commission for the promisee in return for money: *Parkinson* v. *College of Ambulance Ltd* (1925). The Honours (Prevention of Abuses) Act 1925 makes parties to such a contract guilty of an offence.

38. Contracts to commit crimes or torts
Whether in Britain or any foreign friendly nation, e.g. a contract to smuggle goods into the United States of America: *Foster* v. *Driscoll* (1929).

39. Contracts to obtain an unfair benefit from the Government
For example, a promise to use influence to obtain exemption from a legal duty, such as military service: *Montefiore* v. *Menday Motor Components Ltd* (1918).

40. Contracts involving trade with an enemy nation
These are illegal at common law and also under the Trading with the Enemy Act 1939.

41. Contracts to defraud the Revenue
See Alexander v. *Rayson*, **28**, above.

42. Contracts tending to impede the administration of justice
For example, a promise by an accused person to indemnify someone who has stood bail for him: *Herman* v. *Jeuchner* (1885).

43. Contracts prejudical to the freedom of marriage
For example, imposing a general restraint upon a person to prevent marriage, though a particular restraint might be valid if not unreasonable, e.g. a contract forbidding a girl from marrying a particular man.

Marriage brokerage contracts are also in this category and are void, i.e. contracts to arrange marriages for a reward: *Hermann* v. *Charlesworth* (1905).

44. Contracts involving champerty or maintenance
Maintenance means giving financial or other assistance to a party to a law suit, where the maintainer has no sufficient legal or moral interest in the case. Champerty means maintenance with a view of sharing the profits of the action. The Criminal Law Act 1967 states that maintenance and champerty can no longer be punished as a crime or tort, but provides that a contract may still be treated as contrary to public policy or otherwise illegal.

NOTE: A shared commercial interest is sufficient to negative maintenance: *Martell* v. *Consett Iron Co. Ltd* (1955).

Contracts in restraint of trade

These are contracts which seek to restrict a person from freely exercising his trade or profession. For students of mercantile law this is the most important category of illegal contracts.

45. Restraints *prima facie* void

All restraints on trade are *prima facie* void, though they may be enforceable if they seek merely to protect some legitimate commercial interest. By contrast, a restraint which seeks merely to prevent competition is always void: *Morris* v. *Saxelby* (1916).

A restraint may be (*a*) general, i.e. forbidding trading throughout a large area, such as throughout the UK, or Europe, or (*b*) particular, i.e. forbidding trade in some localised area such as a particular town and its environs. General restraints are more disfavoured than particular restraints.

46. When restraints are valid

A restraint will be held void unless the party seeking to enforce it can prove:

(a) that it is reasonable in the public interest;
(b) that it is reasonable as between the parties, i.e. seeks to provide reasonable protection for some legitimate interest of the plaintiff, such as trade secrets or business goodwill;
(c) that the plaintiff has given valuable consideration for the promise he seeks to enforce. In this type of contract consideration is necessary even if the contract is under seal.

Whether a restraint is reasonable or not is a question of law to be decided by the judge; whether the individual restraint under dispute is in fact reasonable is a question of fact in each case.

A restraint which is reasonable between the parties is presumed to be reasonable in the public interest, unless there is some rule of law to the contrary: *Attorney-General of Australia* v. *Adelaide S.S. Co.* (1913).

47. Kinds of restraint
Restraints can be grouped roughly into three categories.

(a) Between employer and employee, to prevent the employee competing with his employer after leaving his job: *see* **48** below.
(b) Between the vendor and the purchaser of a business, to prevent the seller harming the goodwill of the business sold: *see* **50** below.
(c) Between traders, to regulate conditions of trade. These are now largely governed by statute, e.g. the Restrictive Trade Practices Act 1976 and the Resale Prices Act 1976.

48. Restraints upon employees
An employer may compel an employee to sign a covenant promising not to injure the employer's interests either (*a*) during the continuance of the employment (e.g. by passing confidential information to outsiders) or (*b*) after leaving the employment (e.g. by luring away his former employer's customers).

Such agreements are viewed with disfavour by the courts because of the element of coercion: *see* **21** above. They will only be enforced if they satisfy the tests set out in **49** below.

> NOTE: Apart from any express covenant, an employer is entitled to prevent an employee from disclosing trade secrets during the employment or after leaving: *Amber Size & Chemical Co.* v. *Menzel* (1913); or from making a list of the employer's clients with a view to competition after leaving: *Robb* v. *Green* (1895). *See also Thomas Marshall (Exports) Ltd* v. *Guinle* (1978). But even if an express covenant exists and is enforceable the employer loses the right to enforce it if he himself breaks the contract of employment, e.g. by wrongfully dismissing the employee: *General Billposting Co.* v. *Atkinson* (1909).
>
> In *Faccenda Chicken Ltd* v. *Fowler* (1986), the Court of Appeal ruled that an employer could not restrict the use or disclosure of confidential information by a restrictive covenant in the employee's contract of employment unless the information sought to be protected was a trade secret or equivalent to a trade secret. In order to determine whether information fell into this category, it was necessary to have regard to the nature of the employment, the nature of the information itself; whether the employer had stressed the confidentiality of the information to the employee; whether the information could easily be isolated from other non-confidential

information which was part of the same package of information. In the case itself, the court ruled that sales information and prices charged did not come into the category of information which could not be used or disclosed once the contract of employment had ceased.

49. Restraints upon employees: when enforceable

Restraints upon employees will only be enforced if they satisfy the following tests.

(a) The restraint is void unless supported by valuable consideration. The payment of wages is the usual consideration given by the employer. If therefore the covenant is only imposed when the employee is leaving, there may be no consideration for it (unless some special payment is made to bind the contract).

(b) The restraint is void unless the employee has some real capacity to damage the employer and the covenant seeks to guard against such damage. Thus a master is entitled to protection of trade secrets, or to a covenant that an employee in an influential position will not use his influence to seduce the master's clients. Therefore the employee must generally be in some confidential capacity, e.g. a solicitor's managing clerk: *Fitch* v. *Dewes* (1921); but not a mere door-to-door salesman: *Mason* v. *Provident Clothing Co.* (1913); nor a newspaper correspondent: *Leng* v. *Andrews* (1909) (though a newspaper editor might be in a sufficiently confidential capacity). Trade secrets are not restricted to secret formulae for the manufacture of products but can include highly confidential information of a non-technical or non-scientific nature, such as customers' names, which if disclosed to a competitor would cause real or significant harm to the owner and which the owner is entitled to have protected: *Lansing Linde Ltd* v. *Kerr* (1991).

(c) The restraint is void if it seeks merely to restrict or prevent competition.

(d) The restraint must be reasonable, having regard to:

(*i*) the type of employment: *Mason* v. *Provident Clothing Co.* (1913). A boxer-manager agreement was unreasonable and hence unenforceable since it not only imposed restrictions on the manner in which the boxer could carry on his professional activities, but also subjected him to the contractual obligation of fighting in promotions in which the manager had a financial interest and on terms unilaterally imposed by the manager: *Watson* v. *Prager* (1991).

(*ii*) the period of restraint: *Kores Ltd* v. *Kolok Ltd* (1959).

(*iii*) the area of restraint, e.g. a solicitor's managing clerk covenanted not to open a competing practice within seven miles of his former employers. HELD: Reasonable and enforceable: *Fitch* v. *Dewes* (1921).

Examples

(1) A tailor's assistant covenanted not to open a competing business within ten miles of his former employer's. HELD: Void, because in this particular case the assistant had no confidential relationship with customers and the covenant was therefore aimed merely at preventing ordinary competition: *Attwood* v. *Lamont* (1920); *see also*: *Home Counties Dairies Ltd* v. *Skilton* (1970) — milk roundsman.

(2) S was an estate agent with offices in Dartmouth and Kingsbridge. J was employed at the Kingsbridge office and covenanted not to open a competing business within five miles of Dartmouth or Kingsbridge within three years of leaving the employ. HELD: The restraint was too wide, since J had never worked at Dartmouth, but was valid in so far as it related to Kingsbridge. (This was an application of the doctrine of severance: *see* **26** above.) *Scorer* v. *Seymour-Jones* (1966).

(3) A salaried partner in a medical practice agreed not to practise 'in the practice area' (which was physically defined) within a period of three years in the event of the agreement being terminated. The partner later decided to set up as a GP about 100 yards away and well within the defined practice area. HELD: The restraint could be enforced: *Clarke* v. *Newland* (1991).

50. Restraints on sale of a business

Restraints imposed by the purchaser of a business on the seller, preventing the latter from opening another business in such a way as to damage the goodwill of the business sold, are enforced if reasonable in the circumstances.

Restraints of this kind are more readily enforced than those between employer and employee, because they lack the element of coercion which may be present between the parties in contracts of employment.

A restraint of this kind will be reasonable if (*a*) it satisfies the tests set out in **46** above and (*b*) it is intended merely to protect the purchaser's investment in the goodwill of the business bought, i.e. not intended to protect other businesses the purchaser already owned, or merely to prevent ordinary competition.

Examples

(1) N, an inventor of guns, sold his worldwide business to M and promised not to manufacture guns anywhere in the world for 25 years. HELD: Reasonable and binding: *Nordenfeldt* v. *Maxim-Nordenfeldt Co.* (1894) H.L.

(2) S sold his localised business to C (who already had branches all over Britain) and promised not to open a competing business anywhere within ten miles of any of C's branches. HELD: Void. The restraint was more than was necessary to protect the goodwill of the small local business purchased from S: *British Concrete Co.* v. *Schelff* (1921).

5
Discharge of contracts

Discharge by performance

1. Complete performance
In order to effect discharge, performance must be complete and exactly in accord with the terms of the contract.

Partial performance, even if substantial, will not discharge the contract (except in the special cases stated in **2** below).

Example
A sailor, having signed on to receive a lump-sum payment for a complete voyage, died before he completed the journey. HELD: His widow could not claim any part of his wages since he was entitled to payment only if he completed his contracted obligations: *Cutter* v. *Powell* (1795). (NOTE: On the facts this case would now be decided differently, but the general rule it lays down is still valid.)

---

2. Exceptional cases

(a) *Performance prevented by the promisee.* Here the promisor can obtain compensation for work actually done in pursuance of the contract by suing on a *quantum meruit* claim: *see* **30**, below.

(b) *Partial performance accepted.* If the promisee voluntarily accepts less than complete performance where he had genuine freedom of choice, the promisor is entitled to claim payment on *quantum meruit*. For example, A contracted to erect a building for B, and when the work was half done A abandoned the job. B had to complete the building himself, but A sued him for work done. HELD: B need pay nothing under the contract, as he had not freely chosen to complete the building himself, but had been compelled to do so by A's breach: *Sumpter* v. *Hedges* (1898).

(c) *Divisible contracts.* If performance is to be by instalments payment can be recovered for instalments actually completed (unless the intention of the parties appears to be to the contrary).
(d) *Substantial performance,* i.e. where performance is as complete as a reasonable man could expect, even though not strictly in accord with every detail of the contract. This is a question of fact.

Examples

(1) A decorated B's flat for £750, but because of faulty workmanship B had to pay an extra £290 to complete the job. B refused to pay any money at all to A. HELD: A was entitled to recover the £750, less the £290 paid to make good his defective workmanship: *Hoenig* v. *Isaacs* (1952). (2) A installed a defective central heating system for B at a charge of £560. B had to spend £174 to get C to put the system into working order. HELD: There had not been substantial performance of the contract and B need not pay A anything — not even the £385 that A claimed: *Bolton* v. *Mahadeva* (1972).

3. Tender of performance and payment

(a) *Tender of performance.* It is sometimes sufficient if the promisor attempts to perform his side of the contract. Then, if performance is rejected, the promisor is discharged from further liability and may sue for breach of contract if he so wishes.
(b) *Tender of payment.* This relieves the promisor from future liability to make further tenders, but does not discharge him from liability to pay.

Under the Currency and Bank Notes Act 1954, and the Coinage Acts 1971 and 1983, Bank of England notes (and gold coins issued by the Mint) are legal tender for any amount, silver (or cupro-nickel) coins of more than 10p denomination are legal tender up to £10, silver (or cupro-nickel) coins of 10p or less are legal tender up to £5, and bronze coins for any amount up to 20p. (But the debtor should produce the correct amount: the creditor is not obliged to give change: *Robinson* v. *Cook* (1815).)

4. Time for performance or payment

Failure to perform or pay on time may be a breach of warranty but is rarely a breach of condition, i.e. is rarely 'of the essence' of the contract.

(a) *Time of payment* is not of the essence unless otherwise agreed expressly or impliedly. (This rule is statutorily applied to contracts for the sale of goods: S.G.A. 1979, s. 10.)

(b) *Time of performance* is not usually of the essence but may be made so by agreement, and this is usually done in mercantile contracts.

Example

O waived the original delivery date but stipulated a later date as final. HELD: This made the later date of the essence, i.e. a condition, of the contract and failure to deliver on the new date entitled O to rescind the contract: *Rickards* v. *Oppenheim* (1950).

5. Rules with regard to payment of money

(a) Payment of a smaller sum will not usually discharge liability to pay a larger: *Foakes* v. *Beer* (1884), except where the rules in *Pinnel's Case* or the *High Trees Case* apply: *see* 3: 18.

(b) Payment to an agent is usually a good discharge, if the agent is held out by the creditor as having authority to receive money.

(c) Payment by a third party is not a good discharge unless he pays as agent for the debtor: *Smith* v. *Cox* (1940).

(d) Payment to one joint creditor discharges liability to the others: *Kendall* v. *Hamilton* (1879).

(e) Payment by negotiable instrument is conditional payment only, until the negotiable instrument is cashed (or as otherwise agreed). The creditor can always refuse to take a negotiable instrument such as a cheque and can insist on cash.

(f) Payment by post is ineffective if the letter is lost in the post unless the creditor requested this method of payment: *Pennington* v. *Crossley & Son* (1897). But if the creditor did request payment by post, payment is effective once posted, even if the letter is lost in the post: *Norman* v. *Ricketts* (1886).

(g) Payment by cheque is prima facie evidence of receipt (once the cheque has been cashed) but a formal receipt can also be demanded: Cheques Act 1957, s. 3.

(h) Payment by cheque or bill of exchange is conditional, so that the debtor remains liable to pay if the cheque or bill is for whatever reason dishonoured. However, if a person pays a debt by credit card, and the credit card company goes into liquidation before the supplier is reimbursed, the supplier cannot seek further payment from the debtor. However, the credit card company, or any third party to whom it had factored accounts due, could seek payment from the debtor: *Re Charge Card Services* (1988).

6. Appropriation of payments
Where there are several debts outstanding between the parties, it is sometimes important to ascertain what payment has discharged what debt. The following legal rules apply.

(a) The debtor can appropriate any payment to any debt, no matter which is the longest outstanding.

(b) If the debtor makes no appropriation, the creditor can appropriate in any way he chooses, e.g. applying the money to pay off a statute-barred debt: *Seymour* v. *Pickett* (1905).

(c) The rule in *Clayton's Case* (1816). If there is a current account between the parties, subject to constant incomings and outgoings, then if neither party makes any express appropriation the law presumes that the first payment in discharges the earliest outstanding debt.

(d) Certain rules prescribed for credit agreements by the Consumer Credit Act 1974, s. 81.

Discharge by agreement

7. Executory contracts
These are contracts wholly unperformed by either side, which can be discharged by simple waiver. Consideration for the waiver lies in the exchange of promises not to sue to enforce the contract.

8. Executed contracts
These are contracts wholly or partly performed by one party. Discharge of such contracts must be by:

(a) *Deed of release,* for which no consideration is necessary; *or*

(b) *Accord and satisfaction,* i.e. a simple contract agreement (the accord) + valuable consideration (the satisfaction) other than performance of the actual obligations under the original contract. The consideration may take the form of some alternative method of performance, or mere executory promises. But some consideration is necessary to prevent the rule in *Foakes* v. *Beer* coming into operation: *see* 3: **18.**

9.   Substituted agreement
A contract can also be discharged by the parties making a fresh contract in substitution for the old. But this method is available only where the contract is not yet wholly performed on either side, i.e. is still partly executory on both sides.

A new contract substituted for an earlier in this way is called a *novation*.

10.   Variation of contracts
Discharge by agreement may be total or partial. Variation (which may amount to partial discharge) can generally take any form, except that contracts unenforceable unless evidenced in writing can only be varied in writing: *Morris* v. *Baron* (1918). In the case of credit agreements, certain variations are ineffective unless in a prescribed form: Consumer Credit Act 1974, s. 82.

(Total rescission can always be made in any form, e.g. a specialty contract can be rescinded orally: *Berry* v. *Berry* (1929).)

11.   Unauthorised alteration
If one party makes a material alteration to a contract without the consent of the other, the contract is automatically discharged.

A material alteration is one which alters the effect of the contract, e.g. altering the crossing or the amount payable on a cheque.

Discharge by operation of law

12.   By merger
A contract is discharged if it is merged in a higher obligation, e.g. a deed swallows or merges into itself a simple contract on the same terms and between the same parties.

13.   Contracts for personal services
These are automatically discharged by death in most cases.

Contracts of a non-personal nature may survive for the benefit of the deceased's estate.

14. Discharge in bankruptcy

Where a bankrupt obtains his discharge the order automatically cancels liability on all provable debts existing at that date.

15. Lapses of time: Limitation Act 1980

The Act lays down that actions for breach of contract must be commenced within a certain time after the breach occurs, otherwise the right of action lapses, i.e. is statute-barred. (The right of action is not destroyed by lapse of time, it simply cannot be enforced: *see* **17**, below.)

The more important periods of time laid down by the Act are as follows.

(a) Six years for actions for breach of simple contracts.

(b) Twelve years for actions for breach of specialty contracts.

(c) Thirty years in actions of land where the Crown is the plaintiff; twelve years in other cases.

(d) Three years where the claim is for damages for personal injury: Limitation Act 1980. But the period begins to operate only when the plaintiff discovers certain facts, particularly the seriousness of his injury and that it can be attributed to an identified defendant.

(e) Actions under Part I of the Consumer Protection Act 1987 (which allows for claims to be brought for damage to person or property against the producer of defective goods whether negligent or not) expire ten years after the product was supplied: Limitation Act 1980, s. 11A.

(f) In cases of negligence, except personal injury or death, the limitation period is six years. This basic six-year period can be overriden by allowing a further three years from the date when the damage was discoverable: Limitation Act 1980, s. 14A. Where a party seeks to rely on the three-year limitation period in s. 14A in bringing an action for damages for negligence, he must show that he did not possess before the three-year period prior to the date on which proceedings commenced sufficient knowledge of the material facts to enable him to commence proceedings. Section

14B provides a backstop in that no action can be brought once 15 years have elapsed from the date when any action or omission alleged to constitute the negligence occurred. Section 14A is limited to actions for damages for negligence where the duty of care, the breach of which constitutes the negligence relied on, arises solely in tort and does not apply to claims framed in contract: *Société Commerciale de Reassurance* v. *ERAS (International) Ltd* (1992). See also *Iron Trade Mutual Insurance Co. Ltd* v. *J K Buckenham* (1990).
(g) The court has an unfettered discretion to allow an action in respect of personal injury or death to proceed, despite the expiry of the limitation period, if it considers it fair to do so having regard to the degree to which the parties would be prejudiced: Limitation Act 1980, s. 33: *Donovan* v. *Gwentoys Ltd* (1990); *Ramsden* v. *Lee* (1992); *Hartley* v. *Birmingham City DC* (1992).

16. When time runs
The limitation period under the Act is generally calculated from the moment the breach occurs, except where:

(a) the plaintiff was under a legal disability at the date of the breach, e.g. minority or mental incapacity. Here time runs from the date when the disability ceases, or from the time of death if the plaintiff dies while still disabled, whichever occurs first: ss. 22, 31.
(b) the action is based on fraud, mistake, etc. Here time begins to run from the date when the fraud or mistake is discovered by the plaintiff, and not from the date when the cause of action arose: s. 32.

Examples
(1) Eight years after his house was built, A discovered that in breach of contract the builder had laid defective foundations. HELD: He could not have discovered the truth as the builder had concealed the facts, and consequently his right of action was not barred: *Applegate* v. *Moss* (1971).
(2) In order to prevent the Limitation Act operating, the plaintiff's mistake must be as to facts, e.g. not merely ignorance or mistake as to his rights in law: *Central Asbestos Co. Ltd* v. *Dodds* (1972).

17. Acknowledgments and part payments
When a right of action has lapsed it may be revived by the following.

(a) A written acknowledgment constituting an express or implied admission of liability. Thus a letter admitting liability but refusing to pay and relying on the Limitation Act has been held to be a sufficient acknowledgment for this purpose: *Re Coliseum (Barrow) Ltd* (1930). (If the written acknowledgment is lost, its contents can be proved by oral evidence: *Read* v. *Price* (1909).)

(b) A part payment of a statute-barred debt.

Where there is an acknowledgment or part payment, it starts time running again, i.e. the plaintiff has a further six years (or twelve if a specialty contract is involved) in which to commence action: Limitation Act 1980, ss. 29–31.

NOTE: a part payment into a bank current account which is overdrawn operates to revive the right of action for the whole account, including debts incurred more than six years previously: *Re Footman Bower & Co. Ltd* (1961).

Frustration of contracts

18. Supervening impossibility of performance

Where at the outset it is clearly impossible to perform a contract, such contract lacks an essential element and is void, e.g. contracts to walk across the Atlantic.

But sometimes a contract possible when made subsequently becomes impossible to perform, e.g. a lawful contract involving trade between Britain and Russia became impossible to perform when the Crimean War broke out between the two countries: *Avery* v. *Bowden* (1856).

The general rule is that supervening impossibility of performance does not discharge the contract, except where the doctrine of frustration applies.

19. Doctrine of frustration

This has been developed to mitigate hardship which might be caused by the supervening impossibility rule stated above.

Under the doctrine of frustration the courts will imply a term into a contract providing for the discharge of the contract if certain types of impossibility arise after the contract is made: *Cricklewood Property Co.* v. *Leighton's Investment Trust* (1945).

20. Frustration occurs in the following cases

(a) *Where the basis is destroyed.* If the contract depends on the continued existence of something, and that thing is destroyed, e.g. hire of a theatre frustrated by the theatre being burned down: *Taylor* v. *Caldwell* (1863).

(b) *Where there is non-occurrrence of an essential event.* If the contract depends on the occurrence of an event which does not in fact happen, e.g. hire of rooms to watch the coronation procession of Edward VII, frustrated by cancellation of the procession: *Krell* v. *Henry* (1903); contrast *Herne Bay S.S. Co.* v. *Hutton* (1903).

(c) *Where there is death or illness.* A contract for personal services may be frustrated by death or unduly prolonged illness of the employee. What amounts to unduly prolonged illness is a question of fact in each case, e.g. if a concert pianist hired for three performances is ill when due to play at the first, this might amount to frustration: *Robinson* v. *Davison* (1871).

(d) *Where there is government interference.* Where the government prohibits performance for such a period that it would be unreasonable to expect performance after the prohibition ceases: *Metropolitan Water Board* v. *Dick, Kerr & Co. Ltd* (1918).

(e) *Where there is a change in law.* Where a contract legal when made subsequently becomes unlawful through a change in the legal situation: *Avery* v. *Bowden* (1856).

(f) *Where the method of performance is impossible.* If a particular manner of performance is essential, and when the time comes for performance this particular method has become impossible: *Tsakiroglou & Co. Ltd* v. *Noblee and Thorl GmbH* (1962).

Examples _____

(1) A contracted to build for B 78 houses in eight months for £92,000. It was impossible to meet the contract date, and rises in costs added £17,000 to A's bill. There was no clause in the contract to cover this eventuality. The time ultimately taken by A was 22 months. A claimed that the original contract was frustrated by impossibility, and sued for £109,000 on *quantum meruit*. HELD: Contract was not frustrated, and therefore A had no *quantum meruit* claim. He should have foreseen his troubles and written a clause into the contract to cover them: *Davis Contractors Ltd* v. *Fareham U.D.C.* (1956).

(2) Headmaster of school was suspended by his employers after a criminal charge had been made against him, of which he was acquitted six months later. HELD: His enforced absence from work did not frustrate

his contract of employment, since his presence as headmaster was not vital to the continued running of the school: *Mount* v. *Oldham Corporation* (1973).

(3) Property was advertised as being suitable for redevelopment. On the date when the parties entered the contract, they did not know that the Department of the Environment proposed to list the building as being of architectural or historical significance. This happened the following day. This brought the development value of the property down to £200,000 from £1.7m. The court said listing was an inherent risk which the purchaser of property had to bear. Listing did not make the contract radically different and so it was not frustrated: *Amalgamated Investment and Property Co. Ltd* v. *John Walker & Sons Ltd* (1976).

---

21. Limits of the doctrine

Frustration does not occur in the following cases.

(a) Express terms may cover the contingency complained of. The court will refuse to treat the contract as frustrated where to do so would be contrary to the express terms of the contract: *British Movietonews Ltd* v. *London, etc. Cinemas Ltd* (1952) H.L.

(b) Self-induced frustration cannot be pleaded as grounds for discharge, as it may amount to breach of contract.

(c) Although it used to be thought that the doctrine did not apply to leases, the House of Lords ruled to the contrary in *National Carriers Ltd* v. *Panalpina (Northern) Ltd* (1981).

22. Effect of frustration

The contract is discharged for the future (from the date of the frustrating event), but it is not void *ab initio*. Therefore it may be important to ascertain who should bear the loss and who should pay for any services rendered up to the time of frustration.

(a) Before 1943, at common law the loss lay where it fell, i.e. money which had become payable before frustration remained payable, and money paid before frustration was irrecoverable, but money not due until after frustration ceased to be payable: *Chandler* v. *Webster* (1904). This harsh rule was later modified to allow apportionment of loss where there had been total failure of consideration: *Fibrosa Case* (1943).

(b) The Law Reform (Frustrated Contracts) Act 1943 reformed the above position by providing the following.

    (*i*) Money paid before frustration is prima facie recoverable (unless its retention can be justified by expenses incurred by the recipient before frustration).

(*ii*) Money due before frustration ceases to be payable (unless needed to cover expenses as in (*i*) above).

(*iii*) Benefits received before frustration must be paid for, and a party who has incurred expenses before frustration is entitled to compensation therefore.

NOTE: The 1943 Act can be excluded by express agreement, and in any case it does not apply to (*i*) charter parties, (*ii*) carriage of goods by sea, (*iii*) sales of specific goods, (*iv*) insurance contracts.

Breach of contract and remedies

23. Breach of contract
This occurs where one party:

(a) repudiates his obligations;
(b) disables himself from performing his part of the contract;
(c) fails to perform his part of the contract as and when agreed.

24. Anticipatory breach
In (*a*) and (*b*) above the breach may occur before the date fixed for performance, e.g. where A hired B to act as a courier commencing employment on 1st June but wrote to B in May repudiating the agreement, it was held that B was immediately entitled to sue, and need not wait till 1st June for his right of action to accrue: *Hochster* v. *De La Tour* (1853). But a party can ignore such a breach, perform his own side, and later claim damages for breach: *White & Carter Ltd* v. *McGregor* (1962).

25. Effect of breach
The effect depends largely on whether the breach is of a condition or of a warranty: *see* 2: **25–27**.

(a) *Breach of warranty:* the injured party can only sue for damages and must go on with the contract, i.e. the breach does not operate to discharge the contract.
(b) *Breach of condition:* the injured party can choose whether: (*i*) to treat the breach as a breach of *ex post facto* warranty (and sue for

damages while going on with the contract); *or* (*ii*) to treat the breach of condition as automatically discharging the contract.

> NOTE: If he chooses alternative (*ii*) he cannot also sue for damages for breach, since he has indicated a willingness to regard the contract as dead and has therefore waived his right of action for damages (but if he has incurred expense under the contract he can bring a quasi-contractual *quantum meruit* action for compensation). If he chooses alternative (*i*), he keeps the contract alive, and should immediately commence action to enforce it, i.e. should sue for damages or specific performance. If he delays suing, he takes the risk that some unforeseen event may occur to discharge the contract by frustration thus depriving him of his right of action.

Example

A hired B's ship to carry a cargo from Russia. Later B repudiated the contract, thus entitling A either to treat the contract as discharged or to sue for damages. A delayed a decision hoping B would change his mind before the performance date. War broke out between Russia and Britain before the performance date, frustrating the contract. HELD: A had lost his right to sue for damages by his delay: *Avery* v. *Bowden* (1856).

> NOTE: In recent times, a somewhat different approach has been adopted. It has been said that many contractual undertakings cannot readily be called 'conditions' or 'warranties'. Instead, the proper approach, it is said, is to examine the consequences of the breach. If the breach is disastrous, the contract may be taken as terminated, if not disastrous only damages may be claimed: *Hong Kong Fir Shipping Co. Ltd* v. *Kawasaki Kishen Kaisha Ltd* (1962); *Cehave N.V.* v. *Bremer* (1975).

26. Remedies for breach

The common law remedy is damages by way of compensation. In addition there are the discretionary equitable remedies of specific performance and injunction, which are usually available where damages are inadequate to compensate the plaintiff for the breach. *See* **33** below.

27. Damages for breach of contract

The plaintiff can recover financial compensation for his actual loss, provided it is not too remote. Under the rule in *Hadley* v. *Baxendale* (1854) damage is not too remote if:

(a) it is the natural consequence of the breach, e.g. B unduly delayed delivery of a mill-shaft to A's mill, whereby the mill was out of action for a considerable time. A had informed B that the lack of the shaft would necessitate closure of the mill. HELD: A could recover damages for the delay in delivery, but not for loss of profits occasioned by closure of the mill, since there was no way B could have foreseen that his delay would cause the closure: *Hadley* v. *Baxendale* (1854);

(b) although not arising naturally from the breach, the damage caused was something which was within the contemplation of the parties when making the contract. (Thus in *Hadley* v. *Baxendale* the mill-owner could have recovered damages for loss of profits if he had informed the carrier of the likely result of delayed delivery.)

Example

A contracted to supply a boiler to B's laundry and was five months' late in delivery. HELD: B could recover damages for loss of ordinary profits occasioned by the delay since A knew the laundry would be closed pending delivery of the boiler (but B could not recover damages for loss of exceptional profits expected to arise under a valuable contract of which A was not informed): *Victoria Laundry* v. *Newman Industries* (1949); *Parsons* v. *Uttley Ingham* (1978).

28. The measure of damages

Damages for breach of contract are intended to compensate the plaintiff, not to punish the defendant.

NOTE: (1) The plaintiff must mitigate or minimise his loss as far as he reasonably can, he cannot recover additional damages for loss occasioned by his failure to do so: *British Westinghouse Electric & Manufacturing Co. Ltd* v. *Underground Electric Rail Co. Ltd* (1912). Thus if an employee is wrongfully dismissed he can recover damages for loss of wages, but must reduce his loss as much as he can by seeking new employment. He will not recover extra heavy damages if he is out of work for a long time by reason of his own failure to seek work: *Brace* v. *Calder* (1895). (2) Interest on any sum claimed is not allowed unless: (*i*) the parties have previously so agreed, or (*ii*) the claim is on a bill of exchange or promissory note, or (*iii*) the court exercises its statutory discretion to award interest under the Law Reform (Miscellaneous Provisions) Act 1934. (3) The plaintiff must quantify his loss of profit in financial terms. If he cannot do so, he may recover wasted expenditure, even though the expenditure was incurred before the contract was made (provided it was within the contemplation of the parties at the time of contracting): *Anglia Television* v. *Reed* (1971). *See also Cullinane* v. *British 'Rema' Mfg. Co.* (1954). (4) The plaintiff can claim his loss even where his acts of mitigation have made matters worse. It is only necessary that he does what seems reasonable at the time: *Daily Office Cleaning Contractors Ltd* v. *Shefford* (1977). (5) A contract-breaker is not in general liable for any distress, frustration, anxiety, displeasure, vexation, tension or aggravation which his breach of contract may cause to the innocent party. The rule, though, is not absolute. Where the very object of the contract is to provide pleasure, relaxation, peace of mind or freedom from molestation, damages will be awarded if the fruit of the contract is not provided or if the contrary result is procured instead: *Hayes* v. *Charles Dodd* (1990); *Watts* v. *Morrow* (1991).

29. Penalties and liquidated damages

Where the amount of compensation claimed is left to be assessed by the court, damages claimed are called *unliquidated damages*.

But sometimes the parties agree in advance the amount payable in the event of breach. Such an amount is called *liquidated damages*, and in any action for breach of such contract the court will award the pre-assessed sum unless it has been fixed in such a way as to break the rules against penalties.

Liquidated damages are a genuine pre-estimate of the measure of loss which a breach of the contract is likely to cause. A penalty on the other hand is a sum fixed at random to frighten a party into performing his contract: *Dunlop Pneumatic Tyre Co.* v. *New Garage Co.* (1915). In *Lombard North Central* v. *Butterworth* (1987), a lease for a computer provided that in the event of default in payment, the lessors were entitled to all arrears of instalments and to all future instalments which would have been due had the agreement not been terminated. The Court of Appeal ruled that this was an unenforceable penalty clause, since, in the absence of repudiation by the lessee, it obliged him regardless of the seriousness or triviality of the breach to make payment in respect of future instalments.

A sum is a penalty if:

(a) it is extravagant having regard to the maximum possible loss which could result from the breach;

(b) failure to pay a sum of money results in liability to pay a larger sum;

(c) a single sum is payable on the occurrence of any of several events of differing degrees of importance: *Kemble* v. *Farren* (1829).

If a sum is held to be a penalty the court will not award it, but will make its own assessment of damages. The fact that the parties describe a sum as a penalty or a clause as a 'penalty clause' is not decisive. The court will apply the above tests in each case, and if satisfied that the sum is a genuine pre-estimate of loss the court will award it to the plaintiff as liquidated damages.

There is no distinction between a penalty for non-payment of money due under a contract and a penalty for the non-performance of some other obligation under a contract. In addition, there is no distinction between a penalty which requires the payment of money and a penalty which requires the transfer of property: *Jobson* v. *Johnson* (1989).

30. Quantum meruit
Where there has been a breach of condition and the injured party has elected to treat the contract as at an end, he cannot later sue for damages for breach of contract since he has already accepted breach as terminating the contract's existence. However, in such cases, if he has incurred loss, he can bring a quasi-contractual *quantum meruit* action for compensation for work done, expense incurred, etc.: *see* 1: **17**.

A *quantum meruit* (literally 'how much is it worth?') claim can thus arise where:

(a) the defendant has abandoned or repudiated the contract, e.g. where after commissioning a writer to do a series of articles, a magazine closes down before the series is completely written: *Planché* v. *Colburn* (1831). The writer could not sue for breach of contract here because he had not completed his own side of the bargain;

(b) under a void contract one party has done work and the defendant has received the benefit of it: *Craven-Ellis* v. *Canons Ltd* (1936). Here again the plaintiff could not have sued on the contract since it was void;

(c) the parties have agreed to terminate the contract but the plaintiff has performed a substantial part of his own side of the bargain. Here he can sue on a *quantum meruit* claim, but not on the contract since he has accepted termination: *Dakin* v. *Lee* (1916); **(d)** one party has obtained a benefit which he could not reasonably expect to get without paying for it, e.g. where a builder leaves building materials on X's land and X uses the materials, the builder can sue for the value of the materials: *Sumpter* v. *Hedges* (1898) and *see* **2** above.

Similarly, if a grocer by mistake leaves goods at the wrong house and the occupant uses the goods, the grocer could sue for their value.

31. Specific performance

This is a discretionary remedy for breach of contract and consists of a court order compelling the defendant to perform his side of the bargain. It may be awarded in addition to or instead of damages.

Specific performance will only be awarded where:

(a) damages would be inadequate to compensate the plaintiff, e.g. in contracts to sell or lease land, or for the sale of valuable and unique chattels such as rare paintings. It will not be awarded in ordinary contracts for sale of goods where the plaintiff could easily obtain replacement articles with the money received as damages, e.g. in sales of ordinary cars, books, furniture.

Under a contract made in March 1970, the plaintiff agreed to buy all its petrol and diesel fuel from the defendant for at least ten years. The defendant company attempted to terminate the agreement when the market for oil was in an unusual state. The court granted an interlocutory injunction restraining the threatened breach because the court could order specific performance of a contract to sell and purchase chattels which were not specific, or ascertained where, as the evidence showed here, damages would not be an effective remedy: *Sky Petroleum Ltd* v. *V.I.P. Petroleum Ltd* (1974);
(b) the enforcement of the order would not require constant supervision by the court, e.g. not in building contracts or contracts of employment;
(c) the contract is equally enforceable by both parties. Thus a minor plaintiff cannot obtain specific performance of a contract which would not be enforceable against him, since it would be

impossible for the adult defendant party to claim specific performance against the minor (in such cases the minor can of course obtain damages): *Johnson* v. *Agnew* (1980) (CA);

(d) the plaintiff himself has acted fairly and equitably. He cannot obtain specific performance if his own conduct has been tricky or unfair: *Webster* v. *Cecil* (1861): *see* 4: **8**.

32. Injunctions

An injunction is a discretionary court order and is either:

(a) *prohibitory:* forbidding a person to do something; *or*
(b) *mandatory:* commanding a person to do something.

Mandatory injunctions are rarely granted since they might call for supervision by the court, which may not have the resources to enforce the injunction adequately.

Injunctions may take the following forms.

(a) *Quia timet injunctions:* issued to prevent an apprehended injury before it has occurred, but where there is reasonable ground for fearing a breach of contract may occur.
(b) *Interim or interlocutory injunctions:* usually granted pending the decision of a case, e.g. prohibiting the defendant from taking disputed property overseas until the dispute as to its ownership has been settled in court.
(c) *Perpetual:* issued when a dispute has been finally settled, e.g. where an interim injunction is made perpetual when the dispute has been finally settled in court.

33. Injunctions to restrain breaches of contract

An injunction is a suitable additional or alternative remedy to damages where the plaintiff wants to prevent the defendant breaking the contract, or continuing to break it.

Injunctions may be available where specific performance is not. Thus a contract of personal services cannot be enforced by an order for specific performance, since this would necessitate constant supervision by the court. But the court might in such a case grant a prohibitory injunction, forbidding the defendant from breaking the contract (and threatening him with imprisonment if he disobeys).

An injunction will only be granted to restrain a breach of

contract if the clause the plaintiff seeks to enforce is negative in substance, though it may be positive in form. Thus a contract under which a film star is to work exclusively for a plaintiff company appears positive in form, but has a negative meaning, i.e. that the film star must not work for anyone else. An injunction could be granted therefore to prevent the film star working for anyone else: *Warner Bros* v. *Nelson* (1937).

6
Privity, assignment, and negotiability

Privity of contract

1. Doctrine of privity

A contract is a private relationship between the parties who make it, and no other person can acquire rights or incur liabilities under it.

Compare this rule with the separate rule that 'consideration must move from the promisee'. The two rules together mean that a person seeking to sue upon a contract must satisfy the court: (*a*) that he is a party to the contract he seeks to enforce, and (*b*) that he has given consideration for the promise he seeks to enforce (or that the contract is under seal): *see* 3: **9–11**.

Contrast a legal duty with a contractual duty. A legal duty is one which, if not performed, can be sued upon by any person injured by the breach of duty; actions for tort are actions for breach of this sort of duty. A contractual duty is one which is owed only to the other party to the contract, and only that party can sue to enforce it. (Also contractual duties arise by agreement, while legal duties are imposed by the law independently of any agreement between the parties.)

2. Scope of doctrine

The doctrine of privity has two aspects:

(a) no one can acquire rights under a contract to which he is not a party;

(b) no one can incur liabilities under a contract to which he is not a party.

Example
B sold his business to C on condition that C should pay (*i*) £6.50 per week to B for life, and (*ii*) £5 per week for life to Mrs B after B's death. B died and C refused to pay Mrs B, since she was not a party to the contract. HELD: (*i*) Mrs B was not a party to the contract and therefore could not personally enforce it, but (*ii*) as administratrix of her late husband's estate (which was a party to the contract) she could enforce the contract: *Beswick* v. *Beswick* (1968); *Scruttons Ltd* v. *Midland Silicones Ltd* (1962); *N.Z. Shipping Co.* v. *Satterthwaite* (1975).

3. Acquisition of rights

If A and B make a contract whereby B is to pay A to do something for X, X cannot sue A if he fails to do what he promised. It makes no difference if X has given consideration for the promise — he cannot sue unless he is a party to the contract: *Price* v. *Easton* (1833) – nor that B and X are closely related: *Tweddle* v. *Atkinson* (1861).

EXCEPTIONS: (1) *Constructive trust.* Where B is regarded as a trustee for X, X may sue A (and join B as co-defendant) if the contract between B and A is broken. (A constructive trust is one imposed by the courts to prevent injustice, and arises independently of any agreement between the parties.) (2) *Resale Prices Act 1976, s. 26.* A retailer who obtains goods from a wholesaler with notice of restrictive conditions imposed on resale of the goods by the original supplier may be bound by such conditions, even though they arose from the contract between the wholesaler and the supplier (to which the retailer was not a party: *Goodyear Tyre & Rubber Co. Ltd* v. *Lancashire Batteries Ltd* (1958). (3) *Negotiable instruments.* If X is the holder for value of a bill of exchange he may sue the drawer (A) upon the bill: *see* 14: **37, 38.** (4) *Agency.* Where B is secretly acting as agent for X, X can intervene to enforce the contract between A and B, in which case B drops out and the contract subsists directly between A and X. This is called the doctrine of the undisclosed principal: *see* 8: **17.** But it has also been held that where a person makes a contract for a holiday for himself and his family, he can recover damages for everyone for the disappointment suffered when the holiday is a disaster: *Jackson* v. *Horizon Holidays* (1975). (5) *Road Traffic Act 1988, ss. 151, 152.* Persons specified in a third-party car insurance policy can sue the insurance company to enforce the policy for their own benefit. (6) *Law of Property Act* 1925, s. 56 states that a person may take 'an immediate or other interest' under a contract, providing it is in writing. But the

House of Lords has refused to regard this provision as creating a general exception to the doctrine of privity: *Beswick* v. *Beswick* (1968).
(7) *Road Traffic Act 1988, s. 148.* This provides that insurance covers any person driving a motor vehicle with the consent of the owner.

4. Acquisition of liabilities

A contract between A and B cannot impose liabilities on X, save in the following exceptional cases.

(a) Resale Prices Act 1976, s. 26: *see* **3** above.
(b) Commercial usage or trade customs may so provide.
(c) Sale of ships. If X buys a ship from B which has previously been chartered by A, he may be bound by the terms of the charterparty if he has notice of its terms: *Strathcona S.S. Case* (1926).
(d) Restrictive covenants affecting land. These may run with the land, i.e. if X buys land he may be bound by a covenant between A and B, the seller of the land, provided (*i*) X accepts the covenant when buying the land, or (*ii*) the covenant is registered at the Land Charges Registry under the Land Charges Act 1972.

Transfer and assignment of contracts

5. Transfer of contracts

Rights and liabilities under a contract can be transferred in some cases. In this situation, in accordance with the doctrine of privity, if in a contract between A and B, B transfers the contract to X, B drops out of the contract which now subsists between A and X. B thereafter generally has no further rights nor obligations under the contract.

6. Transfer of liabilities

This is only possible where:

(a) the contract so provides; *or*
(b) the parties later so agree. If the parties to a contract agree that it cannot be assigned, any purported assignment is therefore invalid and the intended assignee has no rights under the original contract: *Helstan Securities Ltd* v. *Hertfordshire County Council* (1978).

Transfer is effected by cancellation of the existing contract between A and B and substitution of a new agreement between B an X, i.e. a novation .

NOTE: In a contract between A and B, if performance is not a personal matter, B can always delegate performance to some other person, e.g. his employee. This does not involve transfer of the contract, and privity still exists between A and B who remain fully liable on the contract.

7. Assignment of rights: choses in action

A right or benefit arising under a contract is called a *chose* (or 'thing') *in action*, i.e. a personal right of property which can usually be enforced only by suing (by action) and not by taking physical possession: *Torkington* v. *Magee* (1902). Contrast a *chose in possession*, which is a piece of property capable of actual physical possession, e.g. goods, ships.

Whether the benefit of a contract can be assigned depends on the intention of the parties. Thus a contract of employment cannot usually be assigned, unless otherwise agreed.

Choses in action can be assigned in two ways: (*a*) in accordance with s. 136, Law of Property Act 1925, and (*b*) in accordance with the rules of equity (i.e. any assignment not complying with s. 136).

8. Statutory assignments: L.P.A. 1925, s. 136
Such assignments operate to transfer

(a) the full legal obligation,
(b) the right to enforce the obligation, *and*
(c) power to give a valid discharge.

REQUIREMENTS: (1) The assignment must be absolute, i.e. of the whole debt or other obligation. (2) The assignment must not be by way of charge only. (3) It must be in writing, signed by the assignor. (4) It need not be supported by valuable consideration. (5) Express notice in writing must be given to the obligee by the assignee, to avoid the obligee performing the contract for the benefit of the assignor.

Thus if A owes B £100, B can sell his right to collect payment to X (in the form set out above), and this will entitle X to enforce the debt against A. However, X should notify A of the assignment to avoid A paying B.

9. Effect of statutory assignments

(a) The assignee (X) can sue in his own name to enforce the chose in action, e.g. by suing A for debt.

(b) The assignee (X) takes subject to equities having priority over his assignment, e.g. if A has paid part of his debt to B before receiving notice of the assignment X cannot compel A to pay the full amount (but must try to recover the money from B).

10. Equitable assignments

This means any assignment which though valid fails to comply with the requirements of s. 136, L.P.A., e.g. an oral assignment.

In an equitable assignment the assignee (X) cannot sue in his own name, but must join the assignor (B) as co-plaintiff in any action against the debtor or other obligee (A), or as co-defendant if he refuses. Thus the action will be either *X and B* v. *A*, or *X* v. *B and A*.

> ESSENTIALS: (1) Intention to assign (no particular form is necessary). (2) Notice is necessary to the obligee to prevent him paying assignor: the rule in *Dearle* v. *Hall* (1828). (3) Value is necessary only in assignments of future rights, e.g. the assignor's expectations under a will.

11. Negotiable instruments

Some choses in action possess the quality of negotiability, e.g. cheques and other bills of exchange. These negotiable instruments are freely transferable by mere delivery (with or without endorsement by the transferor), and the transferee usually obtains an indefeasible title free of equities, etc.

Negotiability must therefore be distinguished from assignability. If a chose is merely assignable, the assignee obtains no better rights to the chose than were possessed by the assignor; but if the chose is negotiable, the transferee may obtain a better right than that possessed by the transferor: *see* 15: **2**.

Progress test 1

Law of contracts

1. How does a binding contract differ from other agreements? What kinds of contract are there, and what are their characteristics? (1: **1–4, 5–8**)

2. What is a quasi-contract? When if ever can money be recovered on the grounds of mistake in payment? (1: **12–17**)

3. Distinguish an offer from: (*a*) an invitation to treat, and (*b*) a statement of intention. (2: **1–6**)

Apply the rules of offer and acceptance to the following situations.
- (*i*) Bidding at an auction.
- (*ii*) Putting a coin in a slot machine.
- (*iii*) Display of goods in a shop or self-service store.
- (*iv*) Boarding a bus.

4. Comment on the statement that there cannot be a contract to make a contract. (2: **21**)

A agreed orally to sell his house to B for £110,000 'subject to contract.' The next day C offered A £110,500 for the house and A accepted this offer and sold the house to C. Can B sue A for breach of contract?

Would it make any difference to your answer if the agreement between A and B was in writing? (2: **11, 13;** 3: **3**)

5. In what circumstance may an offer: (*a*) lapse, and (*b*) be revoked? (2: **7, 8**)

6. A wrote to B offering to sell his house for £110,000, the offer to remain open 'until Wednesday noon.' On Tuesday A sells his house to C. What remedies, if any, has B against A? Would it make any difference to your answer if B had paid A 5p to keep the offer open till Wednesday? (2: **9**)

7. When if ever may communication of acceptance be dispensed with? (2: **13**)

8.   What is a tender, and what forms may a tender take?
(2: **15**)

9.   In what circumstances may an offeree be bound by the
terms or a written offer which he has not read? Where such
terms are designed to limit the liability of the offeror, what is
meant by saying that they are interpreted *contra proferentem*?
(2: **17, 18**)

10. In what circumstances may the court imply a term in a
contract?   (2: **22**)

11. Distinguish between conditions and warranties in a contract,
and explain what is meant by *ex post facto* warranties.   (2: **24–28**)
     Why is it important to distinguish between a term of a
contract and a mere representation made during
negotiations?   (2: **30**)

12. What is meant by the proper law of a contract, and why is it
important?   (2: **33, 34**)

13. What contracts are void unless made (*a*) by deed, or (*b*) in
writing? What contracts are merely unenforceable unless
supported by written evidence? What is the distinction between
void and unenforceable contracts?   (3: **1–4**)

14. Define 'consideration'. When if ever is a simple contract
enforceable when unsupported by valuable consideration?
(3: **9–11**)

15. What is a guarantee, and how does it differ from an
indemnity? Is it true to say that a guarantee does not need to be
supported by consideration?   (3: **4**)

16. What formalities govern the transfer of an interest in land?
(3: **8**)

17. Explain the difference between executory, executed, and
past consideration. Why is the distinction between executed and
past consideration important?

A fell into a river and shouted for help. B, hearing the cry, rescued him, and in gratitude A promised B £10,000. A now refuses to pay the money. Can B recover it by an action for breach of contract?   (3: **11, 17**)

18. Explain briefly the rule in *Foakes* v. *Beer* (1884) and any exceptions of which you know.   (3: **18**)

19. What contracts are (*a*) binding on a minor, (*b*) voidable at the minor's option? What must be proved by a shopkeeper suing a minor for the price of goods supplied?   (3: **24–29**)

20. When, if ever, may a contract be avoided at common law on the grounds of mistake (*a*) of law, or (*b*) of fact? What relief is available in equity in cases of mistake?   (4: **1–3, 8**)

21. When if ever may a person who has signed a written acceptance of an offer evade the consequences of his signature?   (2: **16**; 4: **7**)

22. 'Mistakes in the formation of contracts may be common, mutual or unilateral.' Discuss this statement, and explain the cases where such mistakes may avoid a contract.   (4: **1–8**)

23. What is 'misrepresentation' ? When, if ever, is there a positive duty of disclosure imposed on a party to a contract? (4: **12, 19**)

24. Distinguish between innocent, negligent and fraudulent misrepresentation and explain the remedies available for each.   (4: **13, 17**)

25. Explain the importance of the distinction between a mere misrepresentation, and a misrepresentation which has become a term of a contract.   (4: **18**; 2: **22–28**)

26. 'Adequacy of consideration is of itself no grounds for avoiding a contract, but it may be evidence of undue influence.' Explain this statement.   (3: **12**; 4: **20–22**)

27. What is meant by an 'illegal' contract, and what are the consequences of illegality?   (4: **25–29**)

28. Explain briefly the main provisions of the Consumer Credit Act 1974 in regard to loans by professional moneylenders. (4: **32**)

29. Summarise briefly the rules relating to gaming and wagering contracts and their effects.   (4: **33**)

30. 'Restraints of trade are prima facie void.' How far is this true?   (4: **45–47**)

31. Explain briefly the cases in which the courts will enforce covenants by an employee not to compete with his former employer.   (4: **48–49**)

32. State briefly the five ways in which a contract may be discharged.   (Chapter 5)

33. 'To effect discharge, performance must be complete.' What exceptions are there to this rule?   (5: **1–2**)

34. Explain briefly the rules relating to the appropriation of payments by a debtor, or creditor. How does the rule in *Clayton's Case* affect the position?   (5: **6**)

35. Explain what is meant by: (*a*) deed of release; (*b*) accord and satisfaction; (*c*) novation; (*d*) the rule in *Morris* v. *Baron*.   (5: **8–10**)

36. When are rights of action arising under a contract liable to lapse? How may such lapsed rights be revived?   (5: **15–17**)

37. 'Supervening impossibility of performance has no effect on contracts.' Discuss this statement.   (5: **18–22**)

38. A, in Whiteland, and B, in Redland, made a contract for the supply of machines by A, for which B paid in advance. The contract contained a clause stating: 'This contract shall be avoided and the loss shall lie where it falls if war breaks out between Whiteland and Redland.' War does break out, when A has supplied only half the machines. The contract was made in England, and B wants to know whether he can recover any of his money under the Law Reform (Frustrated Contracts) Act 1943. Advise him.   (5: **25, 26**)

39. What is meant by 'anticipatory breach of contract'? A was due to perform a contract on 1 May, but in April repudiated his obligations. On 29 April the contract became illegal through a change in the law. B, the other party to the contract, commenced an action for breach of contract on 30 April. Discuss.   (5: **20–24**)

40. Explain briefly the rule in *Hadley* v. *Baxendale*. What is meant by saying that the plaintiff must mitigate his loss? (5: **27, 28**)

41. Distinguish between penalties and liquidated damages in the law of contracts, and explain when interest may be allowed on sums claimed by way of unliquidated damages.   (5: **28, 29**)

42. 'You cannot both treat a breach of condition as discharging a contract and also sue for damages for the breach.' Discuss this statement. Explain how the plaintiff might have a right of action on a *quantum meruit* claim in these circumstances.   (5: **25, 30**)

43. Explain when the court may award the discretionary remedies of specific performance or injunctions in actions upon contracts.   (5: **31, 32**)

44. The rule that an outsider cannot claim benefits or incur liabilities under a contract is not invariably applicable. Discuss. (6: **1–4**)

45. Why is it easier to transfer the benefit than the burden of a contract? Distinguish between legal and equitable assignments of choses in action, and explain how the effects differ.   (6: **5–10**)

Specimen questions

1. (a) 'In the formation of a contract consideration must be real
       but need not be adequate.' Explain the meaning of this
       statement.
          Does a promise made without consideration ever affect
       the promisor's position?
    (b) Oris, a greengrocer, wished to go to Italy for his annual
       holiday. He requested Robert, a friend and a neighbour,
       to look after his children for two weeks. Robert looked
       after the children while Oris was away. On his return Oris
       told Robert 'I am grateful for your help and promise to
       pay you £500 as a reward at the end of this month.'
          Oris has now changed his mind and refuses to pay £500
       to Robert. Advise Robert.

2. (a) What is a penalty and how does it differ from liquidated
       damages?
    (b) Distinguish between a *quantum meruit* claim and a claim
       for damages. In what circumstances is a *quantum meruit*
       claim appropriate?

3. (a) What is generally the purpose of exemption clauses in
       contracts? In what circumstances are such clauses
       enforced by the courts?
    (b) A bought an electric blanket manufactured by X Ltd from
       B, a dealer in electrical goods, and gave it to C as a birthday
       present. Owing to defective manufacture the blanket
       caught fire the first time it was used and C was badly
       burned. C wishes to recover compensation. Advise him.

4. C went to D's circus, and bought a ticket at the entrance. On
    the back of this ticket there was a printed notice: 'The management
    accept no responsibility for the safety of their audiences.' Just
    before the circus was due to start an announcement was made to
    a similar effect. During the performance the stand upon which C
    was seated collapsed due to the fact that D's workmen had erected
    it carelessly, and C was injured.
       Advise C.

5. On 1st January D wrote to C offering to sell him his motor car for £3500. On 1st June C replied saying, 'I accept your offer, but I consider that £3450 is enough.' D had in fact sold the car to X on 1st May.

C consults you as to his rights: advise him.

6. What are the requirements for establishing a defence of *non est factum* to a contractual claim?

7. J bought a ticket for a world cruise from the agents of K & Co, a shipping line. J was allergic to a certain type of deodorant; so, after he had paid the agent for the ticket and put it away in his wallet, he asked the agents' clerk whether this deodorant was in use on the ship. The clerk said that it was not. There was a statement on the ticket that 'The company accepts no responsibility for any illness or other physical loss occasioned to passengers as a result of the state of the ship or of the use of any preparations or appliances thereon.'

The deodorant in question was in fact in use on the ship. J went on the cruise and became ill as a direct consequence of inhaling it.

Advise J.

8. (*a*) 'An offer and an invitation to treat must be carefully distinguished, but a tender may be either. ' Discuss.

(*b*) In the course of a conversation, A offered to sell his caravan to B for £1000. B replied that he would like time to think it over, and A said 'I will give you three days.' That same day B posted a letter to A enclosing a cheque for £1000 and agreeing to buy the caravan. On the same evening A and B chanced to meet and A informed B that he had just sold the caravan to C for £1200. Advise B.

9. 'No one can claim the benefit of a contract unless he is a party to it.'

Consider this statement.

10. (*a*) Explain the rules the courts will apply in the assessment of unliquidated damages in an action for breach of contract.

(*b*) Golden Films Ltd decided to make a film and engaged Sir

Austin, a famous actor, as the leading man. Before engaging Sir Austin, Golden Films Ltd had already incurred expenses in employing a script editor and a director. Sir Austin's engagements abroad were such that he could not perform the contract. So he repudiated the contract. Golden Films Ltd accepted the repudiation but were unsuccessful in finding a suitable replacement.

Advise Golden Films Ltd whether they can: (*i*) sue Sir Austin for specific performance; (*ii*) recover the expenses incurred before the contract in the form of salaries.

11. (*a*) Explain the equitable remedies for a mistake which is not recognised as an operative mistake at common law.

   (*b*) Justin, an accountancy student, advertised his Mini for sale for £2400. A rogue, posing as 'Sir Richard' the famous film producer, offered to buy the car. Justin accepted 'Sir Richard's' offer and received a cheque signed 'Sir Richard.' He was worried that the cheque might be worthless and was reluctant to let the rogue remove the car. Noticing Justin's hesitation the rogue produced a special identity card authorising 'Sir Richard' to enter the famous Brightwood Studios. Justin, being satisfied about 'Sir Richard's' identity, handed over the log book and allowed him to remove the car. The rogue, now posing as Justin, sold the car to David. David bought the car in good faith. Justin has received a letter from his bank that the cheque signed 'Sir Richard' has been dishonoured.

   Advise Justin as to whether he can sue David and recover the car.

12. (*a*) 'The mere fact that one of the parties to a contract acted under a mistake does not, as a general rule, affect the validity of the contract.' When will a mistake by one of the parties affect the validity of the contract?

   (*b*) B, a builder, submits an estimate to H, a householder, for the erection of a garage. H, who is satisfied with the price quoted, asks B to do the work. While building is still in progress B discovers that he made a mistake in his calculations on which the estimate was based and he asks your advice as to whether he is bound by his estimate which formed the basis of the contract with H.

13. (*a*) Distinguish carefully between conditions and warranties as terms of a contract. How will the court decide whether a contractual term is a condition or a warranty?

(*b*) A, who wished to take his family on a holiday, rents from B a villa for the month of August at an agreed rent. The agreement signed by A and B states *inter alia* that the villa is two hundred yards from the beach and that it has been recently redecorated.

What action may A take if he discovers in July that the villa is a good mile from the beach? Would your answer differ if the villa was in fact only two hundred yards from the beach but had not been decorated for five years? Give reasons for your answer.

14. (*a*) What rules do the courts apply in determining whether or not a covenant in restraint of trade is valid?

(*b*) D sold his newspaper shop to a large company which operated newspaper shops all over Britain. In the contract of sale D convenanted not to open a competing business within five miles of any of the purchaser's branches within five years. Three years later, D, who had become bored with retirement, opened a small newspaper shop three miles from one of the branches of the company that had purchased his business, but over a hundred miles from the shop he had sold. The company now seek an injunction to stop D from trading. Will their application be successful?

Part two

Agency and partnership

7
Agency

Formation of agency

1. Definition of agency

An agent is a person who is employed to bring his principal into contractual relations with third parties.

Since the agent does not contract on his own behalf, he does not need to possess full contractual capacity, e.g. he may be a minor. But the principal must have full capacity to make the contract in question.

> NOTE: Under the doctrine of privity of contract, the agent is an outsider to the contract between principal and third party. Therefore he can only enforce the contract on his own behalf against the third party if he has a personal interest in it, e.g. a lien on proceeds of sale, such as is possessed by an auctioneer: *Chelmsford Auctions Ltd* v. *Poole* (1972).

2. Kinds of agency

(a) *Universal:* an agent appointed to handle all the affairs of his principal. This kind of agency is very rare: it has to be created by deed, and is a form of general power of attorney.

(b) *General:* an agent who has authority to represent his principal in all business of a certain kind, e.g. to manage a branch bank. Such an agent has implied authority to represent his principal in all matters incidental to the business in question. A third party dealing with the agent is not affected by any secret restrictions on the agent's authority: *Watteau* v. *Fenwick* (1893), *see* **13** below.

(c) *Special:* an agent appointed for a particular purpose, not part of his normal business activities, and who is therefore given only limited powers, e.g. where a bank manager is asked by a friend to act as agent in the sale of the friend's house.

(d) *Del credere:* an agent employed to sell goods, who promises to make sure that clients introduced by him to his principal will pay for the goods sold. (NOTE: this is not a contract of guarantee and does not need to be evidenced in writing.)

3. Express appointment

Where the agent is employed to execute a deed on behalf of his principal, his appointment must be by deed and the agency is called a *power of attorney*, e.g. where A is appointed to execute a conveyance of land: *see* the Powers of Attorney Act 1971. Under the Enduring Powers of Attorney Act 1985 powers of attorney may be created which will survive any mental incapacity of the donor and which may make provision regarding the scope of the attorney's authority.

In most other cases the agent's appointment can be in any form.

4. Implied agency

An agency may be implied from certain relationships, e.g. partnership. Thus where a dealer acts as middleman between a hire-purchase finance company and the hirer of goods, there is now an implied agency between the company and the dealer to the extent that the company must accept liability for representations made by the dealer: Consumer Credit Act 1974, *see* Chapter 9.

This can be extremely important, particularly in relation to buying an item, such as a motor car, with money made available by a hire-purchase company. Suppose that money is loaned to a customer of a car dealer because the finance house has an agreement with that dealer by which it provides finance to customers of that dealer. Under the Consumer Credit Act, the dealer is the agent of the finance house. This means that the latter has to take the responsibility for anything said by the dealer, his agent, in negotiating the supply of the car. The effect is that if, for instance, the dealer (the agent) has made a misrepresentation, the customer will be able to take action against the finance house (as principal). The customer will be entitled therefore to rescind the credit agreement and the agreement for the supply of the car.

5. Agency by estoppel

Where P allows third parties to believe that A is acting as his authorised agent, he will be estopped from denying the agency (even if in fact he had no authority at all) if such third parties rely on it to their detriment.

This rule applies even where no agency was ever intended by the principal.

Similarly, a husband, partner or master, who allows his wife, co-partner or servant to act as his agent cannot evade liability on the agent's contracts even after revocation of the agency unless he has expressly notified third parties with whom the agent has habitually been dealing: *Scarf* v. *Jardine* (1882).

Example _____

L owned a house and allowed his wife to induce S to buy it, though he did not give her authority to sell it. S commenced doing repairs to the house and L then decided he did not wish to sell it. S claimed specific performance and L denied that his wife had authority to sell. HELD: L had allowed S to believe Mrs L was a properly authorised agent and was therefore estopped from denying her authority to contract on his behalf: *Spiro* v. *Lintern* (1973).

6. Agency by ratification

Where (*a*) a duly appointed agent exceeds his authority, or (*b*) a person having no authority purports to act as agent, the principal incurs no liability on the contract supposedly made on his behalf: *see* **14** below.

But in such cases the principal may expressly or impliedly ratify the agent's transaction and so accept liability.

Ratification is only possible where:

(a) the agent claimed expressly to be contracting as agent, and named his principal: *Keighley Maxsted* v. *Durant* (1901);
(b) the principal had full contractual capacity both (*i*) at the time of ratification, and (*ii*) at the time the agent made the contract. Thus a company after its incorporation cannot ratify a contract supposedly made on its behalf before incorporation, since it did not exist and therefore had no contractual capacity when the contract was made: *Kelner* v. *Baxter* (1866). But where a person purports to contract as agent for a nonexistent company, he will be liable personally on the contract: Companies Act 1985, s. 36(4);

(c) at the time of ratification the principal had full knowledge of all material facts, or had agreed to dispense with it: *Marsh* v. *Joseph* (1897).

> NOTE: Where ratification takes place it is retrospective, i.e. it dates back to the time when the contract was made by the agent. Thus ratification might defeat an attempted repudiation by the third party, made after the date of contracting and on the discovery by the third party of the agent's lack of authority: *Bolton Partners* v. *Lambert* (1889).

7. Agency of necessity

Commercial agency of necessity may arise in favour of a carrier, shipmaster, etc. providing the person claiming it can prove the following.

(a) That it was impossible to get instructions from the principal, e.g. because communication was impossible: *Springer* v. *G.W. Railway* (1921).
(b) That there was a real and definite commercial necessity, e.g. where the master of a ship sells a cargo to prevent it rotting.
(c) That he acted honestly in the interests of his principal while lacking any instructions.

(These rules probably mean that a commercial agency of necessity will only be implied in favour of a person who is already a duly appointed agent for the principal, and who must exceed his instructions in an emergency. It is doubtful whether a person not already an agent could claim an agency of necessity.)

Termination of agency

8. By act of parties

An agency may be terminated by mutual agreement like any other contract, but in addition the principal may at any time revoke the agent's authority and so prevent him making binding contracts with third parties (though revocation, if unjustified, may leave the agent with a right of action for breach of contract against the principal).

Revocation is not possible in these circumstances:

(a) Where the authority is 'coupled with interest,' i.e. where the agent was appointed to enable him to secure some benefit already owed to him by the principal: *Smart* v. *Saunders* (1848).

(b) A power of attorney (agency granted under a seal) cannot be revoked where it is granted to secure (*i*) a proprietary interest of the grantee, or (*ii*) performance of an obligation owed to the grantee.

The power remains irrevocable so long as (*i*) the grantee continues to possess the proprietary interest, or (*ii*) the obligation remains undischarged, unless the grantor discharges the obligation, dies, becomes bankrupt or incapacitated, or (if a body corporate) is dissolved: Powers of Attorney Act 1971, s. 4.

The Enduring Powers of Attorney Act 1985 makes provision for powers of attorney executed in a prescribed form and expressed to continue in spite of the donor's supervening mental incapacity. Such an enduring power is not revoked by such incapacity but when such incapacity occurs, the power is in effect suspended until registered by the court. Once an enduring power has been registered, it can no longer be revoked by the donor, but only with the consent of the court.

(c) Where revocation would involve personal loss to the agent, the principal may be estopped from revoking without the consent of the agent: *Seymour* v. *Bridge* (1885).

(d) The principal cannot revoke in such a way as to damage the interests of innocent third parties, e.g. by breaking contracts the agent has already made with them.

9. By operation of law

Agency is automatically terminated in the following cases.

(a) By death of principal or agent, save in some exceptional cases.

(b) By bankruptcy or insanity of principal or agent, save in exceptional cases.

Example ———————————————————————————

X employed T as solicitor to sue Y. T commenced the action and brought the case to court. Unknown to T, X had gone insane in the meanwhile. HELD: T's agency was automatically terminated, and he was therefore liable to Y for damages for breach of warranty of authority: *Yonge* v. *Toynbee* (1910).

(c) By frustration: *see* 5: **18.**

(d) By intervening illegality.

(e) By the agent accomplishing his mission.

(f) By effluxion of time, where the agency was created for a limited time.

(g) By the principal becoming an alien enemy.

(h) *See* Enduring Powers of Attorney Act 1985 and **8** above.

Duties of principal and agent

10. Duties of agent

Apart from the obvious duty to obey the principal's instructions, these are as follows.

(a) To exercise due care and diligence on the principal's behalf, plus any special skill he professes to have: *Keppel* v. *Wheeler* (1927). In *Chaudhry* v. *Prabhakar* (1988), the plaintiff asked a close friend, who had some knowledge of motor cars, but who was not a mechanic, to find her a suitable second-hand car to buy. She stipulated that it should not have been involved in any accident. He found one but noticed that the bonnet had been crumpled and straightened or replaced, yet thought the car to be in good condition. He recommended the plaintiff to buy it, which she did. A few months later it became apparent that the car had been in a very bad accident, was poorly repaired and unroadworthy. The court held that a gratuitous agent who offered to buy a second-hand car for another owed that other a duty of care to exercise the degree of care and skill which could be reasonably expected of him in all the circumstances of the case, that degree of skill and care being measured objectively and not subjectively. Since the friend knew that the plaintiff was relying on him, and since he ought to have been put on enquiry by the crumpled bonnet as to whether the car had been in any accident, he was in breach of his duty to take reasonable care.

(b) To disclose promptly to the principal any material information he may receive in execution of his task.

(c) Not to disclose confidential information entrusted to him by his principal.

(d) Not to delegate performance of his duties (*delegatus non potest delegare:* 'a delegate cannot delegate'). But this prohibition is not strictly applied, and the agent may usually delegate performance where required by (*i*) commercial usage or (*ii*) necessity, or (*iii*) where expressly or impliedly authorised by the principal: *De Bussche* v. *Alt* (1878).

(e) Not to let his interest conflict with his duty, e.g. not to compete with his principal. An agent must maintain a high standard of good faith. Thus it is wrong for a broker employed to buy goods to sell his own goods to his principal without full disclosure: *Armstrong* v. *Jackson* (1917). Similarly, an agent should not accept a commission from both parties without his principal's knowledge and consent: *North & South Trust Co.* v. *Berkeley* (1971).

(f) Not to make any secret profit. If, beyond his commission, he receives any extra profit in the course of his duties he must disclose this to the principal.

If he fails to do so: (*i*) the principal can sue him for the amount kept secret; (*ii*) the principal can refuse to pay the agent his commission, and can terminate the agency without notice; (*iii*) the principal can sue the agent and the third party for damages to compensate him for any loss he has sustained; (*iv*) the principal can repudiate the contract (whether or not the bribe was effective); (*v*) the agent and the briber are criminally liable: *Salford Corporation* v. *Lever* (1891): *see* Prevention of Corruption Act 1916.

Examples
(1) E owned property which D offered to purchase. Before contracts had been exchanged, the defendants made an application for planning permission in the name of E and signed as 'agent' for E. Planning permission was given before completion, but unknown to E. HELD: E was entitled to the profits which had accrued to D from the granting of planning permission. D had acted as self-appointed agents and had placed themselves in a fiduciary relationship to E with the result that they were obliged to disclose the application for planning permission: *English* v. *Dedham Vale Properties Ltd* (1978).
(2) In *Logicrose* v. *Southend United Football Club* (1988), M had a controlling shareholding in the defendants as nominee for J who was the defendants' chairman. He negotiated the grant of a licence to the plaintiffs to operate a market on the defendants' land. M, in reaching that agreement, failed to disclose to the defendants' board that their solicitors had strongly advised against that agreement or that, acting on J's instructions, he had required the plaintiffs to pay £70,000 to an offshore company controlled by him. Subsequently M disclosed the payment and accounted for most

of that sum. The defendants served a notice to determine the licence. The plaintiffs claimed the return of £70,000 or damages, and the defendants counterclaimed for rescission. The court gave judgment for the defendants and said that a principal who discovered that his agent had either obtained or arranged to obtain a bribe from the other party to the transaction was entitled to treat it as void *ab initio*. He was also entitled to rescind where, to the knowledge of the other party, the agent had placed himself in a position where his interests and duties conflicted so that he could no longer give disinterested advice; but that in these circumstances, the other party had to have actual knowledge or be blind wilfully to the fact that the agent intended to conceal his dealings from his principal. Since the plaintiffs knew that M was concealing his dealings from his principal, the defendants were entitled to rescind the contract and it was immaterial that the plaintiffs, who had the requisite knowledge, did not know whether M's concealment of his dealings was for his personal interest or not. Where an agent received a bribe, the principal was entitled to recover it from the agent whether the principal elected to affirm or rescind the contract. In recovering the money, there was no implication that he adopted the transaction.

11. Duties of principal

(a) To pay any agreed commission or remuneration and not to prevent or hinder the agent from earning this: *Rhodes* v. *Forwood* (1876).

The agent has a lien over goods belonging to the principal enabling him to retain such goods until his commission is paid.

When commission becomes payable depends on the contract between principal and agent. For example, when the agent is employed to sell goods or land, his commission may become payable:
  (*i*) when he introduces a client (whether sale results or not);
    or
  (*ii*) on completion of the sale, and payment of the price. (The signing of an agreement 'subject to contract' does not amount to completion: *Luxor Ltd* v. *Cooper* (1941).)

(b) To indemnify the agent against liabilities properly incurred in the discharge of his duties: *Christoforides* v. *Terry* (1924).

12. Vicarious liability

A master may be liable for wrongs (torts) committed by his

agent. The extent of this indirect or vicarious liability depends on whether the agent is:

(a) an independent contractor, i.e. an outsider employed to do certain work and told what to do but left free to decide how he will do it. The principal is only liable for his torts if (*i*) he expressly or impliedly commissioned the tort, or (*ii*) he delegated to the contractor performance of a legal duty and the contractor is negligent;

(b) a servant, i.e. a person employed as an integral part of the principal's business, who is told both what to do and how to do it: *Mersey Docks etc.* v. *Coggins* (1947).

The principal is liable for all torts committed by a servant *in the course of his employment,* i.e. where the servant does improperly what he is employed to do properly.

> NOTE: (1) *Course of employment.* What acts are part of the course of employment, or reasonably incidental thereto, is a question of fact in each case: *Chapman* v. *Oakleigh Animal Products Ltd* (1970). Thus a solicitor was held liable where one of his staff gave fraudulent advice to a client of the firm, despite the solicitor's claim that giving fraudulent advice could not be regarded as part of the course of employment: *Lloyd* v. *Grace, Smith & Co.* (1912). But a bus company was held not liable for the negligent driving of a bus conductor who had temporarily taken over the wheel, since this was not what he was employed to do: *Ricketts* v. *Tilling* (1915). (2) *Express prohibition.* The master is vicariously liable if the servant is doing improperly what he is employed to do properly, even if the master has expressly forbidden the particular wrongful act. Thus a bus company was held liable for an accident caused by bus drivers racing to bus stops, despite the fact that the company had expressly prohibited such racing: *Limpus* v. *L.G.O.C.* (1862). A dairy company was liable when a passenger in a milk float was injured through the driver's negligence, even though giving lifts was expressly prohibited: *Rose* v. *Plenty* (1976).

Example _____

A bus conductor (contrary to orders) drove a bus at the depot to enable his own bus to be driven out of the depot, and injured fellow-employees. HELD: He was acting outside the course of his employment and his employers were not vicariously liable for his negligent driving: *Iqbal* v. *L.T.E.* (1973).

The authority of the agent

13. Real and ostensible authority

Extent of the agent's authority depends (*a*) on his contract with his principal, or (*b*) on the law, where this implies a particular authority for particular kinds of agency.

This implied, or ostensible authority, may exceed the agent's actual authority from his principal, and may therefore render the principal liable on contracts made by the agent beyond the limits of his actual authority.

Example ————————————————————————

(1) The manager of a public house was forbidden to order tobaccos by his principal but did so. HELD: The principal was liable to pay the seller, since a manager of a public house would usually have authority to make orders of this kind, and the seller could therefore rely on the agent's ostensible authority in the absence of express knowledge of the limitation imposed by the principal: *Watteau* v. *Fenwick* (1893).

(2) In *Discount Kitchens* v. *Crawford* (1988), it was held that where an employee of company A had had discussions with a potential purchaser, and had then left to join company B but continued negotiations and entered into a contract with the purchaser of goods and services to be provided by company B, the employee could not be said to have fixed company A with any liability since he had not only no actual authority, but he had no apparent authority.

(3) In *Charrington Fuel Oil* v. *Parvant* (1988), it was held that where property changes hands, a request by the owners to previous suppliers of goods (who have no notice of the change) to deliver further goods to the same address, does not amount to a representation that would form the basis of an estoppel on which the ostensible authority concept could be founded, and under which the former owner could be held liable for payment.

————————————————————————

14. Breach of warranty of authority

Every person professing to act as agent for another impliedly warrants that he has authority to make binding contracts on behalf of his principal.

If therefore an agent lacks the authority he professes to have, he is liable to an action for damages for breach of the implied warranty of authority, brought by the person with whom he has been dealing: *Collen* v. *Wright* (1857).

The agent is still liable for damages, even if he was acting in good faith, genuinely believing he had the authority he claimed, e.g. where his authority has been terminated without his knowledge by the death of his principal: *Yonge* v. *Toynbee* (1910).

But he is not liable if his lack of authority was known to the third party at the time of making the contract, or if the third party agreed to exclude the liability for breach of warranty: *Lilly* v. *Smales* (1892).

(Where a dishonest agent deliberately claims authority he knows he does not possess, he is also liable to an action for fraud by the third party whom he has deceived.)

15. Relations between principal and third parties

Generally, once he has made a contract on behalf of his principal the agent drops out of the transaction and privity of contract exists between the principal and the third party: *see* 6: **1–3**.

But the results of an agent's contract differ slightly depending on whether (*a*) he has disclosed the fact of his agency, or (*b*) he has concealed the fact that he is merely an agent for another person.

Each of these possibilities is dealt with separately below.

16. Agent acting for named principal

Here the agent generally incurs neither rights nor liabilities under the contract, and drops out as soon as it is made: *Gadd* v. *Houghton* (1876). Where a person holds himself out as an agent for a named person, but is in fact the agent of an unnamed person, the agent is personally liable: *Savills* v. *Scott* (1988).

EXCEPTIONS: (1) Where the agent agrees to accept personal liability. (2) Where the agent signs a deed he is personally liable thereon and the principal incurs no liability unless the agent was himself appointed by deed (a power of attorney) — in which case the agent drops out and the principal is liable in the ordinary way. (3) Where the agent signs a bill of exchange in his own name, he is personally liable thereon. (To avoid this he should make it perfectly clear that he is signing merely as agent, e.g. by signing 'for and on behalf of' a named principal. A director signing a cheque on behalf of his company should always take this precaution.) (4) Where trade custom makes the agent personally liable, e.g. formerly where an agent acted for an overseas principal, there was a presumption that he accepted personal responsibility; this presumption no longer exists, and the agent is not personally liable in such a case unless it can be shown that he volunteered to accept personal liability: *Teheran-Europe Ltd* v. *S.T. Belton Ltd* (1968). (5) Where the supposed agent is in fact the principal, but purports to contract merely as an agent.

17. Agent acting for undisclosed principal

This covers two possible situations: (*a*) where the agent discloses the fact that he is merely an agent, but conceals the identity of his principal, and (*b*) where he conceals the agency altogether, and appears to be acting on his own behalf.

(a) *Agency revealed: principal concealed.* Here the agent drops out in the normal way, providing he makes it clear when contracting that he does so merely as agent. If he fails to do so he is personally liable on the contract. (The exceptions stated under **16** above apply to this situation.)

(b) *Agency concealed altogether: the doctrine of the undisclosed principal.* Here the third party can enforce the contract against the agent or, when he discovers his identity and existence, against the principal. The third party thus has an option whether to compel the agent to accept personal liability, or to shift liability to the principal as soon as his identity is revealed.

> BUT NOTE: (1) He cannot enforce the contract against both agent and principal. If he sues one he cannot later sue the other. (2) He may be estopped from suing the principal at all if he allows the principal to think he has settled matters satisfactorily with the agent, e.g. by unreasonable delay in taking action against the principal after his identity is revealed: *Heald* v. *Kenworthy* (1855).

Special classes of agent

18. Factors

A factor is a mercantile agent employed to sell goods for a commission 'in the ordinary course of his business,' i.e. a professional buying and selling agent: Factors Act 1889. (A factor differs from a broker in that he has possession of the goods to be sold, while a broker usually does not.)

If a factor has possession of goods with the consent of the

owner for some purpose other than sale but contrary to instructions does sell the goods, the purchaser obtains a good title (providing he did not know of the limitation on the factor's authority). In such cases the principal is legally estopped from denying that the purpose of the factor's possession was sale: Factors Act 1889, s. 2. Such an agent cannot pass good title under the Act, unless he has had continuous physical possession of the goods as factor: *Astley Industrial Trust* v. *Miller* (1968).

A factor has a lien over goods in his possession and power to pledge them for security.

19. Brokers

A broker is a commercial agent employed to make contracts between his principal and others for a commission usually called brokerage. (An agent employed to make non-commercial contracts is therefore not a broker, e.g. a contract to hire a singer for a charity concert.)

Unlike factors, brokers do not have possession of goods for sale, and cannot therefore sell in their own name. They have no lien over goods and no power to lodge them for security.

A broker is primarily agent for the seller of goods, but on making a contract with a purchaser he becomes agent for the purchaser also.

20. Auctioneers: *see* 9: 63–67

21. Position of banks

The relationship between bank and customer is primarily that of debtor and creditor, with the bank usually the debtor (as long as the customer's account is in credit).

In addition, there is a complex implied contract between a bank and its customers, which imposes many duties on the bank similar to those of an ordinary agent: *Joachimsson* v. *Swiss Bank Corporation* (1921).

'The limits of a banker's business cannot be laid down as a matter of law': *Banbury* v. *Bank of Montreal* (1918), but the following general rules apply.

(a) The bank is legally bound to honour its customer's cheques up to the limit of his credit (or agreed loan facilities) but not beyond. Thus if the account is £100 in credit and the customer draws a cheque for £100.50, the bank is theoretically entitled to refuse payment (it cannot legally pay part of a cheque).

(b) The bank has an implied right to charge reasonable commission for its services (and interest on loans).

(c) The bank must not disclose its customer's affairs, save under compulsion of law, e.g. under a court order. In *Re State of Norway's Application (No 1)* (1989), the State of Norway issued letters of request to the High Court in England requesting certain bankers to give evidence in proceedings before a Norwegian court. The witnesses appealed to the Court of Appeal against an order granting the application on the ground that the giving of the testimony would be a breach of their duty of confidence as bankers. The Court of Appeal ruled that in order to determine whether witnesses should be ordered to break their duty of confidence by answering the questions in the letter of request, the court had to consider whether the interest in protecting the confidence was outweighed by the public interest in assisting a foreign court. In the circumstances the balance was against compelling the witnesses to violate their duty of confidence.

(d) Unlike most agents, the bank has a general lien over any of the customer's securities in its possession, e.g. shares, title deeds, insurance policies.

(e) Advice on investment is a service offered expressly by most banks. Where offered, there is an implied duty to exercise care in providing advice, and the bank could be liable in negligence if one of its managers gave negligent advice and so caused damage to the customer: *Woods* v. *Martins Bank* (1958).

(f) A bank is entitled to dispose as it pleases of money deposited by a customer provided it pays his cheques on demand (during business hours) or through a clearing house.

(g) A bank must abide by an express mandate of the customer, and by any express agreement made with him.

(h) The bank is entitled to require that the customer shall exercise reasonable care in drawing cheques. If the bank pays a forged cheque and the forgery was facilitated by the customer's carelessness, the loss falls on the customer and not on the bank: *London Joint Stock Bank* v. *Macmillan & Arthur* (1918).

22. Estate agents

These are agents employed to manage property, and also to buy or sell land or houses for a commission (usually paid by the seller).

The scope of their authority as seller's agents varies, but mere engagement of an estate agent does not confer any authority to receive as agent of the vendor a pre-contract deposit. Where a deposit is paid to the agent in such circumstances, the purchaser is at all times until contract the only person with any claim or right to the deposit and his is a right on demand. The vendor has no such claim or right and no control over the deposit. Accordingly, where a vendor has not authorised an agent to receive a deposit on his behalf, he is not liable to repay it on the agent's default: *Sorrell* v. *Finch* (1976).

With regard to commission, if that commission is payable 'on introducing a person ready, willing and able to purchase', commission will be payable only if the person introduced shows his willingness and ability to buy (not necessarily by a binding contract) and remains so willing and able up to the time of completion. If the purchaser does not complete, no commission is payable even if the purchaser's deposit is forfeited by the vendor. Nor is the vendor bound to claim specific performance of any binding contract. Once there is a binding contract of sale, however, the vendor cannot withdraw except at the risk of having to pay his agent commission, because it is his own fault that the sale has not been completed. In order to give business efficacy to an agency contract under which commission is payable on the agent introducing a buyer, there is an implied term that once a sale contract is concluded with a buyer introduced by an agent, the principal (vendor) will not commit a breach of contract with the buyer which would deprive the agent of his commission. Moreover, if a person who is able to purchase is introduced and expresses readiness and willingness, by an unqualified offer, to purchase, though such offer has not been accepted by the vendor and could be withdrawn, if it is not the vendor but the purchaser who withdraws, the case is entirely different and no commission is payable. Where commission was payable on introducing someone 'willing and able to purchase' leasehold property, and after contract the landlord refused consent to the assignment, it was held that the agent was not entitled to commission because, although the person introduced was financially able to effect the purchase, he was not suitable and acceptable on other grounds, and was therefore not 'able' to purchase. (For statutory regulation of estate agents, *see* 17: **9**.)

23. *Del credere* agents

A factor (*see* **18**) who is responsible for the buyer's bad debts is known as a *del credere* agent. He undertakes to pay the principal if the purchasers he procures do not pay for the goods supplied. Such an agent is an exception to the general rule that the agent incurs no personal liability as regards the contract he is instrumental in forming. Such an agent is usually paid a higher rate of commission, known as a *del credere* commission.

24. Confirming house

A confirming house acts as agent for an overseas customer, finding a supplier and arranging for the shipment of goods. It typically adds an assurance to the bargain made, confirming the contract with the foreign buyer.

25. Canvassing agent

A canvassing agent holds no stock of the contract goods; he deals only with enquiries and solicits orders. The canvassing agent negotiates contracts only on the principal's express authority.

26. Commercial agents

These are given separate status by an EC Directive adopted in 1986 but not yet implemented into UK law. A commercial agent is defined in the Directive as a 'self-employed intermediary who has continuing authority to negotiate the sale or the purchase of goods on behalf of another person, called the "principal", or to negotiate or conclude such transactions on behalf of and in the name of that principal'.

Duties
The Directive states in broad terms that the agent must look after his principal's interests, and that both principal and agent must act dutifully and in good faith. The agent must make proper efforts to negotiate and, where appropriate, conclude the transactions he is instructed to take care of. The main duties of the principal are:

(a) to provide his agent with the necessary documentation relating to the contract goods;

(b) to notify his agent within a reasonable period once the principal anticipates that the volume of commercial transactions will be significantly lower than that which the agent could normally have expected;

(c) to obtain for his agent the information necessary for the performance of the agency contract;

(d) to inform the agent within a reasonable time of the acceptance, refusal or any non-performance of a commercial transaction which the agent had procured for him.

Remuneration.
If the agreement is silent on the matter of remuneration, the Directive will give the agent to be paid the remuneration which is customarily paid for his type of agency in the place where he carries out his activities or else to be paid a reasonable remuneration. An agent will be entitled to be paid commission on:

(a) transactions concluded during the period of agency where

    (*i*) the transaction is concluded either as a result of the agent's action or with a third party whom the agent previously acquired as a customer for transactions of the kind concluded;

    (*ii*) the transaction is concluded with a customer belonging to a geographic area or customer group either entrusted to the agent or within the scope of an exclusive domain; *and*

(b) transactions concluded after the agency has been terminated where

    (*i*) the transaction is mainly attributable to the agent's efforts during the agency and it was concluded within a reasonable time after termination;

    (*ii*) the third party's order reached the principal or the commercial agent before termination.

Due time for payment of commission
The Directive says that the agent' s commission will become due as soon as and to the extent that:

(a) the principal has executed the transaction, *or*

(b) according to his agreement with the third party, the principal should have executed the transaction, *or*

(c) the third party has executed the transaction, or, at the very latest

(d) when the third party has executed his part of the transaction or should have done so if the principal had, as he should have done, executed his part of the transaction.

The commission will have to be paid not later than the last day of the month following the quarter in which it became due. The agent will be entitled to a statement of the commission due to him, showing how it has been calculated, and he can also demand, amongst other things, access to the principal's books in order to check the amount of the commission. The agent's right to commission can be lost only if and to the extent that it is established that the contract between the principal and the third party will not be executed and that fact is due to a reason for which the principal is not to blame.

> NOTE: The Directive is due to be implemented as part of UK law not later than 1 January 1994. You should carefully check your sources of information (legal periodicals and the like) as to whether the Directive is in force.

8
Partnerships

Nature and formation of partnerships

1. Definition of partnership

'Partnership is the relation which subsists between persons carrying on a business in common with a view of profit': Partnership Act 1890, s. 1.

Registered, statutory and chartered companies are specifically excluded from this definition (note also that a non-profit-making association cannot be a partnership).

Capacity to form a partnership is governed by the ordinary rules of contractual capacity: *see* Chapter 3. A minor who remains a partner after becoming 18 becomes liable for the firm's debts incurred after his 18th birthday: *Goode* v. *Harrison* (1871).

The general rule under the Companies Act 1985, s.716, is that a partnership must not consist of more than 20 persons. This does not, however, prohibit the formation of:

(a) a partnership carrying on practice as solicitors and consisting of persons each of whom is a solicitor;
(b) a partnership carrying on practice as accountants and consisting of persons each of whom is a member of a body of accountants established in the UK and for the time being recognised by the Secretary of State, or is a person for the time being authorised by the Secretary of State to be appointed as an auditor either as having similar qualifications obtained outside the UK or as having obtained adequate knowledge and experience in the course of his employment by a member of a body of accountants recognised by the Secretary of State, or as having, before 6 August 1947, practised in Great Britain as an accountant;
(c) a partnership carrying on business as a member of a

recognised stock exchange and consisting of persons each of whom is a member of that stock exchange;

(d) a partnership carrying on business of a description specified in regulations made by the Secretary of State.

Statutory instruments have been made in relation to partnerships consisting of: patent agents, surveyors, auctioneers, valuers, estate agents, land agents and those engaged in land management, actuaries, consulting engineers, building designers and loss adjusters; partnerships formed for the purpose of carrying on business as insurance brokers as long as certain conditions are satisfied, and partnerships formed for the purpose of carrying on business as town planners, three-quarters of whom are members of the Royal Town Planning Institute; member firms of the London Stock Exchange; multi-national firms of lawyers: Partnerships (Unrestricted Size) Regulations Nos. 1, 2 and 4–10, 1968, 1970, 1982, 1990 and 1992.

2.   Tests for establishing partnerships: Partnership Act 1890, s. 2

(a) *Co-ownership* of property does not of itself create a partnership in the property, even though the co-owners share profits.

(b) *Sharing of gross returns* of a business does not of itself indicate a partnership, even if coupled with co-ownership of the property or business.

(c) *Share of profits* is presumptive evidence of partnership, but the presumption can be rebutted by showing that the purpose of sharing was for some other reason, e.g.:

(i) payment of a debt by instalments out of profits;

(ii) remuneration to a servant or agent of the business;

(iii) payment of an annuity or portion to a widow or child of a deceased partner in the business;

(iv) payment of interest (varying with profits) on a loan advanced for use in the business;

(v) payment to the seller of the goodwill of a business (where the consideration is a share of profits).

However, if the business goes bankrupt, the recipient of moneys under (iv) and (v) above is a deferred creditor in the bankruptcy: *see* Chapter 18.

NOTE: Whether a partnership exists therefore depends on the circumstances in each case and the intention of the parties. Sharing losses is stronger evidence of partnership than sharing profits, but is still not conclusive: *Walker* v. *Hirsch* (1884). If executors of a will carry on the testator's business as instructed in the will, they do not automatically become partners: *Re Fisher & Sons* (1912). Even where a partnership exists, a salaried partner on termination of the partnership cannot ask for a winding-up order. He does not share in the equity of the firm, being only entitled to his salary: *Stekel* v. *Ellice* (1973).

3. The firm name

Under the provisions of the Business Names Act 1985, all orders, invoices, business letters, etc. must disclose the true names of all owners of the business (whether individuals or companies) and also the addresses within Great Britain at which they can be contacted. In addition, such information must be displayed on a notice in a prominent position at the business premises. A customer is entitled to ask for a written list of the required information which must be supplied to him immediately. These requirements are relaxed in the case of a partnership which consists of more than 20 members, provided two conditions are satisfied. First, the document must not contain the names of any partners except as signatories; and second, it must state an address at which a full list of partners can be inspected. Actions in contract by a person who has failed to comply with the Act can be dismissed if the defendant can show that he has a claim against that person because of his failure to comply or if he has suffered loss because of such failure. The court can allow the action to proceed if it considers it just and equitable. Failure to satisfy the requirements of the Act is also a criminal offence.

4. Illegal associations

An association may be illegal because of the following.

(a) Its objects are illegal.
(b) Its membership exceeds the statutory limits (*see* **1** above): Companies Act 1985.
(c) It is an association forbidden by law, e.g. a professional partnership between a solicitor and an unqualified person.

The effects of illegality are that (*i*) the members cannot enforce any rights or obligations among themselves, (*ii*) the members cannot enforce any contract against any innocent outsider, and (*iii*) the illegality cannot be raised as a defence in any action brought against them by an innocent outsider.

Dealings with outsiders

5.   Agency of partners

Each general partner is an implied agent for the firm, and can make his co-partners liable on debts incurred by him on behalf of the firm: Partnership Act 1890, s. 5. But he has no implied authority to bind the firm in any matter outside the scope of the firm's business: s. 7.

A person dealing with a partner is not affected by any secret restriction on the partner's agency, unless he knows of it or does not believe him to be a partner: s. 8.

Liability of partners for debts and other contractual obligations is joint: s. 9 (contrast liability in tort). Thus a creditor can sue all the partners jointly, or any one of them for the whole debt. But he has only one right of action, and if he obtains judgment for the whole debt against one (even if the judgment is unsatisfied) he cannot later launch proceedings against the others, since he is taken to have waived his rights against them: rule in *Kendall* v. *Hamilton* (1879). The rule in *Kendall's* case has been modified by s. 3 of the Civil Liability (Contribution) Act 1978 as follows: 'Judgement recovered against one person in respect of any debt or damage shall not be a bar to an action, or to the continuance of an action, against any other person who is (apart from such bar) jointly liable with him in respect of the same debt or damage.'

6.   Extent of implied agency

(a) A partner can bind the firm by the following transactions:
   (*i*)   by selling the firm's goods: *Dore* v. *Wilkinson* (1817);
   (*ii*) by purchasing goods for the firm: *Bond* v. *Gibson* (1808);
   (*iii*) by accepting payment of debts due to the firm: *Porter* v. *Taylor* (1817);

(*iv*) by engaging or discharging employees: *Birkham* v. *Drake* (1841).

(b) In a trading partnership, he has the following additional powers:

(*i*) to borrow money on the firm's credit: *Lane* v. *Williams* (1692);

(*ii*) to sign bills of exchange on behalf of the firm: Bills of Exchange Act 1882;

(*iii*) to employ a solicitor on behalf of the firm: *Tomlinson* v. *Broadsmith* (1896).

NOTE: There is no implied authority (1) to execute deeds — this requires express authorisation by power of attorney: *see* 7: **1–7**; (2) to submit disputes to arbitration; and (3) to give a guarantee in the firm's name, unless the giving of guarantees is within the usual business of the firm.

7. Liability of incoming and outgoing partners

(a) *Incoming partners.* A new partner is not liable (unless otherwise agreed) for debts incurred before he joined the firm: Partnership Act 1890, s. 17(1).

(b) *Outgoing partners.* A retiring partner is not liable for debts incurred after he retired, but is liable for debts incurred before his retirement: s. 17(2). (Release from this liability is by means of a novation under which the remaining partners are substituted for the retiring partner in respect of his liability to the creditors, with the latters' consent.)

But an outgoing partner remains liable if he has allowed creditors to believe him to be continuing in the firm: s. 36. To protect himself from this liability, he must (*i*) give express notice of his retirement to persons who were dealing with the firm before his retirement, (*ii*) notify persons who trade with the firm in the future by advertising his retirement in the *London Gazette*: s. 36(2).

(c) *Death or bankruptcy.* The estate of a deceased or bankrupt partner is not liable for partnership debts incurred after death or bankruptcy: s. 36(3).

(d) *Dormant partners.* A general partner not known to be a member of the firm to creditors seeking to enforce a partnership debt is not liable for debts contracted after his retirement from active participation.

(e) *Holding out.* A person not a partner who holds himself out, or allows others to hold him out, as being a partner in a firm is liable to persons who rely on such representations as though he were in fact a partner, i.e. he becomes a partner by estoppel: s. 14.

(f) *A continuing guarantee* given to a firm is terminated as to future transactions by any change in the membership of the firm: s. 18. This section does not apply where (*i*) there is an agreement to the contrary, (*ii*) the guarantee relates to past transactions, or (*iii*) the guarantee is given by the firm: *see* Chapter 16.

8. Nature of firm's liability

(a) Partners are jointly liable for the firm's contracts, unless otherwise agreed: Partnership Act 1890, s. 9. (The liability may be joint and several if the partners expressly so agree.)

(b) Partners are jointly and severally liable for torts committed on behalf of the firm: s. 12.

(c) The estate of a deceased partner is severally liable for the firm's debts incurred during his lifetime, subject to the prior payment of his own separate debts: s. 9.

> NOTE: Difference between joint and several liability. (1) In joint liability, the plaintiff has only one right of action and he may use this either in suing the firm jointly, or in suing any individual partner separately. But if he sues one alone he waives his right of action against the others, and cannot later sue them even though he obtains judgment against the one sued but is unable to get his money because of that partner's insolvency: *Kendall* v. *Hamilton* (1879). But *see* the modification of this judgment as explained in **5** above. (2) In joint and several liability, the plaintiff has several causes of action. He can sue all partners together, or can sue them separately (in successive actions if necessary). (3) As between the partners themselves, whether the liability is joint or joint and several, they must contribute equally to the damages paid.

9. Notices and admissions

(a) Any admissions or representation by a partner in the course of business and about the firm's affairs are evidence against the firm: Partnership Act 1890, s. 15.

(b) Notice given bona fide to any active partner concerning business matters operates as notice to the firm: s. 16.

Rights and duties of partners

10. Partnership articles
A partnership may arise by express agreement, or by implication, i.e. where persons conduct a business in common with a view of profit: Partnership Act 1890, s. 1. Where a partnership is formed by express agreement (the 'partnership articles'), the rights and duties of the partners among themselves are regulated by that agreement. Where a partnership arises by implication, or wherever the articles (if any) are silent, the rights and duties of the partners are governed by the 1890 Act.

> NOTE: Once formed, a partnership is a relationship requiring the utmost good faith and each partner must disclose to his colleagues all material information coming to his notice: *see* 4: **19**.

11. Rights and duties: Partnership Act 1890, s. 24
Unless otherwise agreed, the following rules apply.

(a) *Equal shares.* Partners are entitled to share equally in capital and profits, and must contribute equally towards losses (agreement to the contrary may be inferred from past dealings).
(b) *Indemnity.* The firm must indemnify a partner against liabilities properly incurred (*i*) in the ordinary course of business, or (*ii*) in anything necessarily done for the preservation of the business.
(c) *Interest on advances.* A partner is entitled to interest at 5 per cent on money (other than capital) advanced to the business (but he is not entitled, before the ascertainment of profits, to interest on capital).
(d) *Management.* Every partner is entitled to participate in management of the business.
(e) *No remuneration.* A partner is not entitled to any remuneration for his services (unless expressly agreed).
(f) *New partners* can only be introduced with the consent of all existing partners. (Notice that there is no implied power to expel partners: *see* **12** below.)
(g) *Disputes as to ordinary matters* may be settled by majority (but change of business requires unanimous agreement).

(h) *Partnership books* are to be kept at the firm's principal place of business and every partner is entitled to inspect them and copy them whenever he thinks fit.

12. Expulsion of partners

A partner can only be expelled from the firm if a power to do so has been conferred by express agreement between the partners: s. 25. Such power must be executed in good faith and in the interests of the firm, otherwise the expulsion is void: *Blisset* v. *Daniels* (1853). It was held in *Hitchman* v. *CBAS Services* (1983) that a clause in a partnership deed which required a particular partner to be a signatory to any notice expelling a partner did not apply when that partner was being expelled.

13. Duties of partners

Apart from any duties imposed by the partnership articles, the following statutory duties are implied.

(a) *Uberrimae fidei*. Partners must render true accounts and full information on partnership matters to their colleagues: s. 28.
(b) *To account* for any benefits derived from the partnership business without the consent of the other partners, i.e. a partner must not make 'secret profits' (cf. agents: *see* 7: **10**).
(c) *Not to compete* with the firm, without the consent of the other partners. Any profits made by such unauthorised competition can be claimed by the firm: s. 30.

14. Partnership property

All partnership property must be held and applied exclusively for the purposes of the firm and in accordance with the partnership articles (if any): s. 20(1).

Whether property is partnership property or not is a question of fact in each case. 'Partnership property' includes the following.

(a) Property originally brought into the partnership stock: s. 20(1).
(b) Property acquired on account of the firm, for the purpose and in the course of the partnership business: s. 20(1).
(c) Property purchased with the firm's money (unless otherwise agreed): s. 21.

(Thus the mere fact that partners are co-owners of land and

share its profits does not make it automatically partnership property, unless it falls into one of the above categories: s. 20(3).)

As between partners, partnership land is treated as personal property: s. 22. Land is conveyed to the partners (or to four of them, if there are more than four) as trustees for sale.

15. Execution against a partner

A creditor who obtains judgment against an individual partner cannot seize partnership property in execution of the judgment: s. 23. His remedy is to appoint a receiver of the debtor partner's share of profits.

By s. 33(2) if a receiver is so appointed, or a partner's share is otherwise charged with payment of his private debts, this entitles the other partners to dissolve the partnership.

16. Assignment of a partner's share

A partner's share in the business is the proportion of the existing assets to which he would be entitled if all the firm's assets were sold and proceeds distributed after discharge of all the firm's debts.

A partner may assign his share (by way of sale, gift, mortgage, etc.) but the assignee does not thereby become a member of the firm, can take no part in management nor inspect books, etc. unless the other partners agree: s. 31.

Thus the assignor remains a partner, though his assignee becomes entitled to his share of profits and of the assets in the event of any distribution. The firm's creditors can therefore sue the assignor for the firm's debts, but the assignor can (unless otherwise agreed) claim indemnity from the assignee: *Dodson* v. *Downey* (1901).

Dissolution of partnership

The effect of dissolution is to terminate the partnership relation and to entitle the partners (unless otherwise agreed) to share the assets after payment of the firm's debts. Dissolution may occur in the ways listed below.

17. By agreement

(a) Under the partnership articles, if they provide a method.
(b) By express and unanimous agreement at any time (overriding the articles).

18. By operation of law

(a) *Expiration.* If entered into for a fixed term or for a single venture, the firm is dissolved on expiration of the fixed term or termination of the venture. (If, however, the partnership is continued beyond the term originally agreed, the rights and duties of the partners remain the same: s. 26.)
(b) *Notice.* If entered into for an undefined term, any partner may determine the partnership at any time by notice to the others: s.26. (If the partnership was originally constituted by deed, the notice must be in writing: s. 26(2).)
The partnership is then dissolved (*i*) from the date stated in the notice or (*ii*) if not stated, then from the date of communication of the notice to the other partners: s. 32.

19. By death or bankruptcy (unless otherwise agreed): s. 33(1)
Also if a partner allows his share to be charged with payment of his debts, this entitles the others to dissolve the partnership if they wish: s. 33(2).

20. By supervening illegality: s. 34
That is, if some event occurs which makes it unlawful for the business to be carried on. The partnership in a firm of solicitors is automatically dissolved when one of the partners forgets to renew his practising certificate: *Hudgell Yeates & Co.* v. *Watson* (1978).

21. By court order: s. 35
The court may order dissolution on the application of any partner in the following cases.

(a) *Mental incapacity* of any partner: Mental Health Act 1983, s. 96.
(b) *Permanent incapacity* of a partner (other than the applicant).
(c) *Conduct prejudicial* to the business (by any partner other than the applicant).
(d) *Breach of the partnership agreement* (by any other than the

applicant). This includes conduct which makes it impracticable for the other partners to carry on.

(e) Where the business can only be carried on at a loss.

(f) Where, in the opinion of the court, it is just and equitable, e.g. where there are only two partners and they are at loggerheads: *Re Yenidje Tobacco Co. Ltd* (1916).

22. Notice of dissolution

To avoid incurring liability after dissolution (e.g. by estoppel) a partner may publish notice of dissolution and can compel his co-partners to join him: s. 37.

23. Effect of dissolution

The authority of partners to bind the firm continues so long as is necessary to wind up the business, provided that the firm is in no case bound by the acts of a partner who has been bankrupted: s. 38.

Also each partner has an equitable lien (*see* 15: **19**) over the firm's assets entitling him to have them applied in payment of the firm's debts, and in payment of whatever is due to partners; this lien can be enforced by injunction forbidding unfair distribution: s. 39.

24. Return of premium: s. 40

To buy entry into an existing firm, a new member sometimes has to pay a premium (in consideration of existing goodwill) in addition to any investment of capital.

On dissolution, he is entitled to demand the return of a proportion of the premium if the partnership was for a fixed term and was dissolved before the expiry of that term, unless dissolution was caused by

(a) agreement, or

(b) misconduct by the party seeking return of the premium, or

(c) death of a partner: s. 40.

The portion returned will usually be in the same ratio to the whole premium as the unexpired term bears to the whole term: *Attwood* v. *Maude* (1868).

25. Dissolution through misrepresentation: s. 41

Where a partnership agreement is rescinded on the grounds of fraud or misrepresentation by any partner, the partner entitled to rescission can also demand the following.

(a) *A lien* on the firm's assets (after payment of debts) for any money he had invested.

(b) *Subrogation*, i.e. a right to stand in the place of any of the firm's creditors for any payment made by him to discharge the firm's debts.

(c) *To be indemnified* by the person guilty of the fraud or misrepresentation against all the firm's debts and liabilities.

(d) *Damages* may also be claimed under the Misrepresentation Act 1967, s. 2, since here rights are without prejudice to other rights.

26. Profits made after dissolution: s. 42

If a partner dies or retires and the other partners carry on the business after the dissolution, without any final settlement of accounts, the outgoing partner or his estate can (unless otherwise agreed) claim:

(a) *such share of profits* after dissolution as is attributable to the use of his share of the assets (after due allowance for the labour and skill of the continuing partners); *or*

(b) *interest* at 5 per cent on the share of the assets. This claim is not exercisable where the articles give continuing partners an option to purchase a deceased or retiring partner's share, and they duly exercise that option.

27. Settling accounts: s. 44

Unless otherwise agreed, the following rules apply.

(a) *Losses* (including deficiencies of capital) are paid first out of profits, next out of capital and lastly (if necessary) by the partners individually in the proportion in which they are entitled to share profits.

(b) *The assets* (including sums contributed to make up losses or deficiencies of capital) are then applied in the following manner:

　　(*i*)　in paying outside creditors;
　　(*ii*)　in repaying advances made by partners (distinct from investment of capital);

(*iii*) in repaying capital to partners;

(*iv*) the residue, if any, is divided among the partners in the proportions in which profits are divisible.

NOTE: Where after paying (*i*) and (*ii*) above there are insufficient funds to repay capital to all the partners in full, deficiencies are shared in the same way as profits: *Nowell* v. *Nowell* (1869). But under the rule in *Garner* v. *Murray* (1904), if such deficiency is attributable to the insolvency of one of the partners, it must (unless otherwise agreed) be borne by the other partners in the proportion of their last agreed capitals (and not in the proportion in which they share profits or losses).

Thus G, M, & W were partners investing unequal capitals. On dissolution (after paying outside creditors) their balance sheet showed:

Liabilities		*Assets*		
G (capital)	£2500	Cash		£1891
M (capital)	£314	W (indebted)	£263	
		Deficiency	£660	
				£923
	£2814			£2814

HELD: (*a*) The firm's loss of £660 must be shared by the partners equally, and (*b*) W's total deficit (£263 + one-third of £660 = £483) must be shared between G and M in proportion to their last agreed capitals, i.e. £2500 and £314 respectively: *Garner* v. *Murray* (1904).

28. Goodwill

This is a partnership asset and means the good reputation and business connections of a firm developed over the years: *Trego* v. *Hunt* (1896).

Unless otherwise agreed in the articles, upon dissolution the goodwill must be sold and the proceeds of sale distributed as capital. Where dissolution is caused by death, the estate of the deceased partner is entitled to share in the proceeds of sale: *Re David & Mathews* (1899).

If the goodwill is not sold and there is no agreement as to its disposal, any partner can carry on the business (even using the firm's name), providing that by so doing he does not expose former partners to liability: *Burchell* v. *Wilde* (1900).

But if by agreement the goodwill is assigned to any person, he can restrain partners from (*a*) soliciting old customers of the firm, or (*b*) using the firm's name (but not from setting up a merely competing business): *Boorne* v. *Wicker* (1927).

29. Sale of goodwill
Where goodwill is sold (either to a partner or to an outsider) the value is divisible among the partners in the same manner as they share profits and losses (unless otherwise agreed).

(a) *Purchaser's rights* (unless otherwise agreed).
    (*i*) He may represent himself as continuing the former business of the vendors.
    (*ii*) He has exclusive rights to the firm's name: *Churton* v. *Douglas* (1859). He has the sole right to solicit former customers of the business bought: *Trego* v. *Hunt* (1896), except where the vendor did not sell voluntarily, e.g. where a bankrupt's trustee sells his business, the bankrupt can recommence business after his discharge and can then solicit any former customers: *Walker* v. *Mottram* (1881).
(b) *Vendor's rights.* He is entitled to open a competing business, unless restrained by a covenant in the contract of sale: *see* 4: **45–50.**

Limited partnerships

30. Limited Partnership Act 1907
This allows a partnership to claim limited liability for some of its members. Limited partnerships are not common, since it is easier and more advantageous to operate a limited registered company.

31. Characteristics of limited partnerships

(a) *Number of partners.* A limited partnership shall not consist of more than 20 partners, of whom at least one must be a general partner: Limited Partnership Act 1907, s. 4(2). This does not apply, however, to a partnership carrying on business as solicitors and consisting of persons each of whom is a solicitor; a partnership carrying on a practice as accountants and consisting of persons who belong to a member of a body of accountants established in the UK and for the time being recognised by the Secretary of State, or a person for the time being authorised by the Secretary of State to be appointed as an auditor either as having similar qualifications obtained outside the UK, or as having obtained adequate knowledge and experience in the course of his employment by a member of a body of accountants recognised by the Secretary of State, or as having before 6 August 1947 practised in Great Britain as an accountant; a partnership carrying on business as a member of a recognised stock exchange and consisting of persons each of whom is a member of that stock exchange. The limit of 20 partners is inapplicable in the case of a limited partnership carrying on one or more of the following activities: surveying, auctioneering, valuing, estate agency, land agency and estate management. Not less than three-quarters of the total number of partners must be members of either the Royal Institution of Chartered Surveyors, and not more than one-quarter of the total number of partners can be limited partners: Companies Act 1985, s. 717; Limited Partnerships (Unrestricted Size) Regulations 1971. Under the Limited Partnerships (Unrestricted Size) (No. 2) Regulations, 1990, an exemption from the size limitations is granted to partnerships formed for the purpose of carrying on business as insurance brokers so long as certain conditions are satisfied. Under the Limited Partnership (Unrestricted Size) No. 3 Regulations 1992, an exemption from the size limitations is granted to a partnership carrying on business as a member firm of the Stock Exchange.

(b) *General and limited partners:* a general partner is fully liable for all debts and obligations of the firm as in an ordinary partnership, and is entitled to participate in management.

A limited partner
- (*i*) contributes a stipulated amount to the firm's capital, and is not liable for the firm's debts beyond that amount (which cannot be withdrawn from the business, except on dissolution),
- (*ii*) cannot participate in management (and if he does so he loses his limitation of liability),
- (*iii*) has no agency for the firm, and

    (*iv*) is entitled to inspect accounts, etc.: Limited Partnership Act 1907, ss. 4, 6.

(c) *Registration:* a limited partnership must register
    (*i*) the firm's name,
    (*ii*) the nature of the business,
    (*iii*) the principal place of business,
    (*iv*) the full names of each partner,
    (*v*) any fixed term for which the partnership is created,
    (*vi*) a statement that the liability of some of the partners is limited,
    (*vii*) the sum contributed by each limited partner (in default of registration the firm cannot claim limited liability: s. 5).

(d) *Majority decisions:* in any ordinary partnership the votes of all partners count, but in a limited partnership only the votes of general (unlimited) partners count, unless otherwise agreed.

(e) *New partners:* in an ordinary firm admission of new members generally requires consent of existing partners: Partnership Act 1890, s. 24. In a limited partnership, unless otherwise agreed
    (*i*) a new partner can be admitted without consent of any limited partner, and
    (*ii*) a limited partner may assign his share to another person (with consent of the general partners, but without the consent of other limited partners): s. 6.

(f) *No dissolution by notice:* a limited partner cannot dissolve the firm by notice: s. 6(5).

(g) *Death, bankruptcy, or lunacy* of a limited partner does not automatically dissolve the partnership: s. 6(2).

(h) *Winding-up:* if a limited partnership is dissolved, the firm's affairs are wound up by the general partners alone, unless the court orders to the contrary: s. 6(3).

(i) *General partner becoming limited partner:* if by agreement a general partner becomes a limited partner, such change in status must be notified in the *London Gazette* and the change confers no limitation of liability until notified: s. 10(1).

Progress test 2

Agency and partnership

1.   Explain how an agency may arise (*a*) by implication, (*b*) by estoppel, (*c*) by necessity.   (7: **4, 5, 7**)

2.   In what circumstances may a person ratify a contract made on his behalf but without his authority?   (7: **6**)

3.   A, a minor, hires X as his agent to buy a house. X contracts to buy the house before discovering that A is a minor. A few days later A reaches his 18th birthday and purports to ratify the contract made by X. Is the ratification effective?   (7: **6**)

4.   'Generally a principal can revoke his agent's appointment at any time.' Discuss.   (7: **8**)

5.   What are the chief rights and duties of an agent, in regard to his principal?   (7: **10, 11**)

6.   Explain briefly: (*a*) ostensible authority of an agent, (*b*) breach of implied warranty of authority by an agent, (*c*) the doctrine of the undisclosed principal.   (7: **13–17**)

7.   In what circumstances may an agent be personally liable on a contract he has made on behalf of his principal?   (7: **16**)

8.   Give an account of the differing types of agent.   (7: **18–26**)

9.   'The limits of a banker's business cannot be laid down as a matter of law.' Discuss.   (7: **21**)

10.   Define a partnership and state the tests outlined by the Partnership Act 1890 for deciding whether a partnership exists or not.   (8: **1, 2**)

11.   Explain what is meant by an illegal association. What information is to be given, and where, as to a firm's name? (8: **3, 4**)

12. To what extent can a partner be regarded as having implied authority to act as agent for his firm?   (8: **5, 6**)

13. In what circumstances may a retired partner continue to be liable for the firm's debts after his retirement?   (8: **7**)

14. Explain what is meant by saying that the liability of partners is generally either joint, or joint and several.   (8: **8**)

15. 'The rights and duties of partners depend on agreement, express or implied, between themselves.' How far do you agree? What are the usual rights and duties of partners?   (8: **10–13**)

16. Explain what is meant by: (*a*) partnership property, (*b*) execution against a partner's share, and (*c*) goodwill.   (8: **14, 15, 28**)

17. In what circumstances may a partner assign his share in a firm, and what is the effect of such assignment?   (8: **16**)

18. Explain briefly the circumstances in which a partnership may be dissolved. What is the effect of dissolution?   (8: **17–23**)

19. On dissolution of a partnership how, in the absence of contrary agreement, are accounts settled?   (8: **27**)

20. Distinguish between, and explain briefly, the rules in (*a*) *Nowell* v. *Nowell* (1869), and (*b*) *Garner* v. *Murray* (1904).   (8: **27**)

21. A and B, partners, sold their business to X two years ago, for an inclusive price to cover goodwill. X now learns that A, trading under his own name, has opened a competing business and is writing to old customers of the A & B firm, saying: 'Please note that A, formerly of A & B, has now opened new premises at 333 New Street.' Explain the legal position.   (8: **28, 29**)

22. What is a limited partnership? How is such a partnership formed, and how does it differ from an ordinary partnership? (8: **30, 31**)

Specimen questions

1. In relation to the law of agency discuss:
   (a) the nature of the duties owed by agent to principal;
   (b) the legal effect of ratification.

2. (a) Describe with examples what is meant by an 'agency by necessity.'
   (b) P, a university professor at a South American university, has asked A, a London bookseller, to acquire for him a library of scientific books due to be sold by public auction and has made funds available for this purpose. A secures the books but is unable to ship them to P because a revolution has broken out in P's country and all shipping is stopped. A finds that he has difficulties in storing the books and he sells them to C, a *bona fide* buyer, at a price 10 per cent higher than paid for them at the auction sale. P now seeks your advice concerning his legal rights against A and C.

3. (a) When, if ever, is an agent personally liable upon contracts made by him on behalf of his principal?
   (b) P appointed A his agent to sell radios on his behalf. A sold the radios to X, without disclosing that he was negotiating the contract as an agent. X paid the agreed price but the radios were not delivered to him, so he wishes to sue for the recovery of the purchase price.
   In the meantime A has sold the radios to Y, who offered him the gift of a car in return for arranging the deal.
   What are the respective rights of X and P in these circumstances?

4. (a) State and explain the duties owed by an agent to his principal.
   (b) E, an estate agent, agreed to find a buyer for S's house. E introduced P, who agreed to buy the house, subject to contract, and left £5000 with E as a deposit. P subsequently withdrew from the sale. P was unable to recover the deposit from E, who had gone into liquidation.

Advise P as to his rights against S.

What would your answer be if E had accepted the deposit as a 'stake holder'?

5.   What rights have (*a*) a retiring partner and (*b*) a purchaser of a firm's business in respect of the goodwill of the business?

6.   (*a*) Explain the distinction between joint and several liability. Why is the distinction important in partnership law?

(*b*) A and B are in partnership as greengrocers. While negligently driving the firm's van on business, A injures X. X is now suing the firm for damages and it is found that A is insolvent. Advise B on the extent of his own liability and that of the firm.

7.   (*a*) 'The duties of a partner to his firm are fundamentally the same as those of an agent to his principal.' Discuss this statement.

(*b*) L, M and N are partners. Having reached the age of 70, L wishes to retire from the business and to assign his share to his son, who has worked in the business for ten years. M and N object to the assignment and wish to purchase L's share themselves. Advise M and N.

8.   What is the essential nature of a partnership?

F and G were in process of forming a company to vend garden equipment. G, without F's knowledge, and in his own name, ordered from E six mowing machines and put them in a shed at the site which had been selected for the company's garden centre. As G is unable to pay the agreed price for the machines, E wishes to claim the money from F.

Advise E.

9.   (*a*) Explain the way partnership property would be applied on its dissolution.

(*b*) John has been a partner in a trading firm of repute. He wishes to retire and has agreed to sell his share of the goodwill to Charles and Peter, the continuing partners.

Advise John as to the steps he must take to protect himself against liability in respect of the debts of the partnership incurred while he was a partner and in respect of the firm's future debts.

10. (a) 'There is normally a right in the principal unilaterally to revoke the agency at any time before the agency has been completely performed by giving notice.' Explain the rule and indicate whether there are any exceptions to it.

(b) Shaw owes Lamb £700. Shaw has appointed Lamb as his agent to collect certain debts owing to Shaw and to deduct 20 per cent of each amount collected until his loan to Lamb is fully repaid. The agreement also provides that Lamb should receive a commission of 5 per cent of all gross amounts collected.

Lamb has collected £3000 and thus recovered £600 of his loan. Now Shaw wishes to cancel the arrangement. Advise Lamb as to his rights in the matter both in respect of the unrecovered balance of the loan and of the commission.

Part three

Mercantile agreements

9

Sale of goods, supply of goods and services, hire and hire-purchase

The law relating to the sale of goods is laid down in the Sale of Goods Act 1979 which consolidated existing law. The law relating to the supply of goods and services is laid down in the Supply of Goods and Services Act 1982 which also consolidated existing law. The law relating to hire and hire-purchase is now contained in the Consumer Credit Act 1974.

The contract for the sale of goods

1. Sale of Goods Act 1979, s. 1

This defines a contract of sale as one 'whereby the seller (*a*) transfers, or (*b*) agrees to transfer the property in the goods to a buyer for a money consideration called the price'. Section 61 of the Act says that 'property' means 'general property' and not merely a 'special property'. In effect, the reference to 'general property' is a reference to the full rights of ownership.

2. Meaning of 'goods', s. 61

Goods means all chattels and tangible things in possession, but not things in action or money (unless the money is traded as goods and not as money, such as an antique coin). 'Goods' also means the following:

(a) *Industrial growing crops*, once they have been severed from the land. Until severance, they are classed as part of the land and are not goods.

(b) *Future goods,* i.e. goods to be made or acquired after the contract has been made.

3.   Sale and agreement to sell

When the property in goods is to be transferred immediately, the contract is known as a 'sale'. If property is to be transferred at some future time, the contract is known as an 'agreement to sell': s. 2. All contracts relating to future goods (*see* **2** above) are agreements to sell: s. 5(3). A common form of an agreement to sell is the conditional sale under which a buyer agrees to buy goods with the price payable in instalments.

4.   Contracts for work and materials

The Sale of Goods Act 1979 does not apply to contracts in which the purchaser is buying the skills of a craftsman and not merely the goods produced by him. Instead, they are governed by the Supply of Goods and Services Act 1982 (*see* **68–74** below). The test usually applied is: is the essential object of the agreement the provision of goods or the exercise of skills?

Example
_____

The employment of an artist to paint a portrait is a contract for the supply of work and materials, since the artist's skill is the main constituent of the contract: *Robinson* v. *Graves* (1935).

_____

5.   Contracts of barter

The 1979 Act lays down that a contract for the sale of goods is one where money is exchanged for goods, so it does not apply to contracts of barter. Here too the transaction is governed instead by the Supply of Goods and Services Act 1982 (*see* **68–74** below). Where a contract is one of part-exchange (a typical example being an old car plus cash in exchange for a new car), that is probably a contract for the sale of goods, certainly where a specific sum is allocated to the trade-in. If a contract of part-exchange is not a contract for the sale of goods, it will be covered by the Supply of Goods and Services Act (*see* **68–74** below).

6.   Sale and loan on security

The Sale of Goods Act does not apply to any transaction in the form of a contract of sale which is intended to operate by way of mortgage, pledge, charge or other security. These are governed by the Bills of Sale Acts 1878–1882 (*see* **16**).

7.   Capacity to contract
Capacity to contract is governed by the ordinary rules as to making a contract: s. 3. The 1979 Act provides that where necessaries are supplied to someone under the age of 18, to a drunkard or someone lacking full mental capacity, that person must pay a 'reasonable price' for them. *See also* Chapter 3.

8.   Form of contract
Any form suffices, written or oral, and a contract may be implied from conduct: s. 4.

9. Price

(a) *Fixed by parties.* The price (*i*) may be fixed at the time of contracting by the parties themselves, or (*ii*) may be left to be determined in the course of dealings between the parties, or (*iii*) may be left to be fixed by some third party: s. 8.
(b) *Fixed by a third party.* Where the contract states that the price is to be fixed by a third party, and he fails to do so, the contract is void: s. 9. But if the purchaser has by then taken the benefit of the goods, he must pay a reasonable price for them. If the third party's failure to fix the price is due to the fault of one of the parties, that party is liable in an action for damages: s. 9(2).
(c) *Where no price is fixed* in any of the ways listed above, the purchaser must pay a reasonable price.

Terms implied by the Sale of Goods Act 1979

10.   Conditions and warranties
The terms implied by the 1979 Act are described as being either 'conditions' or 'warranties'. The former are not defined in the Act, but a warranty is defined as something 'collateral' to the main purpose of the Act, for breach of which the injured party may claim only damages but cannot repudiate the contract: s. 61. In effect, these terms bear their conventional meaning so that a 'condition' is a major term of a contract, while a 'warranty' is a

minor term (*see* 2: **24–32**). The importance of the distinction lies in the remedies available on breach. Where a warranty is broken, the position is as stated above. Where the breach is of a condition, the injured party may both claim damages and elect to terminate the contract.

11. Assessment of terms

If the Act states specifically that a particular term is a condition or a warranty, that of course concludes the matter (*see* **14** below). There will be many cases, however, where nothing is said specifically in the Act. In such cases, the courts will look to other relevant Acts, case law and the intentions of the parties. In recent years, the courts have also developed the theory of the 'innominate term'. If there is no clear guidance as to whether a term is a condition or a warranty, then the effects of a breach of this 'innominate term' will depend on whether or not it goes to the root of the contract: *Cehave N.V.* v. *Bremer* (1975).

12. *Ex post facto* warranties

The buyer is always entitled to treat any breach of condition as a breach of warranty: s. 11(2). This means that he will be able to claim damages but will lose his right to terminate the agreement. In some cases (unless otherwise agreed in the contract), the buyer has to treat a breach of condition as a breach of warranty. This arises where the contract is non-severable and the buyer has accepted any part of the goods: s. 11(4). This does not apply where the buyer is not a trade buyer and the agreement is a conditional sale agreement (*see* **3** above): Supply of Goods (Implied Terms) Act 1973, s. 14(1). In such cases, a condition is to be treated as a warranty when it would have been treated in such a way in a hire-purchase agreement: s. 14(2).

13. Terms and mere representations

It used to be of considerable importance to determine whether some statement made in the course of contractual negotiations was a term of the contract or a mere representation inducing the other party to make the contract. The difference could affect the remedies available if the statement was false. If it was a representation, and was made innocently, then the contract could be terminated, but damages would be unavailable. If, on the other hand, the same statement was a term of the contract, the victim would always be able to claim damages and could also, if the term was a condition, terminate the contract. Now, however, the Misrepresentation Act 1967 has considerably reduced the relevance of the distinction because (*a*) it no longer matters that a representation has become a term of the contract: s. 1, and (*b*) damages and termination are allowed for a negligent misrepresentation and damages can be awarded at the court's discretion for an innocent misrepresentation as an alternative to termination of the contract: s. 2.

14. Implied terms as to title

Section 12 of the 1979 Act, provides as follows.

Subsections 1 and 2

In every contract of sale, other than one to which subsection 3 applies (*see* immediately below), there is:

(a) *an implied condition* that the seller has the right to sell the goods, or, in an agreement to sell (*see* **3** above), the right to sell at the time when the property is to pass, *and*

(b) *an implied warranty* that the goods shall be free of any undisclosed charge or encumbrance and that the buyer shall enjoy quiet possession (subject to any encumbrance or charge disclosed or known to him).

Examples

(1) A purchased a car for £334 from B and resold it to C for £400. A then discovered that the car had never belonged to B who had bought it in good faith from someone with no title. The car was reclaimed by the original owner and A paid off C by refunding him the £400. He sued B for the return of the £334 and was upheld in the Court of Appeal: *Rowland v. Divall* (1923).

(2) In another case, the buyer was entitled to claim for disturbance of quiet possession when a third party validly claimed that he had patent rights over the machine sold by the seller: *Microbeads AC v. Vinhurst Road Markings Ltd* (1975).

Subsection 3

Where it appears from the contract, or can be inferred from the circumstances, that the seller is transferring only such title as he or a third person may have, there is:

(a) *an implied warranty* that all known charges or encumbrances have been disclosed to the buyer; *and*

(b) *an implied warranty* that neither (*i*) the seller, nor (*ii*) any third person to whose claims the sale is subject, nor (*iii*) any person claiming under the seller or such third person will disturb the buyer's quiet possession (subject to any encumbrance or charge disclosed or known to him).

15. Exclusion clauses

The terms as to title cannot be excluded: Unfair Contract Terms Act 1977, s. 6. If such an exclusion clause is or is intended to be incorporated into a consumer contract, a criminal offence is committed: Consumer Transactions (Restrictions on Statements) Order 1976.

16. Correspondence with description: s. 13

In every sale of goods by description, there is an implied condition that the goods shall correspond with their description.

NOTE: (1) Sale by description means that the buyer relies for his information on the description of the goods given by the seller, e.g. in the contract or in preliminary negotiations. Thus, where he buys goods which he has not seen, this must be a sale by description. (2) The question whether goods correspond to their description is 'a test of mercantile character. The question whether that is what the buyer bargained for has to be answered according to such tests as men in the market would apply, leaving more delicate questions of condition, or quality, to be determined under other clauses of the contract or sections of the Act': *Ashington Piggeries Ltd* v. *Christopher Hill Ltd* (1972). In this case, herring meal contaminated with a substance which made it unsuitable for feeding to mink was sold to buyers for use as mink food. It was held by the House of Lords that the goods were still properly described as 'herring meal'. (3) A discrepancy between description and actuality such as could not have been seen on reasonable examination is a breach of this condition, e.g. the buyer examined lace described as 17th century and after purchase discovered it was actually 18th century. HELD: The discrepancy was not discernible on examination and he was entitled to rescind the contract. *Nicholson & Venn* v. *Smith, Merriot* (1947). (4) A seller is liable for breach of s. 13 however free of blame he might be for not providing goods of the contract description. (5) The fact that a description is applied to goods, either in the course of negotiations or in the contract itself, does not necessarily make the contract one of sale by description since, for a sale to be 'by description', the description has to be influential in the sale so as to become an essential term or condition of the contract. The court has to be able to impute to the parties a common intention that the description should be a term of the contract before the sale could be described as being 'by description' and in determining what the intention of the parties is, the presence or absence of reliance on the part of the buyer was a very relevant factor: *Harlington & Leinster Enterprises Ltd* v. *Christopher Hull Fine Art Ltd* (1990)

17. Exclusion clauses

The Unfair Contract Terms Act 1977 states that where the buyer is a consumer, the seller cannot exclude s. 13 Sale of Goods Act. If the buyer is a business buyer, s. 13 can be excluded only if the seller can prove that the exclusion is a reasonable one: s. 6, Unfair Contract Terms Act. In addition, it is a criminal offence to include or to seek to include in a consumer contract a clause excluding s. 13: Consumer Transactions (Restrictions on Statements) Order 1976.

18. Merchantable quality: s. 14 (2)

Where the seller sells goods in the course of a business, there is an implied condition that the goods shall be of merchantable quality, except that there is no such condition:

(a) as regards defects specifically drawn to the buyer's attention before the contract is made; *or*
(b) if the buyer examines the goods before the contract is made, as regards defects which that examination ought to reveal: s. 14(2)(*a*), (*b*).

> NOTE: (1) Goods are of merchantable quality if they are as fit for the purpose or purposes for which goods of that kind are commonly bought as it is reasonable to expect, having regard to any description applied to them, the price (if relevant) and all other relevant circumstances: s. 14(6). (2) A seller is liable for a breach of s. 14(2) however free of blame he might be in not providing goods which are of merchantable quality.

Examples _____

(1) A car is not of merchantable quality if an oil pipe is blocked. This renders the car potentially unsafe since the blockage might lead to the steering seizing up while the car is in the fast lane of a motorway: *Bernstein* v. *Pamson Motors (Golders Green) Ltd* (1987).

(2) A new Range Rover had to be returned several times for repair, but problems remained. It was held that the vehicle was not of merchantable quality even though the defects could be repaired and even though the defects had not destroyed the workable character of the car. The Court of Appeal ruled that when considering if a car was of merchantable quality, there had to be considered not just the owner's purpose of driving the car from one place to another, but his doing so with the appropriate degree of comfort, ease of handling and pride in the vehicle's appearance: *Rogers* v. *Parish (Scarborough) Ltd* (1986).

(3) Where a painting is sold as being the work of a particular artist, and this is discovered later to be untrue, this does not render the painting unmerchantable since it can still be resold, even if at a lower price than was paid for it, and it is still capable of aesthetic appreciation for what it is if not for what it might have been (*see Harlington* case, **16** above).

---

19. Exclusion clauses

The Unfair Contract Terms Act 1977, s. 6 states that where the buyer is a consumer, the seller cannot exclude s. 14(2) Sale of Goods Act. If the buyer is a business buyer, s. 14 (2) can be excluded only if the seller can prove that the exclusion clause is a reasonable one. In addition, it is a criminal offence to include in a consumer contract a clause excluding or purporting to exclude s. 14(2): Consumer Transactions (Restrictions on Statements) Order 1976.

20. Fitness for particular purpose: s. 14(3)

Where the seller sells goods in the course of a business and the buyer, expressly or by implication, makes known to the seller any particular purpose for which the goods are being bought, there is an implied condition that the goods are reasonably fit for that purpose, whether or not it is a purpose for which such goods are commonly supplied, except where the circumstances show that the buyer did not rely or that it was unreasonable for him to rely on the seller's skill or judgement.

By s. 14(4) an implied condition or warranty as to fitness for a particular purpose may be annexed to a contract of sale by usage, e.g. trade custom.

NOTE: (1) Where the goods have only one normal purpose, the seller is assumed to know what they are wanted for. The buyer of a bottle of milk does not have to tell the seller that he wants to drink it, nor does the buyer of a hot-water bottle have to explain what he wants it for: *Frost* v. *Aylesbury Dairies Ltd* (1905); *Priest* v. *Last* (1903). (2) A seller is liable for a breach of s. 14(3) even if he is completely free of blame for the goods not being reasonably fit for their purpose. (3) The instructions accompanying goods are part of the goods themselves. So if the instructions are misleading the goods will not be reasonably fit for their purpose, nor will they be of merchantable quality: *Wormell* v. *RHM Agriculture (East) Ltd* (1987).

21. Exclusion clauses

The Unfair Contract Terms Act 1977, s. 6 states that where the buyer is a consumer, the seller cannot exclude s. 14(3). If the buyer is a business buyer, s. 14(3) can be excluded only if the seller can prove that the exclusion clause is a reasonable one. In addition, it is a criminal offence to include or purport to include in a consumer contract a clause excluding s. 14(3): Consumer Transactions (Restrictions on Statements) Order 1976.

22. Sale by sample: s. 15

In a sale by sample, there is an implied condition that:

(a) the bulk shall correspond with sample in quality; *and*
(b) the buyer shall have a reasonable opportunity to compare the bulk with the sample; *and*
(c) the goods shall be free of any defect rendering them unmerchantable, and which would not be apparent on reasonable examination of the sample.

NOTE: (1) Where part only of the goods are not up to sample, the buyer must still accept or reject all of the goods, unless the contract is severable, i.e. in instalments, in which case each instalment must be treated separately. (2) Mere display of a sample during negotiations does not make the contract a sale by sample. There must be an agreement, express or implied, to that effect. (3) The seller is liable for a breach of s. 15 even if he is completely free of any blame.

23. Exclusion clauses

The Unfair Contract Terms Act 1977, s. 6 states that where the buyer is a consumer, the seller cannot exclude s. 15 Sale of

Goods Act. If the buyer is a business buyer, s. 15 can be excluded only if the seller can prove that the exclusion clause is a reasonable one. In addition, it is a criminal offence to include or purport to include in a consumer contract a clause excluding s. 15: Consumer Transactions (Restrictions on Statements) Order 1976.

Passing of ownership and risk

24. Passing of ownership

The transfer of the legal property in the goods is important for assessing who bears the risk of loss or deterioration, etc.

The position depends (*a*) on whether the contract is a sale or an agreement to sell, and (*b*) on whether the goods are specific and ascertained, or unascertained: *see* below.

25. Specific and ascertained goods

(a) *Specific goods* means goods identified and agreed upon at the time of making the contract: s. 61(1).

Goods are not specific merely because the source of supply has been agreed, e.g. '500 tonnes of coal from stack no. 2'.

(b) *Ascertained goods* means goods identified and agreed upon after the making of the contract.

(c) *Unascertained goods* means goods not yet identified and agreed upon, but merely described, e.g. the coal in (a) above.

26. When the property passes

(a) *Specific and ascertained goods:* The property in them passes whenever the parties intend it to pass. The intention of the parties may be (*i*) stated in the contract or (*ii*) left to be ascertained by the court from the circumstances: *see* 27 below.

(b) *Unascertained goods:* The property passes only when they become ascertained, i.e. no property can pass in unascertained goods.

27. Tests of intention

Where the contract does not state when the property is to pass, the court will apply the following tests to ascertain the intentions of the parties.

(a) *Unconditional contract for sale of specific goods in a deliverable condition*: the property passes when the contract is made (even if delivery is postponed): s. 18(1).

The risk then passes to the buyer, even though the seller retains a lien for unpaid purchase money: s. 20.

(b) *Sale of specific goods not in a deliverable state:* the property does not pass until (*i*) the seller puts them into a deliverable state, and (*ii*) the buyer is notified thereof: s. 18(2).

(c) *Sale of specific goods in a deliverable state*, but requiring some additional act such as weighing, measuring, testing, etc. to fix the price: the property does not pass until (*i*) the seller has done the required act, and (*ii*) the buyer is notified thereof: s. 18(3).

(d) *Goods delivered on approval or on sale or return, etc.:* the property does not pass until (*i*) the buyer signifies acceptance, or adopts the goods (e.g. by using them), or (*ii*) the buyer retains the goods for an unreasonable time or beyond any agreed time limit. What is a reasonable time is a question of fact in each case: s. 18(4).

(e) *Contract for sale of unascertained or future goods:* the property passes when (*i*) the seller unconditionally appropriates goods of the required description to the contract, (*ii*) puts them in a deliverable state, and (*iii*) notifies the buyer: s. 18(5).

(Appropriation by the seller includes delivery to the buyer or to a carrier on behalf of the buyer, provided the seller has not reserved a right of disposal: s. 18(5). If a right of disposal is reserved, property does not pass until the seller's conditions are satisfied: s. 19(1). Where the goods are shipped on a bill of lading to the order of the seller or his agent, it is presumed that a right of disposal is reserved: s. 19(2).)

28. Perishing of specific goods

(a) *If before the contract is made*, the contract is void: s. 6 (and *see Couturier* v. *Hastie* (1857), 4: **4**). This is a simple case of common mistake as to the existence of the subject-matter of the contract.

(b) *If after the contract is made*, and before the property passes to the buyer; the contract is void: s. 7. (But if the destruction was due to the fault of either party, the contract would not be void: instead the innocent party could sue for breach of contract.)

(c) *If after the contract is made*, and after the property has passed to the buyer: the buyer bears the loss and must pay for the goods.

'Perished' means destroyed or so changed or deteriorated as to defeat the purpose of the contract. But mere deterioration does not amount to perishing unless it causes the goods to become valueless: *Horn* v. *Minister of Food* (1948).

29. Passing of risk

Unless otherwise agreed, the risk will pass to the buyer only when the property in the goods passes to him.

Note that passing of risk is independent of possession, e.g. if the property in the goods has passed to the buyer, the risk falls on him even though the seller has not yet delivered the goods.

> NOTE: (1) Where performance of the contract is delayed by the fault of one party, the risk of loss or damage falls on that party: *Sterns Ltd* v. *Vickers Ltd* (1923). (2) Where delivery involves a sea journey, the goods remain at the seller's risk unless he gives the buyer reasonable notice (so that he can insure the goods): s. 32(3). (3) Where delivery is to a distant place, and the seller agrees to deliver at his own risk, the buyer must nevertheless accept the risk of any necessary deterioration incidental to the long journey: s. 33.

Nemo dat quod non habet

There is a general rule of law that *nemo dat quod non habet* ('No one can give what he has not got'). As applied to the sale of goods, the rule means that a seller of goods cannot give a better title to the purchaser than he himself possesses. Thus a purchaser who buys stolen goods from a thief can get no valid title to them, since the thief has no title: *see* **14** above.

The Sale of Goods Act 1979 lays down important exceptions to this general rule and these are stated below.

30. Estoppel

Where the true owner is estopped from denying the actual seller's right to sell the purchaser will get a good title.

Example _____

A allowed some of his property wrongfully to be detained by S, and also allowed B to think that S was entitled to the property. S sold the goods to B. HELD: B got a good title, as A was estopped from denying S's right to sell: *Pickard* v. *Sears* (1837).

31. Orders for sale

Where a person not the owner sells goods (*a*) under a court order, or (*b*) under a legal power of sale, e.g. the power of sale given to a legal mortgagee, the purchaser gets a good title.

Example

A deposits goods with B for B to repair them, and then fails to collect and pay for the repaired goods. B has a statutory power to sell the goods: Torts (Interference with Goods) Act 1977, and *see* 12: **6.**

32. Factors Act 1889, s. 2

The purchaser will get a good title if he buys in good faith from a factor, with whom the owner deposited the goods (even though the factor may have no actual authority to sell).

A factor is a mercantile agent whose ordinary business is the buying and selling of goods in his possession: Factors Act 1889, s. 1, *see* 7: **18** above.

33. Sale of Goods Act 1979, ss. 24 and 25

(a) *Seller in possession after sale.* If the buyer of goods allows the seller to remain in possession of them (or in possession of documents of title thereto) the seller can resell the goods to a second purchaser who will get a good title. The seller can then be sued in damages by the first buyer: s. 24. It is irrelevant whether the buyer has consented to the seller's retention of possession or not: *Worcester Works Finance* v. *Cooden Engineering Co. Ltd* (1971).

(b) *Buyer in possession after sale.* If the seller allows the buyer to get possession of goods (or documents of title thereto) before paying for them, the buyer can sell the goods and pass a good title: s. 25(1). (The seller can then only sue the original buyer for damages.) These provisions do not apply where the buyer is obtaining the goods under a conditional sale agreement (*see* **3** above) and where the credit allowed does not exceed £15,000: s. 25(2).

34. Writs of execution

If a person fails to pay a debt when ordered by the court, a writ may be issued empowering the sheriff to seize his chattels and to sell them in satisfaction of the debt. The sheriff then has power to give a good title, although he is not the owner of the goods sold: Supreme Court Act 1981, s. 138.

35. Sale under voidable title

The purchaser from a seller whose own title is voidable will get a good title, provided (*a*) he had no knowledge of any defect in the seller's title and (*b*) the seller's title had not been avoided at the time of the sale.

Example
───

A rogue obtained jewels on credit from P by fraud and sold them to B before P discovered the fraud. HELD: P could avoid the rogue's title to the jewels on the grounds of fraud, but since he had not done so before B bought the jewels B got a good title: *Phillips* v. *Brooks* (1919), *see* 4: **6.**

It appears that where the other party cannot be found, avoidance is effective as soon as the victim exhibits clear intention to avoid, e.g. by reporting the fraud to the police: *Car & Universal Finance Co.* v. *Caldwell* (1964).

───

36. Market overt

The purchaser normally gets a good title if he buys in a market overt (open market).

The term 'market overt' covers (*a*) all shops in the City of London, and (*b*) elsewhere, all markets established by statute, charter or custom as open markets.

A bona fide purchaser for value without notice of any defect in the seller's title will get a good title, provided:

(a) the sale is in accordance with the customs of the particular market;
(b) the sale took place in public, e.g. in the public part of a shop;
(c) the market dealer was the seller, not the purchaser;
(d) the goods were openly displayed, and were of a class the seller normally deals in;
(e) the sale took place in the normal opening hours of the market, e.g. between sunrise and sunset: *Reid* v. *Metropolitan Police Commissioner* (1973).

NOTE: The market overt provisions do not protect a purchaser where: (1) the transaction took place in Scotland; (2) the goods sold belong to the Crown; (3) the sale took place in a private part of the shop or stall, e.g. behind a curtain.

Performance of the contract

37. Delivery

It is the duty of the seller to deliver the goods, and of the buyer to accept and pay for them: s. 27. Unless otherwise agreed, payment and delivery are normally concurrent: s. 28.

Delivery means voluntary transfer of possession from one person to another. It may be actual or constructive, e.g. by handing over documents of title, or authority for the buyer to obtain the goods from some person in whose possession they are: *Central Newbury Car Auctions* v. *Unity Finance* (1957).

Delivery may also be by the seller agreeing to hold the goods as agent for the buyer: this is known as 'attornment'.

38. Time and place of delivery

(a) *Time of delivery.* Where the seller is to send the goods to the buyer but no time is fixed, they must be sent within a reasonable time and delivery must be at a reasonable hour: s. 29(3).

The seller usually bears the expense of putting the goods into a deliverable condition, and he must take reasonable care to see that they reach the right person: s. 29(6).

(b) *Place of delivery* (unless otherwise agreed) is the seller's place of business, or if he has none then his residence: s. 29(2).

If the sale is of specific goods known by both parties to be lodged at some other place, then delivery is to be made at that place: s. 29(2).

39. Delivery to a carrier

Where the seller is to send the goods, delivery to a carrier (as agent for the buyer) whether named by the buyer or not, is *prima facie* proper delivery to the buyer: s. 32(1). In such cases the seller must make a reasonable contract with the carrier, otherwise the buyer is entitled to refuse to be bound: s. 32(2).

40. Delivery of wrong quantities: s. 30

(a) *If less than ordered* the buyer may reject the lot; if he accepts the lesser quantity he must pay a proportionately reduced price.

(b) *If more than ordered*, the buyer may reject the lot, or may accept the agreed quantity only (if this is possible). The buyer may also accept all the goods, in which case he must then pay a proportionate price.

(c) *If goods ordered are mixed* with goods not ordered, the buyer may accept those ordered and reject the others (if it is possible to separate them, otherwise he must accept or reject the lot).

41. Delivery by instalments

Delivery is presumed to be in one transaction, unless it was expressly agreed that it should be by instalments.

If instalments are to be paid for separately on delivery, it is a question of fact whether failure to deliver one instalment justifies repudiation of the whole contract: s. 31.

The test is: is the breach regarding one instalment sufficiently fundamental to injure the contract as a whole? It is relevant to consider the likelihood of the breach being repeated. In *Regent OHG* v. *Francesco of Jermyn Street* (1981), the plaintiffs were manufacturers of menswear. They agreed to sell 62 suits to the defendants, who owned a retail shop. Delivery was to be by instalments. The number and size of the instalments was to be left to the plaintiffs' discretion. The defendants later informed the plaintiffs that they wished to cancel the order but the plaintiffs insisted on delivery of the suits which were in production. Because of shortage of cloth, one consignment was delivered one suit short, the plaintiffs having previously informed the defendants of the fact. The defendants, consistent with their wish to cancel the entire order, rejected delivery of all the consignments. The plaintiffs were forced to sell the suits elsewhere at a much lower price and brought an action against the defendants for non-acceptance. The defendants contended short delivery of one instalment amounted to short delivery on the whole contract, and the plaintiffs having delivered a quantity of goods less than they contracted to sell, they were entitled under s. 30 Sale of Goods Act to reject all the goods even though the parties had agreed on delivery in instalments. The plaintiffs contended that the contract was divisible into separate instalments and that under s. 31, whether the short delivery was a repudiation of the whole contract or merely a severable breach depended on the terms of the contract and the relevant circumstances. The court held that the plaintiffs were entitled to damages for the following reasons. First, on its true construction, the contract was divisible even though the number and size of the individual deliveries were not fixed in advance but were left to the plaintiffs' discretion. It followed that s. 30 (*see* **40** above) did not apply to the contract and that the defendants were not entitled to cancel the contract under s. 30 because of short delivery of one suit. Second, in any event, where the nature of the delivery of goods was short delivery in one instalment, the more flexible provisions of s. 31 were to apply in preference to those of s. 30. Applying s. 31, the short delivery of one suit, in all the circumstances, could not be said to go to the root of the whole contract and did not entitle the defendants to repudiate the whole contract.

42. Acceptance by the buyer

(a) The buyer is entitled to examine goods not previously seen, before accepting them: s. 34. Generally, the place of delivery is the place of examination, unless otherwise agreed.

(b) The buyer accepts: (*i*) when he so informs the seller, or (*ii*) except where the buyer was unable to exercise his right under s. 34 to examine the goods, when he does some act of ownership, e.g. sells the goods, or (*iii*) keeps the goods an unreasonable time without notifying the seller that he wishes to reject them: s. 35. In *Bernstein* v. *Pamson Motors* (1987), a buyer of a new car had it for approximately three weeks during which time he drove some 140 miles. The High Court ruled that enough time had run against him with the result that he was unable to reject the car.

(c) If the buyer rejects the goods, when entitled to do so, he is not bound to return them to the seller, but only to notify the seller of rejection so as to enable the latter to collect them: s. 36.

(d) If the buyer's rejection amounts to repudiation of the contract, the seller has an immediate right of action. The same applies when the buyer keeps the goods for an unreasonable length of time without making up his mind. In such a case the seller's damages will be measured as the amount of loss caused by the wrongful retention: *Long* v. *Lloyd* (1958).

43. Delivery by sea

In contracts for the carriage of goods sold by sea, various special terms are usual. These may be expressly agreed between the parties, but more often they rely on one of the established customary agreements with the implied terms that these contain.

The most common of these standard agreements are f.o.b., c.i.f., and ex-ship contracts: *see* below.

44. F.o.b. (free on board)

Under such a contract, the seller's duties (unless otherwise agreed) are as follows.

(a) To deliver the goods to a named port of shipment.
(b) To put the goods on board ship at his own expense.
(c) To negotiate a reasonable bill of lading or other contract of carriage, and forward it to the buyer (who pays the freight).
(d) To notify the buyer of shipment, so as to enable him to insure the goods at sea. (If the seller fails to do this the goods will travel at his risk; otherwise the goods will be at the buyer's risk.)

Once the goods are shipped the property in them (and usually the risk) passes to the buyer. If the seller is prevented from putting the goods on board, e.g. by a strike, the property and risk remain with him: *Colley* v. *Overseas Exporters* (1921).

45. C.i.f. (cost, insurance, freight)

Here the seller's duties go further than in an f.o.b. contract, and are as follows.

(a) To deliver the goods to the port of shipment at his own expense, and to see them safely on board.
(b) To insure the goods during transit.
(c) To negotiate a suitable bill of lading or other contract of carriage and to forward this to the buyer to enable him to claim the goods on arrival at the port of destination. (Purchase money is not normally paid until the documents of title reach the buyer.)

Once the goods are delivered to the ship the risk passes to the buyer (and should be covered by his insurance). The property in the goods passes to the buyer when the goods are shipped, unless the seller reserves a right of disposal in which case property does not pass until the price is paid.

The buyer is entitled to reject the documents of title, and/or the goods. Acceptance of one does not bind him to accept the other. But the buyer must pay the price when he receives the documents of title, even though he has not yet examined the goods. (It is also the buyer's responsibility to pay unloading charges and transport from the port of destination to any further inland destination.)

46. Ex-ship

Here the seller is bound to arrange the shipment of the goods to the port of destination, and to such further inland destination as the buyer may stipulate. The buyer is not bound to pay for the goods until they are unloaded from the ship and all freightage charges paid. The goods travel at the seller's risk, but he is not bound to insure them (though of course he usually does).

Rights of an unpaid seller against the goods

47. Unpaid seller

The term includes any person who is in the position of seller, though not himself the owner, e.g. a factor. The seller is unpaid as long as any part of the purchase price is outstanding.

Payment by a negotiable instrument is conditional only, i.e. is not effective until the negotiable instrument has been honoured. However, payment by means of a credit card is unconditional. If the credit card company goes into liquidation before it has paid the suppliers who took the particular card, the suppliers have no right of recourse against the customers. The company can, however, pursue the debts as can any third party to whom the company may have sold its receivables: *Re Charge Card Services* (1988).

48. Differing situations

The seller may have to contend with two different legal situations: (*a*) where the property has not passed to the buyer, and (*b*) where the property has passed to the buyer. His rights differ in these two cases and are examined below.

49. Property not passed to buyer

Here the seller may

(a) withhold delivery if the price is unpaid or not tendered, or if the buyer is insolvent, or

(b) if part of the goods have been delivered, he may withhold the remainder: s. 39.

It has become increasingly common in recent years for sellers to incorporate into their contracts a 'retention of title' clause. These have many forms but they usually stipulate that the seller retains the property in the contract goods until such time as the buyer has paid off all amounts under the contract. Sometimes this is extended to all amounts owing under the particular contract and any other contract outstanding between the same parties. The validity of these clauses was first upheld in *Aluminium Industrie* v. *Romalpa* (1976). The position would appear to be that since the goods supplied by the seller start off as his property, and since the clause allows him to retain his title, no charge is conferred over the property within the Companies Act 1985 and it does not need to be registered to be valid: *Clough Mill* v. *Martin* (1984). It was also said in that case that if a seller exercises his rights under a retention clause and repossesses the goods and resells them while the contract still subsists, he is only entitled to resell the amount needed to discharge the balance of the outstanding price and if he sells more he is accountable to the buyer for the surplus. However, if the contract had been terminated, as by an accepted repudiation, the seller can resell the goods as owner uninhibited by any contractual restrictions and therefore while he would have to refund any part of the purchase price paid by the buyer, which would be recoverable on the ground of failure of consideration, he is entitled to retain any profit on the resale. It was also said that if goods which are subject to a retention clause are incorporated in or used as material for other goods, it is to be assumed that the newly manufactured goods are owned by the buyer of the original goods, subject to a charge created in favour of the seller by the retention clause unless the use of the original goods leaves them in a separate and identifiable state, in which case it is possible for the seller to retain ownership of them. *See also*: *Re Bond Worth* (1980); *Borden (UK) Ltd* v. *Scottish Timber Products* (1981); *Re Peachdart* (1983); *Hendy Lennox (Industrial Engines) Ltd* v. *Puttick Ltd* (1984) and *Re Andrabell* (1984). It should be added that a buyer against whom a retention clause is incorporated can still make a valid resale of the goods as a person who has agreed to buy goods: *see* **33**(*b*) above.

50. Property passed to buyer
Here the seller has the following rights.

(a) Lien: *see* **51** below.
(b) Stoppage in transit: *see* **54** below.
(c) Re-sale: *see* **58** below.

51. Lien: s. 41
The seller's lien is a right to retain possession of goods until payment or tender of payment. A lien arises when:

(a) goods have been sold without any agreement as to credit; *or*
(b) goods have been sold on credit, but the period of credit has expired; *or*
(c) goods have been sold on credit and the buyer has become insolvent (whether the period of credit has expired or not).

52. Lien is lost when
(a) goods have been delivered to a carrier for transmission to the buyer, without the seller reserving a right of disposal; *or*
(b) the buyer or his agent lawfully obtains possession of the goods; *or*
(c) the seller waives his lien: s. 43.

53. The seller may exercise a lien
(a) when in possession merely as agent for the buyer;
(b) where part delivery has taken place (the lien extends over the remainder of the goods);
(c) if the seller breaks his contract while the buyer is solvent, he will still be entitled to claim a lien if the buyer subsequently becomes insolvent.

54. Stoppage in transit: s. 44
This means a right to stop the goods when they are on their way to the buyer (and after they have left the possession of the seller). The right arises when:

(a) the goods are in transit (*see* **55** below); *and*
(b) the buyer becomes insolvent. (The buyer is insolvent if he has ceased to pay his debts as they fall due in the ordinary course of business or he cannot pay debts as they become due: s. 61.)

55. Meaning of transit

Goods are in transit until the buyer accepts them, i.e. if in the hands of a carrier prior to delivery, or if rejected by the buyer when delivered: s. 45.

> NOTE: Where goods are in the possession of a carrier, the position depends on whether he is agent for the seller or for the buyer (a question of fact in each case). If he is agent for the seller, then the goods are still in the possession of the seller and his right is one of lien, not stoppage. If he is agent for the buyer, transit is over, and the seller has no right of stoppage. (The carrier may become agent for the buyer either by appointment as such, or by notifying the buyer that he holds the goods on his behalf, i.e. that they await collection.)

Transit ceases when the goods reach their ultimate destination, but not some intermediate destination (unless further instructions are conveyed to the carrier to send them on, in which case transit has ceased).

56. How stoppage is effected

This is done by the seller (*a*) taking possession of the goods or documents of title thereto, or (*b*) giving notice to the carrier of his exercise of the right of stoppage.

If the seller wrongfully stops the goods, e.g. where the buyer is solvent, he is liable for damages for the tort of conversion if the property has passed to the buyer, or for damages for breach of contract if the property has not yet passed to the buyer.

If a carrier wrongfully delivers stopped goods to the buyer, he is liable for damages to the seller. And if he wrongfully obeys the seller's instructions to stop transit, he is liable for damages to the buyer.

57. Transit ceases when

(a) goods reach their destination and possession is transferred to the buyer or his agent;

(b) the buyer or his agent obtains delivery before they reach their destination;

(c) a carrier wrongfully refuses to deliver the goods to the buyer or his agent;

(d) the goods have reached their destination and the carrier has notified the buyer that he holds them as his agent;

(e) goods are delivered to the master of the buyer's ship, or of a ship which the buyer has chartered.

> NOTE: Sale by the buyer does not affect the seller's right of stoppage, unless the seller has assented thereto.

58. Resale: s. 48

The contract is not necessarily rescinded by the exercise by the seller of his rights of lien or stoppage, nor does the seller automatically thereby acquire a right to resell the goods to another purchaser.

The seller has a right of resale after exercise of his rights of lien or stoppage in transit where:

(a) the goods are perishable; *or*

(b) the price has not been paid within a reasonable time after notice was given by the seller of his intention to resell; *or*

(c) such right was expressly reserved by him in the contract.

In addition to the above, the seller may also have a right of action for damages for breach of contract: *Ward* v. *Bignall* (1967).

Actions for breach of contract

59. By the seller: s. 49

He has the following rights of action.

(a) For the price.
   (*i*) Where the property in the goods has passed to the buyer and he has failed to pay for them.
   (*ii*) Where the price is payable on a certain day and has not been paid, the seller can sue for the price notwithstanding that the property has not passed to the buyer or the goods have not yet been appropriated to the contract.

(b) Damages for non-acceptance. This action lies where the buyer has refused to accept the goods and the property has not passed to him: s. 50(1).

The measure of damages is the estimated loss directly and naturally resulting to the seller: s. 50(2). Where there is an available market for the goods, the measure of damages will therefore normally be the difference between the contract price and the market price at the date of breach: s. 50(3).

In determining whether there was an available market, if the seller actually offered the goods for sale there was no available market unless there was one actual buyer on that day at a fair price. If, on the other hand, there was only a hypothetical sale, there would be no available market unless on the relevant day there were in the market sufficient traders potentially in touch with each other to evidence a market in which the seller could, if he wished, sell the goods. The market price on a hypothetical sale is the fair market price for the total quantity of the goods if they have to be sold on the relevant day, but taking into account the price which might be negotiated within a few days with other potential buyers who were not part of the market on that day only because of difficulties of communications: *Shearson Lehman* v. *Maclaine Wilson (No. 2)* (1990). Where there is no available market, the seller is entitled to damages for loss of his bargain: *Thompson* v. *Robinson* (1955) and *Lazenby Garages Ltd* v. *Wright* (1976).

60. By the buyer

(a) *For non-delivery.* The buyer can recover damages calculated in the same manner as in **59** above: s. 51(1).

(b) *For recovery of price*, where this has been paid and the goods have not been delivered.

(c) *For specific performance*, where the contract is for sale of specific or ascertained goods. But such an order is discretionary, and the court may award damages instead: s. 52.

(d) *For tort* (conversion) if the property has passed to the buyer and the seller has wrongfully detained or disposed of the goods.

The action for detinue was abolished by the Torts (Interference with Goods) Act 1977.

(e) *For breach of condition* the buyer can reject the goods, or, if he chooses, accept them and sue for damages for breach of an *ex post facto* warranty: *see* 2: **28**.

(f) *For breach of warranty*, the buyer can only sue for damages; he cannot reject the goods.

> NOTE: The Consumer Protection Act 1987 gives the Government power to lay down standards of safety in the manufacture of goods to protect consumers. Any person injured by defects in such goods (whether he is the actual buyer or not) can sue the seller, the manufacturer or any importer — whoever is more appropriate. (Exemption clauses cannot remove this liability.)

Auction sales

61. Auction sales

An auction is a sale at which the auctioneer (as agent for the seller) invites persons present to bid (offer) for goods sold.

The bidder is the offeror, and can withdraw his bid at any time before the auctioneer accepts it, usually by knocking with a hammer.

The general rules laid down by the Sale of Goods Act apply to sales of goods by auction; therefore if the sale is of specific goods the property in them will pass to the buyer as soon as the hammer falls, i.e. as soon as the contract is made: s. 57(2).

Each lot put up for sale becomes the subject of a separate contract.

62. Position of auctioneer

Auctioneers require to be licensed annually: the Auctioneers Act 1845.

(a) *Agent for the seller*. The auctioneer is primarily agent for the seller, but on accepting a bid he becomes also agent for the buyer. Thus his signature on a memorandum of sale would be binding on both seller and buyer: *Cohen* v. *Roche* (1927).

> NOTE: He has a lien on the goods for his charges and has a right of

action for the price against a buyer who has taken delivery and has failed to pay. He has implied authority to receive payment in cash, but no implied authority to sell on credit.

(b) *Auctioneer's warranties.* Independently of any liability as agent, he impliedly warrants on his own behalf:
- (*i*) that he has authority to sell the goods;
- (*ii*) that he knows of no defect in the seller's title;
- (*iii*) that he will give possession upon payment of the price, and that the purchaser's possession will not be disturbed by the seller or by himself.

(He does not warrant the seller's title in a sale of specific goods, unless he fails to make it clear he is merely acting as agent: *Benton* v. *Campbell, Parker & Co. Ltd* (1925).)

63. Auctions with and without reserve

(a) *Auctions with reserve.* This means any auction which is announced as being (*i*) subject to a reserve price being reached, and/or (*ii*) subject to the seller himself reserving a right to bid.

If a reserve price has been announced and the auctioneer inadvertently accepts a bid at a lower price, the buyer cannot enforce the sale.

(b) *Auctions without reserve.* These are the normal auctions, and in such sales the seller cannot legally bid, either personally or through an agent. If he does so, the buyer can treat the sale as fraudulent: S.G.A., s. 57(4), (5).

64. Bidding rings

It is a criminal offence for any dealer to make an agreement supported by consideration to abstain from bidding at any sale which he attends: Auctions (Bidding Agreements) Act 1969. (A 'dealer' is any person who makes it his business to attend auctions for the purpose of buying goods for resale.)

If a dealer is convicted under this enactment, the buyer can claim damages for fraud against any person who is a party to the agreement (and providing the buyer is innocent of any complicity). Also the seller can avoid the sale, unless the goods were bought by an innocent purchaser.

NOTE: The Auctions (Bidding Agreements) Act 1969 attempted to prevent operation of 'rings', by enabling the courts to ban participants from auction for from one to three years and to order restoration to the seller of the property sold. (The Act must be displayed at auctions, but is of doubtful value.)

65. Mock Auctions Act 1961
It is a criminal offence to promote or conduct a 'mock auction', i.e. an auction at which:

(a) articles are sold to a bidder for a sum lower than his highest bid, or where part of the price is refunded; *or*
(b) the right to bid is restricted to persons who have already agreed to buy one or more other articles; *or*
(c) an article is offered as a gift by way of inducement.

Contracts for the supply of goods and services

66. The Supply of Goods and Services Act 1982
This Act, which deals only with implied terms, applies to many contracts where ownership or possession of goods passes but where the contract is not a contract of sale, *see* **1, 4** and **5** above. It does not apply to contracts of hire-purchase, *see* below. A typical case covered by the 1982 Act is a contract for work and materials, *see* **4** *above*. If a plumber is employed to install a tap, the contract is for work and materials and is governed by the Act.

67. Implied terms
Where ownership of goods passes, the supplier of the goods is under identical obligations as to title, description, merchantable quality, fitness for purpose and sample as the seller of goods under a contract of sale, *see* **14, 16, 18, 20** and **22** above and ss. 2–5.

68. Exclusion clauses
The implied terms as to title cannot be excluded: Unfair Contract Terms Act 1977, s. 7(3A). In relation to the other implied terms, these cannot be excluded in contracts with consumers, but in business to business contracts the terms can be excluded provided the particular exclusion clause is reasonable: s. 7(2),(3).

69. Contracts of hire
The 1982 Act provides that the owner of goods which are hired

out is subject to a condition that he has a right to transfer possession, or will have that right where possession is to be transferred at a date later than the contract itself: s. 7(1). There is also an implied warranty that the person taking the goods on hire will have quiet possession except insofar as that possession is disturbed by the owner of the goods or some other person entitled to the benefit of a charge or encumbrance disclosed or known to the hirer before the contract was made. In addition, there are conditions as to description, sample, merchantable quality and fitness for purpose identical to those in contracts for the sale of goods *see* **14, 16, 18, 20** and **22** above and *see* ss. 8–10.

70. Exclusion clauses

The terms as to description, sample, merchantable quality and fitness for purpose cannot be excluded in contracts with a consumer: Unfair Contract Terms Act 1977, s. 7(2). In contracts between businesses, those terms can be excluded if the exclusion clause is a reasonable one: s. 7(3). The terms as to transferring possession and the assurance of quiet possession can be excluded in consumer and business contracts if the exclusion clause is reasonable: s. 7(4).

71. Supply of services

Where services are supplied under a contract, whether or not the ownership or possession of goods is also transferred:

(a) The supplier must provide his services with reasonable care and skill: Sale of Goods and Services Act, s. 13.
(b) Where the time for carrying out the service is not fixed by the contract, left to be determined in a way agreed in the contract or determined by the course of dealing between the parties, the supplier must carry out the service in a reasonable time: s. 14.
(c) Where no charge is agreed in advance, left to be determined in a way agreed in the contract, or determined by the course of dealing, only a reasonable charge can be made: s. 15.

72. Exclusion clauses

Liability for any act of negligence resulting in death or personal injury cannot be excluded: Unfair Contract Terms Act

1977, s. 2(1). Where the negligence results in any other kind of loss, liability can be excluded only if the exclusion clause is reasonable: s. 2(2). In so far as breach of contract is concerned, the duty to exercise reasonable care and skill can only be excluded if the exclusion clause is reasonable. In business-to-business contracts, however, this is only the case if the contract is on written standard terms: s. 3.

Contracts of hire, hire-purchase and conditional sale

73. A contract of hire

Such a contract arises where a person agrees to hire goods for a particular or indeterminate period. Such contracts are sometimes called contracts of bailment. A contract of hire-purchase is one where a person hires goods for a specified period and has an option to purchase the goods hired, often at the end of the period of hire. During the period of hire, he is a mere bailee of the goods: *see* Chapter 12. Such a contract must be distinguished from contracts of conditional sale (*see* **3** above) where the buyer agrees to pay off the price in instalments, but commits himself at the outset to making the purchase.

74. Regulating hire and hire purchase businesses

The Consumer Credit Act 1974 creates a system for controlling regulated consumer hire and consumer credit agreements. These are defined as follows.

(a) *A regulated consumer hire agreement* is an agreement with a non-corporate hirer where the agreement must run for at least three months and the rental does not exceed £15,000: s. 15.

> NOTE: Goods hired from the public utilities such as British Gas or British Telecom are not covered by the definition: s. 16(6).

(b) *A regulated consumer credit agreement* is an agreement with a non-corporate borrower for any kind of financial accommodation (and includes hire-purchase agreements) providing the accommodation does not exceed £15,000: s. 8.

> NOTE: An agreement is not regulated if it is exempt. Generally, agreements are exempt if they cover mortgage loans made by local

authorities, friendly societies and insurance companies: s. 16(1),(2). There are also exemptions for agreements where the number of payments does not exceed a specified number or the rate of interest does not exceed a particular percentage: s. 16(5); Consumer Credit (Exempt Agreements) Order 1989.

75. Licensing of businesses

A business providing any kind of regulated agreement must be licensed by the Office of Fair Trading: s. 21(1). A local authority, however, does not need to apply for a licence nor does a body corporate empowered by a public general Act naming it to carry on a business: s. 21(2),(3).

76. Type of licence

A licence issued by the OFT is either standard or group: s. 22(1). Standard licences cover individual applications and last for ten years. Group licences cover a particular group where the OFT feels that this would be better than having members of the group apply individually for a licence: s. 22(1)(*b*). The Law Society has a licence covering solicitors in practice. Where a licence is refused, an appeal may be made to the Secretary of State for Trade and Industry, and from him to the High Court: ss. 41, 42.

77. Unlicensed trading

An offence is committed by a business which needs a licence but which does not have one: s. 39. In addition, agreements made by an unlicensed trader cannot be enforced by him unless he has been granted an order by the OFT: s. 40. Appeals against refusals of an order are as in **76** above.

78. Form and content of agreements

Agreements which are regulated consumer hire and regulated consumer credit agreements have to be in the specified form: ss. 60, 61; Consumer Credit (Agreements) Regulations 1983. If the prescribed formalities are not observed, then the agreement is 'improperly executed' and it can only be enforced on a court order: ss. 61, 65.

79. Copy requirements

The customer under a regulated consumer hire or consumer

credit agreement is entitled to copies of the agreement within strictly controlled time limits: ss. 62–64; Consumer Credit (Cancellation Notices and Copies of Documents) Regulations 1983. If these requirements are not observed, then the agreement is improperly executed with the consequences referred to in **78** above: ss. 62(3), 64(5), 65.

80. Terms implied into agreements

As regards hire-purchase agreements, the Supply of Goods (Implied Terms) Act 1973 implies conditions and warranties which are identical to those implied in contracts for the sale of goods (*see* **14, 16, 18, 20** and **22** above). The position with regard to exclusion clauses is also identical (*see* **15, 17, 19, 21** and **23** above). With regard to conditional sales, these are contracts of sale covered by the Sale of Goods Act.

81. Statutory right of cancellation

If the negotiations leading up to a regulated consumer hire or consumer credit agreement included oral representations made in the presence of the customer, the agreement may be cancelled by the customer for any reason. His right to cancel lasts in most cases for five days from the day following his receipt of his copy of the agreement (*see* **79** above).

NOTE: An agreement cannot be cancelled if (*i*) the credit extended is a mortgage loan or a bridging loan, or (*ii*) the agreement was signed by the customer on the other party's business premises, or (*iii*) the agreement is secured on land.

82. Statutory right to withdraw

The customer has a right to withdraw from any regulated consumer credit or consumer hire agreement before it is made: s. 57(2). In addition, where the agreement is to be secured on land, certain formalities must be followed: ss. 58(1), 61(2); Consumer Credit (Cancellation Notices and Copies of Documents) Regulations 1983. If these requirements are not observed, then the agreement is improperly executed with the consequences referred to in **78** above: ss. 61(2), 65.

83. Statutory right of termination

The customer under a hire-purchase or conditional sale agreement can, if the agreement is regulated (*see* **74**) terminate it any time. His liability is to bring his payments up to at the most one half of the total price and any installation charges: ss. 99, 100. If the agreement is a regulated consumer hire agreement (*see* **74**), the customer can terminate the agreement at any time when it has lasted 18 months: s. 101(1), (3).

> NOTE: (1) A conditional sale agreement for the purchase of land cannot be terminated after the property has passed to the customer: s. 99(3), and a conditional sale agreement for the purchase of goods cannot be terminated if the property has passed to the customer who has transferred it to a third party: s. 99(4). (2) A hire agreement cannot be terminated if (*i*) the goods are hired out for business purposes, or (*ii*) if the goods are selected by the customer and then acquired by the other party from a third party, or (*iii*) if the rental payments exceed £900 a year: s. 101(7).

84. Liability

In many hire-purchase or conditional sale transactions, there are in fact three parties involved. Thus, A wishes to buy a car and arranges to take one stocked by B, a dealer, who offers to arrange terms through C, a finance company. B then sells the car to C who lets it out to the customer, A. A therefore has no direct contract with B. However, it has been ruled that A has a right to sue B for any misrepresentation or breach of the 'collateral' contract between himself and B (i.e. a contract whereby A agrees to hire or buy the car from C in return for B arranging a hire-purchase or conditional sale): *Andrews* v. *Hopkinson* (1956). Furthermore, anything said by the dealer in the negotiations preceding the contract with the finance company is said by him as agent of the finance company who must therefore take responsibility for what is said: Consumer Credit Act, s. 56. The foregoing provisions apply to all goods, not just cars, but the CCA only applies to regulated consumer hire or regulated consumer credit agreements (*see* **74** above).

85. Joint and several liability

In certain circumstances, a customer will buy goods direct from a dealer with credit extended to him by a third party. In such cases his contract for the supply of the goods, unlike the position discussed in **84** above, will be directly with the dealer. If the customer has any claim against the dealer for misrepresentation or breach of contract under a regulated consumer credit agreement, he has the same claim against the party who extended the credit who is therefore 'jointly and severally' liable with the dealer so long as there was some kind of business tie-up between the dealer and the party providing the credit: Consumer Credit Act, s. 75(1). This means that each is responsible to the customer for the full amount of his loss.

> NOTE: (1) These provisions do not apply if the credit was not provided in the course of a business: s. 75(3)(*a*). (2) These provisions do not apply if the cost of the particular item was £100 or less or was more than £30,000: s. 75(3)(*b*). (3) If the creditor is sued by the customer, he will be able to seek compensation from the dealer, subject to any agreement made between them: s. 75(2). (4) If the breach or misrepresentation entitles the customer to rescind the agreement, he will also be entitled to rescind the credit agreement: *UDT* v. *Taylor* (1980).

86. Supply of information

Customers under regulated agreements are entitled, on payment of 50p, to a copy of the agreement and to a statement of account. This information must be supplied within 12 working days of receiving a request in writing. If this is not done, the agreement cannot be enforced while the default continues. If default in supplying the information extends for a month, a criminal offence is committed: Consumer Credit Act, ss. 77, 78 and 79; Consumer Credit (Prescribed Period for Giving Information) Regulations 1983. Customers who have 'running account' credit agreements (whereby they have a credit limit and can keep borrowing up to that limit) are also entitled to regular information without having to make a separate request: s. 78(4).

87. Default notices

No action can be taken to enforce or terminate a regulated agreement unless due notice has been given in the prescribed form giving a minimum of seven days' notice: Consumer Credit Act, ss. 76, 87, 88 and 98; Consumer Credit (Enforcement, Default and Termination Notices) Regulations 1983.

88. Statutory rebate

The customer under a regulated consumer credit agreement (*see* **74**) has a right to pay off the agreement early. If he does so, he is entitled to a rebate of credit charges: ss. 94, 95; Consumer Credit (Rebate on Early Settlement) Regulations 1983.

89. Protected goods

When the customer under a regulated hire-purchase or conditional sale agreement has paid all the installation charges and at least one-third of the total price, the other party cannot recover the goods in the event of a breach of contract without a court order. If he does recover the goods without a court order, the agreement is terminated and all sums paid in the past can be recovered: ss. 90, 91.

90. Extortionate credit bargains

The rules relating to extortionate credit bargains apply to all agreements for the provision of credit, whether or not regulated. If the court finds that the bargain is extortionate, it can reopen matters to do justice between the parties: s. 137. A bargain is extortionate if:

(a) it requires the customer or a relative to make payments which are grossly exorbitant; *or*
(b) it otherwise grossly contravenes ordinary principles of fair dealing: s. 138.

NOTE: These provisions do not apply to hire agreements. However, where goods hired out under a regulated consumer hire agreement are repossessed, the customer can apply to the court for relief from sums paid or to be paid: s. 132.

91. Ancillary credit businesses

The Consumer Credit Act also lists five 'ancillary credit businesses'. These are: credit-brokerage, debt-adjusting, debt-counselling, debt-collecting and the operation of a credit reference agency. The provisions of **75–77** above apply in such cases.

92. Powers of the court

On application the court has the power to issue time orders

(time to pay or remedy a breach); protection orders (for protecting property subject to the particular agreement); return orders (for the handing over by customer of goods to which a regulated consumer hire purchase or conditional sale agreement relates) and transfer orders (passing of title to customer under regulated hire-purchase or conditional sale agreement of some of the goods, return to other party of balance): ss. 129, 313, 133.

In exercising its discretion under the Act to make, if it is just so to do, a time order providing for payment by instalments of any sum owing and for postponement of the recovery of any security or possession of any land to which the agreement relates, the court is to have regard not only to the debtor's position, but also to the creditor's interest. This means that, where there has been a long history of default on the part of the debtor, it would not be just to require the creditor to accept the figure offered by the debtor and make a time order if the instalments which he can afford will not meet the accruing interest and there is no realistic prospect of his financial position improving: *First National Bank* v. *Syed* (1991).

Specimen questions

1. (*a*) What terms as to quality or fitness for purpose are implied by law in a contract for the sale of goods? To what extent, if at all, is it possible for a seller to exclude liability for the breach of such terms?

    (*b*) In the course of his employment with the Lawmark Company, Watkins was sent to take delivery of a machine which the company was buying from the Metalwork Company. Watkins examined the machine superficially and failed to notice that an important working part was defective. He took delivery and, due to the faulty part, the machine did not work. The Lawmark Company wish to know their rights (if any) against the Metalwork Company.

2. (*a*) Describe in outline the principal exceptions to the rule '*nemo dat quod non habet*' whereby a person cannot pass a better title to goods than he himself possesses.

(b) Robin is an absent-minded person. One day he goes off to work without locking up his house. Sly, a thief, lets himself in and steals a valuable clock which he sells to Tom, a private collector. Tom buys in good faith, paying Sly £1000. Robin now wishes to know whether he can recover the clock from Tom.

3. (a) What remedies has the buyer of goods against the seller where the latter has been guilty of a breach of contract?

(b) Some months before the investiture of the Prince of Wales, W, a Welsh shopkeeper, orders from M, a manufacturer, a large quantity of commemorative drinking mugs for delivery one week before the investiture. In fact, the mugs are delivered to him one week after the investiture. State with reasons whether W will be legally entitled: (i) to refuse to accept delivery of the mugs, and (ii) to claim damages.

4. (a) When does the property in goods sold 'on sale or return' pass to the buyer?

(b) Jack has been supplied with a colour television-set by Televisions Galore Ltd on two weeks' approval. After a week, Jack sold the set to Jim and went abroad. Jim bought the set in good faith and was not aware of the circumstances. Advise Televisions Galore Ltd whether they can recover the set from Jim. What is Jack's legal position?

5. James, a client of yours, wishes to introduce credit facilities in his shop. Explain to him the nature of a hire-purchase and conditional sale contract, and explain to him the formalities which are necessary for the creation of a valid hire-purchase or conditional sale contract under the Consumer Credit Act 1974 and explain to him the legal consequences of the failure to comply with these formalities.

6. What remedies has an unpaid seller of goods against the goods themselves?

A, whose business was in London, had agreed to send a consignment of diamonds to B in Newcastle. A hired a car from an independent firm and gave the diamonds to the driver with the instructions to deliver them at B's address. No sooner had the car left London than A heard that B was insolvent and this was in fact the case. A then telephoned X, a friend in Newcastle, and asked X to get the diamonds back for him. X met the car outside B's office and told the driver to give them to him, but at that moment B came out and persuaded the driver to give them to him instead. The diamonds are now in the hands of B's trustee in bankruptcy from whom A claims them.

7. (a) Define a contract for the sale of goods and explain what is meant by 'goods' in this context.
    (b) A agreed in writing to sell a yacht to B, but when the agreement was signed they had not yet fixed a price. What would be the legal position if:
      (i) the agreement stated that 'the price shall be mutually agreed at a later date'; *or*
     (ii) the agreement stated that 'the price shall be fixed by C'; or
    (iii) no price was mentioned in the agreement at all.

8. The Fruitex Co. Ltd contracted to sell to the Supplies Co. Ltd a consignment of canned fruit at an exceptionally low price. By written notice they stated that they gave 'no guarantee as to the merchantability of the contents of any item included in the consignment'. The goods having been delivered, the Supplies Co. Ltd discovered that all the contents of the cans were defective and unsaleable. The Fruitex Co. Ltd now threaten to sue the Supplies Co. Ltd for the price.

9. The Computer Co. Ltd contracted to deliver 144 electronic devices to the Communications Co. Ltd in a year. Delivery to be made at the rate of twelve devices a month. After three months, the Communications Co. Ltd discover that all the devices are seriously defective. They have now indicated that they wish to repudiate the contract.

10. On 1 January, Higgs agreed to sell his lawnmower to Watts 'on 1 February'. On 8 January, there was a freak storm and the shed in which Higgs kept the mower was struck by lightning and

was entirely destroyed together with the mower. On 1 February Higgs claimed the price of the mower from Watts. Is Higgs entitled to do so, or could Watts claim that he no longer has to pay because the goods have been destroyed?

10
Carriage of goods

Carriage of goods, whether by land, water or air, is usually conducted by persons who make carrying their business and who fall within the category of 'common carriers'.

Common carriers

1. Common carriers

A common carrier is one who offers for hire to transport from place to place, either by land, air or water, the goods of anyone wishing to employ him.

The law traditionally imposes special duties on common carriers, above and beyond those imposed on people who casually, for hire or otherwise, carry goods.

> NOTE: A private carrier is a person who carries goods for another in pursuance of some special agreement, e.g. a warehouse company delivering goods to a ship: *Consolidated Tea & Lands Co.* v. *Oliver's Wharf* (1910). A private carrier's responsibility is that of an ordinary bailee: *see* 12: **2**.

Common carriers are rare today. The Transport Act 1962 expressly states that British Rail is not a common carrier. The Transport Act 1968 makes a similar provision regarding the National Freight Corporation, and the Transport (London) Act 1969 also states that the London Transport Executive is not a common carrier.

2. Position of common carriers

The carrier is bound to carry all goods offered to him at a fair price (which may be demanded in advance), unless

(a) he has no space,
(b) the goods are of a kind he does not profess to carry, or
(c) the destination is not on his normal route, or
(d) the goods are dangerous or inadequately packed.

If he unjustifiably refuses to carry goods he may be prosecuted and/or sued for damages.

(Many carriers evade classification as common carriers by reserving in advance the right to refuse to carry any goods at will. Thus A offered to carry various types of goods, while reserving the right to reject any, and to charge varying rates according to the kinds of goods carried, the destination etc. HELD: He was not a common carrier: *Belfast Ropework Co. Ltd* v. *Bushell* (1918).)

3.   Duties of carriers
It is the duty of any carrier (whether common or not):

(a) to deliver at the place directed. This is discharged by delivery at the right place, not necessarily to any particular person;
(b) to deliver within a reasonable time, allowing extension of time for unforeseeable delays such as unexpected strikes: *Sims* v. *Midland Rly* (1913);
(c) to obey the instructions of the consignor as to alterations of delivery etc.;
(d) not to deviate unnecessarily from his agreed route.

The carrier's rights are:
(a) to demand reasonable payment (in advance, if desired),
(b) to refuse goods not properly packed;
(c) to claim a lien on the goods carried for his charges.

NOTE: A common carrier has at common law a particular lien allowing him to retain the particular goods until his charges are paid. He has no right to use or otherwise dispose of the goods in the absence of express agreement.

4.   Liability of common carrier
He is an insurer for the safety of the goods he carries, from the moment they are received by him until they are delivered. He is therefore liable for all damage to the goods, whether occasioned by negligence or not, except where the damage is caused by the following.

(a) *Act of God:* an act of nature of such extraordinary description or degree that no reasonable person could be expected to guard against or foresee it, e.g. lightning, freak winds, earthquake, etc.
(b) *Queen's enemies:* the forces of a State with which this country is at war, e.g. capture of the carrier's ship by an enemy warship, but not damage by rioters, rebels, etc., since they are not the forces of an enemy State.
(c) *Inherent vice in the goods carried:* some latent defect in the goods themselves, over which no one has control and against which the carrier cannot guard, e.g. in animals, disease not visible when consigned, but not mere normal unruliness or stupidity.
(d) *Fault or fraud of the consignor:* although the carrier is bound to insure the safety of the goods, he is not liable for harm caused directly by the negligence of the consignor, e.g. through bad packing.

5. Measure of damages
This will be either the value of the goods, assessed at destination on the date of scheduled delivery, or loss attributable to delay or depreciation, etc.

Provided that the carrier must not be made liable for damage other than that which: **(a)** flows naturally and directly from his breach of duty; plus **(b)** such additional damage as he should reasonably have foreseen at the time of making the contract: *Hadley* v. *Baxendale* (1854), and *see* 5: **27**.

6. Modification of carrier's liability
Save where prohibited by statute, common carriers may vary their legal liability by contract; but the courts interpret exemption clauses strictly, and as far as possible to the disadvantage of the carrier. Exemption clauses by private carriers are less strictly interpreted and may even protect the carrier against liability for theft by his servants: *John Carter Ltd* v. *H. Hanson Haulage (Leeds) Ltd* (1965). But no exemption clause will protect any carrier against a fundamental breach (*see* 2: **18** above), e.g. where he consigns a valuable cargo to another carrier without the owner's consent: *Garnham, Harris & Elton Ltd* v. *Alfred W. Ellis (Transport) Ltd* (1967).

NOTE: The Unfair Contract Terms Act 1977 controls and invalidates the use of certain exclusion clauses, except where these are authorised by statute. Clauses excluding or limiting liability arising from negligence causing death or personal injury are void. Where negligence results in some other kind of damage, such as damage to personal property, clauses of this kind are only valid if proved to be reasonable. Other clauses valid only if reasonable are (providing the contract is with a consumer or on the other party's written standard terms): those excluding or restricting liability for breach of contract and those which purport to allow no performance of the contract or one which is substantially different from the performance which was reasonably expected. The first Schedule to the 1977 Act states, however, that the provisions on negligence resulting in death or personal injury apply to contracts for the carriage of goods by ship or hovercraft, but that the other provisions only apply in favour of a person dealing as a consumer. Furthermore, the same Schedule makes special provision for the carriage of goods by ship or hovercraft in pursuance of a contract which either specifies that as the means of carriage over part of the journey to be covered, or makes no provision as to the means of carriage and does not exclude that means. The position here is that the above provisions concerning negligence resulting in death or personal injury apply. The other provisions do not extend to the contract as it operates for and in relation to the carriage of the goods by that means, except in favour of a person dealing as a consumer.

7. Liability of consignor

The consignor must notify the carrier if goods are dangerous, e.g. explosives or combustibles. He is also deemed to warrant the fitness of goods to be carried, and is liable for damages for breach of warranty even if ignorant of an unfitness which causes harm to the carrier.

Carriage by land

8. The principal statutes

The Carriers Act 1830, the Transport Act 1962, the Transport Act 1968 and the Transport Act 1985 are the principal statutes governing carriage by land. Otherwise, the applicable rules are those of common law, stated in the preceding section.

9. Carriers Act 1830

This applies only to common carriers (but not to carriage of goods by sea). The main provisions of the Act are as follows:

(a) The carrier is under no liability for loss or damage to packages containing certain articles, worth all told more than £10, unless at the time of consignment the consignor notified the carrier of the true value and contents of the package. (The carrier may then charge a higher fee for the increased risk. The carrier must post notice of such extra charges at his office; otherwise he is not allowed to charge them. When such higher fee is charged, the consignor may demand a receipt for any payment made.)

Articles covered include: gold, silver, gems, watches, bills and securities, paintings and engravings, title deeds and some other documents, glass, china, furs, etc.

(b) A notice alone cannot limit or reduce the carrier's liability: there must be express agreement to that effect.

(c) The Act gives no protection to the carrier for loss or damage caused by the crime of the carrier's servants, or the carrier's own negligence. (But the burden of proof is on the consignor.)

(d) A carrier is only liable for the real value (of which he may require proof), i.e. he need not accept the consignor's assessment.

10. Carriage by rail

This is governed by the various Transport Acts, and the Act of 1962 stipulates that British Rail is not to be regarded as a common carrier (and is therefore not subject to the Carriers Act 1830). Contracts for carriage of goods by rail are governed by the BR Rules, which envisage two main types of agreement:

(a) *Board's risk conditions.* The Board is liable for any loss, misdelivery or damage, unless it can prove Act of God, seizure under legal process, default of consignor (e.g. bad packing, or inherent vice in goods), or wastage through normal conditions.

It may also evade liability for casualty if it can prove it has exercised reasonable care, or there has been fraud by the consignor.

The Board is also usually liable for loss caused by deviation from the scheduled route causing delay unless it can prove that the deviation was not caused by any negligence.

The Board has a general lien for carriage charges and

expenses, and other charges outstanding against the owners. Goods may be sold if not claimed within a reasonable time.

(b) *Owner's risk conditions.* The Board's liability is lower, so are the carriage charges. The Board is not liable for loss, damage, deviation, misdelivery, delay or detention, save where such is proved to have been caused by wilful misconduct of the Board's servants, including gross negligence.

Negligence is presumed where loss arises through non-delivery of the whole consignment.

> NOTE: Damageable goods improperly packed. The Board may refuse such goods, and where it agrees to carry them it is only liable if (*a*) there is wilful misconduct, or (*b*) damage would have occurred even though the goods have been properly packed, and (*c*) the Board would have been liable under Board's risk conditions.

11. Termination of rail transit

Transit ceases when (*a*) the goods are delivered, or (*b*) the sender exercises his right of stoppage in transit, *see* 9: **54**, or (*c*) where it is agreed to take goods to a particular depot to await collection — here transit ceases one day after notice of arrival.

12. Notice of claims

This must be served on the Board within three days of termination of transit, and any claim must be made within seven days. (If the claim is for non-delivery, the times are extended to 28 days and 42 days from commencement of transit.)

13. Passengers' luggage

To make the Board liable, the passenger must prove (*a*) that BR assumed control of the luggage, and (*b*) that the luggage was 'personal luggage,' i.e. for the personal use of the passenger.

Assumption of control is a question of fact in each case. Putting luggage in the guard's van is indicative of assumption of control, but the fact that the passenger took the luggage into the compartment with him does not of itself rule out the possibility that BR has assumed control.

14. Railway passengers

The Board is not a common carrier of passengers and

therefore may refuse any passenger, and does not insure passengers' safety.

The Board can lay down any limitation on contractual or other liability for the safety of passengers, save that it cannot impose conditions which (*a*) negative liability for death or injury, or (*b*) prescribe a time limit for the enforcement of claims therefore. This was laid down in the Transport Act 1962, s. 43(7). This was repealed and replaced with equivalent provisions by the Unfair Contract Terms Act 1977.

15. Carriage by road

Where a passenger is carried by road transport, in public service vehicles, the contract cannot negative in any way claims for bodily injury or death of the passenger: Road Traffic Act 1960, s. 151.

Ordinary common carriers are under the usual liabilities of common carriers. Private carriers are liable only for negligence, or as otherwise agreed.

Carriage of goods by road within Britain is largely free of statutory restrictions, save those laid down by the Carriers Act 1830, and the various Road Traffic Acts. Where goods are to be transported internationally within the EC and some other countries, carriage is governed by the detailed provisions of the Carriage of Goods by Road Act 1965 and the Carriage of Passengers by Road Act 1974. Reference should also be made to the Carriage by Air and Road Act 1979. Road transport between England and Jersey falls outside the Act: *Chloride Batteries* v. *F & W Freight* (1989).

Carriage by air

16. Carriage by air

The Carriage by Air and Road Act 1979 governs international carriage between the UK and countries which are parties to the various international conventions dealing with carriage by air.

Under the Act the carrier is liable for loss of goods or injury to passengers, unless he can establish one of the specified defences, e.g.:

(a) that all reasonable precautions were taken for safety of goods;
(b) that loss or injury was due to negligent pilotage or navigation.

Maximum liability (*i*) for death or injury is 250,000 francs, and (*ii*) for loss or damage to goods is 250 francs per kilo (unless agreed otherwise). The maximum liability for goods may be increased by Order in Council, up to 25,000 francs per kilo.

The Carriage by Air Acts (Application of Provisions) Order 1967 applies similar rules to carriage by air within the UK, i.e. 'non-international' carriage. A contract of carriage made and to be performed wholly within the territory of a single foreign state or between two foreign states is outside the 1967 Order: *Holmes* v. *Bangladesh Biman Corp.* (1989).

Carriage by sea

17. Carriage by sea

The owner of a ship may be a common carrier, and as such (if not protected by contract) is an insurer of goods carried, subject to the usual general defences, e.g. Act of God.

Carriage by sea is arranged under a contract called a contract of affreightment, either in the form of a charterparty or a bill of lading.

NOTE: Carriage by sea is governed by the normal common law rules relating to common carriers, save as amended by the Hague Rules as enacted for Britain by the Carriage of Goods by Sea Act 1971.

18. Implied undertakings by shipowners

(a) *That the ship is seaworthy*, i.e. is fit for the particular voyage contemplated. This is an absolute warranty, and breach of it renders the owners liable irrespective of any question of fault or negligence on their part, unless liability is modified by the contract.

Bad stowage may amount to unseaworthiness if it endangers the safety of the ship (not merely the safety of the cargo): *Elder Dempster* v. *Zochonis & Co.* (1924). Where the steering system fails soon after the commencement of a voyage, this raises a rebuttable presumption that the system was not in proper working order when the voyage began and that the particular vessel is unseaworthy: *Phillips Petroleum Co.* v. *Cabaneli Naviera* (1990)

If the shipper discovers unseaworthiness before the voyage commences, he may repudiate the contract.

NOTE: The warranty is not absolute in bills of lading governed by the Carriage of Goods by Sea Act 1971.

(b) *That the ship will be ready* (*i*) to load cargo and (*ii*) to sail, on the agreed date. (If delay is fundamental, the shipper may repudiate the contract; otherwise he can only sue for damages.)

(c) *That the ship will not deviate unnecessarily.* Deviation to save life is permissible, but deviation to save property is not (except in bills of lading governed by the Carriage of Goods by Sea Act 1971).

Most contracts contain a deviation clause allowing the ship to call at agreed ports in any order, and to make other necessary and pre-agreed deviations. But such clauses are strictly construed.

19. Liability of shipowners

The Merchant Shipping Acts 1894–1988 provide that, regarding British ships, no owner, charterer, manager, or operator, etc., shall be liable for damage for which he is not personally or jointly responsible in the following cases:

(a) *Loss or damage by fire* (even though caused by unseaworthiness).

(b) *Loss caused by robbery* of such articles as jewels, watches, gold, silver, etc., unless the true value was declared by the consignor at the time of contracting.

(c) *Where loss of life or bodily injury* is caused to passengers, or damage to goods (or to persons other than passengers), by negligence or default in navigation, the damages payable by the owners are limited to (*i*) 206.67 drawing rights per ton of the ship's weight for injury to persons, and (*ii*) 66.67 drawing rights for injury to goods.

(d) *The dangerous nature of any goods* must be notified to the shipowner, who may refuse to carry dangerous goods, or charge additional sums, etc.

20. Freight

The shipowner's carriage charges are called freight and usually become payable only when he has delivered the goods, or when he is prevented from delivering them by some fault of the consignor. Unless otherwise agreed, the person responsible for paying freight is the consignor.

Freight may take the following forms.

(a) *Advance freight*, payable before the goods will be delivered. If through no fault of the shipowner the goods are lost (e.g. through one of the excepted perils, *see* **4** above), liability to pay freight remains.

(b) *Lump sum freight*, i.e. a sum payable by a charterer for the use of the ship. If the ship is ready on the agreed date but no cargo is loaded, the charterer still becomes liable to pay the freight.

(c) *Pro rata freight*, i.e. a reduced sum payable where (by agreement) the cargo is delivered at some port other than that originally agreed.

(d) *Dead freight*, i.e. a sum payable by way of compensation for loss of revenue where a charterer fails in a promise to provide a full and complete cargo.

21. General and particular average

Three types of proprietary interest are risked in sea voyages: the ship (owner's interest), the freight (charterer's interest), and the cargo (cargo owner's interest). Loss sustained by any one interest must usually be borne by that interest alone, and is called a particular average loss, e.g. cost of damage to the ship, falling on the owner alone.

But if one interest suffers loss by reason of damage or expense incurred on behalf of the whole venture (i.e. on behalf of all three interests), such loss must be averaged out over all three interests, and the other two must contribute compensations to the interest which has sustained loss, i.e. a general average assessment is made. (*See also* 11: **26**.)

General average contributions can only be claimed where:

(a) the danger was common to all, and was real danger, e.g. not a false alarm;

(b) the party claiming contribution must not have caused the danger;

(c) the interest against which contribution is claimed must have been saved.

22. The Athens Convention 1974
This Convention was enacted by the Merchant Shipping Act 1979, and provides, as from 10 November 1989, for limitations on a shipowner's liability.

Bills of lading

23. Bill of lading
This is a document signed by the master, the shipowner, or his agent, specifying the goods shipped and setting out the terms of carriage.
Such a document is a receipt, evidence of contract, and a document of title to the goods. A bill of lading is not a negotiable instrument, but does entitle the holder to delivery of the goods; and property in the goods passes to the transferee of a bill on indorsement of the bill to him.

24. Carriage of Goods by Sea Act 1971
This Act (based on the international Hague Rules) governs all bills of lading for the carriage of goods from any port in Great Britain or Northern Ireland.
The 1971 Act provides the following.

(a) There is no absolute warranty as to seaworthiness: s. 3.
(b) Bills governed by the Act must contain (*i*) particulars of identification of the goods (by 'leading marks' stamped upon them), (*ii*) the number of pieces shipped, (*iii*) the condition of the goods as they appear on inspection. This statement is evidence of their receipt in the stated condition.
The shipper is deemed to guarantee the accuracy of particulars furnished by him to the carrier.
(c) Statements as to apparent condition of goods refer only to external appearance, i.e. defects apparent on reasonable inspection.
(d) A bill of lading is *prima facie* evidence of receipt by the carrier of the stated goods, but the master's signature does not estop the owner from proving (*i*) that the goods were not in fact shipped, or (*ii*) that the owner's agent acted without authority — where this

happens the agent himself may be liable for breach of warranty of authority: *V/o Rasnoimport* v. *Guthrie and Co. Ltd* (1966).

(e) The Act implies that the shipowner will (*i*) use reasonable diligence to make the ship seaworthy, (*ii*) properly man and equip it, (*iii*) provide adequate hold storage, refrigeration plant, etc., and (*iv*) use reasonable care in loading and unloading, or that his agents will do so. (The burden of proving compliance with these requirements is on the shipowner.)

(f) Excepted perils. The shipowner is not liable for damage due to (*i*) negligence or default by the master, crew, etc., in navigating or managing the ship at sea (not in dock), (*ii*) fire, (*iii*) accidents of navigation, (*iv*) Act of God, (*v*) war, (*vi*) strikes and lock-outs, (*vii*) riots and civil commotion, (*viii*) saving life or property at sea, (*ix*) wastage due to inherent vice in the goods, (*x*) inadequate packing, or other fault of the consignor, (*xi*) latent defects not discoverable by careful inspection.

These exemptions only apply provided that loss is not occasioned by the negligence or default of the carrier or his servants or agents, including stevedores: *Leesh River Tea Co. Ltd* v. *British India S.N. Co. Ltd* (1966).

(g) The carrier cannot contract out of or reduce his liability under the Act. However, when the value of the goods is declared beforehand the carrier may limit his liability to 666.67 units of account per package or unit, or 2 units per kg, whichever is the higher. There are special provisions for containers. *See* the Merchant Shipping (Sterling Equivalents) (Various Enactments) (Amendment) Order 1986.

The defences given to the carrier are extended to his servants or agents. Neither he nor they are entitled to limit the damage if it resulted from acts *or* omissions done with intent to cause damage, or recklessly, and knowing damage would probably result.

Charterparties

25. Charterparties

A charterparty is a contract whereby a charterer hires a ship for the carriage of cargo on a particular voyage (a voyage charter) or for a period of time (a time charter). Possession of the ship and control of the crew usually remain with the owner, but occasionally the ship is completely leased to the charterer (a charter by demise), and he may provide his own crew.

A charterparty differs from a bill of lading in that it deals with the whole ship, while a bill does not.

26. Form of charterparty

It must be in writing and usually contains the following.

(a) A statement of the ship's tonnage (so that its cargo capacity can be assessed). A substantial inaccuracy in tonnage gives rise to a right of action for breach of warranty.

(b) A statement of the ship's whereabouts, which is a condition of the contract and if untrue entitles the charterer to repudiate the contract: *Behn* v. *Burness* (1863).

A charterparty may also contain a paramount clause, i.e. one which stipulates that the liability of the shipowner shall be limited in the manner provided by bills of lading covered by the Carriage of Goods by Sea Act 1971.

27. Usual terms

In a voyage charter the following terms are usually included.

(a) An undertaking by the owner that on the agreed date the ship will be seaworthy, fully provisioned and ready to sail when loaded to the agreed port of destination.

(b) An 'excepted perils' clause, protecting the owner from liability for loss caused by Act of God or the Queen's enemies, restraint of princes (interference by a foreign state), barratry (wilful default by the master, mutiny by the crew, etc.) and perils of the sea, e.g. natural disasters, storms, icebergs.

(c) An undertaking by the charterer to complete loading and unloading within a certain number of days (called 'lay days') and to pay compensation (called 'demurrage') for undue delay.

Sometimes the charterparty also provides that if the charterer completes loading and unloading more quickly than agreed, the freight charge shall be reduced; the reduction is called dispatch money.

28. Shipowner's implied undertakings

The following undertakings by shipowners are implied by law in all charterparties.

(a) That the ship will be seaworthy. Damage to certain foodstuffs was found to be due to inadequate insulation. This meant that the vessel was 'uncargoworthy' and that this amounted to unseaworthiness: *Ben Line Steamers* v. *Pacific Steam Navigation Co.* (1989).

(b) That it will be ready to load and sail on the agreed dates (substantial delay may amount to breach of condition; trifling delay is merely breach of warranty).

(c) That the ship will not deviate from its route except for good cause, or as agreed in the contract. A time-chartered ship on a voyage from New Hampshire to Turkey was damaged when she went aground in the course of leaving a berth in the inner harbour at Boston to which she had diverted for bunkers and the refitting of a cargo boom. It was held that, as Boston was the usual bunkering on such a voyage, the deviation from the outer harbour where the bunkering took place was reasonable: *The Al Taha* (1990).

Good cause usually means where necessitated by (*i*) the safety of the ship, or (*ii*) for the purpose of saving life (not merely property).

29. Full and complete cargo

A charterparty sometimes binds the charterer to provide the ship with a full and complete cargo, i.e. as much as the ship can safely carry (excluding deck loading, unless otherwise agreed). If a particular quantity of cargo is agreed (usually measured in tons), the charterer discharges his obligation if he provides approximately that quantity, even though he fails to take all available space.

If the charterer fails to provide the agreed full and complete cargo, the shipowner (unless otherwise agreed) can:

(a) charge the charterer dead freight, i.e. damages for loss of revenue for the unoccupied space; *or*

(b) deviate from his route to collect supplementary cargo.

30. Cesser and lien clauses

These are usually inserted and provide the following.

(a) *Cesser clause*: the charterer's liability under the charterparty is to cease as soon as the agreed cargo is loaded.

(b) *Lien clause*: the master and owners are given a lien on the cargo for the unpaid freight and for demurrage charges.

Specimen questions

1. State the forms which bills of lading or charterparties may take, and mention what undertakings by the shipowner or carrier are implied in every contract of affreightment.

Explain what is meant by 'deviation' and state the effect thereof. In what circumstances is deviation allowable by statute or otherwise?

2. (*a*) Who is a 'common carrier' and how does his position in law differ from that of a 'private carrier'?

(*b*) Miss E contracted with G, a local removal man, that he move her furniture from London to Brighton. One of the conditions of the contract was that G would not be responsible for loss or damage by fire. During transit one of the removal men carelessly dropped a cigarette in the van. The van caught fire and Miss E's furniture was lost. Consider with reasons whether Miss E will be able to recover damages from G.

3. (*a*) What is a bill of lading and what are its functions? What is the legal effect of a statement in a bill of lading that the goods are 'in apparent good order and condition'?

(*b*) What provisions are implied in a bill of lading to which the Carriage of Goods by Sea Act 1971 applies?

4. The K Shipping Co. agreed to carry a cargo of pig iron for the J Co. from the UK to Australia. It was within the terms of the charterparty that the ship should call at a port in the Island of Rebellia. Upon approaching that island, the ship's captain was warned by a radio message from Rebellia that there was a revolution in progress, and that shipping should avoid the port. The captain nevertheless entered the harbour whereupon the vessel was seized by the rebels. When it was released six months later the voyage was continued. At the time of delivery of the cargo at Sydney, the price of pig iron having fallen heavily, J Co. made much less profit on the sale of it there than they would have made but for the delay.

Consider the rights of J Co.

11
Insurance

Nature of insurance

1. Nature of insurance

A contract of insurance is one which has as its object indemnification of the insured against loss, or the payment of a sum of money to the insured or nominees on the happening of a stated event.

The document of contract is usually called a *policy*, and the person seeking to be insured is the *proposer*.

NOTE: (1) The insurance broker in the field of non-marine insurance is the agent of the insurer: *Stockton* v. *Mason* (1978). (2) The Unfair Contract Terms Act 1977 does not apply to contracts of insurance (*see* 2: 18). (3) Where an insurer makes a contract of insurance that he is not allowed by statute to make, the insured's only remedy is to claim the return of his premium since he cannot claim under the insurance policy: *Re Cavalier Insurance Co.* (1989).

2. Insurance not a wager

Distinguish carefully between an insurance contract (which is valid and enforceable) and a wager (which is void: *see* 4: 34).

(a) A wager is a contract to pay money on the ascertainment of some uncertain future event. What renders this void is that the parties have nothing to lose, apart from the money staked on the wager, e.g. a wager on the outcome of a horse race.

(b) An insurance contract is a contract to provide compensation to the insured in the event of him suffering some apprehended harm to some insurable interest, e.g. his property, or his health. Here the insured would suffer harm (to property or health) irrespective of the contract, and the contract is simply an attempt to provide him with compensation if the apprehended danger materialises.

(If the insured had no 'insurable interest,' the contract would be a wager and therefore void.)

3. Insurance is *uberrimae fidei*
The parties to any insurance contract must make full disclosure of all material facts at the time of contracting, otherwise the contract will be voidable by the other party.

This duty falls primarily on the proposer, who must disclose to the insurer all facts which might influence a prudent insurer whether to accept the risk or not, or whether to charge a higher premium. Thus a motorist proposing an accident insurance must disclose any previous motor accidents, and a householder proposing burglary insurance must disclose the true value of the property to be insured.

Failure to disclose such material facts (and any alterations in them subsequent to the making of the contract) entitles the insurer to avoid the contract. The insurer may even require the proposer to warrant the truth of immaterial matters, and breach of such warranty will then also render the contract voidable: *Roselodge Ltd* v. *Castle* (1966).

Examples _____

(1) In a mortgage application form, one of the clauses asked whether the applicant requested insurance cover. There was no separate proposal form; but one of the questions was: 'Are there any other matters which you wish to be taken into account?' The applicant answered in the negative. He did not disclose that he had several convictions including one for robbery, for which he had received twelve years' imprisonment. It was held that the applicant was obliged to disclose such facts as a reasonable or prudent insurer might have treated as material, and therefore to disclose his record for this could affect the moral hazard which the insurers had to assess. The absence of a proposal form did not modify that duty in any way. This meant that the insurance company could avoid the policy so far as it affected the applicant's interest: *Woolcott* v. *Sun Alliance and London Insurance Co.* (1978).

(2) In his insurance proposal form, a serving soldier based in army barracks gave as his occupation 'government service' and his parents' address as his postal address. This was held to be a material non-disclosure

which entitled the insurers to avoid the policy: *Mark* v. *West Yorkshire Insurance Co.* (1989).

(3) The owner of a hotel occasionally held discotheques on the hotel premises. He filled out an insurance policy saying 'no' to the question whether the premises were used for any other purposes than those of a hotel. It was held that, although the discotheque was a material fact which ought to have been disclosed, it was part and parcel of the whole hotel operations and there was therefore no need to disclose it in an answer to the question: *Roberts* v. *Plaisted* (1989).

(4) In a contract of insurance, there is an obligation of the utmost good faith on both parties: the duty on the insurer extends at least to disclosing all facts known to him which are material either to the risk sought to be insured or the recoverability of a claim under the policy which a prudent insured would take into account in deciding whether or not to place the risk for which he sought cover with the insurer: *Banque Financière de la Cité* v. *Westgate Insurance* (1990).

NOTE: Under the Rehabilitation of Offenders Act 1974 those convicted of certain offences can, where the appropriate time has passed, deny on an insurance form that they have been convicted of such an offence.

4. Double insurance

If the insured takes out simultaneous policies against the same risk, so providing insurance beyond the extent of his potential loss, he can still recover only the amount of his actual loss.

Thus if X's house is worth £100,000 and he takes out two fire policies (each for £100,000) with two different insurers, he still cannot recover more than the amount of his real loss if the house is destroyed by fire, i.e. a maximum of £100,000. But he can choose which insurer to call upon, and the insurer who pays out on the policy is then entitled to contribution from the other.

Example ─────────────────────────────────

In one case, the insured had his car insured under policies with different insurers. When the insured was later involved in an accident, the resulting claim was settled by one of the insurance companies. This company learned of the other policy and claimed a 50 per cent contribution from the other company. The latter resisted the claim on the ground that the insured had not given notice of any claim within the stipulated time, it had a good defence to any claim made by the insured and was therefore not liable to make a contribution. It was held that,

although the second company would not have been liable to contribute
if it had avoided the policy at the time of the accident, the fact that the
insured had chosen only to seek an indemnity from it did not absolve the
second company from its liability to contribute, and it was irrelevant that
the latter would have had a defence if a claim had been brought by the
insured. The first company was therefore entitled to a 50 per cent
contribution: *Legal & General Assurance Society Ltd* v. *Drake Insurance Co.
Ltd* (1989).

Life insurance

5. The contract of life insurance
This is a contract under which the insurer promises to pay a
stated sum upon the death of the person whose life is insured.

The consideration for the insurer's promise is the payment by,
or on behalf of, the insured of certain sums called premiums.

NOTE: (1) *Insurable interest.* The contract is void unless the
proposer has an insurable interest in the life insured: Life Assurance
Act 1774 (LAA), s. 1. A person has an insurable interest in his own
life, and the following have insurable interests in each other's lives:
(*i*) husband and wife, (*ii*) employer and employee, (*iii*) creditor and
debtor (and guarantor). But there is no insurable interest between
parents and children, brothers and sisters, etc., unless the person
seeking the insurance is financially dependent on the person whose
life is insured. (2) The name of the person who is to receive the
moneys payable under the policy must be inserted in it: LAA., s. 2.
A policy taken out by a husband or wife, and designated as being for
the benefit of his or her spouse, creates a trust of the moneys payable,
so that the moneys payable are not liable to death duties on the death
of the insured: Married Women's Property Act 1882, s. 11. (3) *Suicide
of insured.* If the insured commits suicide while sane the sum assured
by the policy is irrecoverable: *Beresford* v. *Royal Insurance* (1938). But
since the Suicide Act 1961, suicide is no longer a crime and so no
question of public policy arises. Insurers may still reject a claim since
the risk does not cover loss due to the wilful act of the insured, unless
the policy expressly so provides. So insurers may still reject a sane
suicide, unless the policy otherwise provides. If the insured commits
suicide while of unsound mind, the policy moneys are recoverable
(unless the contract provides otherwise). (4) *Profiting under policy from
own crime.* It is a rule of public policy that a wrongdoer cannot profit
from his own crime. In one case, the defendant purchased a house

with another whom he subsequently murdered. The house was purchased subject to a mortgage, and the loan was secured on an endowment policy taken out on the lives of the defendant and the deceased. The building society claimed under the policy and applied the proceeds to pay off the mortgage. The question arose as to whether the defendant was entitled to the amount representing his share of the net proceeds. It was held that, since the defendant was claiming under a fund which would not have come into existence but for his criminal act, he was barred by the rule of public policy from benefiting from his own criminal act. It was also held that, as no valid claim could have been made under the insurance policy by the defendant, the personal representatives of the deceased were the persons to whom the equity of redemption in the insurance policy belonged. This meant that they were to be treated as having provided the policy proceeds that were applied by the building society in repayment of the mortgage, and were as a result entitled to claim a contribution from the defendant: *Davitt* v. *Titcumb* (1989).

6. Assignment of life policies

A life policy may be assigned either by delivery and endorsement of the policy, or by delivery with an accompanying instrument of assignment.

Written notice of the assignment must be given to the insurer, who must acknowledge receipt thereof: Policies of Assurance Act 1867, s. 3. Where are competing claims, the date of receipt by the insurer of the notice of assignment regulates all questions of priority of the competing claims: P.A.A. 1867, s. 6.

As with other assignments of choses in action, the assignee takes his assignment subject to equities arising before receipt of notice by the insurer. The assignee can sue in his own name to enforce the policy.

NOTE: It appears that a person may take out a policy on his own life, and then assign it to another who has no insurable interest, without invalidating the policy. Thus the assignee of a policy, who has no insurable interest, may still be able to enforce it: for this reason life policies can be assigned as securities — *see* below.

7. Assignment by way of mortgage

A life policy can be used as security for a loan (e.g. by a bank). The methods by which this can be achieved are as follows.

(a) *Legal assignment to the creditor* (who must then give the notice to the insurer required by the P.A.A. 1867).

> NOTE: (1) The assignment must be under seal. (2) The assignee can sue in his own name. (3) The insurer holds the policy moneys for the benefit of the assignee. (4) The assignee gains priority from the date of registration.

(b) *Equitable assignment to the creditor*, by deposit of the policy plus a memorandum of the reasons for deposit. On redemption of a legal mortgage of a policy, the mortgagee reassigns the policy to the mortgagor. When an equitable mortgage is redeemed, no formal reassignment is necessary: the lender merely cancels the memorandum of deposit and returns the policy.

8. Life policies as securities

They have several advantages and disadvantages as securities.

Advantages

(a) Methods of mortgaging are simple;
(b) the surrender value of the policy is increased by each payment of premium, so that the value of the security will appreciate as long as premiums are paid;
(c) the policy can be realised immediately (if, for instance, the insured fails to pay his premiums when due) by surrender to the insurer;
(d) death of the insured makes the moneys assured immediately available.

Disadvantages

(a) The mortgagee is to some extent at the mercy of the person paying the premiums, and his default may invalidate the policy;
(b) the insurer may be able to avoid the policy if the proposer failed to disclose all material facts;
(c) suicide of the insured may invalidate the policy;
(d) the policy may contain provision for avoidance by the insurer on breach of various covenants by the insured.

Fire insurance

9. The contract

A contract of fire insurance is one providing for indemnification of the insured up to a certain amount in the event of injury or loss by fire, caused to a specified property during a specified time.

The insured can only recover for actual loss: *Castellain* v. *Preston* (1883).

The proposer must have an insurable interest in the property insured: Life Assurance Act 1774, s. 1. Owners, tenants, trustees and mortgagees have insurable interests, but a shareholder in a company has no insurable interest in the property of the company.

> NOTE: To discourage people setting fire to their own property in order to get insurance money, the Fire Prevention (Metropolis) Act 1774, s. 83 provides that any person interested in the property (such as a tenant, mortgagee, etc.) can compel the insured to use the money in repairing and reinstating the damaged premises.

10. Average clauses

A fire policy often contains an average clause which provides that the insured can only recover such proportion of the loss caused by fire as the value of the policy bears to the value of the property insured.

Thus, if property worth £150,000 is insured for only £75,000 and fire damage is caused to the extent of £75,000, the insurer can refuse to pay more than half this amount.

11. Subrogation

On payment of all moneys due under the policy, the insurer is entitled to be subrogated to the rights of the insured, i.e. to pursue any remedies available to the insured in contract or tort in respect of the loss. Thus if the fire was caused by the negligence of X, the insurer (after paying out on the policy) could sue X for his negligence.

If the insured forestalls this right of subrogation by discharging or waiving any claim against such third parties, the insurer is likewise discharged from liability under the policy to the same extent: *Phoenix Assurance Co.* v. *Spooner* (1905).

Subrogation is only available where the insurer has paid the whole claim of the insured, and any action can only be brought in the name of the insured.

12. Excepted perils

Risks covered include loss by fire (even though caused by the insured's own negligence, but not if caused by his wilful default), and loss occasioned by a fire brigade in putting out the fire.

Excepted perils include riot, civil commotion, war, explosion, and sometimes Act of God.

A policy will not cover consequential loss (such as loss of profits of a business), unless expressly so agreed.

Accident, burglary and other forms of insurance

13. The contract

The same general rules apply as with life and fire insurance. Note that burglary insurance is a form of indemnity insurance (i.e. compensation for actual loss), while accident insurance is often lump-sum insurance (i.e. stipulating for the payment of a lump sum on the occurrence of a specified event).

Policies in this class usually provide that notice of the burglary, accident, etc. must be given to the insurer within a specified time, failing which the insurer may be discharged from liability: *Re Williams & Thomas* (1909).

14. Burglary insurance

The policy usually provides cover against house-breaking and theft from the premises insured. Cover is restricted to the premises agreed.

15. Accident policies

These usually provide for the payment of a lump sum in the event of death by accident, and of smaller sums in other eventualities. Provision may also be made for payment of weekly sums during disability, sickness, etc.

The policy usually covers only accidents (or sickness) to the insured alone, though other persons may be included if so desired.

(a) *Accidents to the insured.* Cover is for personal injury or death, caused by chance or by the negligent or intentional act of any third person, e.g. assault. It will not cover injuries deliberately self-inflicted.

(b) *Accidents to third parties* (e.g. to passengers in the insured person's car, or a visitor to his premises etc.). Such cover gives the injured person a right to sue the insurer for the sum assured if

(*i*) the insured becomes bankrupt, or makes any composition with his creditors, *or*

(*ii*) is a company which goes into liquidation. Otherwise only the insured can sue: Third Parties (Rights against Insurers) Act 1930.

NOTE: All motorists must be insured against injury to third parties and in addition passengers must be covered by the driver's insurance (even if they have agreed to travel at their 'own risk'): Road Traffic Act 1988. A person injured by a car who obtains judgment against the motorist can recover the damages awarded in that action from the motorist's insurer: Road Traffic Act 1988, ss. 151–153. In such policies, restrictions on the insurer's liability because of the age or condition of the assured or of the car (provided the car is roadworthy), or of the load carried, are void.

The Motor Insurer's Bureau (MIB) — established in 1946 following an agreement with the Ministry of Transport, and consisting of virtually every insurer transacting motor insurance — satisfies judgments in respect of claims within the scope of the Road Traffic Acts where the injured party has been unable to claim damages: *see Limbrick* v. *French & Farley* (1989). By an extension to the agreement in 1968, the MIB also covers victims of hit-and-run drivers. The Green Card system is an international extension of the concept behind MIB.

Marine insurance

16. The contract

This is a contract whereby the insurer (underwriter) promises to indemnify the insured against loss caused by maritime perils: Marine Insurance Act (MIA) 1906, s. 1.

Maritime perils means perils at sea, but the policy may be extended to cover inland navigation: MIA, s. 2.

17. Insurable interest
The insured must have an insurable interest in the vessel, or in the maritime venture at the time of the loss: s. 5.

Persons having insurable interests include mortgagees of a ship, lenders of money on security of the ship and/or freight ('bottomry'), or on the security of the cargo ('respondentia'), the master and crew to the extent of their wages, the owners of the ship, cargo, etc., and the underwriter himself (who can thus re-insure against his own risk as insurer).

18. Duty of disclosure
The contract, like all insurance contracts, is *uberrimae fidei* and full disclosure must be made of facts which materially affect the risk.

Matters need not be disclosed if: (*a*) they diminish the risk, or (*b*) are waived, or (*c*) may be deemed to be known in the ordinary course of trade.

Where the contract is made by an agent, he must disclose all facts which are known (or should be known) to his principal.

19. Kinds of policy

(a) *Voyage policies*, to insure for a voyage from one place to another, i.e. a particular voyage.

(b) *Time policies*, which provide cover for a stated period. (This must not be longer than twelve months, subject to any renewals at the end of the twelve months.)

(c) *Mixed policies*, i.e. a combination of voyage and time cover.

(d) *Valued policies*, where the value insured is specified.

(e) *Unvalued policies*, where the value insured is not specified but is left open for assessment in accordance with customary usage if the occasion arises.

(f) *Floating policies*, where the name of the ship is left blank so that the policy is available for any ship owned by the insured.

(g) *Open cover*. This is not an actual insurance policy, but a contract to issue a policy at a given time or on the occurrence of a particular event.

(h) *Re-insurance*, where the underwriter himself insures against his own liability under a marine insurance policy.

20. Measure of indemnity

The assured can only recover for actual loss. If the loss is total, he is entitled to the maximum sum assured by the policy whatever that may be.

In the case of partial loss the position is as follows.

(a) *Partial loss to ship.* The insured can recover the cost of repairs, or the amount of depreciation if the ship is not repaired.

(b) *Partial loss of goods.* The insured can recover the value of goods lost, or if the policy is a valued policy the loss calculated as a proportion of the total amount assured.

21. Warranties

In marine insurance the word 'warranty' is largely used in the same sense as the word 'condition' in ordinary contracts, and means that the assured undertakes absolutely that something shall be done or some requirement fulfilled, or affirms or denies the existence of particular facts.

Such a warranty must be exactly complied with, otherwise the policy will be avoided: MIA 1906, s. 33.

Warranties may be expressed or implied by the 1906 Act.

Example

A contract of marine insurance contained a warranty to the effect that no vessel would enter a prohibited zone. A vessel did so in breach of warranty. It was ruled that, in policies of marine insurance, it was settled that any statement of fact bearing on the risk introduced into the written policy was to be construed as a warranty and that compliance with that warranty was a condition precedent to the attaching of the risk. This meant that if the warranty was not complied with the insurer was discharged from liability as from the date of the breach of the warranty. In the present case, this meant that, once the vessel had entered the prohibited zone in breach of warranty, it was uninsured: *Bank of Nova Scotia* v. *Hellenic Mutual* (1991).

22. Implied warranties

(a) In a voyage policy (*i*) that the ship shall be seaworthy at the start of the voyage: s. 39, (*ii*) that the ship is normally fit to carry any goods insured: s. 40.

(b) Generally, (*i*) that the adventure is legal: s. 41, (*ii*) if cover is granted for the ship in port, that she shall be reasonably fit to meet the hazards of the port: s. 39.

(There are no implied warranties covering (*i*) the nationality of the ship, or (*ii*) the seaworthiness of a ship covered by a time policy, or (*iii*) that goods insured are seaworthy.)

23. Premiums
These must normally be paid before the policy is issued, and are returnable as and when agreed, or where the policy is void for any reason, or where in an unvalued policy the venture has been over-insured: s. 84.

24. Risks covered
These include all the normal risks of sea journeys, loss from fire, pirates or thieves, barratry (wilful misconduct by master or crew), and collision (up to three-quarters of the damage sustained).

The insurers are only bound to compensate for direct loss, and consequential loss (e.g. loss of profits) requires express cover.

25. Loss may be total or partial
Total loss may be either actual or constructive.

(a) *Actual.* The property covered is destroyed or is so changed as to have changed its character entirely, or where the assured is deprived of its use. (Actual loss may be presumed if a ship is missing for an unreasonable time, and no information can be obtained as to its whereabouts).

(b) *Constructive.* The property covered is reasonably abandoned in circumstances which make it appear that total loss is inevitable, e.g. where the crew leaves a sinking ship, of which no more is heard.

(Where there is constructive total loss, the insured may treat it as partial loss if he wishes, or may relinquish his property to the insurer who may salvage it if possible. In the latter case he must give notice of abandonment to the insurer, and acceptance of such notice is conclusive evidence that the insurer admits liability.)

26. General average loss
Where a general average loss has occurred, the assured may recover the total value assured from the insurer who may then (by

subrogation) recover his due contribution from the other parties' liability.

(For meaning of 'general average', *see* 10: **21**.)

27. Assignment of policy
Unless prohibited by the contract, a marine policy can be assigned by indorsement: s. 50. The assignment is subject to equities in the normal way. It may be made either before or after loss.

28. Discharge of insurer
In a voyage policy the insurer is automatically discharged if the ship (*a*) sails from a port other than specified in the policy, or (*b*) deviates unreasonably from the scheduled route (in which case discharge dates from the time of deviation).

Deviation is excused (*a*) where authorised by the policy, or (*b*) where for the purpose of saving life (not property), or (*c*) where necessary to obtain medical aid for any person aboard the ship, or (*d*) where necessary for the safety of the ship, or (*e*) otherwise where caused by circumstances beyond the control of the master or his employer.

State supervision

29. Insurance Companies Act
A company is not able to start an insurance business unless authorised by the Secretary of State for Trade and Industry under the Insurance Companies Act 1982 or unless exempted under the Act. A person authorised under that Act is also counted as an authorised investment business under the terms of the Financial Services Act 1986. An insurance company with its head office in the UK must possess the standard solvency margin. The 1982 Act lays down detailed regulations for companies to deposit accounts and statements of their business with the Secretary of State, to apply assets relating to long-term business alone thereto, and a number of other matters designed to prevent or give warning of insolvency. The Act also provides for a cooling-off period in relation to long-term policies. Those who work as Lloyd's brokers are subject to the regime provided by the Lloyd's Acts 1871–1982.

30. Policyholders' protection

If an insurance company fails, the Policyholders' Protection Board, appointed under the Policyholders' Protection Act 1975, takes over. The Board is financed by levies on insurance companies authorised to conduct business in the UK under the Insurance Companies Act 1982. The Board ensures that insured persons are not left without cover.

31. Brokers

These are required to be registered under the Insurance Brokers (Registration) Act 1975. If not registered, a business commits an offence if it describes itself as an 'insurance broker', or if it indicates in any way that it is registered.

Specimen questions

1. Explain the expression 'insurable interest' in connection with a contract of marine insurance; and state what persons possess an insurable interest in such a contract.

2. (*a*) What is the nature of a contract created by a fire insurance policy?
   (*b*) A is insured with several companies in respect of the same property to an amount exceeding the value of the property. In the event of a loss through fire what are the rights of A and the insurance companies?

3. Adam made a proposal to an insurance company for an insurance on his life for £50,000. On the proposal form he answered various questions truthfully and disclosed all relevant facts. A few days later, but before the proposal was definitely accepted, Adam was taken ill with pneumonia. Subsequently the company accepted the proposal and the first premium was paid. Two days later Adam died of pneumonia and the company learned for the first time of his illness. Is the company liable to pay the £50,000?

4. (*a*) What is meant by a warranty in a contract of marine

insurance? How does it differ from a warranty in a contract for the sale of goods?

(*b*) What warranties are implied in a contract of marine insurance?

5. In respect of a contract of insurance explain what is meant by
   (*a*) an insurable interest;
   (*b*) subrogation.

Give examples of the former and illustrate the operation of the latter by reference to a set of facts which you may devise for this purpose.

6. Give an account of the statutory control of the insurance market.

12
Bailment

Nature and kinds of bailment

1. Definition of bailment

A bailment is a delivery of goods by one person to another for some limited purpose, on condition that when the purpose has been accomplished the goods shall be returned.

The bailment may be simple or exclusive. In an *exclusive bailment* the bailee (i.e. the person to whom the goods are bailed) can during the continuance of the bailment retain the goods against anyone, including the bailor, e.g. a pledge or pawn of goods: *see* 15: **9**. In a *simple bailment* the bailee can defend his possession against anyone, except the bailor.

2. Duties of bailee

These are defined by common law, though the duties of an 'involuntary bailee' are now regulated by the Unsolicited Goods and Services Acts 1971 and 1975: *see* **3** below.

(a) *To take reasonable care of the goods* bailed to him. If goods are lost or damaged the onus is on the bailee to prove that he did exercise reasonable care, irrespective of whether the bailment was for reward or was gratuitous: *Houghland* v. *R. R. Low (Luxury Coaches) Ltd* (1962).

(b) *To return the goods* in accordance with the contract. If he fails to do so, he is liable for loss or damage notwithstanding the exercise of reasonable care. If he entrusts goods to a servant who steals them, the bailee is liable in conversion to the bailor: *Shaw & Co.* v. *Symmons & Sons Ltd* (1917).

(Contracts of bailment frequently contain a clause restricting the duty of care or excluding it, but if the bailee returns the goods to the wrong person he has no protection from such a clause: *Alexander* v. *Rly Executive* (1951), and *see* **5** below.)

NOTE: (1) The burden of proving exercise of reasonable care is on the bailee. Therefore if he has lost the goods or they are damaged when returned, it is for the bailee to prove that loss or damage was not due to his negligence. (2) If goods are lost or damaged while in his custody, and the bailee cannot show how this happened, he is liable: *Houghland* v. *R. R. Low Ltd* (1962); *Levison* v. *Patent Steam Carpet Cleaning Co. Ltd* (1977); *Port Swettenham Authority* v. *T. W. Wu & Co.* (1978); *Mitchell* v. *London Borough of Ealing* (1978). (3) If goods are lost while in his custody it is not enough for the bailee to show that he was reasonably careful to protect them; he must show also that he made reasonable efforts to recover them: *Coldman* v. *Hill* (1919). (4) The bailee is liable for the negligence or dishonesty of his servants, if he did not use reasonable care in selecting them, e.g. where he entrusts goods bailed to a known thief: *Williams* v. *Curzon Syndicate Ltd* (1919). But he is not generally liable for wrongs committed by his independent contractors, or by servants if he can show he was reasonably careful in his selection of them. (5) If the bailee professes a particular skill, he is liable if he fails to exercise that skill, even if the bailment is gratuitous: *Wilson* v. *Brett* (1843). (6) The bailee is not liable for loss or damage occasioned by Act of God (inevitable and unforeseeable accident), robbery with violence, or war. (7) Where there is no express contract between the parties, the duties of the bailee arise from the law of tort: *Chesworth* v. *Farrar* (1966). (8) A bailee's duty to guard against possible loss includes a duty to take reasonable care to prevent damage to the bailed property by the deliberate act of a third party: *Lockspeiser Aircraft* v. *Brooklands Aircraft* (1990). (9) Once a bailor's claim for damages has been settled, a bailee cannot pursue any additional claim. The owner of a car obtained damages when it was damaged. A second party who had the authority of the owner to use the car, and was therefore a bailee, also claimed for damages for loss of use. This further claim was rejected: *O'Sullivan* v. *Williams* (1992).

3. Involuntary bailees

By the Unsolicited Goods and Services Acts 1971 and 1975, where a person becomes an involuntary bailee, e.g. has unsolicited goods delivered to him by post, so that he cannot easily refuse to take delivery, the following rules apply.

(a) The goods become the property of the recipient:
    (*i*) after 30 days, if he has served notice on the sender with a demand for removal of the goods, *or*
    (*ii*) after six months, if no notice has been given to the sender.
(b) These rules do not apply if the goods were sent for the purposes of the recipient's trade or business.

It is illegal to present an invoice for goods known to be solicited.

4.   Duty of bailor

In the case of a gratuitous bailment, a bailor is under a duty to disclose any defect in the goods of which he is aware: *Coughlin* v. *Gillison* (1899). It may be that he is also under a duty to take reasonable steps to ensure that the goods are safe and must disclose defects of which he ought reasonably to be aware: *Griffiths* v. *Arch Engineering* (1968).

In the case of a contract for hire, the Supply of Goods and Services Act 1982 implies terms as to merchantable quality and fitness for purpose which apply to contracts for the sale of goods, as well as identical provisions as to description and sample: *see* Chapter 9. The 1982 Act also implies a condition on the part of the bailor that he has a right to transfer possession, and also implies a warranty as to quiet possession. Under the Unfair Contract Terms Act 1977, none of these implied terms can be excluded or restricted, except that, in business-to-business contracts, the terms relating to merchantable quality, fitness for purpose, description and sample can be excluded or restricted subject to the requirement of reasonableness.

5.   Particular contracts

The bailee may by express terms seek to exclude liability for negligence, particularly in bailments for reward. Such terms must be clear and unambiguous and are generally construed against the bailee as far as possible, under the *contra proferentem* rule: *Morris* v. *C. W. Martin & Sons Ltd* (1965); *Levison* v. *Patent Steam Carpet Cleaning Co. Ltd* (1977).

Thus the bailee loses the protection of such exemption clauses if he breaks the contract in some other way, e.g. by delivering goods to the wrong person: *Alexander* v. *Rly Executive* (1951).

Examples _____

(1) If the bailment is a contract for personal service, the bailee loses the protection of exemption clauses if he breaks his contract by delegating performance to another, e.g. where a laundry accepted articles 'at owner's risk entirely' and then delivered them for cleaning to another firm which lost them: *Davies* v. *Collins* (1945).

(2) The bailee is liable if he deviates from the contract, and cannot then rely on exemption clauses, e.g. where he undertakes to store goods at a certain warehouse but in fact warehouses them elsewhere and they are lost: *Lilley* v. *Doubleday* (1881).

(3) The bailee also loses the benefit of exemption clauses if he or his agent misrepresents the effect of the clauses: *Curtis* v. *Chemical Cleaning & Dyeing Co.* (1951).

_____

6. Bailee's power of sale

A bailee cannot sell or otherwise dispose of goods bailed unless:

(a) the contract so provides; *or*

(b) a right of sale is conferred by statute.

Otherwise if he sells goods bailed he is liable for damages for the tort of conversion, i.e. converting to his own use and disposition goods to which another is entitled.

A statutory power of sale of uncollected goods is given by the Innkeepers Act 1878, and the Torts (Interference with Goods) Act 1977.

For the 1977 Act to apply, the goods must be in the control or possession of the bailee, where:

(a) the bailor is obliged to take delivery or could give directions as to their delivery; *or*

(b) the bailee could impose such an obligation, but cannot trace or communicate with the bailor; *or*

(c) the bailee can reasonably expect to be relieved of any duty to safeguard the goods on giving notice, but cannot trace or communicate with the bailor.

The Act makes special provision for goods accepted for repair or other treatment, goods accepted for valuation or appraisal, and the storage, warehousing and the like, of goods.

If the bailor fails to collect his goods after the prescribed notice has been given (or after the bailee has made reasonable attempts, but failed, to give such notice) the bailee may sell the goods. He must account over to the bailor less the costs of sale and sums outstanding.

7.   Types of bailment

(a) *Deposit (depositum)* means goods are deposited for safe custody, e.g. in a cloakroom. The bailee cannot use the goods and must (subject to any terms of the contract) exercise reasonable care of them while in his possession. He must return them to the bailor, and no exemption clause will protect him if he delivers them to the wrong person: *Alexander* v. *Rly Executive* (1951).

(b) *Loan for use (commodatum)*. The bailee is entitled to use the goods loaned and is not liable for fair wear and tear unless he deviates from the conditions of the loan.

(c) *Hire (locatio rei)*. The bailee must take reasonable care of the goods and use them in accordance with the terms of the contract. He is not liable for loss by robbery, accidental fire occasioned without negligence, etc. In a hire for reward the owner cannot usually reclaim the goods save in accordance with the terms of the contract, i.e. the bailment is exclusive.

Hiring is automatically determined (even in hire-purchase contracts) if the hirer attempts to sell the goods: *Helby* v. *Matthews* (1895). For bailor's duties, *see* **4** above.

(d) *Innkeepers*. They are bailees of their guests' luggage in certain circumstances: *see* **8** and **9** below.

(e) *Deposit for work to be done (locatio operis faciendi)*, e.g. deposit for repair or alteration. The bailee must take care of the goods and hand them to the true owner or his agent when requested, but he has a lien over the goods for his charges and need not return them until his charges are paid.

(f) *Pawn or pledge (vadium)* of chattels as security for a loan: see **15: 9**.

(g) *A consumer hire agreement*. This is an agreement capable of lasting for more than three months and where the rental does not exceed £15,000: Consumer Credit Act 1974, s. 15. Various formalities attach to such agreements. The hirer (the bailee) also has the right to terminate most agreements after 18 months: s. 101.

NOTE: A hire-purchase agreement is *not* a consumer hire agreement.

8. Innkeepers and guests
A hotel or innkeeper is one who holds himself out as ready to receive all travellers who:

(a) are willing to pay a reasonable price for accommodation offered; *and*
(b) come in a condition fit to be received: Hotel Proprietors Act 1956, s. 1.

An innkeeper must accept all travellers provided he has enough room and they are willing to pay and are in a reasonably fit condition to be received. Failure to accept bona fide travellers renders him liable to an action for damages: *Browne* v. *Brandt* (1902), and possibly to prosecution.

Any person is a traveller who calls for a meal or a drink: *Williams* v. *Linnitt* (1951). But he is only entitled to protection for his luggage if he stays to take sleeping accommodation.

9. Innkeepers' liability
The inn or hotel keeper is an insurer of his guests' luggage (but not of their pet animals, cars, etc.), and can only evade liability for loss or damage by showing that it was caused by: (*a*) Act of God, (*b*) war, (*c*) guest's own negligence (though leaving luggage in an unlocked room is not usually such negligence: *Brewster* v. *Drennan* (1945)), or (*d*) inherent vice in the goods themselves.

By the Hotel Proprietors Act 1956, the innkeeper's liability is restricted to £50 for any one article or a total of £100 for any one guest, unless:

(a) loss or damage was caused by the wilful default or negligence of the innkeeper or his servants; or
(b) the goods were expressly deposited with the innkeeper for safe custody in some place specially provided, e.g. the hotel safe.

A notice of these restrictions on liability must be given to the guest before or at the time of registering (when the contract is made), and a notice placed in the room is therefore inadequate: *Olley* v. *Marlborough Court Hotel* (1949). Such notice must be prominently displayed at or near the reception office and/or in the main hall of the hotel. If not so displayed the innkeeper loses the protection of the 1956 Act.

10. Innkeepers' lien

The innkeeper has a right to retain all a guest's luggage for non-payment of his charges. The lien does not extend to things over which the innkeeper owes no duty of care, e.g. the guest's car or pet animals.

The lien is lost if the guest is allowed to remove the goods; there is no power to detain the guest himself.

By the Innkeepers Act 1878, the hotelier is given a statutory right to sell such goods as are subject to his lien, and reimburse himself for his charges out of the proceeds of sale. The right to sell becomes exercisable when the goods have been retained for six weeks; and one month's notice of the sale must be given to the guest to give him a final chance to pay the bill.

Specimen questions

1.   To what extent is the borrower of goods loaned to him for use under a duty to take care of the goods?

B deposited a motor van with a firm of garage proprietors for sale on commission upon the terms of a printed document which stated that 'customers' vehicles are driven by our staff at customers' sole risk.' While the van was being demonstrated to a prospective buyer, it was damaged through the negligence of one of the staff. Discuss the legal position.

2.   Explain the nature of a bailment. Mention three forms which bailment may take, and explain the nature of the consideration which will support a contract of bailment.

B contracted to warehouse D's furniture at B's depository in Chelsea, but B warehoused a part of the furniture at a depository in Fulham. The furniture warehouse at Fulham was destroyed by fire. Discuss the legal position.

3.   (a)   Define the term 'bailee.' What are the duties of a bailee of goods?

   (b)   Fred has received an unsolicited parcel of goods from

Inertia Sales Ltd. Fred has written to Inertia Sales Ltd informing them that he does not wish to buy the goods sent and that he wishes them to be removed from his premises as soon as possible.

For six weeks Fred did not hear from Inertia Sales Ltd and eventually decided to sell the goods.

Now Fred has received a letter from Inertia Sales Ltd demanding payment and threatening legal proceedings if the payment is not made by return of post.

Advise Fred.

Would your answer be different if Fred had not written to Inertia Sales Ltd requiring them to remove the goods?

4. What duties are imposed on a bailor as to the quality of the goods he supplies?

13
Arbitration and awards

Arbitration

1. Reference to arbitration

Arbitration in mercantile disputes is now mainly governed by the Arbitration Act (AA) 1950, the Arbitration Act 1975 and the Arbitration Act 1979. A dispute may be referred to arbitration in the following ways.

(a) *By order of the court.* The Rules of the Supreme Court provide that the court may refer settlement of disputes to official referees, Masters of the Court, registrars, district judges, etc. The reference may relate to a specified issue (e.g. the costs in an action before the court), or to the whole dispute. Reference by the court usually occurs in cases where some special technical or local knowledge is required, and all the parties consent to the dispute going before a specially qualified arbitrator.

(b) *By certain statutes* which may provide that disputes arising under the statute are to be settled by arbitration. The statute may then lay down special rules for the conduct of the arbitration (otherwise the Arbitration Act 1950 will normally apply).

(c) *By consent of the parties*, out of court, e.g. under an arbitration clause in a contract. An arbitration agreement is a *'written agreement to submit present or future differences to arbitration, whether an arbitrator is named therein or not'*: AA, 1950, s. 32. An agreement to submit to arbitration is not an exclusion clause: Unfair Contract Terms Act 1977, s. 13. Oral agreements are valid but are not covered by the Arbitration Acts.

(Contrast a valuation, which is made before any dispute arises and in order to forestall disagreement.)

(d) *The Arbitration Act 1975* provides for the recognition of arbitration agreements with an international element, and the consequent staying of court proceedings concerning disputes which should be arbitrated, and the recognition and enforcement in the UK of arbitral awards made in other countries party to the New York Convention on the Recognition of Foreign Arbitral Awards. For the position where an English court is the enforcing court of the country whose law applies, *see Hiscox* v. *Outhwaite (No. 1)* (1991).

2. Arbitration agreements

If in a contract there is an arbitration clause, the court may stay any proceedings respecting the agreement and refer the dispute to arbitration: 1950 Act, s. 4 and 1975 Act, s. 1.

The court may stay proceedings in the following circumstances:

(a) If the dispute is within the scope of the arbitration clause.

(b) If the applicant has not in any way consented to proceedings being brought before the court, e.g. by filing a defence.

(c) Where the applicant is willing to do anything necessary to assist arbitration.

(d) Where the contract stipulates that no right of action is to accrue under the contract until the arbitration procedure described therein has been resorted to: *Scott* v. *Avery* (1856).

(e) If there is no reason in the interests of justice to refuse the application.

(f) Where an order for summary judgment is sought under RSC Order 14, and the relevant contract includes an arbitration clause, it is all the more necessary that a stay should be granted and that full-scale argument in the Order 14 proceedings should not be permitted. In the case of a commercial arbitration, this will be even more the case, especially when the dispute turns on construction, or the implication of terms or trade practice, since arbitrators in the same business or trade are as well or better able than the court to judge what was intended by the particular words or phrases: *Home Insurance* v. *Mentor Insurance* (1989).

(g) Where one party ignored a court order to pay a sum into court to secure the amount in dispute in an arbitration, the court has the power to order a permanent stay of his claim in the arbitration:

Richco International Ltd v. *International Industrial Food Co. SARL* (1989).

Example _____

(1) An action was brought alleging fraud, and the defendant sought a stay of proceedings to have the matter referred to arbitration under the terms of the agreement. This was opposed by the plaintiffs. The Court of Appeal ruled that where a party alleging fraud opposed a stay, and the party accused of fraud wished to proceed to arbitration, the allegation of fraud was not by itself sufficient reason for the court to oppose the stay. Instead, the court had a discretion dependent on all the circumstances of the case. Since the parties had agreed, without reservation, that disputes between them should go to arbitration, and since the plaintiffs' wish to proceed with their action was not a sufficient reason for refusing a stay, a stay would be granted so that the matter could be referred to arbitration: *Cunningham-Reid* v. *Buchanan-Jardine* (1988)

(2) *See also Home & Overseas Insurance Co. Ltd* v. *Mentor Insurance Co.* (1989) where the Court of Appeal ruled that, where there is an arbitration clause, the court should not, on an application made to it prior to the arbitration, permit full-scale argument on the terms of the agreement between the parties, since the parties have agreed on their chosen tribunal and the defendant is entitled *prima facie* to have the dispute decided by that tribunal in the first instance.

NOTE: Reasons for refusing the application (Arbitration Act 1950, s. 24) include (*i*) suspected bias of the arbitrator, e.g. where he is an associate or relative of one of the parties to the dispute, (*ii*) the fact that allegations of fraud are being made against one of the parties to the dispute, (*iii*) the fact that the dispute involves a point of law and is therefore best left to the court.

Example _____

A dispute arose between a boxer and his manager in relation to their contract. The contract was in the form prescribed by the British Board of Boxing Control. The Board was also named as arbitrator in the event of any dispute. It was held that the Board 'is not or may not be impartial' for the purposes of the 1950 Act. The court also said that 'fraud' in the Act is to have its ordinary meaning as having dishonesty as an essential ingredient: *Watson* v. *Prager* (1991)

Refusal to enforce Convention awards is permissible, e.g.

where the party to the arbitration agreement is under some incapacity: Arbitration Act 1975, s. 5.

3. Construction of arbitration agreements

The Arbitration Act of 1950 implies the following clauses in arbitration agreements, unless expressly excluded by the parties.

(a) Reference is to a single arbitrator, unless otherwise stated. (If reference is to two arbitrators, they must appoint an umpire to decide between them, by a casting vote.)

(b) Parties to arbitration must submit to examination on oath, must produce necessary documents if ordered, etc. Witnesses may also have to submit to examination on oath.

(c) The arbitrator's award is final and binding, but he can always make an interim award, pending final decision.

(d) Arbitrators can apportion costs, and any provision in the agreement that any party must pay his own costs however the arbitration is decided is void.

(e) Arbitrators can order specific performance, except in contracts relating to land.

(f) The parties may alter the arbitration agreement by mutual consent, but the arbitrator cannot. (The court may rectify the agreement at any time, but not so as to introduce new matter; as to rectification, *see* 4: **9**.)

(g) The time for making the awards may be fixed by the agreement; if not, then a reasonable time is implied, and can be extended by the courts.

(h) If the contract itself is assignable and is assigned, any arbitration clause in it is also assigned: *Shayler* v. *Woolf* (1946). *See also Montedipe SpA* v. *JTP-RO Jugotanker* (1990). An equitable assignee of a claim under a pending arbitration does not automatically become a party to the arbitration on the assignment taking effect in equity: the assignee must first give notice to the other side and submit to the jurisdiction of the arbitrator. If he does not do so, and if the assignor, being a corporation, is dissolved in the meantime, the arbitration and any award made in it lapses and becomes a nullity since an arbitration requires two or more parties and there cannot be a valid award when one of the two parties has ceased to exist: *Baytur SA* v. *Finagro Holding SA* (1991).

(i) Death or bankruptcy of any party to the agreement does not affect the validity of the agreement or the arbitrator's appointment.

(j) An arbitration agreement may be revoked by the court if (*i*) the arbitrator shows bias, or (*ii*) there is any question of fraud involved in the dispute.

Conduct of proceedings

4. The arbitrator

Any person can be an arbitrator, even though personally interested in the subject-matter of the dispute.

Reference to an arbitrator is presumed to mean a single arbitrator, unless otherwise stated. If a dispute is referred to a single arbitrator and none is appointed (or the one appointed refuses to act), and the parties fail to agree on a replacement, any party can serve seven-days' notice demanding appointment. If then no appointment is made, he can appeal to the court: Arbitration Act 1950 s. 10; *Tritonia Shipping Inc.* v. *South Nelson Forest Products Corpn* (1966).

If reference is to two arbitrators and one is not appointed, the appointor of the other arbitrator can serve similar seven-days' notice and on expiry of the notice can make his own appointment (subject to the court's power to invalidate such appointment).

If reference is to three arbitrators, an award by two of them is binding.

An arbitrator's authority is irrevocable (unless otherwise agreed). But the court may revoke his appointment, or remove him, or nullify the arbitration agreement entirely. Grounds for removal would include misconduct, bias, fraud, or failure to act with reasonable speed: s. 23. When removing an arbitrator, the court may appoint a replacement: s. 25. Only exceptional circumstances (such as misconduct) will justify the court allowing revocation of the appointment: *City Centre Properties Ltd* v. *Tersons Ltd* (1969).

An arbitrator or valuer in a commercial dispute is presumed to be entitled to reasonable remuneration, unless otherwise agreed, and he has a lien for his fees on the subject-matter of the award. The courts have said that, while it is not improper for a party appointing an arbitrator to agree his fees before appointment, it is contrary to an arbitrator's judicial status, once the appointment has been made, for him to bargain unilaterally with only one party for his fees. Any agreement thus reached probably constitutes misconduct and is liable to render the arbitrator vulnerable to imputations of bias: *K/S Norjarl A/S* v. *Hyundai Co. Ltd* (1991). It was said in the same case that, although it was not improper for an arbitrator to stipulate at the time of appointment for a commitment fee to be payable even if arbitration did not take place, an arbitrator was not unilaterally entitled, once appointed, to change the terms of his contract by demanding a commitment fee unless there was a significant and substantial change in the commitment required of him which justified the payment of a further fee. The court said that where the arbitrator is a barrister, a commitment fee should not extend to payment of the entire fee for the hearing before it has started. A modest proportion of the fees for the hearing should normally suffice to cover the period between settlement and the time by which a barrister arbitrator can reasonably expect to find substitute employment. An arbitrator (unlike a valuer) is not liable for negligence in making his award: *Sutcliffe* v. *Thackrah* (1974); *Arenson* v. *Casson Beckman* (1975); *Campbell* v. *Edwards* (1976).

> NOTE: A judge of the Commercial Court may act as a sole arbitrator (or as an umpire) with permission of the Lord Chief Justice. Appeals from such judge/arbitrator are to the Court of Appeal, not to the High Court: Administration of Justice Act 1970, s. 4.

5. Conduct of proceedings

(a) The arbitration agreement may provide rules for governing proceedings, e.g. the customs of a particular trade.

(b) The arbitrator is entitled to call for examination on oath, discovery of documents, presentation of pleadings in writing, etc., unless otherwise agreed.

(c) At the hearing the arbitrator may exclude persons other than the parties.

(d) The arbitrator fixes the time and place of the hearing and must notify the parties. If any party fails to attend, the arbitrator can proceed in his absence but must first give reasonable notice of his intention to do so.

(e) The arbitrator must hear both sides, and obey the ordinary rules of evidence. Improper rejection of evidence is grounds for setting the award aside, but not if it was caused by mere honest mistake as to its value: *Falkingham* v. *Victorian Rly Commissioners* (1900).

(f) Attendance of witnesses can be compelled by writ of *sub poena* issued by the High Court, at the arbitrator's request. Any witness giving false evidence on oath is guilty of the crime of perjury: Perjury Act 1911, s. 1.

(g) In commercial cases where an umpire is appointed, arbitrators may appear before him and give evidence as witnesses: *Bourgeois* v. *Weddell & Co.* (1924).

(h) The arbitrator can state his award in the form of a 'special case' for the opinion of the court, and can be ordered to do so if the court thinks fit: s. 9. The special case may state a question of law for the court's decision, or may relate to the award itself. A clause in the arbitration agreement prohibiting the stating of a special case is void: *Czarnikov* v. *Roth, Schmidt & Co.* (1922). The court does not construe special cases rigidly, and may draw inferences from the facts: *Universal Cargo Carriers Corpn* v. *Citati* (1958). Statement of the special case renders the arbitrator *functus officio* and terminates his jurisdiction.

> NOTE: Where there is a clear-cut point of law involved arbitrators must 'state a case' on request by a party to the arbitration: *Halfdan Grieg & Co.* v. *Sterling Coal & Navigation Corpn* (1973).

(i) The Arbitration Act 1979 places strict limits on the judicial review of arbitration awards.

The Act provides that no appeal lies to the Court of Appeal from the High Court in an arbitration matter unless leave is given and the High Court certifies that the case raises a question of law of general public importance or should for some other reason be considered by the Court of Appeal. The test for giving leave to appeal to the Court of Appeal is whether the question of law is worthy of consideration by the Court of Appeal, for example because there is sufficient doubt as to the correctness of the judge's decision to warrant such consideration or because the decision of the Court of Appeal would add significantly to the clarity and certainty of English commercial law: *Geogas SA* v. *Trammo Gas Ltd* (1991). When this case was taken to the House of Lords, the House ruled that a decision of the Court of Appeal on the grant of leave is final and unappealable, and so the House of Lords has no jurisdiction to entertain an appeal from a decision of the Court of Appeal granting or refusing leave to appeal from a decision of the High Court in respect of an arbitration. When exercising its discretion to grant leave to appeal to the High Court from an arbitration award in regard to a point of law which was not brought before the arbitrator, the court is not barred from granting leave to appeal by the fact that the point was not argued before the arbitrator, but that is, however, a factor to be taken into account in the exercise of that discretion. Accordingly, where all the necessary facts have not been found because of the failure to argue the point in the arbitration, that will be a powerful factor against granting leave, although the court may in very special circumstances remit the award for further facts to be found, with a view to granting leave. On the other hand, if all the necessary facts have been found, the judge should give such weight as he thinks fit to the failure to argue the point in the arbitration and should in particular consider whether the new point is similar to the points argued before the arbitrator or whether it is totally different: *Petraco (Bermuda) Ltd* v. *Petromed International SA* (1988).

(j) The courts have the jurisdiction under the 1950 Act to extend the time limit for commencing an arbitration contained in the arbitration agreement, whether or not the arbitrators themselves have such power under the agreement. The courts will exercise this discretion to enable relief to be given from undue or unreasonable hardship which would otherwise be suffered by a party to an arbitration agreement if he was deprived of the opportunity to pursue a contractual claim by the operation of a restrictive contractual time limit in circumstances in which he ought reasonably to be excused his failure to comply with it: *Comdel Commodities Ltd* v. *Siporex Trade SA* (1990).

When considering an application for an extension of time to appoint an arbitrator to hear a claim, the existence of any potential claim by the applicant against his solicitor for negligence in failing to appoint an arbitrator within the agreed time limit is relevant to the question whether the applicant would suffer undue hardship if an extension were not granted. However, because it is more difficult for such an applicant to pursue a secondary claim against his solicitor than his primary claim against the respondent (since the respondent would not participate in the secondary claim), the applicant may suffer undue hardship if the court were to refuse an extension of time in circumstances where the degree of fault on the part of the applicant is not grave and there is no allegation of any prejudice suffered by the respondent: *Unitramp SA* v *Jenson & Nicholson Pty Ltd* (1992).

6. The award

(a) The arbitrator can make his award at any time, unless otherwise stated in the agreement. If a time is fixed by the Arbitration Act 1950 or any other statute, the court generally has power to extend the time limit.

(b) The award may be verbal or in writing, or in such form as the agreement expressly requires.

(c) The Administration of Justice Act 1982 inserts a provision into the Arbitration Act 1950 which allows an arbitrator to award interest on awards or any sums paid before the award, unless the arbitration agreement contains a term to the contrary. The rate of interest payable varies in conjunction with that payable under the scheme for judgment debts in the Supreme Court (*see* the Judgments Act 1838, s. 17). Under the Judgment Debts (Rate of Interest) Order, the rate of 15 per cent has been fixed in relation to judgment debts.

(d) Costs are generally in the discretion of the arbitrator, which must be fairly exercised but need not be supported by reasons: *Perry* v. *Stopher* (1959).

7. Requisites of a valid award

(a) It must be certain in meaning (though the court may assist interpretation where necessary, and may rectify mistakes in expression).

(b) It must be final (though this does not prohibit the making of interim awards, pending final decision of the dispute).

(c) It must be possible and reasonable.

(d) It must settle all the points referred to arbitration, but must not deal with matters outside the reference.

(If part of the award is valid and part void, the court may apply the doctrine of severance to separate the good from the bad and enforce the valid parts.)

8. Remission to arbitrator

The award is final, but the court has power to remit any matter back to the arbitrator for re-consideration any time within three months of the award being made: s. 22.

Grounds for remission are (*a*) defect in the award, sufficient to justify setting it aside, (*b*) serious omission through inadvertence, (*c*) formal defect, (*d*) mistake by the arbitrator, (*e*) technical misconduct by the arbitrator, (*f*) discovery of new and material evidence.

The jurisdiction of the court to remit an award to an arbitrator is wholly unlimited and extends to any case where, although the arbitrator has acted with complete propriety, some aspect of the dispute has not, due to some mishap or misunderstanding, been considered and adjudicated on as fully as or in a manner which the parties were entitled to expect, and where it would be inequitable to allow any award to take effect without further consideration from the arbitrator: *King* v. *Thomas McKenna Ltd* (1991).

9. Setting awards aside

An award may be set aside because of (*a*) misconduct of the arbitrator, (*b*) uncertainty or lack of finality in the award, (*c*) illegality of the contract on which the award was made.

(In a reference by consent of the parties, mistake is rarely grounds for setting aside the award unless it is a mistake of law.)

There is a presumption of finality in arbitration awards, so leave to appeal against the arbitrator's award in a case involving the regulation of future property rights should not be granted unless there was a strong *prima facie* case that the arbitrator was wrong in law: *Ipswich BC* v. *Fisons plc* (1990).

10. Enforcement of awards

Enforcement is as follows:

(a) in the same manner as a judgment of a court,
(b) by action in the court to enforce the award,
(c) by court order for specific performance.

Arbitration agreements are subject to the Limitation Act 1980, and rights of reference or enforcement of any award may lapse thereunder.

11. Consumer arbitration agreements

The Consumer Arbitration Agreements Act 1988 was enacted to cover the growing trend for contracts made with consumers to contain clauses requiring disputes to be referred to arbitration. Section 1 of the Act provides that such a clause is unenforceable unless the consumer gave his written consent after the differences in question had arisen or where he has submitted to arbitration in respect of those or other differences. These provisions only apply if the proceedings would be within the jurisdiction of the county court: *see* the High Courts and County Courts Jurisdiction Order 1991. The provisions of s. 1 do not apply to an arbitration agreement which is other than a domestic arbitration agreement, nor does the section apply to contracts within Sch. 1 of the Unfair Contract Terms Act 1977. This relates to insurance contracts; contracts relating to land; contracts relating to intellectual property rights; contracts relating to companies; contracts relating to carriage; contracts of employment; and contracts relating to certain diseases resulting from employment in the coal industry. The courts are also empowered by s. 4 of the 1988 Act not to apply s. 1 where there is no detriment to the consumer. The court can only make such an order if proceedings would fall outside the small claims limit (presently £1000), or if the consumer has submitted to arbitration in pursuance of the agreement.

Specimen questions

1. (*a*) In what ways may a reference to arbitration be made? What is the effect of an oral submission?
   (*b*) What are the main advantages and disadvantages of arbitration?

2. Define an arbitration agreement, and state to what arbitration agreements the Arbitration Acts 1950 and 1979 apply.

   Where one party to an arbitration agreement commences legal proceedings concerning the subject-matter of the agreement, mention the circumstances in which the court may stay the proceedings.

   R rendered services to a sanitary authority under an agreement whereby disputes were to be referred to the authority's surveyor. Disputes arose which would probably lead to a conflict of interest between R and the surveyor. If R commences proceedings against the authority, ought the court in your opinion to stay the proceedings?

3. A contract provided for any dispute between the parties to it to be referred to arbitration. A dispute has arisen and been properly referred to a single arbitrator, who has made a valid award.

(*a*) Can either party appeal against the award?
(*b*) How can the award be enforced?

4. State five of the provisions which, unless a contrary intention is expressed, are included in every arbitration agreement.

5. State the conditions upon which an award obtained in an arbitration conducted in a foreign country may be enforced in England.

6. A contract between a British subject and a French company provided that disputes arising under it should be determined by arbitration in France. An arbitration held in France has resulted in an award being made in favour of the British party to the contract, and he desires to enforce the award in England. Can he do so, and if so, subject to what conditions?

7. Explain the difference between an arbitrator and an umpire. In what circumstances may an arbitration award be set aside?

8. State the main requisites of a valid arbitration award and examine the grounds upon which an award may be set aside.

9. In what circumstances is a consumer bound to refer a dispute to arbitration?

Progress test 3

Mercantile agreements

1. Distinguish between an agreement to sell, and a contract for the sale of goods. How do such contracts differ from contracts for the supply of work and materials? (9: **1, 3, 4**)

2. In what circumstances must the injured party treat a breach of condition in a contract for the sale of goods as though it were a breach of warranty? (9: **12**)

3. Summarise briefly the conditions and warranties implied by the Sale of Goods Act and explain how such terms can be excluded from contracts covered by the Act. (9: **14–23**)

4. Explain the meaning of the following phrases in connection with the sale of goods: (*a*) sale by sample; (*b*) sale by description; (*c*) merchantable quality. (9: **16–23**)

5. 'Generally in a sale of goods there is no term implied that goods shall be of any particular quality or that they shall be fit for any particular purpose.' How far do you agree? (9: **16–23**)

6. A enters B's shop and asks for soap. B, who runs a general store, sells him soap intended for washing poodles. A uses the soap to wash his own hair and as a result goes bald. Has A any remedy under the Sale of Goods Act? (9: **20–21**)

7. A buys a car from B in reliance on B's assertion that the car has not done more than 20,000 miles. At the time of purchase A signs a contract which states: 'This contract overrides and excludes all conditions and warranties implied by the Sale of Goods Act, and all representations made by the seller.' A now finds that the car has done 100,000 miles. What is his legal position? (9: **14–23**)

8. Distinguish between specific, ascertained and unascertained goods and explain why the distinction is important. (9: **24–29**)

9. When, if ever, may a purchaser of goods get a better title than was possessed by the person from whom he bought the goods? (9: **30–36**)

10. Explain briefly the rules laid down by the Sale of Goods Act regarding: (*a*) delivery of wrong quantities, (*b*) delivery by instalments, and (*c*) time and place of delivery. (90: **38, 40–41**)

11. Summarise the duties of the seller in f.o.b., c.i.f. and ex-ship contracts and explain the meaning of these technical terms. (9: **44–46**)

12. What are the rights of an unpaid seller, and what does this term mean? (9: **47–58**)

13. What is the position of an auctioneer as agent for the seller and the buyer of property? (9: **62**)

14. 'Hire-purchase is much more hire than purchase.' Discuss. (9: **73**)

15. What conditions and warranties are implied by the Supply of Goods (Implied Terms) Act 1973 and to what contracts does this Act apply? (9: **80**)

16. A is persuaded to take a car on hire-purchase through the misrepresentation of B, the dealer. The car is sold by B to a finance company, which then lets the car to A on hire-purchase. Later A discovers the misrepresentation, and wishes to know whether he can sue B for damages. Explain the legal position. (9: **84, 85**)

17. What is a common carrier, and what are his duties and liabilities at common law? How far can such duties and liabilities be modified by contract? (10: **1–6**)

18. Explain briefly the main provisions of: (*a*) the Carriers Act 1830, and (*b*) the Transport Act 1962. (10: **9, 10**)

19. How far is a railway company liable for the safety of (*a*) passengers, and (*b*) passengers' luggage?   (10: **13, 14**)

20. Explain briefly the meaning and significance of the following: (*a*) bill of lading, (*b*) charterparty, (*c*) freight, (*d*) demurrage, (*e*) general average.   (10: **17–21**)

21. State briefly the main provisions of the Carriage of Goods by Sea Act 1971, with regard to bills of lading.   (10: **24**)

22. Write short explanatory notes on the following: (*a*) voyage charter, (*b*) paramount clause in charterparty, (*c*) full and complete cargo.   (10: **26, 29**)

23. How does an insurance contract differ from a wager? What is meant by 'insurable interest' (*a*) in life insurance, and (*b*) marine insurance?   (11: **2, 5, 17**)

24. State the main provisions of the Policies of Assurance Act 1867, with regard to the assignment of life insurance policies. Explain how such a policy can be used as security for a loan.   (11: **6, 7**)

25. Explain the significance of the average clause in a fire insurance policy. In what circumstances can the insurer claim subrogation to the rights of the insured?   (11: **10, 11**)

26. What is meant by a warranty in a marine insurance contract, and what warranties are implied under the Marine Insurance Act 1906?   (11: **21, 22**)

27. In connection with marine insurance, explain the following terms: (*a*) bottomry, (*b*) respondentia, (*c*) constructive total loss, (*d*) general average loss.   (11: **17, 25, 26**)

28. Explain how the state supervises insurance business.   (11: **29, 30**)

29. Explain briefly the following: (*a*) *depositum*, (*b*) *locatio rei*, (*c*)

Torts (Interference with Goods) Act 1977, (*d*) innkeepers' lien. (12: **6, 7, 10**)

30. What are the duties of a bailee? How far is a bailee liable for loss occasioned by the negligence of his employees? (12: **2**)

31. Explain the main provisions of the Hotel Proprietors Act 1956. (13: **8, 9**)

32. How may reference to an arbitrator occur? (13: **1**)

33. In what circumstances may the court stay proceedings, and refer a dispute to arbitration under an arbitration agreement? (13: **2**)

34. What are the principal powers of an arbitrator under the Arbitration Act 1950 as amended by the Arbitration Act 1979? How may an arbitration award be enforced? (13: **3, 4–6, 10**)

Part four

Negotiable instruments

14
Negotiable instruments

Negotiability

1. Meaning of negotiability

Certain classes of chose in action, called 'negotiable instruments,' can be transferred (or negotiated) without the formalities necessary in assignments of choses in action under s. 136 of the Law of Property Act (LPA) 1925 or the rules of equity.

A negotiable instrument is a document evidencing an obligation, which (*a*) is transferable by mere delivery (or by delivery plus indorsement), (*b*) such delivery operating to transfer all legal rights to the obligation evidenced, (*c*) is free of any defects in the transferor's title.

(A negotiable instrument payable to bearer, such as a bank note, is transferable by delivery alone. One payable to the order of a specified person, such as most cheques, is transferred by delivery of the instrument indorsed (signed) on the back by the payee or other transferor.)

2. Characteristics of negotiable instruments

(**a**) Title passes by delivery (or by delivery plus indorsement); whereas a legal assignment of an ordinary chose in action must be in writing under s. 136, LPA, and any assignment not in writing is merely equitable: *see* 6: **8**.

(**b**) No notice is necessary to the debtor or other obligee; whereas ordinary assignments must be notified under s. 136, LPA or the rule in *Dearle* v. *Hall*: *see* 6: **8, 10**.

(**c**) The holder can sue in his own name; whereas an equitable assignee of an ordinary chose in action cannot.

(**d**) A bona fide transferee for value takes free of any defects in the transferor's title; whereas an assignee of an ordinary chose gets no better title than his assignor had.

(e) A transferee in due course (*see* **38** below) takes free of any defences which could have been raised by the debtor against the transferor; whereas any defence available against an assignor of an ordinary chose in action can be raised against the assignee.

3.   Examples of negotiable instruments

A chose in action may become negotiable either (*a*) by statute, or (*b*) by mercantile custom judicially recognised.

Instruments negotiable by statute include bills of exchange and promissory notes. Instruments negotiable by custom include bank notes, share warrants, bearer debentures, and exchequer bills.

> NOTE: The following are not negotiable instruments, though they are freely transferable: bills of lading, Post Office orders, share certificates, IOUs and receipts.

Example _____

A postal order and a £5 note are stolen from X. The thief sells both to Z. (*a*) The bank note is a negotiable instrument payable to bearer and Z becomes the legal owner of it: X cannot recover it from Z and can only sue the thief. (*b*) The postal order is transferable, but not negotiable; therefore the seller of it cannot give a better title than he has himself. The thief has no title, therefore Z can get no title; X can recover the postal order or its value from Z (who can only sue the thief for damages).

4.   Who can sue on a negotiable instrument?

If a negotiable instrument is dishonoured (i.e. not paid when due), a holder for value can sue any person who signed the bill before it came into his possession.

The persons who may be liable are: (*a*) the drawer, i.e. the person who first issued the instrument, (*b*) the acceptor, i.e. the person (if any) who has accepted liability on the instrument, and (*c*) any indorser, i.e. any person who has transferred the instrument to another and indorsed it to effect the transfer (he will also have a right of action against accommodation parties, i.e. persons who have signed an instrument merely to lend the credit of their names to the instrument).

EXCEPTIONS: A signatory may avoid liability in the following cases: (*a*) where he signed under a fundamental mistake as to the nature of the document: *see* 4: **1–7**; (*b*) where his signature was forged (since, then, he has not signed it himself), unless he is estopped from denying the genuineness of the signature, e.g. where he facilitated the forgery; (*c*) where he signed *sans recours* ('without recourse'), indicating that he accepted no liability on the instrument; (*d*) where for some reason the law will not allow him to be sued, e.g. minors, bankrupts, enemy aliens.

Bills of exchange

5. Bills of Exchange Act (BEA) 1882

This Act codified the law relating to cheques and other bills of exchange, the most important kinds of negotiable instruments.

(Most of the rules laid down by the Act as applying to bills of exchange generally apply also to cheques, which are bills of exchange drawn on a banker. But since cheques are bills payable on demand, the rules relating to presentation for acceptance do not apply to them.)

6. Bills of exchange defined

A bill of exchange is an 'unconditional order in writing, addressed by one person to another, signed by the person giving it, requiring the person to whom it is addressed to pay on demand, or at a fixed or determinable future time a sum certain in money to or to the order of a specified person or to bearer': BEA 1882, s. 3(1).

The person issuing the order is called the drawer, and the person to whom it is addressed is the drawee. If the bill is made payable to a named person, or to his order, it is an order bill and he is the payee. Otherwise a bill may be payable to bearer, and such a bearer bill is transferable by mere delivery (without any indorsement). An order bill, however, requires to be indorsed by the payee to effect transfer.

NOTE: The definition of bills of exchange should be memorised, and the comments on the definition at **7–13** below studied carefully.

7.   'Unconditional order'

It must be a positive order to pay, not a mere request or authorisation. The usual wording is 'Pay X . . .', though 'Please pay X . . .' is also regarded as unconditional.

An order is not unconditional if:

(a) it gives the drawee a discretion whether to pay or not, e.g. 'Pay X, if satisfied with goods consigned';

(b) it orders payment from a particular fund, e.g. 'Pay X out of my current account.' (But where an unconditional order to pay is merely coupled with mention of a particular fund, for the guidance of the drawee, this is sufficiently unconditional);

(c) it requires the drawee to do something more than to pay money, e.g. 'Pay X and notify me in writing'.

8.   Parties to a bill

The three necessary parties are the drawer, the drawee, and the payee (or bearer). One person may fulfil two different capacities, e.g. where he draws a bill payable to himself, or payable to the drawee (such as a cheque on X Bank and payable to the bank in payment of a debt). In such cases the bill is fully valid and can be negotiated in the normal way.

But where the drawer and drawee are the same legal person (e.g. where a branch of a company draws a bill on its head office), the order is not strictly a bill of exchange, but a promissory note in favour of the payee: BEA, s. 5(2).

A bill is also treated as a promissory note if the payee is a fictitious person or lacks contractual capacity: BEA, s. 5(2).

9.   Addressed to drawee

He must be identified with reasonable certainty (depending on the circumstances).

A bill can be addressed to joint drawees (e.g. to X, Y, and Z), but not to alternate drawees (e.g. to X, Y, or Z).

NOTE: An instrument made payable to 'cash' is not payable 'to the order of a specified person or to bearer' and therefore is not a bill of exchange: *Orbit Mining & Trading Co. Ltd* v. *Westminster Bank Ltd* (1963).

10. Dating a bill

If a bill is undated the holder may insert what he believes to be the correct date of issue (which may be necessary for calculating time for payment).

If an incorrect date is inserted the bill is nevertheless enforceable by a holder in due course as though the date were correct: BEA, s. 12.

A bill should bear the correct weekday date, but is not invalid merely because it is post-dated, ante-dated, or Sunday-dated.

Any date appearing on a bill is presumed to be the correct one unless the contrary is proved: BEA, s. 13.

> NOTE: By BEA, s. 45, the drawer and indorsers are discharged from liability if the bill is not presented for payment on the due date. BEA, s. 12 (*see* above) therefore protects a holder in due course against s. 45, where he has in good faith relied on an incorrect date.

11. Consideration and capacity

(a) *Consideration.* Bills of exchange require to be supported by consideration like other simple contracts, but note the following:

  (*i*) *consideration is presumed, in favour of a holder.* Thus the normal burden of proof is reversed; in other contracts the person seeking to enforce the contract must prove that he has given consideration, in bills of exchange it is for the defendant to show that no consideration has been given;

  (*ii*) *past consideration suffices,* i.e. any antecedent debt or other obligation: BEA, s. 27.

(b) *Capacity to contract* by bill of exchange is generally co-extensive with ordinary contractual capacity: *see* Chapter 3. Thus a minor incurs no liability by signing a bill, but adult signatories to the same bill would be fully liable.

12. Sum payable

A bill must order the payment of a 'sum certain in money,' i.e. not in goods or services, etc. (Note also that the words used are 'sum certain,' not 'a certain sum' which could mean an unspecified sum.)

(a) A sum may be certain within the meaning of the Act even though it is to be paid:

(*i*)   with interest (usually calculated from the date of the bill);

(*ii*) by instalments; *or*

(*iii*) according to some indicated rate of exchange, e.g. where a bill drawn in pounds in Britain is payable in dollars in the USA: BEA, s. 9(1).

(b) Where the sum payable is stated in both words and figures (though this is not legally necessary) which do not agree, the sum denoted by the words is the amount payable: BEA, s. 9(2).

13. Order and bearer bills

A bill may be drawn payable to bearer, or to the order of the drawer, payee, or (sometimes) drawee: BEA, s. 3(1).

(a) *Order bills* are those payable to a named payee or some person designated by him. A bill is an order bill if:

(*i*)   the bill itself so states; *or*

(*ii*) it is payable to a specified person without further words prohibiting transfer, e.g. 'Pay X' or 'Pay X or order.' (But a bill payable to 'X only' is not an order bill and in fact is not really a negotiable instrument at all, but an ordinary chose in action. Such a bill is enforceable by X, but if X sells it to Y, Y cannot enforce it against the drawer or drawee except through the agency of X.)

(b) *Bearer bills* are those transferable by mere delivery. A bill is a bearer bill if:

(*i*)   the bill itself so states;

(*ii*) the last or only indorsement is in blank (*see* **27**,(*g*) below); or

(*iii*) the bill is payable to a fictitious or non-existent person: BEA, ss. 7(3) and 8. (A non-existent person is one of whose existence the drawer is unaware, or who does not exist at all. A fictitious person is one of whose existence the drawer is aware, but who was not intended by the drawer to receive payment: *Bank of England* v. *Vagliano Bros* (1891).)

14. Inland and foreign bills

(a) *An inland bill* is one which is or purports to be (*i*) both drawn and payable within the British Isles, or (*ii*) drawn within the British Isles upon some person resident therein: BEA, s. 4(1).

(b) *Foreign bills* are all other bills. But unless the contrary appears on the face of the bill, the holder may treat it as an inland bill.

15. Bills in a set

A set of bills means a bill executed in duplicate, triplicate, etc. The payment of one part of a bill in a set discharges the other parts also: BEA, s. 71.

But if the drawee mistakenly accepts two or more parts of the same bill he will be liable on each part accepted as if it were a separate bill. Similarly a holder who indorses several parts is liable on each.

16. Inchoate instruments

Where a person signs a blank piece of paper and delivers it to another, intending it to be converted into a bill, it operates as authority to fill it up as a complete bill for any amount, using the signature already upon it as that of drawer, acceptor, or indorser: BEA, s. 20(1).

Such a bill can only be enforced against the original signer if it is:

(a) filled up within a reasonable time of delivery, *and*
(b) completed strictly within the limits of the authority given: s. 20(2).

But after completion the bill is fully enforceable in the usual way. Thus where S signs an inchoate instrument and delivers it to X with authority to complete it for not more than £100, if X fills it up for £1,000 he cannot force S to accept liability for that amount. But if X sells (negotiates) the bill to H, who takes it in good faith and without notice of the £100 limit, H as a holder in due course could enforce the bill for the full £1000 against S. (As to the meaning of 'holder in due course,' *see* **38** below.)

17. Material alterations: s. 64

The following alterations are material: amount, date, payee's name, terms of acceptance, place for payment, crossings on a cheque, altering order to bearer. (Alteration of the place where drawn is material if it changes an inland bill into a foreign bill, or vice versa.)

Effect

An unauthorised alteration discharges from liability all persons who became party to the bill before the alteration, unless they expressly or impliedly assent to the alteration: BEA, s. 64.

Apparent and non-apparent alterations

The effect of s. 64 differs slightly where the alteration is not apparent.

(a) *Alteration is not apparent*: a holder in due course can enforce as if it had not been altered, i.e. with the alteration deleted: s. 64.

(b) *Alteration apparent*: all parties prior to the alteration are discharged from liability (even against a subsequent holder in due course). But the bill will be valid and enforceable as between persons who became parties subsequent to the alteration.

Example

S draws a cheque for £100 in favour of X, who fraudulently alters the amount to £1000 and sells (negotiates) it to Y who negotiates it to Z. Here: Z can enforce it against Y and X, even if the alteration is apparent; but he has no remedy against S unless he is a holder in due course and the alteration was not apparent (when he can make S liable for the unaltered amount).

Cheques

The provisions of s. 64 apply to cheques, but note if a cheque is altered and the drawer later authorises the alteration (usually by initialling it) the effect is (*a*) the drawer is bound by the cheque as altered, (*b*) other parties are protected by s. 64 unless they too have assented to the alteration.

18. Overdue bills

A bill is deemed to be overdue in the following circumstances.

(a) Bills payable on demand are overdue when they have been in circulation for an unreasonable time.
(b) Other bills are overdue when the date fixed for payment has passed without the bill being presented: BEA, s. 36.

Effect of a bill being overdue is that it can still be negotiated, but a transferee can get no better title to it than his transferor had, i.e. he cannot be a holder in due course.

(A holder in due course is one who takes a bill in good faith and for value before it is overdue, and he gets a perfect legal title to the bill irrespective of any defects in his transferor's title.)

19. Lost bills

If a bill is lost before it is overdue, the holder can compel the drawer to issue a replacement (though he cannot compel any other parties to sign the copy): s. 69.

Where this happens the drawer can demand security from the holder to guard against the possibility of having to pay twice over, i.e. on the original bill and on the replacement.

20. Bills as conditional payment

A creditor who receives a cheque or other bill in settlement of his debt is not regarded as finally paid, since he has not received cash but merely a contractual right to obtain cash under the terms of the bill.

Payment by bill of exchange therefore is conditional, i.e. subject to a condition that if the bill is dishonoured the creditor shall have a right of action for the debt against the debtor.

Signature, delivery and indorsement

21. Meaning of negotiation

A bill is negotiated when it is transferred in such a way as to constitute the transferee the holder of the bill, i.e. by delivery of a bearer bill, or by delivery plus indorsement of an order bill: BEA, s. 31.

Negotiation may be prohibited by clear words written on the face of the bill, e.g. by marking the bill 'not negotiable.'

NOTE: The addition of the words 'not negotiable' has differing effects in cheques and other bills. (*a*) A cheque crossed 'not negotiable' remains transferable, but the transferee gets no better title than his transferor possessed, i.e. the instrument descends to the status of an ordinary assignable chose in action: *see* **52** below. (*b*) Any other bill marked 'not negotiable' ceases to be transferable altogether: *Hibernian Bank* v. *Gysin & Hanson* (1939). (*c*) A cheque or other bill marked 'not transferable' ceases to be transferable altogether (and therefore is not really a bill of exchange).

22. No liability without signature

Liability on a bill is incurred only by a person who has signed it, either as drawer, acceptor or indorser: s. 23.

(a) *Signature in an assumed name*, or on behalf of a firm, confers full liability: s. 23.

(b) *Transfer by delivery*. A person who transfers a bill by delivery without indorsement (i.e. a bearer bill) is not liable upon it (except to his immediate transferee): s. 58.

(c) *Indorsement by a stranger*. A person who is not a party to a bill but who signs it for any reason is fully liable on the bill, by reason of his signature, to a holder in due course: s. 56.

(d) *Agent's signature*. Any agent signing a bill incurs full personal liability unless he makes it clear that he signs merely on behalf of someone else, e.g. by signing '*per pro*' or 'for and on behalf of' his principal: s. 26. Thus a company director who signs a cheque merely as 'director' or 'manager' will be personally liable on the cheque: he should sign 'J. Jones, director, *per pro* X Co. Ltd.'

Example

Directors of a company signed a cheque on which the ampersand was omitted from the name 'X. & Co. Ltd.' HELD: The company was not properly named and the directors were personally liable on the cheque: *Hendon* v. *Adelman* (1973).

23. Signature *sans recours*

The drawer or any indorser can negative or limit his liability by clear words accompanying his signature on the bill: s. 16.

(a) Signature *sans recours* ('without recourse') negatives all liability of the signer on the bill.

(b) Signature *sans frais* ('without expenses') limits the signer's liability to the actual value of the bill, i.e. excludes liability for any expenses arising through dishonour and subsequent action for enforcement.

24. Forged signatures: s. 24

'Where a signature on a bill is forged or placed thereon without the authority of the person whose signature it purports to be, the forged or unauthorised signature is wholly inoperative' and no rights can be acquired by reason of such signature (unless the party against whom enforcement is sought is for some reason estopped from denying the genuineness of the signature).

> NOTE: (1) *Forged or unauthorised*. A forged signature is one which is false or altered, e.g. where X signs S's name to a cheque, or alters a signature to that of another person. An unauthorised signature is where X signs his own name, but without authority to do so, e.g. where an agent without authority to do so signs a cheque on behalf of his principal. (2) *Ratification of unauthorised signatures*. An unauthorised signature can be ratified by the person by whose authority it purports to be made, thus validating it. (A forgery cannot be ratified in any circumstances since falsely making or altering any document is a criminal offence, and as such can never be validated: Forgery and Counterfeiting Act 1981). (3) *Estoppel*. If a person knows that his signature to a bill has been forged, but leads others to believe that the signature is genuine he will be estopped from denying the genuineness of the signature and will be fully liable on the bill, e.g. where S habitually lets his wife forge his signature to cheques and obtain cash thereon, he may be estopped from denying the genuineness of such signature if a dispute later arises.

25. Effect of forged signatures

(a) *Forgery of drawer's signature*: the bill is void since it fails to satisfy the definition in BEA, s. 3(1) of an order 'addressed by one person to another, signed by the person giving it'.

(But the bill will remain valid as between subsequent parties to it, e.g. X draws a cheque in favour of himself on S's bank and forges S's signature as drawer. He then negotiates the cheque for value to Y. Here S incurs no liability on the bill (unless estoppel applies), but Y has full rights of action against X.)

(b) *Forgery of the acceptor's signature*: the acceptor incurs no liability, but a holder has full rights against other persons whose signatures are genuine, i.e. the drawer and indorsers.

(c) *Forgery of indorsement*: if the bill is an order bill indorsement is vitally necessary to effect legal transfer; therefore any forgery of such indorsement nullifies transfer. Thus the transferee gets no title to the bill, and has no claims against persons who became parties to it before the forgery. (But by s. 55 the bill will be valid and enforceable as between parties subsequent to the forgery.)

Example

S draws a cheque in favour of A, who negotiates it to B. X steals it from B and negotiates it (by forging B's indorsement) to Y who negotiates it to Z. Z can enforce the bill against Y (and X) and Y can claim compensation from X. But neither Y nor Z have any claims against S, A, or B. (But B could compel S to issue another cheque, on giving adequate security.)

NOTE: In cases (*a*) and (*c*) above no person who takes the bill subsequent to the forgery can be a holder in due course (though by ss. 54 and 55 he may have the legal rights of such a holder against persons who became parties subsequent to the forgery).

26. Delivery of bills

No person is liable upon a bill unless he has (*a*) signed it, and (*b*) delivered it. An order bill must have the signature of the transferor on it in order to effect a valid transfer; but a bearer bill is transferable by delivery without indorsement.

NOTE: (1) *Importance of delivery.* No person is liable on a bill even if he has signed it, if he can prove positively that he did not deliver it, either actually or constructively. Delivery means deliberately and unconditionally transferring possession to another: BEA, s. 21(1). Thus if a bill is stolen from X, he has not delivered it and he (and prior parties) incur no liability except under (2) below. (2) *Delivery presumed.* (*i*) Delivery is conclusively presumed in favour of a holder in due course, who can thus enforce a bill even against a person who can show that he did not deliver it: s. 21(2). (*ii*) Delivery is also rebuttably presumed in favour of any holder (though here it can be disproved so as to avoid liability): s. 21(3). (3) *When delivery is rebuttably presumed.* Delivery is not presumed conclusively where (*i*) the bill was not complete or was irregular when it left the possession of the party to be charged, e.g. an inchoate instrument, or (*ii*) where the person seeking to enforce it is not a holder in due course. (4) *Conditional delivery.* Where a bill is delivered subject to the fulfilment of some condition, delivery is incomplete until the condition is satisfied, and the bill is not enforceable between the parties to the conditional delivery. (But such bill is fully enforceable by a holder in due course: *see* (2) above.) (5) *When deliverer liable.* Although a person who delivers a bill without signing it is not generally liable on the bill, he impliedly warrants (*i*) that he will indemnify his immediate transferee (but no one else), (*ii*) that the bill is genuine, and (*iii*) that he is entitled to transfer it. (This warranty does not apply if the transferee has not given value for the bill.)

27. Valid indorsements

An order bill requires the indorsement of the transferor in order for the transfer to be effective.

Requirements of valid indorsements are as follows.

(a) It must be written (on the back of the bill). The signature of the indorser is sufficient, without further words indicating transfer: s. 32(1). Indorsement may be in ink, print, pencil, etc. (but banks discourage indorsements in pencil, since they are easily obliterated; and indorsement by rubber stamp on a cheque will not usually be accepted by a bank).

(b) Partial indorsement is ineffective. The indorsement must relate to the full value of the bill: s. 32(2).

(c) Where there are several payees, all should indorse (unless one has authority to indorse on behalf of the others, e.g. in a partnership): s. 32(3).

(d) Manner of indorsement should correspond exactly with the drawing, e.g. if the payee's name is misspelt he should indorse in the misspelt version (adding the correct spelling if he wishes): s. 32(4).

(e) *Allonge*. Where there is insufficient space on the bill for further indorsements, an additional piece of paper (called an allonge) may be glued to the bill to receive further indorsements.

(f) Indorsement by agent. An agent is personally liable as indorser unless he makes it clear that he indorses only on behalf of another, e.g. by indorsing '*per pro*' his principal.

(g) Blank and special indorsements. If the indorser merely signs his own name (without adding that of the transferee), the indorsement is said to be in blank and the bill becomes payable to bearer (so that it can be further negotiated by mere delivery).

If the indorser adds the name of the transferee the bill is specially indorsed and is payable to order, i.e. if the transferor wishes to negotiate it further he must himself indorse the bill. (Thus by means of its indorsement, an order bill may be converted into a bearer bill at any time, and vice versa.)

28. Restrictive and conditional indorsements

(a) A restrictive indorsement is one which prohibits further transfer or limits transferability, e.g. 'Pay X only, signed J. Smith,' or an indorsement indicating that the indorsee is to receive payments only as agent for the indorser: s. 35(1).

By this means an indorser can deprive the bill of its negotiability. This will not affect the rights of the transferee as against the indorser, but will prevent him passing a full title to any further transferee: s. 35(2).

(b) Conditional indorsement is one which makes payment or transfer subject to some condition, e.g. 'Pay X, after his marriage to Z.' Such a condition can be ignored by the payer: s. 33.

(c) Indorsement *sans recours*. If the indorser seeks to restrict his liability to the transferee by indorsing *sans recours*, or *sans frais* (*see* **23** above), the transferee can refuse to accept the bill with this indorsement. If he does take the bill so indorsed, he is bound by the restriction.

(d) Faculative indorsement is one in which the indorser waives some of his legal rights in favour of the transferee, e.g. indorsement with 'notice of dishonour waived': s. 16(2). In such a case the transferee and subsequent transferees can enforce the bill against the indorser without giving notice of dishonour, etc.

Liability of parties

29. Parties to a bill

A party means a person who is liable on the bill, i.e. the drawer, acceptor, and indorsers.

However, the payee (before he indorses the bill) has rights under it, and can also be described as a party.

30. Order of liability

(a) *Before acceptance* the drawer is the principal debtor and primarily liable.

(b) *After acceptance*, the drawee takes over primary liability (and the drawer and indorsers are merely sureties for him).

(c) *After indorsement*, the indorser becomes liable as a surety for the value of the bill. The holder can thus enforce the bill against the drawer, the acceptor (primarily) and any indorsers. He can sue any one or he can sue any combination of them, and each is liable for the full value of the bill.

(As between themselves the parties have no right of contribution: contrast guarantors, *see* 16: **9–10**. But any party who has been made to pay the full amount on the bill has a right of action for that amount against his immediate transferor.)

31. The drawer: s. 55

(a) *Liability*. He engages that (*i*) on due presentment it will be paid according to its tenor, and (*ii*) if dishonoured, he will compensate the holder or any indorser who has suffered loss thereby (provided necessary proceedings on dishonour are taken).
(b) *Estoppel*. He is precluded from denying to a holder in due course the existence and capacity of the payee.

32. The drawee/acceptor

He is the person to whom the order is addressed. He is under no liability on the bill unless and until he accepts it, after which he assumes primary liability (and is called *the acceptor*).

Where a bill is not payable on demand it must be presented to the drawee for him to signify his acceptance of liability (or to reject it), and later presented to him again for payment. A bill payable on demand, such as a cheque, is merely presented for payment without any prior presentation for acceptance.

(a) *Liability*. He engages that he will pay the bill on due presentment for payment according to its tenor.
(b) *Estoppel*. He is precluded from denying (*i*) the existence, capacity and signature of the drawer, and (*ii*) the existence and capacity of the payee of an order bill (though he may deny the validity or genuineness of the payee's indorsement): s. 24.

33. Indorsers

They are people (including the payee) who indorse an order bill in order to transfer it.

(a) *Liability*. They engage (*i*) that on due presentment the bill will be accepted and paid according to its tenor, and (*ii*) that if it is dishonoured they will compensate the holder (or any indorser who is compelled to pay it) providing necessary proceedings for dishonour are taken: s. 66.
(b) *Estoppel*. An indorser is precluded from denying (*i*) to a holder

in due course — the genuineness of the drawer's signature and of all indorsements prior to his own, and (*ii*) to a later indorser — the validity of the bill or his own title when he indorsed it.

(Remember that any person signing a bill otherwise than as drawer or acceptor incurs the full liability of an indorser.)

34. Accommodation party

This means a person who has signed a bill as drawer, acceptor or indorser without receiving value therefore.

An accommodation party is liable on the bill to any holder for value, but not to the person whom he has accommodated, i.e. the person to whom he lent the credit of his name.

An accommodation bill is one of which the acceptor is an accommodation party: s. 59(3), i.e. a person who accepts for the honour of the drawer or some other party. (When a bill is not accepted by the original drawee, some other person may step in to accept the bill to save the drawer or any indorser from being sued for dishonour. This is called 'acceptance for honour.')

35. Referee in case of need

The drawer or any indorser who fears that a bill may not be accepted by the drawee may designate some other person in addition to the drawee as 'referee in case of need,' to whom the holder may apply for payment (if he wishes) in the event of dishonour by the drawee: s. 15.

If the referee accepts liability, the bill becomes an accommodation bill and he is said to be accepting for honour of the drawer or any indorser on whose behalf he intervenes: ss. 65–68.

36. Fictitious and non-existing payees: s. 7

Where the payee of a bill is a fictitious or non-existing person, the bill may be treated as payable to bearer (and can be negotiated without the indorsement of such payee): s. 7(3).

(a) *Fictitious payee* means someone whom the drawer did not intend to receive payment, though he may be an existing person and may be named by the drawer as payee.

Examples ————————————————————————————————

(1) V's clerk G obtained V's acceptance of bills G had forged, and apparently drawn by a customer of V in favour of X, a person known to V. G then forged X's indorsement to the bills and obtained their value. HELD: The clerk was the real drawer of the bills, and he knew of X's existence but did not intend him to obtain payment, therefore X was a fictitious payee and the bills were payable to bearer: *Bank of England* v. *Vagliano Bros* (1891).

(2) A clerk induced his employer to draw cheques payable to X, to whom the employer owed money. The employer intended X to be the payee, but the amounts of the cheques were forged by the clerk, who later forged X's indorsements and obtained payment. HELD: The cheques were not payable to a fictitious payee since the drawer intended X to receive payment, though not of the amounts stated. Thus the cheques were order bills, needing a valid indorsement by X to effect transfer, therefore the forged indorsements by the clerk were ineffective and the transferee obtained no title: *Vinden* v. *Hughes* (1905).

———

(b) *Non-existing payee* means someone (living or not) of whose existence the drawer is unaware, even though he may have intended him to receive payment.

Example ————————————————————————————————

A clerk induced his employer to draw cheques in favour of X (an actual person), by pretending that the money was owing to X. The clerk then forged X's indorsements and obtained the value of the cheques. HELD: X was a non-existing payee, and these cheques were therefore bearer bills. Consequently transfer would have been effective without indorsement at all: *Clutton* v. *Attenborough* (1897).

———

37. Holder: meaning and position

(a) *Meaning.* He is the payee or indorsee of a bill, who is in possession of it, or the bearer of a bearer bill: s. 2. Thus a person who takes an order bill by means of a forged indorsement is not a holder, since he is neither the indorsee of it, nor the bearer of a bearer bill.

(b) *Position.* He can enforce the bill (*i*) against any person who has signed it, and (*ii*) against the transferor from whom he obtained it, whether that person signed it or not.

To have full rights of enforcement he should (*i*) have given value himself (in which case he is probably a holder in due course: *see* below), or (*ii*) have obtained it from a person who has given value for it (in which case he is a holder for value: *see* **39** below).

But in any case the law presumes in favour of any holder that his possession is supported by valuable consideration, and in any action brought by the holder it will be for the defendant to disprove this presumption (not for the holder to prove the existence of consideration): *see* **11** above.

38. Holder in due course: s. 29

(a) *Meaning.* He is a holder who has taken a bill (*i*) complete and regular on the face of it, (*ii*) before it was overdue and without notice that it had been dishonoured (if such was the case), (*iii*) in good faith and for value, and (*iv*) without notice of any defect in the transferor's title: s. 29(1): *see* **66** below. In *Mackenzie Mills* v. *Buono* (1986), the defendant imported furniture from suppliers in Italy. Following discussions between the defendant and the suppliers as to the quality of the furniture, payment was made by a post-dated cheque in exchange for a promise that the suppliers would replace certain defective items. A number of the cheques were dishonoured. A further cheque was endorsed by the suppliers and handed over to the plaintiffs, a firm of solicitors who were acting for the suppliers in their dispute with the defendant. At that time the suppliers owed the plaintiffs some £500 in respect of costs already incurred in respect of the dispute. That cheque too was dishonoured on being countermanded by the defendant. In an action on the cheque, the plaintiffs obtained judgment for the full amount of the cheque with interests and costs. The defendant appealed, contending that the plaintiffs were not holders in due course of the cheque, not having given any value for it. The court held that, the cheque having been given in payment for the furniture in anticipation of the defective items being replaced, it was clear that as between the defendant and suppliers value had been given for it, notwithstanding that in proceedings between them the defendant could be in a position to contend that the consideration originally given for it had wholly failed. It followed that the plaintiffs were deemed to be holders of the cheque for value and therefore were holders in due course.

NOTE: (1) That the payee cannot be a holder in due course, since he did not take the bill by the process of negotiation, i.e. he was one of the original parties to the issue of the bill: *R. E. Jones Ltd* v. *Waring & Gillow Ltd* (1926). (2) A person who derives his title through a forged indorsement cannot be a holder in due course, since a holder is a person who derives his title through a valid indorsement (s. 2) and a forgery is an invalid and inoperative indorsement (s. 24). The Consumer Credit Act 1974 has imposed certain restrictions on the holder in due course in relation to negotiable instruments taken under regulated agreements. These are explained in **66** below.

(b) *Rights.* A holder in due course can sue on the bill in his own name, and defeat any defences arising from defects of title or arising from the relations of the parties before he took the bill.

Thus the only defences that can be raised against his claims are

(*i*) that he does not satisfy the definition given in s. 29(1), e.g. that the bill was overdue when he took it, or had some patent defect (such as disagreement of words and figures of the amount),

(*ii*) that a forged indorsement vitiates his title,

(*iii*) that issue, acceptance or negotiation of the bill were produced by fraud, coercion or illegality (in which case the holder in due course can still enforce the bill but only if he can prove positively that, subsequent to the alleged fraud, coercion or illegality, value has in good faith been given for the bill, i.e. the burden of proof shifts to the holder): s. 30(2).

(c) *Presumption in favour of holder.* Every holder of a bill is presumed to be a holder in due course until the contrary is proved.

(d) *Good faith.* Negligence of the holder (e.g. failure to make reasonable enquiries) does not preclude him from being a holder in due course, i.e. does not necessarily amount to bad faith.

39. Holder for value

(a) *Meaning.* He is a holder of a bill for which value has at some time been given; he need not have given value himself.

(b) *Rights.* He can enforce the bill against all persons who became parties prior to the giving of such value. (Remember also the presumption in favour of all holders that value has been given for the bill.)

He can sue on the bill in his own name, but he obtained no better title than his transferor possessed. Thus if a holder in due course gives the bill as a present to V, V is a holder for value (since value has been given by the holder in due course) and has as good a title as his transferor, i.e. in this case a perfect title.

Example
_____

S draws a cheque in favour of A, who indorses it for value to B, who gives it gratuitously to C who gives it gratuitously to D. Presuming all indorsements are valid, D is a holder for value (even though he did not himself give value) and can enforce the cheque against all persons who became parties prior to value being given, i.e. against S and A, but not against B or C.

_____

Acceptance, payment and dishonour

40. Acceptance of bills of exchange

Bills not payable on demand must be accepted by the drawee as a prerequisite to payment. (Bills payable on demand, including cheques, bypass this intervening stage and proceed straight to payment.)

(a) *Drawee's liability.* The drawee is under no liability to holders of the bill until he accepts liability, by signing across the face of the bill. (Though he may be liable to damages for breach of contract to the drawer if he improperly refuses to accept a bill which he was contractually bound to accept.)

Acceptance is signified by the drawee signing across the face of the bill, with or without addition of the date or such words as 'accepted': s. 17.

(b) *When made.* Acceptance may be made at any time, even before the drawer's signature of the bill (though usually after). A bill may be accepted when overdue or when previously dishonoured: s. 18. If a bill payable after sight is dishonoured by non-acceptance but the drawee later changes his mind and accepts it, the holder is entitled to have the acceptance back-dated to the date when it was first presented for acceptance: s. 18(3). This may be important, e.g. where a bill is payable three months after sight by the drawee.

(c) *Kinds of acceptance.* Acceptance may be either general (unqualified acceptance of the bill as drawn) or qualified. The holder is entitled to general acceptance, and may treat the bill as dishonoured if only a qualified acceptance is offered: s. 44(1). If he takes a qualified acceptance he loses his right of recourse against prior parties to the bill (except such of them as authorised him to do so): s. 44(2).

(d) *Kinds of qualified acceptance*:

(*i*) conditional, e.g. 'Accepted subject to deduction for expenses';

(*ii*) partial, e.g. for part only of the sum specified;

(*iii*) local, i.e. payable only at a particular place. (Merely naming a place for payment is general acceptance, unless it is to be made only at the place named);

(*iv*) qualified as to time, e.g. 'accepted payable in six months' where the bill specified three months;

(*v*) acceptance by some only of several joint drawees.

41. Presentment for acceptance

A bill payable after sight must be presented for acceptance within a reasonable time and if not so presented the drawer and all indorsers prior to presentation are discharged from liability: s. 40(1).

Presentment is only necessary where:

(a) the bill is payable after sight or after demand (since presentation will enable calculation of the period after which the bill shall be payable);

(b) there is an express stipulation for presentment;

(c) the bill is payable elsewhere than at the residence or place of business of the drawee, e.g. at a bank. (But the drawee for his own convenience may nominate his bank or some other place as the place for payment, in which case the bill is said to be domiciled. Domiciling a bill is not qualified acceptance, unless it is done in such a way as to prohibit the holder from seeking payment anywhere else.)

42. Presentment for acceptance is excused

and the bill may be treated as dishonoured where:

(a) the drawee is dead, bankrupt, lacks capacity or is a fictitious person;

(b) presentment is impossible, e.g. because the drawee cannot be found;

(c) acceptance is refused: s. 42(2).

43. Presentment for payment

A bill not payable on demand must be presented for payment on the due date (as fixed by the bill, e.g. three months after acceptance, or 'after sight').

(a) Presentment must be at a reasonable hour on a business day, and at the proper place: s. 45(3).

(b) Delay in presentment is excused if due to circumstances beyond the holder's control: s. 46(1).

(c) A bill not presented within due time is not invalidated, but it cannot be enforced against any person who drew or indorsed it unless such person's signature was added within a reasonable time. (Compare the position of the drawer of a cheque, who is discharged by delay only to the extent he has suffered damage: s. 74 and *see* **48** below.)

(d) Presentment for payment may be excused where:

    (*i*) after reasonable diligence it cannot be effected, e.g. because the acceptor cannot be found;

    (*ii*) the drawee is a fictitious person;

    (*iii*) presentment has been waived: s. 45(2).

(e) A bill is dishonoured by non-payment when

    (*i*) it is properly presented but payment is refused or cannot be obtained, *or*

    (*ii*) presentment is excused: s. 47(1).

An offer of partial payment can be treated as dishonoured, or it can be accepted and the bill treated as dishonoured for the balance.

> NOTE: Formerly three 'days of grace' were added to the due date for the benefit of the drawee but to bring English law into line with international usage these were abolished by the Banking and Financial Dealings Act 1971.

44. Procedure on dishonour

The holder of a dishonoured bill must notify the fact of dishonour to all prior parties against whom he reserves a right of action; persons not so notified are discharged. The 1882 Act, however, does not contain any requirement as to the giving of notice of protest or of dishonour to a guarantor, and any failure in regard to protest and dishonour will not discharge the guarantor's liability: *G&H Montage GmbH* v. *Irvani* (1990).

Similarly, any indorser must reserve his rights of action by notifying parties prior to himself. But even where it is known that a bill will be dishonoured on presentation on maturity (because, for example, of the drawer's insolvency) notice of dishonour must not be given until dishonour has actually occurred: *Eaglehill Ltd* v. *Needham Builders Ltd* (1972).

Inland bills
Notice of dishonour can be in any form, oral or written, providing it clearly identifies the bill: s. 49(5). Return of a dishonoured bill is sufficient notice to the drawer: s. 49(6). Notice must be given within a reasonable time of dishonour: s. 49(12).

Foreign bills: noting and protesting
Formal notice of dishonour is required in the case of foreign bills (and is optional in the case of inland bills). Formal notice is achieved by getting the bill re-presented by a notary public (or, if none can be found, by a householder in the presence of witnesses), who notes on the bill the answer obtained, if any. The notary or householder then issues a formal certificate of dishonour (called the *protest*), setting out the circumstances of dishonour. The protest and a copy of the noted bill are then sent by the holder to the person or persons he intends to make liable.

45. Circumstances under which notice of dishonour is dispensed with

(a) When after exercise of reasonable diligence it cannot be given, e.g. where the address cannot be found.
(b) When waived, expressly or by implication, by the person entitled to notice.
(c) *As regards the drawer*:
   (*i*) where drawer and drawee are the same person,
   (*ii*) where the drawee is a fictitious person or lacks capacity,

    (*iii*) where the drawer is the person to whom presentment for payment was made,

    (*iv*) where the drawee was under no obligation to the drawer to accept the bill, *or*

    (*v*) where the drawer has countermanded payment.

(d) *As regards the indorser*:

    (*i*) where the drawee is a fictitious person or has no capacity, and the indorser was aware of this when he indorsed,

    (*ii*) where the indorser is the person to whom the presentment was made, *or*

    (*iii*) where the bill was accepted or made only for the indorser's accommodation.

46. Discharge of bills

This occurs by the following means.

(a) By payment in due course, i.e. to a bona fide holder without the payer having notice of any defect in the holder's title: s. 59.

    Note that by s. 60 where a banker, in reliance on a forged indorsement, pays a bill drawn on him in good faith and in the ordinary course of business, the bill is effectively discharged and the bank incurs no liability. (The Cheques Act 1957, s. 1, reduces the importance of this rule by providing that indorsements are no longer necessary in most cases.)

(b) By an acceptor becoming the holder of all rights on the bill at or after its maturity: s. 61.

(c) By renunciation by the holder of all rights against the acceptor: s. 62. (Renunciation must be in writing, or the bill must be delivered up to the acceptor.)

(d) By intentional cancellation by the holder or his agent: s. 63. (Unintentional cancellation is ineffective.)

(e) By material alteration of the bill or its acceptance, without the consent of all parties liable upon it, e.g. by alteration of date, amount, etc.: s. 64.

Cheques

47. Definition

A cheque is a bill of exchange drawn on a banker and payable on demand: Bills of Exchange Act 1882, s. 73. It is not necessary that the words 'on demand' should appear on a cheque, since all bills are treated as payable on demand where no time is specified for payment: s. 10.

48. Stale and overdue cheques

(a) A *stale cheque* is one which has been in circulation for a considerable period of time. Banks generally refuse to honour a cheque more than six months old.

(b) An *overdue cheque* is one which has been in circulation for an unreasonable time: s. 36. (A person who takes an overdue cheque cannot be a holder in due course.)

> NOTE: (1) *What is a reasonable time?* This depends on all the circumstances of each case. Thus where a cheque is intended by the drawer to be presented within two or three days; failure to present within that time might amount to unreasonable delay: *Wheeler* v. *Young* (1897). By contrast, if a cheque was issued overseas for payment in Britain, time would have to be allowed for its transmission to Britain in computing what is a reasonable time. (2) *Discharge of drawer.* If not presented within a reasonable time the drawer is discharged to the extent of any damage he suffers from the delay. In the absence of such damage he remains fully liable for six years, after which his liability is statute-barred: Limitation Act 1980. (3) *Summary on delay in presentation*: (*a*) bills other than cheques — drawer and indorsers completely discharged: Bills of Exchange Act 1882, s. 45; (*b*) delay with regard to cheques: indorsers discharged under s. 45; drawer discharged only to extent of damage suffered: s. 74. (4) *Damage suffered by drawer.* Example: A drew a cheque for £100 in favour of B, who failed to present it for some time. When drawn, A's account had funds to meet the cheque, but during the intervening time the bank went into liquidation. HELD: B could claim for the money as a creditor of the *bank*, but A was under no liability and B had no claim against him: *Wheeler* v. *Young* (1897).

49. Undated and post-dated cheques

(a) *Undated cheques.* A banker is not bound to honour such a cheque, but it must be remembered that any holder is entitled to fill in the correct date: s. 20(1). Any date appearing on a bill is presumed to be the correct date.

(b) *Post-dated cheques.* These are not really cheques, since they are not payable on demand. However, a banker is entitled to pay a post-dated cheque when it falls due. If he pays it before its date he cannot debit the customer's account, and must bear the loss if the customer stops the cheque before its due date.

(Post-dated cheques are frequently used today instead of bills of exchange payable at some time after sight, e.g. where a purchaser of goods issues a post-dated cheque for goods to be delivered later, thus being entitled to stop the cheque if the goods are not delivered when agreed.)

50. Payment by cheque

(a) *Conditional payment.* Payment by any bill is conditional only. A creditor is entitled therefore to refuse payment by cheque, and in any case payment is not effective until the cheque is honoured. (But a creditor who takes a cheque in payment may be estopped from action against the debtor if the cheque is dishonoured because he negligently failed to demand payment himself. But the cheque will remain enforceable by other parties against the drawer for six years: Limitation Act 1980.)

(b) *Cheques through the post.* If a cheque is sent through the post and is lost, the loss falls on the sender, unless the creditor requested this method of payment. Such a request will not be implied; it must be express: *Pennington* v. *Crossley & Son* (1897).

(c) *Cheques as evidence of payment.* An unindorsed cheque which appears to have been paid by the banker on whom it was drawn is *prima facie* evidence of receipt by the payee of the sum stated on the cheque, even without the payee's indorsement: Cheques Act 1957, s. 3.

51. Crossings on cheques

The object of crossing a cheque is to convey instructions that it is not to be paid otherwise than through a bank, or to make some other stipulation as to the manner of payment: s. 76. A crossing is a material part of a cheque and any unauthorised alteration of a crossing is unlawful (s. 78) and discharges the cheque: s. 64.

The drawer or any holder may cross a cheque, or add to an existing crossing, e.g. where the holder of a cheque crossed generally adds the words 'not negotiable.'

Crossings are usually intended as instructions to the paying banker, but a crossing 'account payee' is an instruction to the collecting banker.

52. Types of crossing

(a) *General crossing:* indicated by drawing two transverse lines across the face of the cheque, thus / /, with or without the addition of the words '& Co.' between the lines (or such other words as 'not negotiable': *see* (c) below). The effect of such a crossing is to make the cheque payable only to a collecting banker, i.e. it precludes the paying banker from paying cash for the cheque across the counter.

(b) *Special crossing:* indicating the name of a particular banker, with or without the addition of two transverse lines. The effect is that the paying banker must pay the cheque only to the collecting banker named on the crossing, and to no other.

(c) *'Not negotiable':* this general crossing deprives the cheque of its negotiability, and it becomes an ordinary transferable chose in action, i.e. it can be assigned, but the assignee obtains no better title than was possessed by his assignor: s. 81.

Thus where a clerk took a blank cheque from his employer, which was already crossed 'not negotiable,' and fraudulently made it payable to P, it was held that the employer could recover the value from P (who had obtained cash), since the clerk had no title to the cheque and P could get no better title than the clerk had: *Wilson & Meeson* v. *Pickering* (1946).

(d) *'Account payee'* (or *'Account payee only'*): originally, this was not a statutory crossing, though it was recognised and obeyed by banker's custom, with the effect that a collecting bank which collected for some person other than the named payee could be liable in negligence. This has now been given statutory backing by the Cheques Act 1992.

53. Alterations on a cheque

Any material alteration on a cheque or other bill discharges from liability any party to the bill who did not assent to the alteration. On a cheque, alterations of date, amount, name of payee, or of any crossing would be material.

Bankers therefore should not pay a cheque unless any alteration is initialled by the drawer, and where the words 'or order' have been altered to 'bearer' the normal practice is to insist on the drawer's full signature by way of assent.

(Note the distinction between apparent and non-apparent alterations: *see* **17** above.)

54. Indorsements

The general rule about indorsements applies to cheques. The Cheques Act 1957, s. 1 dispenses with the need for an indorsement where the apparent payee or indorsee of a cheque is paying it into his own account. But the Committee of the London Clearing Banks has decided that though these provisions dispense in law with the necessity of a banker requiring to see a payee's indorsement in all cases, bankers will in practice insist upon the payee's indorsement except where a cheque is paid into a bank for the credit of the payee's account or for the credit of a joint or partnership account where the payee is one of the account holders.

Therefore indorsement will be required in the following situations:

(a) If the payee, or his transferee, presents the cheque to the drawee bank for payment over the counter (only possible in the case of an open cheque). A banker disregarding the requirement as to indorsement would not be acting in the ordinary course of business and would as a result be outside the protection afforded by s. 1. No indorsement is, however, required where the customer presents his own cheque for payment;

(b) Order cheques which are to be paid into an account other than that of the original payee, i.e. order cheques which have been negotiated;

(c) If the payee combines cheques and receipt forms marked 'R'.

55. Duty of bankers as to crossed cheques

The banker is liable to the true owner for any loss occasioned where:

(a) he pays a cheque which is crossed specially to more than one banker (unless the additional special crossing merely indicates that one of the bankers named is to collect merely as agent for the other);

(b) he pays a cheque crossed generally otherwise than to a bank, i.e. treats it as an open cheque;

(c) he pays a cheque crossed specially otherwise than to the banker named in the crossing or his agent: Bills of Exchange Act, s. 79.

56. Protection of paying banker

The drawee bank is statutorily protected against liability if it pays in the following circumstances.

(a) *Cheques with forged indorsements:* provided they are paid (*i*) in good faith, and (*ii*) in the ordinary course of business: BEA, s. 60.
(b) *Crossed cheques:* provided the bank pays a cheque drawn upon it (*i*) in accordance with the crossing, (*ii*) in good faith, and (*iii*) without negligence: BEA, s. 80.
(c) *Cheques not indorsed or irregularly indorsed:* provided the cheque is drawn on the bank and is paid (*i*) in good faith, and (*ii*) in the ordinary course of business: Cheques Act 1957, s. 1.

57. Protection of collecting banker

A collecting banker, that is one who presents a cheque to the drawee bank on behalf of a customer, is protected from liability where he receives payment for a customer who has no title or defective title, provided he does so (*i*) in good faith, and (*ii*) without negligence (whether or not the cheque is crossed): Cheques Act 1957, s. 4.

Section 4 applies only to customers. A person becomes a customer as soon as he opens an account, i.e. where the bank obliges someone, not having an account, by cashing his cheques from time to time, this does not make such person a customer: *Commissioners of Taxation* v. *English, Scottish & Australian Bank Ltd* (1920). The following have been held to amount to negligence by a collecting bank.

(a) Opening an account for someone without making adequate enquiries about him: *Hampstead Guardians* v. *Barclays Bank* (1923).
(b) Collecting payment for a customer of a cheque made out to the customer's employer without making enquiries: *Underwood Ltd* v. *Martins Bank* (1924).
(c) Paying into a customer's private account a cheque payable to him in an official capacity: *Ross* v. *London County Bank* (1919).
(d) Receiving payment for a customer of cheques clearly

indicating they are payable to him only as agent for someone else: *Bute (Marquess)* v. *Barclays Bank* (1955).

(e) Where a bank uses a computer to identify the branch on which a cheque is drawn and a customer with accounts at two branches alters a cheque from branch A to draw it on branch B and the computer fails to recognise the change, if the computer directs the cheque to branch A, which pays the cheque, the bank may be liable for negligence: *Burnett* v. *Westminster Bank Ltd* (1966).

Where a collecting banker is negligent he may be sued for damages for the tort of conversion by the true owner of the cheque.

Where the customer's own negligence in drawing cheques contributes to the loss the amount recoverable from the banker is reduced under the Law Reform (Contributory Negligence) Act 1945: *Lumsden & Co.* v. *London Trustee Savings Bank* (1971).

NOTE: There is no corresponding duty of care imposed on the drawer or acceptor of any bill: *Scholfield* v. *Londesborough* (1896). In an action for breach of contract for failing to honour a cheque, the customer is not entitled to claim damages for vexation and disappointment: *Rae* v. *Yorkshire Bank* (1987).

If a bank has credited the customer's account with more than it should have done, the customer is not generally entitled to retain the extra sum. However, if the customer has relied on the misleading statement and altered his position in reliance on it, the bank cannot reclaim the money. In *United Overseas Bank* v. *Jiwani* (1977), the bank was able to reclaim the money, even though part had been used to buy a hotel, since it was established that the customer would have made the purchase anyway and did not rely on the bank.

58. Termination of banker's authority: BEA, s. 75
A banker's authority to pay a cheque drawn by his customer is terminated by the following.

(a) *Countermand of payment*, written or oral, though if oral countermand is made, it is the practice to insist on written confirmation and merely to postpone payment pending receipt of confirmation.

(b) *Notice of the customer's death.* Observe that it is not the death which terminates the authority, but notice of the death.

(c) *Notice of the mental incapacity* of the customer.

(d) *Notice of the presentation of a bankruptcy petition against* the customer. Note that if the bank receives notice of an act of bankruptcy committed by the customer, it can still pay out to the customer himself but should not pay out cheques drawn by him in favour of third parties (otherwise it may be liable to make good such payments to the trustee in bankruptcy): *Re Keever* (1966).

(e) *The making of a receiving order* in bankruptcy against the customer.

(f) *The service of a garnishee order* attaching the balance of the customer's account, i.e. a court order addressed to a debtor commanding him not to pay the stated debt to his creditor but to hold the money pending further orders from the court (which may eventually direct that the money shall be paid to some other person).

(g) *Notice of a breach of trust*, i.e. when a customer is about to use trust funds for his own purposes.

(h) *Notice of a defect in the presenter's title*.

(i) *Insufficient credit* in the customer's account, or where payment would increase the customer's indebtedness beyond some agreed limit. The bank is entitled to refuse to pay a cheque if it exceeds the customer's entitlement by as little as a penny, and it cannot pay part of a cheque. If it wrongly refuses to honour a cheque properly drawn, it is liable to the customer for damages for breach of contract, but is not liable to the holder. A bank may also be liable for damages for libel if it makes a defamatory comment unjustifiably on a cheque, e.g. where it wrongly marks a cheque 'No funds.'

(j) *Where money is paid into a trust account*, a bank is liable if it knowingly assists in a dishonest and fraudulent design on the part of the trustees: *Rowlandson* v. *National Westminster Bank Ltd* (1978).

59. Duties of the customer
It is the duty of the customer, in drawing a cheque, to take usual and reasonable precautions to prevent forgery and fraud.

Examples _____

(1) M's clerk was entrusted with the task of filling in M's cheques for signature. The clerk prepared a bearer cheque on which the sum payable was not mentioned in words and which bore the figures £2.0s.0d. M

signed it. The clerk then added the words 'one hundred and twenty pounds' and placed a '1' and a '0' either side of the '2' in the spaces which he had left. The clerk obtained payment of the cheque. It was held that the bank could debit the client's account to the full amount of the cheque since the loss was caused by M's failure to ensure that the cheque could not be altered in the way it was: *London Joint Stock Bank* v. *Macmillan* (1918). (2) A dishonest employee forged cheques on his employer's account over more than six years, taking around HK$5.5m. The company did not check thoroughly its monthly statements and did not detect the loss. The court required the bank to make good the loss, ruling that the company was not required to check its bank statements nor to operate a system of control which would aid the bank in detecting fraud. A bank could impose such a duty, but it would have to do so expressly in the terms of its contract with the customer: *Tai Hing Cotton Mill Ltd* v. *Liu Chong Hing Bank Ltd* (1985).

Where an agreement for the purchase of traveller's cheques contains an express condition that the purchaser should properly safeguard the cheques against loss or theft, the whole of his conduct should be considered when deciding whether he had in fact properly safeguarded them. Taking into account the facts that the plaintiff had carried the cheques in a transparent bag instead of concealing them about his person, and that he had fallen asleep because he was tired and had been drinking, he could not be said to have properly safeguarded the cheques and he was therefore not entitled to a refund: *Braithwaite* v. *Thomas Cook Ltd* (1989). In another case, the contract contained an express obligation on the part of the bank to refund lost or stolen cheques. There was no implied term that this was subject to the customer not being reckless or negligent, with the result that the bank had to make a refund even though the cheques were stolen largely as a result of the customer's negligence: *Elawadi* v. *BCCI* (1989).

Promissory notes and miscellaneous instruments

60. Promissory note: BEA, s. 83

This is an unconditional promise in writing by one person to another, signed by the maker, and engaging to pay on demand or at a fixed or determinable future time a sum certain in money to or to the order of a specified person, or to bearer.

A promissory note is inchoate and incomplete until delivery to the payee or bearer: s. 83.

61. Difference from bills of exchange

(a) Acceptance of a note is never necessary, since there is no drawee.

(b) A promissory note (unlike a bill) cannot be drawn in a set.

(c) The maker is the person liable to pay. (In a bill, the drawer is only liable until the drawee accepts.)

(d) A promissory note must contain an unconditional promise to pay. (The acceptor of a bill may make a conditional promise to pay.)

(e) A promissory note is a promise to pay; a bill is an order to pay.

(f) A bill may be treated as a promissory note where (*i*) drawer and drawee are the same person and (*ii*) the drawee is fictitious or lacks capacity: s. 5(2).

62. Bank notes

These are promissory notes payable to bearer. When presenting a note for payment it is not necessary for the bearer to reveal how he came by the note, but if the circumstances aroused suspicion the bank would be entitled to refuse payment until satisfied of good faith; if, however, the bearer sued the bank for its refusal, the burden of proving bad faith would rest on the bank.

63. Joint, and joint and several notes

Where a note is issued by two or more persons, their liability may be joint or joint and several, depending on the circumstances.

(a) *On a joint note*, each maker is fully liable for the whole amount, but a person suing to enforce the note has only one cause of action and can sue all, or one or any combination, but cannot later bring a second action against parties not sued in the first. If the maker of a joint note dies, his estate ceases to be liable on the note.

(b) *On a joint and several note*, each maker is fully liable but a holder has several rights of action, e.g. he may sue all, or any one, or bring successive actions against the makers. The death of a maker does not relieve his estate from liability on the note.

NOTE: Where a note runs 'I promise to pay' and is signed by two or more makers, it is deemed to be a joint and several note: s. 85.

64. Miscellaneous banking instruments

(a) *Bankers' drafts.* These are drafts to order payable on demand, drawn by an office of a bank upon itself or upon some other office of the same bank: Bills of Exchange Act (1882) Amendment Act 1932. Drafts may be crossed, and the crossing has the same effect as the crossing on a cheque (*see* **51–52** above). The Cheques Act 1957 extends the protection given bankers by the BEA to cover bankers' drafts.

(b) *Conditional orders.* These are documents ordering payment of money subject to the fulfilment of some stated condition. They may be crossed like cheques, and the Cheques Act 1957 extends the provisions of the BEA protecting bankers to conditional orders.

Note that a document apparently a cheque may in fact be a conditional order, e.g. a cheque stating on it that payment is not to be made unless an attached receipt form is signed. But the mere fact that a cheque contains a receipt form does not make it a conditional order, unless payment is made conditional on the signing of the receipt.

(c) *Dividends and interest warrants.* These are drafts issued by a company and ordering its bank to pay the stated sum to a named person. They can be crossed like cheques, and are covered by the protections given by the Cheques Act 1957.

(d) *Deposit receipts.* These are acknowledgments by a banker that he holds funds to a certain amount for the depositor. They are not negotiable instruments.

65. Quasi-negotiable instruments

The following documents have some of the qualities of negotiability, but not all, and are therefore not negotiable instruments.

(a) *Bills of lading*: receipts for goods shipped, signed by the carrier or his agent. A bill of lading is a document of title to the goods specified therein, and possession of the bill entitles the holder to delivery of the goods. But it is not a negotiable instrument, so that a transferee gets no better title than was possessed by his transferor.

(b) *Dock warrants*: documents issued by a dock or warehouse company acknowledging that it holds certain goods on behalf of the person named, or his indorsee. They are documents of title assignable by delivery plus indorsement, but they are not negotiable instruments and the indorsee gets no better title than his transferor.

(c) *American share certificates* usually have a transfer form printed on the back, and the owner can sign this form leaving the name of the transferee blank. This then operates as a power of attorney to a subsequent transferee to fill in his own name or the name of another, the person named being entitled to apply to the company for registration as a shareholder. Such transferee gets no better title than his transferor.

(d) *I.O.Us.* These are merely written admission of the existence of a debt (with an implied promise to pay at some future date). They are not negotiable but can be assigned under s. 136, Law of Property Act 1925.

Note that if the document contained an express promise to pay, it would be a promissory note.

66. Negotiable instruments under the Consumer Credit Act 1974

Sections 123–125 of the Act impose the following restrictions on the use of negotiable instruments taken under regulated agreements.

(a) A creditor or owner is not able to take a negotiable instrument in payment other than a bank note or cheque.

(b) Where a cheque is taken, it must be negotiated direct to a bank.

The Act further provides that a negotiable instrument cannot be taken as any kind of security for a regulated agreement. If any of the foregoing provisions is not complied with, the agreement under which the relevant sum is payable is enforceable on a court order.

Where a negotiable instrument is taken in contravention of the Act, the person taking it is not a holder in due course (*see* **38** above). If that person further negotiates the instrument, the holder can enforce the instrument but the creditor or owner under the regulated agreement must indemnify the consumer who gave him the instrument. If a cheque is taken, which it can be, but it is not negotiated as it should be directly to a bank, that constitutes a defect in title. This means that any subsequent holder who knew or ought to have known of the defect in the cheque cannot enforce it. If he neither knew nor ought to have known, and enforces the cheque, the consumer has the same right of indemnity as in the case of an improperly taken negotiable instrument.

Progress test 4

Negotiable instruments

1. How would you define a negotiable instrument? What are the characteristics of such an instrument, and how does it differ from other choses in action? (14: **1–3**)

2. What persons are liable on a negotiable instrument and to whom? (14: **4**)

3. Define a bill of exchange. Explain what is meant by saying that a bill must be unconditional. What is a conditional order and what is its effect? (14: **6, 7, 64**)

4. What is meant by saying that there must be three parties to a bill of exchange? What is the effect where the drawer and drawee are one and the same person? (14: **8, 61**)

5. X is the holder of an undated cheque, and when he presents it to his bank the bank refuses to take it. Explain why the bank refused it and what X can do to remedy the situation. (14: **10, 49**)

6. 'A cheque is an exception to the rule that past consideration is no consideration.' Discuss. (3: **17**; 14: **11**)

7. What is meant by saying that a bill must order the payment of a 'sum certain' and not a 'certain sum' of money? (14: **12**)

8. Distinguish between order and bearer bills, and explain how each can be negotiated. Distinguish also between non-existing and fictitious payees.   (14: **13, 36**)

9. Explain briefly the meaning of: (*a*) inland and foreign bills; (*b*) bills in a set; (*c*) inchoate instruments.   (14: **14–16**)

10. What is, and what is the effect of, a material alteration of a bill? Why is it important to distinguish between apparent and non-apparent alterations?   (14: **17, 53**)

11. What is meant by an overdue bill? How does an overdue cheque differ from a stale cheque?   (14: **18, 48**)

12. X owes Y £100 and draws a cheque for that amount in favour of Y. The cheque is lost or stolen before Y is able to present it to his bank. Y now maintains that he has not been paid. What is the legal position?   (14: **19, 20, 50**)

13. What is meant by the negotiation of a bill? Explain the effect of marking a bill or a cheque 'not negotiable'.   (14: **21**)

14. X negotiates a bearer bill to Y for value and later, when the bill is dishonoured, X maintains that he is under no liability (*a*) to Y, or (*b*) to any person to whom Y has negotiated the bill. What is the legal position? Would it make any difference to Y's position if he had not given value?   (14: **11, 22**)

15. Explain the effect of the following signatures on a bill of exchange: (*a*) signature of a stranger; (*b*) agent's signature; (*c*) signature *sans recours*; (*d*) signature *sans frais*.   (14: **22, 23**)

16. 'A forged or unauthorised signature is wholly inoperative on a bill of exchange.' Discuss this statement, distinguishing between forged and unauthorised signatures and explaining how estoppel may operate to prevent a person whose signature has been forged from denying that he signed the bill.   (14: **24**)

17. Distinguish carefully between the effect of forgery of the signature on a bill of: (*a*) the drawer; (*b*) the drawee; (*c*) an indorser.   (14: **25**)

18. What is meant by the delivery of a bill? What is conditional delivery and what is its effect?   (14: **26**)

19. 'Delivery is presumed in favour of any holder of a bill of exchange.' Explain this statement, and state the cases where delivery is not presumed conclusively.   (14: **26**)

20. 'An order bill is transferable by delivery plus indorsement.' Explain this statement, and explain also what is meant by a valid indorsement.'   (14: **26, 27**)

21. Explain the following terms: (*a*) blank and special indorsements; (*b*) restrictive indorsements; (*c*) conditional indorsement; (*d*) indorsement *sans recours*.   (14: **27, 28**)

22. In what order are the parties to a bill liable upon it? Explain carefully the liability of: (*a*) the drawer; (*b*) the drawee; (*c*) an indorser.   (14: **30–33**)

23. Explain the significance of the following terms: (*a*) referee in case of need; (*b*) accommodation party; (*c*) accommodation bill; (*d*) fictitious payee; (*e*) non-existing payee.   (14: **34–36**)

24. Distinguish carefully between the following terms in relation to bills of exchange: (*a*) holder; (*b*) holder for value; (*c*) holder in due course.   (14: **37–39**)

25. What are the rights of a holder in due course and of a holder for value?   (14: **38, 39**)

26. What is meant by saying that neither a payee of a cheque nor the paying banker can be a holder in due course?   (14: **38, 56**)

27. When does a bill of exchange require acceptance by the drawee in order to render it payable? What is, and what is the effect of, qualified acceptance?   (14: **40, 41**)

28. When is presentment for acceptance (*a*) necessary; (*b*) unnecessary?   (14: **41, 42**)

29. Explain the following: (*a*) days of grace, (*b*) noting and protesting, (*c*) presentment for payment.   (14: **43, 44**)

30. When is presentment for payment excused?   (14: **43**)

31. When is a bill dishonoured (*a*) by non-acceptance, and (*b*) by non-payment?   (14: **40, 44**)

32. When is notice of dishonour necessary and when is it unnecessary? What form should such notice take (*a*) in the case of inland bills, and (*b*) in the case of foreign bills?   (14: **44, 45**)

33. What is a promissory note and how does it differ from a bill of exchange? What is the distinction between (*a*) joint notes and (*b*) joint and several notes?   (14: **60, 61, 63**)

34. Define the following, and explain how far they are subject to the provisions of the Cheques Act 1957: (*a*) bankers' draft, (*b*) conditional order, (*c*) dividend warrant, (*d*) deposit receipt. (14: **64**)

35. Some instruments are negotiable by statute, and others are negotiable by custom; others again have some of the characteristics of negotiable instruments, but not all. Explain this statement.   (14: **3, 65**)

36. Define a cheque. How does a cheque differ from an ordinary bill of exchange?   (14: **6, 47**)

37. An overdue cheque is one which has been in circulation for an unreasonable time. What is meant by 'unreasonable time' in this context?   (14: **48**)

38. The effect of delay in presenting a cheque differs from the effect of delay in presenting other bills. How?   (14: **48**)

39. 'A banker is not bound to honour an undated or post-dated cheque.' Do you agree?   (14: **49**)

40. On 1 June X sent to his insurance company a cheque to cover the insurance on his car. The cheque arrived on 2 June. On 2 June X was charged by the police with driving an uninsured vehicle, since his insurance had expired in May. Explain why the prosecution would succeed.   (14: **50**)

41. What is the object of crossing a cheque, and what types of crossing are legally recognised?   (14: **51, 52**)

42. When does a banker's authority to pay a cheque drawn upon him cease?   (14: **58**)

43. State and explain briefly the protections given to paying bankers by statute.   (14: **56**)

44. A collecting banker who collects a cheque for the wrong person may be liable in tort to the true owner. What form does this liability take, and when does it arise?   (14: **57**)

45. Explain the significance of the Consumer Credit Act 1974. (14: **66**)

Specimen questions

1. As a general rule, a bill of exchange must be presented for payment in order to retain the liability of the drawer and of the indorsers.

You are required to state:

(*a*) those circumstances which excuse delay in presentment for payment; and
(*b*) those circumstances which make it unnecessary to present the bill at all.

2. (*a*) How does the Bills of Exchange Act 1882 define the

following terms: (*i*) a general acceptance; (*ii*) a partial
acceptance; (*iii*) a local acceptance?

(*b*) The holder of a bill for £1000 drawn at one month after
date presents it to the drawee for acceptance. The
drawee accepts the bill payable two months after date.
What type of acceptance has been given, and what steps
should the holder take?

3. (*a*) What condition must be fulfilled before a person may
be regarded as a 'holder in due course'? How does his
legal position differ from that of the 'holder'?

(*b*) Ivor has received the following cheques, in good faith
and for value, from John:

(*i*) a cheque crossed 'a/c payee only' payable to
Stephen Cole and indorsed by him;

(*ii*) a cheque crossed 'not negotiable' payable to and
indorsed by P. Offerman, who obtained it by fraud;

(*iii*) a crossed cheque payable to 'Christine Dickens or
order', on which Christine Dickens' indorsement
has been forged.

Ivor had no knowledge of the history of these cheques
when he received them. Advise him as to whether he
has a good title to them.

4. L drew a cheque for £1300 payable to M in payment for a
motor cycle. M specially indorsed the cheque to N in payment for
a picture, and N specially indorsed it to O, telling him that the
money was to be used for O to have a holiday. Instead of using the
cheque as directed, O specially indorsed it to P as a gift.

As the cheque has been dishonoured, P wishes to know his
rights against all the parties concerned. Advise him.

5. L drew a cheque for £100 in favour of X and gave the cheque
to Y (L's secretary) to remit to X. Y indorsed the cheque by forging
X's signature, and negotiated it to M in return for goods.

Advise L as to his rights.

6. Jones transferred the following cheques to Brown:

(*a*) an uncrossed cheque payable to Smith whose
indorsement had been forged by Jones;

(*b*) a cheque crossed 'not negotiable' payable to Jones and indorsed by him, which Jones had obtained by fraud;

(*c*) a cheque crossed 'a/c payee' payable to Jones and indorsed by him.

Brown had no knowledge of the history of the cheques and gave value to Jones for them. Advise Brown whether he has a good title to any of these cheques.

7. (*a*) What is meant in the law relating to bills of exchange by a holder in due course? Why is it important to ascertain whether the holder of a bill is a holder in due course?

(*b*) D owed £100 to C for goods supplied. When payment fell due, D drew a cheque for £100 in C's favour and sent it to him. Subsequently, however, D stopped payment of the cheque before C had cashed it. Will C have a right of action on the cheque against D? Would your answer be the same if the cheque had been drawn in C's favour by D's friend, F, acting at D's request and F had stopped payment? Would, in this case, C have a right of action against F? Give reasons.

8. Williams sells goods to Thomas at the price of £100 and Thomas gives Williams a cheque for the amount, payable to 'Williams or order'. What are Williams' rights and liabilities in each of the following situations:

(*a*) Williams loses the cheque and asks Thomas for another, but Thomas declines to give one.

(*b*) Williams indorses the cheque to Rees to satisfy a debt of £85 which he owes to Rees. The cheque is subsequently dishonoured and Thomas cannot be traced. Rees claims the sum of £100 from Williams.

9. A buys goods from B and asks B to accept C's cheque for part of the money and the balance in cash. He explains that he has no banking account of his own and that C's cheque is crossed. B agrees to this and the goods are given to A and he hands B the cheque and cash as arranged. The cheque is payable to 'A or order,' but B omits to obtain A's indorsement. He subsequently discovers his mistake.

(*a*) Is B entitled to ask for A's indorsement?

(*b*) Will B's rights against C be affected if he finds A obtained the cheque by fraud?

10. (*a*) Allen sells a typewriter to Baker, an infant, who pays for it by his cheque. Allen indorses the cheque to Cook who takes it in good faith and for value. The cheque is dishonoured on presentation. Can Cook enforce payment of the cheque against A or B?

(*b*) Davis, by mistake, draws a cheque payable to Evans, who does not exist. The cheque is negotiated by Franks by a forged indorsement to Green, who takes it in good faith and for value. Can Green enforce payment of the cheque?

11. (*a*) Explain the rights and duties of a paying banker and a collecting banker in relation to cheques.

(*b*) How is a banker's authority to pay a cheque drawn on him by his customer terminated?

12. (*a*) What is a bill of exchange? How does a cheque differ from other bills of exchange?

(*b*) What is meant by the 'negotiation' of a bill of exchange? How does the addition of the words 'not negotiable' affect the transferability of (*i*) bills of exchange generally, and (*ii*) cheques?

Part five

Securities

15
Securities

Summary of property law

1. Understanding of property law

Students who are required to study the subject of securities need at least a background knowledge of the law of property. This section is intended to provide a superficial outline to facilitate understanding of the law relating to securities, but students who have no prior knowledge of the subject would be well advised to make a more detailed study of property law.

2. Ownership and possession

The owner of property is the person who has the maximum legal rights over the property (including the right to actual possession). He may however part with possession, without surrendering ownership, e.g. where the owner lends property to another.

Ownership is a legal concept; possession is a state of fact, and involves actual control over the property. When the owner of land leases it to a tenant, the tenant acquires legal possession and can assert his right of control against anyone (even against the owner, if the owner in breach of the lease attempts to regain possession).

3. Transfer of ownership

(a) *Personal property.*
   (*i*) Chattels can be transferred by mere delivery, with intention to pass ownership (and not merely possession).
   (*ii*) Choses in action require to be assigned either in accordance with the method laid down by s. 136 of the Law of Property Act 1925 or equity or in accordance with some

particular method laid down for particular choses, e.g. share transfers.

(b) *Real property.* Freehold land (and also leasehold) should be transferred by deed if legal ownership is intended to pass. Any attempted conveyance which is not by deed operates to transfer only an equitable interest in the property.

A deed is not necessary in the following cases.

(*i*) Leases for a term not exceeding three years.

(*ii*) Assents by personal representatives. A deceased person's land vests in his personal representatives and they can transfer it to the beneficiaries under the deceased's will (or upon his intestacy) by a mere written assent.

(*iii*) Disclaimers by a trustee in bankruptcy need only be in writing.

(*iv*) On redemption of a mortgage of land, the land revests in the mortgagor as soon as the mortgagee signs a receipt for the mortgage moneys.

Securities generally

4. Meaning of 'security'

A security is some right or interest in property given to a creditor so that, in the event of the debtor failing to pay his debt as and when due, the creditor may reimburse himself for the debt out of the property charged.

Both real and personal property may be charged with repayment of a debt in this way. (Real property means freehold land, and personal property includes leasehold land and all movable property, such as chattels and choses in action.)

5. Forms of security

(a) *Mortgages.* A mortgage is an assurance to the creditor of the legal or equitable interest in property as security for the discharge of debt, subject to a proviso that on repayment of the debt the property shall revert to the borrower.

The characteristic of a mortgage is that possession of the property remains vested in the mortgagor (the borrower), while the mortgagee (the lender) obtains some or all of the rights of ownership, or the right to obtain ownership if the debtor defaults.

Land is the form of property most usually mortgaged, but chattels can be mortgaged by conditional bill of sale (*see* **12** below), and choses in action (such as insurance policies) can be mortgaged by assignment subject to a condition that on repayment the chose shall revert to the borrower.

(b) *Pledges or pawns.* A pledge is a deposit of chattels with a lender as security for a debt. If the pledgee is a professional lender upon this type of security (a pawnbroker) the pledge is called a pawn. A pledge differs from a mortgage in that the lender obtains possession of the chattel, while the borrower retains ownership.

(c) *Liens.* A lien is a right to retain property until a debt is paid (a possessory lien) or to seek a court order for sale of the property (equitable lien). A lien differs from mortgages and pledges in that it arises by implication of law from certain situations, while mortgages and pledges are the result of express agreement between a borrower and a lender.

6. Appropriate formalities

The Consumer Credit Act 1974 lays down various requirements concerning formalities for securities provided in relation to regulated agreements.

(a) Any security must be in writing and must conform to requirements laid down in regulations yet to be made as to form and content: s. 105.

(b) A security instrument must be properly executed (i.e. signed in the prescribed manner; embodying all the terms of the security; its terms are readily legible; and a copy is provided at the proper time): s. 105.

(c) Failure to observe the requirements of **(a)** or **(b)** means that the security is enforceable against the surety on an order of the court only: s. 105.

(d) If an application for an order is dismissed other than on technical grounds, the security is to be treated as ineffective: ss. 105 and 106.

(e) Regulations yet to be made may provide for any matters relating to the sale or other realisation of securities: s. 112.

(f) The Consumer Credit Act cannot be avoided by the use of a security: s. 113. For example, where a hire-purchase agreement is terminated under s. 100, the hirer is not liable for more than 50 per cent of the total purchase price. Section 113 would make it impossible for a security to be used so as to obtain more than 50 per cent.

7. Land mortgages

Where a prospective regulated agreement is to be secured on land, the prospective mortgagor must receive a copy of the unexecuted agreement which contains a prescribed notice indicating his right to withdraw from the prospective agreement: Consumer Credit Act, s. 58. This agreement must be sent by post to the mortgagor for signature not less than seven days after the copy was given. During the 'consideration period', the mortgagee must not communicate in any way with the mortgagor except at the mortgagor's specific request. The 'consideration period' runs from the date when the copy of the unexecuted agreement is first given and expires seven days after the day the unexecuted agreement is sent for signature; or its return, with signature, by the mortgagor, whichever comes first: s. 61. A land mortgage securing a regulated agreement is enforceable on an order of the court only: s. 126.

8. Legal and equitable interests

In English property law a distinction is drawn between legal interests in property (which are enforceable in any court and against any person), and equitable interests (which are personal rights against a particular individual and are not enforceable against other persons, save in certain exceptional circumstances: *see* below). Both legal and equitable interests in property can be used as security for loans, but the limited enforceability of equitable interests makes them less acceptable securities.

Differences between legal and equitable interests:

(a) *Creation.* A legal interest is one created in the correct form for the particular type of property, e.g. a deed of conveyance to create a legal interest or estate in land. An equitable interest is either (*i*) the result of an informal creation, e.g. a conveyance of land not under seal, or (*ii*) the result of a transfer of an existing equitable interest, since these cannot be converted into legal interests (even by conveyance under seal).

(b) *Enforceability.* If a person has a legal interest in property his claims are enforceable against all comers, and are indefeasible. But the holder of an equitable interest in property can

> (*i*) enforce his interest only against the person through whom he derives it, i.e. the owner of the parallel legal interest in the property, *and*
>
> (*ii*) can have his interest in the property destroyed if the legal owner sells the property to a purchaser for value without notice of the equitable interest attaching to the property.

(c) *Parallel interests.* In any one piece of property there may be parallel legal and equitable interests, vested in different persons. Thus, in a trust, the legal owner of property is compelled to hold the property as trustee for the benefit of the beneficiary, that is the owner of the equitable interest. (And the beneficiary's claims are enforceable only against the trustee, and can be extinguished if the trustee sells the property to a purchaser who buys without knowing of the beneficiary's interest.)

9. Legal and equitable mortgages

Just as there can be parallel legal and equitable ownership of property, mortgages can also be either legal or equitable. And where there are several mortgages of a piece of land some may be legal and others equitable.

Where the mortgagee obtains a legal interest in the property charged his mortgage is a legal mortgage; if he obtains merely an equitable interest, his mortgage is equitable (and is a weaker security).

Pledges and mortgages of personalty

10. Mortgages of personalty

The method of mortgaging personalty is to transfer legal ownership to the mortgagee, subject to a condition for retransfer on repayment of the loan.

The method of mortgaging therefore depends on the method of transfer of legal title appropriate to the particular form of personalty.

(a) Chattels are transferable by delivery without the need for any accompanying document, but in order to provide the mortgagee with documentary evidence (while leaving possession in the hands of the mortgagor) a conditional bill of sale is normally used: *see* **12** below.

(b) Choses in action are transferable by assignment, either legal (under the Law of Property Act 1925, s. 136) or equitable: *see* 6: **7**.

In some cases particular statutes lay down special requirements for the assignment of particular choses in action (e.g. insurance policies, copyrights, etc.), and these requirements would have to be observed in the mortgage of such a chose.

11. Pledge or mortgage

Where chattels are to be mortgaged, a conditional bill of sale must be used. But this procedure is not popular: *see* **12** below.

An easier method of using small chattels as security is to pledge them, i.e. to deliver possession to the lender subject to a condition that he shall return the chattels on repayment of the loan. But pledging is only appropriate in connection with smaller chattels, which can be easily moved or stored. Larger chattels, such as pianos, motor cars, collections of furniture or paintings, etc. must normally be mortgaged by bill of sale.

12. Conditional bills of sale

An absolute bill of sale is a documentary assignment of chattels, giving title with or without delivery of the chattels comprised. Since chattels can pass by delivery, without documentation, and since most sales take effect in actual or constructive delivery, absolute bills of sale are rarely used. Their only use today is where the purchaser requires for some reason documentary evidence of his purchase, e.g. where he is buying goods for export and may have to prove to the customs authorities that he is the owner of the goods.

A conditional bill of sale is one used as documentary evidence of a mortgage of chattels, i.e. it transfers ownership to the mortgagee (while leaving the mortgagor in possession as bailee for the lender), subject to a condition that the chattels shall be reassigned to the borrower on repayment of the loan.

13. Form of conditional bills of sale

These must comply with the requirements of the Bills of Sale Acts 1878 and 1882, as follows.

(a) The bill must be by deed, attested by at least one witness; otherwise it is void.

(b) The bill must be registered at the Central Office of the Supreme Court within seven days of creation; otherwise it is void.

(c) Consideration for the bill must be truly stated therein.

(d) Interest payable and date for repayment must be stated in the bill, together with any other conditions.

(e) The chattels comprised in the bill must be inventoried, and the inventory must be attached to the bill on registration.

(f) The lender's remedy under a conditional bill of sale which has been properly registered and drawn is seizure of the chattels. The right to seizure arises

    (*i*) on failure to repay the loan as agreed,

    (*ii*) on bankruptcy of the borrower, *or*

    (*iii*) on any fraudulent dealing by the debtor with the chattels with the intention of removing them from the lender's power, e.g. an attempted sale to another person.

> NOTE: A conditional bill of sale takes its priority from the date of registration. Therefore a bill created earlier than a rival may rank after the rival if registered later. Because of the technicalities and publicity involved, bills of sale are not popular forms of security. They are sometimes taken by professional moneylenders, but very rarely by non-professional moneylenders such as bankers. From a borrower's point of view a pledge offers an easier way of raising money on security of chattels; the difficulty here is that a pawnbroker will not usually take a pledge of large and cumbersome chattels, which may then only be useful as security if someone can be found who is willing to take a conditional bill of sale (e.g. pianos, cars, collections of paintings, etc.).

14. Pledges

A pledge of chattels involves actual or constructive delivery of chattels to the lenders. Constructive delivery might be by giving the pledgee the key to a warehouse in which the goods are stored.

The pledgor remains the legal owner of the goods, and the pledgee becomes a bailee who must return the goods on repayment as agreed. The pledgor is entitled to demand a receipt for deposit of the goods. The pledgee owes a duty of care for the goods while in his possession, and if they are lost or damaged through his negligence he must make good the loss. (But if the goods were taken from him by robbery with violence, he is generally excused liability.) The pledgee generally has no right to use the goods deposited unless otherwise agreed. The pledgee has a possessory lien over the goods entitling him to retain them until repayment, even if there is no written agreement stating the purpose of deposit.

15. Pawnbrokers

The Consumer Credit Act 1974 replaces the controls which were formerly imposed on pawnbrokers by the now-repealed Pawnbrokers Acts 1872–1960. Pawnbrokers must be licensed as creditors under the 1974 Act by the Office of Fair Trading. The person who takes an article in pawn must provide a receipt. This must be in the form prescribed by the Consumer Credit (Pawn-Receipts) Regulations 1983. If the receipt is lost, the borrower may provide a statutory declaration which must be in the form prescribed by the Consumer Credit (Loss of Pawn-Receipt) Regulations 1983, or, if the lender agrees, give him a written statement in the form prescribed by those Regulations. The latter alternative is possible only where the amount of the loan exceeds £25. Copies of the pawn agreement must be provided, and the agreement must be drawn up in the manner specified by the Consumer Credit (Agreements) Regulations 1983 and the Consumer Credit (Cancellation Notices and Copies of Documents) Regulations 1983. Breach of these provisions means that the agreement can be enforced against the debtor only on a court order. Breach of the provisions relating to copies is an offence.

Redemption

The article given in pawn can be redeemed during the period for which credit is extended. There is, however, a guaranteed minimum redemption period of six months. If the pawn-receipt is tendered while the redemption period lasts, the goods must be handed over if payment is made of the money owing. The lender need not redeem the goods, however, if he knows or ought reasonably to suspect that neither the person taking the goods is unauthorised to receive them nor owns the article in question. If the goods are handed over to an unauthorised party, and the lender has no reason to suspect that the person taking the goods is unauthorised, then the lender incurs no liability in tort to the real owner. It is a criminal offence, however, to refuse redemption of the article without reasonable cause. If the pawn is not redeemed by the end of the redemption period, it remains redeemable to the time when it is realised, unless the article has already become the lender's property. If the credit limit under the agreement is not more than £25, and if the redemption period is six months, the goods in question become the property of the lender if the redemption period has passed without redemption. If an application has been made to the court for a time order, the goods instead become the lender's property within the five days following the end of the redemption period. If the credit limit is more than £25, or if the redemption period is not six months, the goods become realisable by the lender.

Realisation
The lender may not sell the article unless he has given the period of notice in the form and giving the details required by the Consumer Credit (Realisation of Pawn) Regulations 1983. Once the goods have been sold, the lender must provide the debtor with a statement of the amount realised and the expenses. If the net proceeds cover the cost of redemption, the debt is discharged and any surplus must be handed over. If the proceeds are insufficient, the balance remains payable. The debtor can challenge the amount realised, the expenses charged, or both.

Liens

16. Definition
A lien is a right over the property of another arising by operation of law (independently of any agreement), and gives the lienor a right (*a*) to retain the property until the owner has settled some debt owed to the lienor (a common law or possessory lien), or (*b*) to sell the property in satisfaction of the debt (an equitable lien).

A lien must be distinguished from a deposit of chattels by way of pledge. A pledge is security derived from express agreement; a lien generally arises independently of agreement.

17. Common law or possessory liens

These arise where the creditor has actual possession of some of the debtor's property, and obtains a right to retain such property until an outstanding debt is paid.

NOTE: (1) A common law lien cannot arise independently of possession, i.e. the creditor is not entitled to obtain possession solely for the purpose of claiming such a lien. (Cf. equitable liens: *see* **19** below.) (2) A common law lien is exercisable only by detaining the goods until the debt is paid, i.e. there is no right of sale, save in some exceptional cases where a right of sale is given by statute. A statutory right of sale is given to innkeepers (Innkeepers Liability Act 1878), unpaid sellers of goods (Sale of Goods Act 1979), and repairers (Torts (Interference with Goods) Act 1977). (3) A common law lien is extinguished by (*i*) agreement, express or implied, (*ii*) payment of the debt, (*iii*) loss of possession, or (*iv*) taking security for the debt. (4) A common law lien may be general or particular, i.e. may be available against any goods of the debtor coming into possession of the creditor, or only against the particular goods in connection with which the debt was incurred. Thus a carrier has a particular lien for his freight charges, while stockbrokers and factors have general liens. A banker's lien is also a general lien: *see* **20** below.

18. Maritime liens

A maritime lien is one attaching to a ship, in favour of the shipmaster (for disbursements and wages), seamen (for their wages), salvors (for charges in connection with salvage), etc.

The lien is exercised against the ship itself, not against the owners, and it arises independently of possession. A notice of lien is affixed to the ship, and proceedings may be taken in the Admiralty Court to arrest the ship. If the lien is not discharged, the ship will not be allowed to leave harbour, and a court order for sale may be given to the lienor.

If the owner of a ship subject to a lien sells the ship, the purchaser takes it subject to the lien, i.e. becomes responsible for discharging the lien.

19. Equitable liens

Unlike common law liens these are not founded on possession, and can be exercised by a court order for sale of the property subject to the lien. But like all equitable rights they can be extinguished by the owner selling the property to a bona fide purchaser for value without notice of the lien.

Equitable liens arise mainly in connection with the sale of land, e.g. a vendor of land who has given possession to the purchaser has a lien over the land for unpaid purchase money, and a purchaser who hands over a deposit before obtaining possession has a lien for his deposit.

20. Banker's lien

This is a general possessory lien arising at common law, but unlike other common law liens it gives the banker a right of sale of securities subject to the lien.

NOTE: (1) The lien arises out of a general course of dealing, and covers 'All securities deposited with them as bankers, by a customer, unless there be an express contract, or circumstances that show an implied contract, inconsistent with the lien': *Brandao* v. *Barnett* (1846). (The lien therefore usually arises by implication from the relationship, but it appears that it may also be granted expressly unlike other liens.) (2) Property subject to the lien includes all securities coming into the banker's possession in the ordinary course of dealing, e.g. promissory notes, bills of exchange, foreign bonds, etc. It does not cover securities deposited merely for safe custody, unless at some time the customer agrees to allow the banker to hold these as security for an advance (in which case they are subject to an equitable mortgage, rather than a lien). (3) The banker's lien has been called an 'implied pledge' (*Brandao* v. *Barnett*) which appears to confer a power of sale, at least in so far as it affects negotiable securities. The Bills of Exchange Act 1882, s. 27 provides that any person having a possessory lien over a bill is deemed to be a holder for value to the extent of his lien, and can therefore sell and transfer the bill.

Guarantees and indemnities

Nature of guarantee

1. Definition of guarantee

A guarantee, or surety contract, is an undertaking 'to be answerable for the debt, default, or miscarriage of another': Statute of Frauds 1677, s. 4.

Guarantees may be either specific or continuing.

(a) A *specific guarantee* relates to one isolated debt only. (Where a bank accepts a specific guarantee of a single loan, a separate account should be opened for that loan, otherwise the guarantee may be cancelled out by operation of the rule in *Clayton's Case, see* **5:6**.)

(b) A *continuing guarantee* is one covering a series of transactions, e.g. a guarantee of an overdraft on a current account at a bank. (A bank, in order to enforce such a guarantee of an overdraft, should stipulate expressly in the guarantee form that the guarantee shall cover the final balance. Otherwise it will be interpreted as covering only the overdraft as it existed at the date of the agreement, and payments in after that date would thus reduce the guarantor's liability.)

2. Characteristics of guarantees

(a) *Three parties*: principal creditor, principal debtor and guarantor (or surety).

(b) *Primary liability to pay* must attach to the principal debtor. The surety only becomes liable to pay if the debtor defaults.

(c) *The guarantor has no interest in the contract* between the principal debtor and the principal creditor, except in so far as he agrees to accept liability if the debtor fails to pay.

3. Form of guarantees

The Statute of Frauds, s. 4 requires any contract of guarantee to be evidenced in writing, by some sufficient note or memorandum *see* 3: **4–5**. (This requirement does not apply where the guarantee is part of some larger transaction, e.g. a contract of agency.) A contract of guarantee can be made enforceable under s. 4 either by having a written agreement signed by the guarantor or his agent, or by having a note or memorandum of the agreement, which could be signed by the guarantor or his agent. In the latter case, the intention or capacity of the person signing the memorandum is irrelevant since all that is necessary under s. 4 is the existence of a note or memorandum of a promise to answer for the debt, default or miscarriage of another person signed by the party to be charged: *Elpis Maritime Co.* v. *Marti Chartering Co.* (1991). The courts have also held that, where the terms of a written guarantee have been orally altered, they may be relied upon in defending a claim, although they cannot be sued upon: *Re a Debtor* (1991). When a property owner deposited title deeds with a bank as security for a customer's overdraft, there was effectively a guarantee of the overdraft to the extent of the property's value, and the guarantee needs to be supported in writing under the Statute of Frauds: *Deutsche Bank* v. *Ibrahim* (1991).

Guarantees require to be supported by consideration, but the consideration does not need to be stated in the written memorandum: Mercantile Law Amendment Act 1856. (Thus the consideration may be proved by independent oral evidence if necessary.) Guarantee bonds do not require consideration.

NOTE: (*a*) Representations made in order to assist someone to obtain credit must be in writing, personally signed by the party making the representation. Otherwise the representation is not actionable: Statute of Frauds Amendment Act 1828. (*b*) Guarantees can also be securities within the Consumer Credit Act 1974: *see* 15: **6**.

4. Guarantees not *uberrimae fidei*

Neither the principal creditor nor the principal debtor is under any legal duty to disclose to the guarantor facts which might influence him against entering into the contract. Thus if A offers to guarantee B's bank account, the bank is under no obligation to reveal matters which show that B is a bad risk: *Wythes v. Labouchere*.

NOTE: (1) Active misrepresentation by the creditor (or by the debtor with the creditor's knowledge) will be grounds for rescission. D, an illiterate farmer, guaranteed a loan to his son by P, the bank. D believed that the loan and guarantee related to the purchase of farm land and, when D asked the bank officials, their answers tended to confirm that view. In fact, the guarantee also covered an overdraft for the son's business. The bank did not know that D was illiterate. When the son's business collapsed, the bank sued D on the guarantee. The Court of Appeal held that the bank had been guilty of misrepresentation and in breach of its duty not to mislead. In addition, D had shown that the document was fundamentally different from the one he thought he was signing and that there was no carelessness on his part. His pleas of *non est factum* (i.e. that this document could not be regarded as his) succeeded: *Lloyds Bank v. Waterhouse* (1991). (2) Active concealment of material facts may amount to misrepresentation, e.g. keeping silent about some facts so as to put facts disclosed into a deceptive light. The New Zealand Court of Appeal has held that a creditor's failure to disclose to a guarantor a material fact known to him will vitiate the guarantee if the non-disclosure amounts to a misrepresentation. This will be the case where the fact is inconsistent with the presumed basis of the contract of guarantee: *National Mortgage and Agency Co. of New Zealand Ltd v. Stalker* (1933). (3) Once the contract of guarantee is made, the creditor owes a duty of the utmost good faith to the guarantor, who is entitled to be discharged if this duty is not observed. Thus the creditor must disclose material facts coming to his knowledge and affecting the guarantor's risk, but need not disclose mere suspicions. For example, A guaranteed B's bank account, and B overdrew on the guaranteed account to pay off debts to another creditor. The bank suspected that A was being defrauded, but did not disclose this. HELD: They were under no duty to do so: *National Provincial Bank v. Glanusk* (1913). (4) Guarantees in the nature of insurance are *uberrimae fidei*, e.g. 'fidelity guarantees' (of the character and good faith of some third person). Thus A gave a fidelity guarantee in respect of L to L's employer, B. B omitted to disclose that L had misappropriated some of B's money and was only being retained in employment in reliance on A's guarantee bond. HELD: L's former dishonesty should have been disclosed, and A was not liable on his guarantee: *London General Omnibus Co. v. Holloway* (1912).

5. Indemnity contracts

An indemnity contract is one in which the indemnifier promises to preserve the other party from loss. Unlike a guarantee (*a*) it is a contract of primary liability, (*b*) it does not require written evidence, and (*c*) there are only two parties, i.e. the indemnifier and the person he promises to indemnify.

Example _____

In *Birkmyr* v. *Darnell* (1704) guarantees and indemnities were distinguished thus:

A and B enter a shop and B asks X for goods on credit. Then (*i*) if A says to X, 'Give B the goods, and if he does not pay for them I will,' this is a contract of guarantee (since A will only become liable if B defaults, i.e. A's liability is secondary to B's); (*ii*) if A says to X, 'Give B the goods and I will see that you get paid,' this is an indemnity since A accepts the principal or primary liability for the debt.

_____

NOTE: An indemnity may be a security within the Consumer Credit Act 1974: *see* 15: **6**.

6. Capacity to contract

Capacity to guarantee is generally co-extensive with normal contractual capacity, but note the following:

(a) A partner as guarantor has no power to bind his firm unless (*i*) so authorised by his co-partners, or (*ii*) giving guarantees is part of the firm's normal business. Even where he has authority, he cannot bind the firm in a guarantee under seal unless (*i*) he is so authorised by deed (power of attorney), or (*ii*) all the partners sign the guarantee deed.

(b) Guarantees by married women are enforceable only against their separate estates. (Thus a bank considering a guarantee from a married woman cannot take her husband's status into account in assessing the value of her guarantee.)

(c) Trading companies have implied power to borrow money, but there is probably no implied power to give guarantees. (Thus a bank, before accepting a guarantee from a company, must examine the memorandum and articles of the company to make sure there is power to give guarantees.)

7. Position of creditor

His rights against the guarantor are dependent on the terms of the contract. But a continuing guarantee by or to a partnership is revoked as to future transactions by any change in the constitution of the firm: Partnership Act 1890, s. 18.

8. Joint and several guarantees

Sometimes several persons join in giving a guarantee, and the liability of such co-guarantors may then (depending on the agreement) be joint, or several, or joint and several.

(a) *Joint guarantors.* Each guarantor is personally liable for the full amount, but the creditor has only one cause of action against them and should therefore sue all in one action. If he elects to sue just one of the guarantors, he cannot later sue the others since he has exhausted his one cause of action, and is taken as having waived his claims against the others: the rule in *Kendall* v. *Hamilton* (1879). The rule in *Kendall's* case has been modified by the Civil Liability (Contribution) Act 1978, s. 3 which states that: 'Judgment recovered against any person liable in respect of any debt or damage shall not be a bar to an action, or to the continuance of an action, against any other person who is (apart from any such bar) jointly liable with him in respect of the same debt or damage'.

Also on the death or bankruptcy of a joint guarantor, his estate is discharged from all liability. (As between themselves joint guarantors have a right of contribution for any sums paid beyond their fair share of liability.)

(b) *Several guarantors.* Each is fully liable for the whole debt, and can be sued separately and successively, i.e. the creditor has several rights of action and the rule in *Kendall* v. *Hamilton* does not apply. Further, the death or bankruptcy of a several guarantor does not release his estate from liability for claims arising before the death or bankruptcy.

(c) *Joint and several guarantors.* Here the creditor can either sue them jointly or separately and successively, and death or bankruptcy has the same effect as in **(b)** above. (From the creditor's point of view therefore a several, or joint and several guarantee is preferable, e.g. bank guarantees are nearly always drafted on the basis of joint and several liability.)

Position of the guarantor

9. Liability of the guarantor

This arises only when the principal debtor has defaulted, and not until then.

The surety's liability depends partly on the terms of the contract and partly on the following rules of law.

(a) If the transaction between the creditor and the principal debtor is void, the surety is not bound by his guarantee. With regard to guarantees of contracts made by minors, s. 2 of the Minors' Contracts Act 1987 makes such a guarantee enforceable against the guarantor, even though the main contractual obligation may not be enforceable against the minor.

(b) The creditor may be entitled to treat the guarantor as a principal debtor, unless he makes it clear that he is a surety only and only secondarily liable.

(c) The creditor is under a legal duty not to prejudice the guarantor in any way, e.g. by increasing his liability by allowing release of any co-guarantor. (In such a case the guarantor can demand release also: *see* **11–17** below.)

(d) If the surety goes bankrupt, the creditor can prove in the bankruptcy for the amount guaranteed. (Bank guarantees usually provide expressly for this contingency, and for the bankruptcy of the debtor.)

(e) When he has accepted liability to the creditor, the guarantor immediately acquires a right of action against the debtor for the value of the guarantee. But this right does not arise until he has accepted liability himself (even though he has not yet actually paid the creditor): *Ascherson* v. *Tredegar Dry Dock Co.* (1909).

(f) Where a loan is secured by way of a mortgage on company shares and by a guarantee executed by a surety, the creditor is not obliged to sell the shares before they become worthless even though, at the time of the debtor's default, they covered the amount of the loan. The surety remained liable under the contract of guarantee and the creditor was entitled to sue him instead of pursuing his claim against the debtor or selling the mortgaged securities: *China and South Sea Bank Ltd* v. *Tan* (1989).

(g) The guarantor of a holding company's liability to a bank is also liable for its subsidiary's debt if the guarantee, on its true construction, having regard to all the circumstances of its execution, was intended by the parties to secure an inter-available facility as between companies in the group, and not merely a direct advance to the holding company: *Bank of Scotland* v. *Wright* (1990)

(h) Sureties who gave a landlord a guarantee that the tenant would perform the covenants in the lease were held not to be entitled to take advantage of their own wrongdoings to avoid their contractual liability. Their failure to ensure timely registration of an assignment of the lease did not prevent them from being liable to the landlord for the tenant's failure to pay rent: *Cerium Investments* v. *Evans* (1991).

10. Rights of the guarantor

(a) *Indemnification by debtor.* The surety can sue the debtor for all sums properly paid under the guarantee plus damages for any additional loss. But he cannot recover the whole value of the guarantee if he was only made to pay a smaller sum. (This right to compensation arises as soon as he actually accepts liability to the creditor; but he cannot sue the debtor until he has actually paid the creditor himself.) However, a person who, without being asked to do so, guarantees payment of another's debt is not entitled on paying the debt to be indemnified by the principal debtor: *Owen* v. *Tate* (1975).

(b) *Set-offs and counter-claims.* If sued by the creditor, the surety can avail himself of any set-offs or counter-claims which the debtor has against the creditor, e.g. where he is sued on a £1000 guarantee and finds that the creditor owes the debtor £200 for goods or services, he is entitled to set off the £200 against the guarantee and so reduce his own liability to £800.

(c) *Delivery of securities held by the creditor.* On paying his guarantee to the creditor, the surety is entitled to possession of any securities the debtor may have earlier deposited with the creditor in respect of the same debt, even if the surety did not know of them when he made his guarantee.

(d) *Hotchpot.* A co-guarantor who has received securities from the principal debtor (or creditor) must share the benefit of them with other co-guarantors, even though they may have been unaware of their existence when they became guarantors.

(e) *Contribution from co-guarantors.* If one surety pays the whole debt, he is entitled to compensation from co-sureties (in a joint, or joint and several guarantee), even if (*i*) their guarantees are contained in different instruments, or (*ii*) he did not know of the existence of the co-sureties when he signed his own guarantee.

This right is implied by equity, and is independent of contract. (It may however be modified by contract.)

Discharge of guarantor

Unless otherwise agreed, a guarantor is automatically discharged in the following circumstances.

11. Unauthorised variation of terms

The guarantor is automatically released if the debtor and creditor vary the contract between them, without the guarantor's knowledge and approval (even though the variation is not prejudicial to the guarantor).

Example _____

A guaranteed D's overdraft. Without A's knowledge the bank allowed D to open a second account into which he paid substantial sums, while leaving his existing overdraft undiminished. HELD: This amounted to an unauthorised variation of the guarantee and A was discharged: *National Bank of Nigeria Ltd* v. *Awolesi* (1964).

12. Creditor relinquishes securities

If the creditor relinquishes securities of the debtor held by him in respect of the debt guaranteed, this automatically releases the guarantor (unless otherwise agreed).

13. Creditor omitting to do something to protect the surety

If the creditor omits to do something he reasonably should do for the protection of the guarantor, this operates as automatic release, e.g. where he fails to register an equitable mortgage granted to him by the debtor, since such a mortgage may be void if not registered (and the surety would be entitled to a transfer of such mortgage on payment of the guarantee).

14. Unauthorised extension of time to the debtor

If the creditor makes a binding agreement to grant the debtor an extension of time for payment of the debt, this automatically releases the surety. In *Unigate* v. *Bentley* (1986), D gave a guarantee in consideration of a payment of £325,000 by P to a particular company. The guarantee related to performance by BV, the company in question, of its obligations under an agreement between P and BV. The money was to be repaid to P in the event of certain circumstances specified in the agreement. D contended that the final date for completing certain tests specified in the agreement had been extended by mutual agreement between P and BV and that as a consequence it had been prejudiced because the date on which he could pay the money and exercise his right of indemnity had been postponed without his consent and that he was accordingly discharged from liability under the guarantee. The court dismissed D's argument, saying that the type of prejudice contended for was strictly confined to cases where the surety had guaranteed the payment of a debt on a fixed time and that date was postponed by agreement between the parties. This was not such a case.

> EXCEPTIONS: (1) Where the extension was expressly or impliedly sanctioned by the original guarantee agreement (as in bank guarantees in some cases). (2) Where judgment has already been obtained against the surety and the principal debtor together. (3) Where there are several distinct debts, extensions of time in respect of one debt will only discharge the surety in respect of that debt alone.

15. Release of co-surety

This is where the creditor discharges any co-surety, thus depriving the remainder of their rights of contribution against the surety discharged: *Smith* v. *Wood* (1929).

16. Revocation

This is only possible where the consideration for the guarantee is divisible, i.e. in continuing guarantees, which can always be revoked as to future liabilities (unless otherwise agreed).

Specific guarantees cannot generally be revoked, and revocation of a continuing guarantee does not affect liability for debts already incurred.

Also if the consideration for any guarantee is a forbearance to sue (i.e. a promise by the creditor not to sue the debtor for the debt, in reliance on the guarantee), it appears that the guarantee is irrevocable.

17. Release of debtor

Release of the debtor automatically releases the surety, unless the creditor expressly or impliedly reserves his rights against the surety in the original contract (as is usually done in bank guarantees). However, a creditor's acceptance of a debtor's wrongful repudiation of a contract does not discharge a guarantor from liability under his guarantee, though the action against him is not to repay the debt but to pay damages for breach of contract: *Maschi* v. *Lep Air Services* (1972).

18. Death of guarantor

It depends on the terms of the contract whether his death will discharge his estate from liability under his guarantee. Thus bank guarantee forms usually stipulate that the guarantee shall remain operative until the bank receives notice of the guarantor's death.

Death of joint guarantor discharges his estate from liability, but surviving joint guarantors remain liable.

19. Bankruptcy of guarantor

The creditor can prove for the debt in the guarantor's bankruptcy: Insolvency Act 1986, s. 322. If the surety obtains his discharge from bankruptcy, this operates in most cases to release him from his guarantee: s. 281. In addition, under the 1986 Act, s. 345, the court can discharge a contract between the bankrupt and another party, on the latter's application and on such terms as the court thinks equitable.

20. Change in constitution of firm

A continuing guarantee given to a firm, or to a third party regarding transactions by a firm, is automatically revoked as to future liabilities by any change in the constitution of the firm, e.g. on the death or retirement of any partner: Partnership Act 1890, s. 18.

21. Limitation Act 1980

The creditor's rights against the guarantor are statute-barred after six years (twelve years if the guarantee was under seal), but time begins to run only when the debt becomes due from the principal debtor.

Thus bank guarantee forms usually stipulate that the guarantor shall not become liable until the bank formally notifies him that it proposes to call in his guarantee. Time then begins to run only after the bank makes this formal demand, even though the debtor may have become liable considerably earlier: *Bradford Old Bank* v. *Sutcliffe* (1918).

The Act also bars the guarantor's claim for indemnification against the debtor, and for contribution from co-sureties, after the limitation period has elapsed.

22. Effect of forgery

R and F were directors of B Ltd which wished to lease equipment from L Co. They signed a form of guarantee which guaranteed the obligations of 'B Company Ltd'. (Later, the word 'company' was deleted in manuscript by someone who added squiggles to the deletion to represent the signatures of R and F and to indicate their assent to the alterations. It was held that the alterations, although forgeries, did not render the guarantee unenforceable. It was said that a forged alteration applied to a document does not render it void unless it goes to the whole essence of the instrument: *Lombard Finance* v. *Brookplain Trading* (1991).)

Progress test 5

Securities

1. What is a security, and what forms may it take? (15: **4, 5**)

2. Distinguish between legal and equitable interest in property, and explain how ownership of the various forms of property can be transferred at law. (15: **3, 8**)

3. How can personalty be (*a*) mortgaged, and (*b*) pledged? What sort of chattels are suitable for pledging? (15: **10–14**)

4. Explain briefly the main provisions of (*a*) the Bills of Sale Acts, and (*b*) those provisions of the Consumer Credit Act dealing with pawnbroking. (15: **13, 15**)

5. What is a lien? Distinguish between possessory, equitable and maritime liens. (15: **16–19**)

6. When, if ever, does a lien confer a power of sale? (15: **16–20**)

7. Define a guarantee. How does it differ from an indemnity contract, and what form must it take? (16: **1, 3, 5**)

8. Guarantees are not *uberrimae fidei* contracts, but once formed a guarantee imposes similar duties upon the creditor. Explain. (16: **4**)

9. Distinguish between joint, and joint and several guarantees. (16: **8**)

10. What are the rights and liabilities of a guarantor under a contract of guarantee? (16: **9, 10**)

11. In what circumstances is a guarantor discharged from liability? (16: **11–15**)

12. In what circumstances may a guarantor revoke his guarantee? (16: **16**)

13. G guaranteed D's overdraft to the amount of £1000. Later the bank allowed D to increase his overdraft to £1200. What effect, if any, has this on G's liability? (16: **11**)

14. In what ways, if any, does capacity to act as a guarantor differ from normal contractual capacity? (16: **6**)

Specimen questions

1. 'Guarantees are subject to the ordinary rule of English law that all contracts, except those under seal, must be supported by consideration.'

   (*a*) Explain the meaning of the term 'consideration' in this quotation.
   (*b*) Is there any provision in English law which requires that a contract of guarantee shall be in any particular form?
   (*c*) In relation to a contract of guarantee, is there any provision in English law which *either* requires that the consideration must be stated in the written agreement, *or*, on the other hand, provides that the consideration need not be stated there?

2. E and F were partners in a furriers' business. G asked E whether the firm would guarantee G's overdraft with the H Bank up to £1000. Without consulting F, E agreed and he gave the H Bank a written guarantee in the name of 'E and F, furriers'.

G has now failed to settle his overdraft and F consults you as to his legal position.

Advise him.

3. What special rules govern a contract of suretyship?

X, who was employed in A's shop, stole some money from the till. When A discovered the theft he told X that he would overlook it but, nevertheless, thought it wise to obtain a guarantee of X's fidelity. This A asked B to do, and B signed a document to that effect. A did not tell B about the theft. Later X stole £50 from the till and absconded.

Advise A.

4. (*a*) How far is it true to say that a creditor is not bound to disclose to a prospective guarantor facts about the debtor which might influence him against becoming guarantor?
   (*b*) In what circumstances is a contract of guarantee automatically discharged?

5. (*a*) Distinguish between a possessory lien, a maritime lien and an equitable lien.
   (*b*) Eddy, a solicitor, acted for Roy and had possession of

the title deeds to Roy's land. Roy mortgaged his land to Allan and the deeds remained with the solicitor who acted for both parties. Roy fails to pay Eddy the legal fees and Eddy claims a lien over the title deeds.

Advise Allan.

6. State the essentials of a contract of guarantee.

A & Co. were stockbrokers who agreed with B that he should have half the commission earned as a result of his introductions and that he should pay half of any losses which might be sustained from them. Explain whether or not this is a contract of guarantee.

7. (a) An executor finds that the deceased had, during his life-time, given a continuing guarantee.
      (i) In what circumstances would the guarantee be revoked by death?
      (ii) If it is revoked, what action should the executor take?
   (b) Jones gives Brown a continuing guarantee for the due fulfilment by a partnership firm, Robinson & Co., of its business transactions with Brown. A partner in the firm retires and another partner is taken in. What effect, if any, has the change in the partnership on Jones' guarantee?

8. When one of two sureties has paid the debt to the creditor what remedies are available to such surety against:
   (a) the debtor,
   (b) the creditor, and
   (c) the co-surety?

9. G signed a guarantee in respect of the banking account of C. The latter is unable to repay his overdraft, and the bank has demanded payment from G under his guarantee. G wishes to deny liability on the ground that the bank failed to disclose to him: (i) that C's wife had served a prison sentence and (ii) that C's wife had authority to draw on C's account. Advise G whether or not he is liable to the bank.

10. A customer has applied to his bank for an overdraft of £1000,

and he has offered as security a life policy on his own life for £5000 with profits, the surrender value being £990.

Explain what is meant by 'surrender value,' and describe the steps which should be followed to enable the bank to obtain a legal mortgage of this policy.

11. (*a*) Define a guarantee and explain how it differs from an indemnity contract.

 (*b*) P orally hired A as his agent for the sale of some valuable paintings, and as part of the contract A guaranteed P against failure of any of A's clients to pay for the paintings they bought. State with reasons whether the guarantee is enforceable.

Part six

Consumer protection and competition law

Consumer protection and fair trading

There are a number of enactments which directly relate to the protection of the consumer. For the most part, these involve the criminal law.

Trade Descriptions Act 1968

1. **Trade Descriptions Act 1968**
   This is probably the most important consumer protection statute. Section 1 provides that no one may apply a false trade description to goods or supply goods to which a false trade description has been applied. The following are the descriptions laid down by the Act which constitute trade descriptions:

   (a) quantity, size or gauge;
   (b) method of manufacture, production, processing or reconditioning;
   (c) composition;
   (d) fitness for purpose, strength, performance, behaviour or accuracy;
   (e) any physical characteristics not included in the previous paragraphs;
   (f) testing by any person and results thereof;
   (g) approval by any person or conformity with a type approved by any person;
   (h) place or date of manufacture, production, processing or reconditioning;
   (i) person by whom manufactured, produced, processed or reconditioned;
   (j) other history including previous ownership or use. This part

of the Act has often been used to convict car dealers who turn back the odometer.

In the context of the car trade, a practice has grown up of dealers applying disclaimers which seek to disclaim the accuracy of the odometer and thus to avoid the making of a false trade description. The rule laid down by the court in *Norman* v. *Bennett* (1974) is that a disclaimer will only be of effect if it is as 'bold, precise and compelling' as the false description (i.e. the wrong mileage) which it seeks to disclaim.

Example
_____

The defendants applied a disclaimer notice by means of a sticker to all odometers by means of a sticker which read: 'Trade Descriptions Act 1968. Dealers are often unable to guarantee the mileage of a used car on sale. Please disregard the recorded mileage on this vehicle and accept this as an incorrect reading'. This was held to be an adequate disclaimer: *Newham London Borough Council* v. *Singh* (1988).

_____

2.   Strict liability

An offence under s. 1 is an offence of strict liability. This means that a person is guilty even if he had no intention to commit an offence: an offence automatically arises if goods are described falsely. However, s. 24 of the Act provides that a person charged with an offence is entitled to an acquittal if he can prove (the burden of proof is on him) that

(a) the commission of the offence was due to a mistake or to reliance on information supplied, to the act or default of another person, an accident or some other cause beyond his control; *and*
(b) he took all reasonable care and exercised all due diligence to avoid the commission of such an offence by himself or any person under his control.

Both limbs of this defence have to be satisfied, and most attempts to use it fail at **(b)** because the courts have interpreted it very strictly.

Example
_____

A company imported pencils which broke the law because of excessive lead in the paint coating. The company had obtained assurances that the product complied with the law and had obtained written assurances to that effect. It was held that they had not shown due diligence since they were a large enough concern to have sampled the product, which they had not done: *Boots* v. *Garrett* (1980).

3. Section 14 of the Trade Descriptions Act

This extends the law to catch false statements as to services, facilities and accommodation. Unlike s. 1, however (*see* above) s. 14 does not give rise to offences of strict liability. An offence only arises if the person charged knew that the statement was false or if he made the statement recklessly.

Example

An advertisement indicated that certain items were available carriage-paid. The advertisement was later amended to add further items. The advertisement continued to state that carriage would be paid. However, the intention was that carriage would only be paid only if both the original and the added items were ordered. One person who ordered just one set of items was charged carriage. It was held that an offence had been committed since the false statement had been made recklessly, as no thought had been given as to whether it was ambiguous: *MFI* v. *Nattrass* (1973).

If a person is charged with an offence in front of magistrates, then the penalty is a maximum fine of £2000. Serious cases will be taken to the Crown Court where a fine can be imposed (no maximum is set) and there is a maximum sentence of two years, There can be a combination of fine and sentence.

4. The 'by-pass' provision

Section 23 allows the prosecution to charge the person whose act or default caused another to breach the provisions of the Act. If, therefore, a manufacturer were to supply a retailer with a falsely labelled product, any offence by the retailer could be said to have been caused by the act or default of the wholesaler who could therefore be charged. In such a case, the prosecution could also charge the retailer but it is not required to.

5. Trading Stamps Act 1964

When trading stamps are delivered to customers by retailers, the Act requires each stamp to show a cash value. The law does not lay down what this value has to be, and a common amount seems to be 0.01p. The Act further provides that when a customer has collected 25p worth, he has an absolute right to redeem the stamps for cash. If the stamp does not state a cash value, the promoter of the scheme is liable to a maximum fine of £100; the maximum fine is £50 in the case of any other person. In any shop where trading stamps are available, a notice must be displayed indicating how much has to be spent to obtain one stamp of a given cash value. The maximum fine for an offence is £50.

Catalogues

If the trading stamps scheme provides for the redemtion of the stamps for gifts (which is always the case), there is no requirement to publish a catalogue. However, if one has been published, then the Act states that it must contain the name of the promoter and the address of his registered office. Similarly, there is no obligation to issue a stamp book, but, if one is issued, then it must contain that information. The maximum fine for an offence is £400. In addition, a copy of any current catalogue must be placed in every shop where trading stamps are available in a place where it can be 'conveniently consulted' by shoppers. The maximum fine for an offence is £50.

6.   Section 4 of the Trading Stamps Act 1964

Where a customer does redeem his stamps for gifts, s. 4 of the Act implies the following warranties:

(a) that the promoter of the scheme has a right to give the goods in exchange;

(b) that the goods are free from any undisclosed charge or encumbrance and that the customer will have 'quiet possession' of the goods except so far as it is disturbed by any person he knew to have the benefit of any such charge or encumbrance;

(c) that the goods are of merchantable quality, except where

    (*i*) a defect is drawn to the customer's attention before the goods are obtained, *or*

    (*ii*) if the customer examines the goods beforehand and should have seen the particular defect.

It was necessary for the Act to provide these warranties since

redeeming stamps for goods is not a sale of the goods within the
Sale of Goods Act 1979.

> NOTE: the terms implied are warranties not conditions. This means
> that, in the event of a breach, the customer is only entitled to
> damages. Note too that there is no implied term that the goods are
> reasonably fit for their purpose.

Fair Trading Act 1973

7. The Fair Trading Act 1973

There are four main consumer protection aspects to this Act.
First, it created the post of Director-General of Fair Trading, who
is charged with the function of keeping commercial practices
under review so far as they affect consumers. *Second,* the Act also
established a body called the Consumer Protection Advisory
Committee. References can be made to the Committee in relation
to consumer trade practices. If such a reference is accompanied by
specific proposals for the control of that practice, the Committee
is then entitled to say that it does not agree with the reference; that
it would agree with it if it were modified in a given way; or that it
accepts it entirely. If it takes either of the last two options, the
proposals for reform then go to the Secretary of State for Trade
and Industry. He can then (*a*) accept the original proposals, or (*b*)
accept the proposals with the suggested changes, or (*c*) he can take
no action. If he opts for (*a*) or (*b*), the proposals must be laid before
each House of Parliament in the form of a statutory instrument
which must then be subject to a vote.

So far, three statutory instruments have emerged via this
procedure: the Mail Order Transactions (Information) Order
1967/1812; the Consumer Transactions (Restrictions on
Statements) Order 1976/1813; the Business Advertisements
(Disclosure) Order 1977/1918. There is also provision in the Act
for some advisory references to the Committee. These will detail
specific consumer trade practices without giving any proposals for
reform. To date, there have been no such references.

Third, the Act also provides for written assurances to be
obtained by the Director-General of Fair Trading from traders
who persisted in a course of conduct which is (*a*) detrimemtal to
the interests of consumers and (*b*) is unfair. A course of conduct is

deemed to be unfair if it consists in breaches of the criminal or civil law. Traders who fail to give the requested assurance, or who give an assurance but breach it, can be made the subject of a court order, breach of which is contempt of court. There have been occasions where jail sentences have been imposed following contempt.

Fourth, the Fair Trading Act also requires the Director-General of Fair Trading to obtain codes of practice with trade associations where those codes will offer guidance in safeguarding and promoting the consumer interest. Codes have been obtained covering: caravan sites; cars; double-glazing: electrical goods; funerals; furniture; launderers and dry cleaners; mail order buying; motorcycle industry; package holidays; photography; shoes; party plan selling; postal services; telecommunication services.

8. Pyramid selling

The Fair Trading Act also controls pyramid selling in conjunction with the Pyramid Selling Schemes Regulations 1989. Pyramid selling is not made illegal, but there are controls imposed on the way it is conducted and advertised.

Estate Agents Act 1979

9. Estate Agents Act 1979

The Act provides for the Director General of Fair Trading to ban estate agents from practice if they have:

(a) committed offences under the Act itself or failed to comply with certain obligations under the Act;

(b) been convicted of any offence involving fraud or violence;

(c) have committed discrimination in the course of estate agency work;

(d) engaged in a practice which has been declared undesirable (*see* the Estate Agents (Undesirable Practices) (No. 2) Order 1991/1032);

(e) been convicted of a specified offence (*see* the Estate Agents (Specified Offences) (No. 2) Order 1991/1991).

The Act does provide for regulations to be made specifying for minimum standards of competence, but no such regulations have been made.

The Act states that all clients' moneys received in the course of estate agency work are held on trust. Section 14 also requires client's money to be paid into a client account. Further provisions are made in the Estate Agents (Accounts) Regulations 1981/1520.

10. Section 18 of the Act

This provides that, before an estate agency contract is made, the agent must give the client:

(a) particulars of the circumstances in which the client will become liable to pay;
(b) particulars of the amount of remuneration for carrying out estate agency work (or, if that cannot be ascertained, details of how remuneration will be calculated);
(c) particulars of payments which do not form part of the agent's remuneration for carrying out estate agency work or a contract or pre-contract deposit;
(d) particulars of any amounts payable under **(c)** above or, if not possible, details of how the amounts will be calculated.

If there is a breach of these requirements, the contract can only be enforceable on a court order.

The Act does contain provisions forbidding estate agents from taking a pre-contract deposit in excess of a prescribed limit, but these provisions have not been brought into force.

11. Section 21 of the Act

This states that an estate agent who has a personal interest in any land shall not enter into negotiations for the purchase or sale of any interest in that land until he has disclosed to that person the nature and extent of that personal interest. The Act also says that where the result of a proposed sale would result in the agent having a personal interest in the land, the same rules apply.

Section 21 goes on to provide that an estate agent may not receive a contract or pre-contract deposit in respect of the purchase of any land in which he has a personal interest, or of a personal interest in any land.

Failure to comply with any of the provisions of s. 21 are expressly stated not to give rise to any criminal offence, or any ground for a civil claim, though a breach can be taken into consideration by the Director General of Fair Trading when considering whether to ban a person from estate agency work (*see* **9** above)

12. Due diligence defence

In any proceedings for an offence under the Act, s. 28 provides that the defence of all due diligence applies. This differs from the defence available under the Trade Descriptions Act in that the first limb of the defence available under the latter has not been repeated (*see* **2** above).

Consumer Credit Act 1974

13. Consumer Credit Act 1974

The Act provides for a system of positive licensing. Parties who wish to engage in the business of consumer credit or consumer hire, where the credit provided or the rental payments do not exceed £15,000, must apply to the Office of Fair Trading for a licence and show that they are fit and proper persons to hold a licence.

Unlicensed trading is a criminal offence, and agreements made while unlicensed are unenforceable, except where an order has been made by the Director General of Fair Trading.

14. Regulations

The 1974 Act also provides that agreements for credit or hire must be made in the form prescribed by regulations (*see* the Consumer Credit (Agreements) Regulations 1983 as amended). If agreements are not made in the proper form, they can only be enforced on a court order. There are also provisions for cancelling agreements. The basic rule is that an agreement can be cancelled for any reason if it is an agreement where the prior negotiations included oral representations made in the customer's presence. The 'cooling-off' period normally runs for five days following the day when the customer received a copy of the agreement or a notice of cancellation rights. The Act also contains detailed provisions with regard to advertisements and quotations, and default and termination notices (*see* 9: **74–92**)

15. Ancillary credit businesses

The provisions of the 1974 Act regarding licensing (*see* **13**) also apply to 'ancillary credit businesses'. These are: credit reference agencies; debt collectors; debt adjusters; debt counsellors and credit brokers. The Act contains provisions for correcting mistakes in the files of a credit reference agency.

Consumer Protection Act 1987

16. Price indications

The Price Marking Order 1991/1382 sets out how the selling price of goods is to be indicated. As a rule, prices must be inclusive of VAT or indicate the amount of VAT payable if the price is quoted exclusive of VAT. There is no requirement for the price of goods to be stated in advertisements. Misleading price indications are governed by the provisions of the Consumer Protection Act 1987, which repealed and replaced those provisions of the Trade Descriptions Act 1968, which dealt with misleading price indications. Section 20 provides that an offence is committed if a price indication is misleading as to the price of any goods, services, accommodation or facilities. Section 23 states that the Act covers new houses where the freehold is being disposed of and new houses where a lease of more than 21 years is being disposed of.

17. Misleading price indications

Section 21 of the Act states that a price indication is misleading if it indicates

(a) that the price is less than it is;
(b) that its applicability does not depend on matters on which it does in fact depend;
(c) that the price covers matters in respect of which an additional charge is made;
(d) that a person who in fact has no such expectations, (*i*) expects the price to be increased or reduced, or (*ii*) expects a price to be maintained;
(e) that the points by which consumers might be expected to judge the validity of a relevant price comparison are not in fact what they are.

Example

An advertisement states (*i*) that the price of a cinema seat is £1, but does not state that this is for afternoon performances only; (*ii*) that goods will be delivered carriage free, but does not state that this is only within the particular area; (*iii*) that goods should be bought at current prices which will be held until a given date, when in fact it is known that there will be no price increase after that date; (*iv*) that the price of a particular make of computer has been reduced, but does not indicate that its range of functions has also been reduced. In all these cases, there would be an offence.

18. Code of practice on price indications

Section 25 of the 1987 Act provides for the Secretary of State for Trade and Industry to issue a code of practice which gives practical guidance as to avoiding misleading price indications and which promotes good practice as to such indications. It is expressly stated that the code is not binding, but that compliance with it or breach of it may be taken into account in determining whether an offence has been committed. The relevant code is the Code of Practice for Traders on Price Indications.

19. Liability

Where an offence is committed under the 1987 Act, the penalty before the magistrates is a maximum fine of £5000. If the case is taken in the Crown Court, the penalty is a fine. No prison sentence can be imposed. The Act also applies the due diligence defence in the manner provided for in the Estate Agents Act (*see* **12**).

20. Product safety

This is dealt with by the Consumer Protection Act 1987 and by the Food Safety Act 1990

21. Liability for defective products

Part 1 of the 1987 Act implements an EC Directive on liability for defective products. Under the Act, a producer of a defective product is liable for all the damage which it causes whether he has been guilty of negligence or not. In addition, liability also extends to anyone who claims to be a producer, as by putting his name or mark on the product and the first importer of the product into the Common Market. Own-branders will therefore be within the Act. In addition, any supplier of the defective product will be liable if

(a) an injured party asks the supplier to identify any of the parties previously mentioned in the above paragraph;
(b) that request is made within a reasonable time after the damage occurs and when the person making the request cannot find out the information for himself; *and*
(c) the supplier within a reasonable time from making the request fails to comply with the request or to identify his own supplier.

22. Game and agricultural produce

The Act does not apply to game or agricultural produce if, at the time of its supply, it has not yet undergone an 'industrial process'. If, for example, vegetables are sold in the state they were when harvested, they would be outside the Act. If, on the other hand, they have been washed, sliced or otherwise prepared for the market, then that would be an 'industrial process' and the particular product would then be within the Act.

In the case of damage to property, no claim can be made if the value of the claim does not exceed £275. If it does, then the claim can cover the first £275 of damage. In addition, no claim can be made if the particular property damaged was not of a type which is ordinarily intended for private use or consumption, and if it was not intended by the person injured for his own private use or consumption, or occupation.

23. Defences

In certain cases, a person will have a defence to a claim for damages. These are:

(a) the defect in the product was attributable to compliance with binding requirements;
(b) the defendant did not supply the product to anyone;
(c) the supply was not in the course of a trade or business, and the defendant was not in any of the categories **(a)–(c)** in **21** above or

was so only by virtue of things done with no intention to make a profit;

(d) the product was not defective when supplied by the producer, the 'own-brander' or the first importer into the Common Market;

(e) the scientific and technical knowledge at the time was not such that a producer of products of the same description might be expected to have discovered the defect if it had existed in the products while they were under his control.

A defence is also created for those who design components for other products. If the defect in the other product is wholly attributable to its design, or to compliance by the producer of the component part with instructions given to him by the producer of the product into which his component was incorporated, then no liablility falls on the producer of the component.

24. Consumer Protection Act 1987, Part II

The Act also imposes certain criminal penalties in relation to defective goods. Part II of the Act provides for a 'general safety requirement'. It is an offence to supply consumer goods which fail to comply with this requirement, which requires goods to be reasonably safe having regard to all the circumstances. 'Consumer goods' are defined as those which are ordinarily intended for private use or consumption. The definition is expressly stated to exclude: growing crops or things comprised in land by virtue of being attached to it; water, food, feeding stuff or fertiliser; gas supplied by an authorised person; aircraft (other than hang-gliders) or motor vehicles; controlled drugs or licensed medicinal products; tobacco.

The penalty for breach of the general safety requirement is a fine not exceeding £5000, a sentence not exceeding six months, or a combination.

25. Defences

The offence described above is not absolute in that certain defences are available when goods have been supplied in breach of the general safety requirement. No offence arises in relation to anything which resulted from compliance with any binding obligation; or from any failure to do more than is required by (*a*) safety regulations (*see* **26** below); (*b*) standards of safety which have been approved; (c) any provisions in law which impose such requirements as are designated. So far, many standards have been approved under (b) but no requirements have been designated under (c).

In addition, a defendant has a defence if:

(a) he reasonably believed that the goods would not be used or consumed in the UK;
(b) the following conditions are satisfied
   (*i*) the goods were for sale by retail, *and*
   (*ii*) he had no reasonable grounds for believing that the goods failed the general safety requirement nor knew that they failed the requirement;
(c) it was indicated that the goods were not new and provided for the acquisition of an interest in the goods by the person supplied.

The due diligence defence also applies in the manner provided for by the Estate Agents Act (*see* **12** above).

26. Safety regulations

The 1987 Act also contains provisions for the making of safety regulations. This power to make safety regulations only applies to goods other than the following: growing crops and things comprised in land by virtue of being attached to it; water, food, feeding stuff and fertiliser; gas supplied by an authorised person; controlled drugs and licensed medicinal products.

A number of safety regulations have been made under the 1987 Act (such as the Furniture and Furnishings (Fire) (Safety) Regulations 1988) and a number of other safety regulations made under statutes now repealed are also treated as having effect as if made under the Act.

The penalty for breach is a maximum fine of £5000, a sentence not exceeding six months, or a combination. The due diligence defence applies as described in **25** above.

27. Dangerous goods — prohibition notices

The Act also gives other powers to deal with dangerous goods. The Secretary of State for Trade and Industry is empowered to serve a prohibition notice on any person banning the supply of goods considered to be unsafe. The Secretary of State also has the power to require a person to issue a notice to anyone about unsafe goods which that person supplies. The power to make a prohibition notice applies in relation to goods which can be subject to safety regulations (*see* **26** above); but the power to make a notice to warn also applies to growing crops or things comprised in land by virtue of being attached to it. The power to make prohibition notices has been sparingly used, but no notices to warn have ever been issued. Breach of a notice or order carries the same penalties as for a breach of safety regulations (*see* **26** above) and the due diligence defence as set out in **25** above also applies.

28. Suspension notices

The Act also empowers local enforcement authorities to issue suspension notices where it has reasonable grounds for supposing that goods contravene any safety provision. A 'safety provision' is a reference to the general safety requirement (*see* **24**), safety regulations (*see* **26**) and a prohibition notice (*see* **27**).

The penalties for breach of a suspension notice, which can last for up to six months, are as set out in **26** above, the defence of due diligence also applying. Appeals may be made against the imposition of a suspension notice to the magistrates' court. A notice is to be set aside only if the court is satisfied that there has been no contravention of any safety provision. A further appeal may be made to the Crown Court.

29. Forfeiture orders

Local authorities are also empowered by the Act to apply to the magistrates for a forfeiture order. An order may only be made if the court is satisfied that there has been a contravention of a safety provision in relation to the goods. The definition of a 'safety provision' here is the same as that given in **28** above, with the addition of a suspension notice. Where a forfeiture order is made, then the goods are to be destroyed. However, the court can allow the goods, instead of being destroyed, to be supplied to someone who carries on the business of repairing or reconditioning the goods, or to be supplied by way of scrap. Appeals against forfeiture orders may be made to the Crown Court.

Food Safety Act 1990

30. The Food Safety Act 1990

The Act makes it a criminal offence for any person to sell to the prejudice of a buyer any food which is not of the 'nature or substance or quality' demanded by him.

*Examples*_____

(1) A tin of peas contained a caterpillar. Even though the caterpillar was entirely harmless, the court ruled that an offence had been committed: *Smedleys Ltd* v. *Breed* (1974).

(2) A straw in a bottle of milk also gave rise to an offence: it was not necessary to show that the extra matter was deleterious: *Barber* v. *Co-operative Wholesale Society* (1983).

The penalty for breach is, in the case of offences charged in the magistrates' court, a maximum fine of £20,000, a sentence not exceeding six months, or a combination. If the case is taken before the Crown Court, the penalty is a fine, or a maximum sentence of two years, or a combination. The single-limb due diligence defence also applies, so a defendant need only prove that he exercised all due diligence to avoid commission of the particular offence.

_____

31. Food safety requirements

The 1990 Act also makes it an offence to provide food which does not comply with the food safety requirements. Food does not comply with these requirements if

(a) it has been rendered injurious to health;
(b) it is unfit for human consumption; *or*
(c) it is so contaminated that it would not be reasonable to expect it to be used for human consumption in that state.

The penalties and the defence of due diligence are as set out in the preceding paragraph.

Local authority officers are empowered under the Act to inspect food and to provide for its seizure if it appears that the food is in breach of the food safety requirements. A Justice of the Peace may condemn the food and order that it be disposed of or destroyed so as to prevent it from being used for human consumption.

32. Improvement notices

The 1990 Act contains provisions empowering a local authority to issue an improvement notice where it has reasonable grounds for believing that the proprietor of a food business is failing to comply with certain regulations. The notice must specify the measures which are to be taken to rectify matters, giving at least 14 days to take them. If the proprietor of a food business is convicted of a relevant offence, and the court is satisfied that the health-risk conditions are fulfilled with respect to that business, the court can issue a prohibition order.

These provisions apply to any regulations which make provision for

(a) requiring, prohibiting or regulating the use of any process or treatment in the preparation of food; *or*
(b) for securing the observance of hygienic conditions and practices in connection with the carrying out of commercial operations with respect to food or food sources.

33. Emergency action

Section 12 of the 1990 Act provides for emergency prohibition notices and orders to deal with circumstances which pose an imminent risk of injury to health. An emergency prohibition notice may be issued by a local authority where satisfied that the health-risk condition is satisfied. Application must be made to the magistrates' court for the issue of an emergency prohibition order within three days of the service of the notice. It is an offence knowingly to contravene an emergency prohibition notice or order. An appeal against the decision of the court to make an emergency prohibition order can be made to the Crown Court.

Section 13 provides for emergency control orders. This empowers the Minister for Agriculture, Fisheries and Food to make orders in respect of commercial operations with respects to food, food sources or contact materials which may involve imminent risk of injury to health. The Minister may give directions for the prevention of commercial operations and may do anything else which appears to him to be necessary or expedient for the purpose of control orders. It is an offence knowingly to contravene an emergency control order. The penalty for breach of these sections is as given in **30** above, except that the maximum fine in front of the magistrates' is £5000. The due diligence defence as described in that paragraph also applies.

34. Food premises
The 1990 Act makes provision for the registration and licensing of food premises. Provided an application is made in the due form, local authorities have no discretion to refuse that application.

Miscellaneous matters

35. Medicines Act 1968
Medicinal products cannot be marketed unless they have a product licence. In addition, it is an offence to supply such a product which is not of the nature, substance or quality demanded by the purchaser (cf. **30** above).

36. Cancellable agreements
It has already been pointed out (**14** above) that certain consumer credit and consumer hire agreements are cancellable. Following adoption of an EC Directive, this right to a 'cooling-off' period was extended by the Consumer Protection (Cancellation of Contracts Concluded away from Business Premises) Regulations 1987/2117. The Regulations apply, subject to various exceptions (such as milk supplied door to door by the milkman), to contracts made at the consumer's home or at the home of another person, or to the consumer's place of work, where the trader's visit was unsolicited.

The Regulations also apply to contracts made during an excursion organised by the trader away from his business premises. The Regulations will also apply to visits made at the request of the consumer where the goods or services concerned were not those in relation to which the visit was requested and where the consumer did not know that the supply of the other goods and services formed part of the trader's business activities. The Regulations further apply to an offer made by a consumer in the foregoing circumstances.

Where a contract is within the Regulations, it is not enforceable unless the documentation formalities are complied with. These formalities include the provision of a cancellation notice. The right to cancel extends for a period of seven days following the making of the contract.

37. Timeshare properties

These are properties for which a person agrees a specified period of the year when he will have rights of occupancy. Often, though not always, they will be overseas properties. The selling methods used in relation to the sale of timeshares, particularly inducing consumers to attend presentations by the offer or promise of gifts, which often never materialised or which were subject to conditions, such as the purchase of a timeshare, not indicated in the advertising, received adverse attention. Some of these practices were caught by s. 14 of the Trade Descriptions Act (*see* 3), but no specific legislation directed at timeshare was enacted until the passing of the Timeshare Act 1992. This Act applies to 'timeshare agreements', which are agreements for timeshare accommodation for a period of not less than three years, and to 'timeshare credit agreements'. These latter arise where a creditor offers credit to a person seeking timeshare accommodation and the creditor knows or has reasonable cause to believe that the credit is to be used to finance a timeshare agreement. The Act will apply if the agreement is subject to UK law or if one or both parties is in the UK when the agreement is entered into.

38. Cancellation rights

In the case of both a timeshare agreement and a timeshare credit agreement, the consumer must first have received notice of his right to cancel the agreement. Such notice must entitle the consumer to cancel for at least 14 days after the day on which the agreement was entered into. In the case of a timeshare agreement, but not a timeshare credit agreement, an offence is committed if the notice is not provided. If the above notice is not given, then notice of cancellation can be given at any time. On cancellation, monies paid shall be recoverable. Provision is also made for the repayment of any credit which may have been provided in terms which allow for the credit to be repaid free of interest. The cancellation rights are inapplicable in the case of agreements cancellable under the provisions of the Consumer Credit Act 1974 (*see* **14** above).

39. Offences and defences
Where an offence is committed, the penalty is a fine not exceeding £5000 before the magistrates, or a fine with no maximum if the case is before the Crown Court. The due diligence defence applies as in the Estate Agents Act (*see* **12** above), and there is provision for prosecuting the person whose act or default is responsible for commission of the offence (*see* **4** above).

Specimen questions

1.   XYZ Co. operates as a motor dealer, specialising in the sale of new and second-hand cars. It also takes cars in part-exchange from members of the public, and buys cars from other dealers when it is short of a particular make or model. The company knows that other dealers occasionally turn back odometers and that members of the public have been known to do the same. On one particular occasion, it sells a second-hand car which had had its odometer turned back, although this was not known to XYZ Co. In its view, the state and condition of the car was entirely consistent with the mileage appearing on the clock.

Is the company guilty of an offence? Is there anything it could do to guard against the possibility of a criminal prosecution?

2.   'The provisions of the Trade Descriptions Act 1968, in relation to the applications of false trade descriptions, impose strict but not absolute liability'.

Discuss this statement in relation to s. 1 of the Act and the application of the due diligence defence.

3.   A firm of tailors buys cloth from a representative. The rep assures them that the cloth is all wool. Suits are made up from the cloth and these are then advertised as being 100 per cent wool. In fact, the cloth is a man-made fibre. The representative's employers now seek your advice as to whether they can be prosecuted for the offence committed by the tailors.

4.   DEF Co. are tour operators. Their speciality is organising tours to the Indian sub-continent. Because of the nature of the climate, they endeavour to ensure that all rooms are air-conditioned. A representative of DEF pays a visit to one of the hotels and discovers that no air-conditioning is installed, but he is shown copies of contracts which indicate that it will be installed before the holiday season gets under way. Their assurance is accepted and, three months later, the first tourists visit the hotel. They quickly find out that the air-conditioning has not been installed. They seek your advice as to whether any liability exists on the part of the operators.

5. In what circumstances may the holder of trading stamps redeem them for cash or goods?

6. John obtains a colour television with the trading stamps which he has collected. The set is obtained from a redemption shop run by the promoter of the trading stamps scheme. After a couple of weeks or so, the set produces only black and white pictures and no amount of re-tuning will correct the fault. What are John's rights and remedies in this situation?

7. The Fair Trading Act 1973 sets out a procedure by which commercial trade practices can be controlled by the enactment of statutory instruments. Explain how this system works and say how you would like to see it reformed.

8. GHI Ltd operate a television repair service from back-street premises. The service they provide is far from efficient. Over an 18-month period, they are twice taken to the county court for failure to make proper repairs, and in each case judgment is given to their customers. In addition, around a dozen customers, through their solicitors, seek redress for poor and dilatory repairs, and these claims are settled without recourse to legal proceedings. Moreover the company is convicted twice under the Trade Descriptions Act 1968, in relation to false descriptions applied to certain second-hand goods which they were selling.

Explain the procedures by which the Office of Fair Trading can seek to ensure that GHI Ltd cease offending.

9. 'Estate agents are not subject to a positive licensing system enabling them to set up in business, but they are subject to what might be called a system of negative licensing'.

Explain this statement by reference to the powers of the Director General of Fair Trading under the Estate Agents Act 1979.

10. Richard, a house-owner, places his house on the market through XYZ estate agents. The asking price is £200,000. There is an exchange of correspondence between Richard and the firm in the form of a short letter from him asking the firm to act for him, and from the firm agreeing to act 'on our normal terms and rates'. The firm finds a willing buyer and obtains from him a deposit of £50,000 which it states to be its minimum and a contract of sale and purchase goes through. When presented with the estate agent's bill, Richard declines to pay saying that it is far too high. The purchaser also complains saying that the deposit demanded by the firm was above average, and he seeks to recover the amount of interest which he could have earned had at least part of the deposit been left in his building society account.

    Advise the parties.

11. What are the rules binding an estate agent in relation to a personal interest which he may have in any land; and what are the penalties provided for breach of such duties?

12. 'Unlike the Estate Agents Act 1979, the Consumer Credit Act 1974 provides for a system of positive licensing to be imposed on those who wish to provide credit or hire by way of business'. Discuss this statement, and state the nature of the penalties attached to unlicensed trading.

13. What rules apply as to how the price of goods is to be marked, and what must a trader do to ensure that customers know how much VAT they will be paying?

14. The MegaSave Emporium offers a special promotion on refrigerators, advertising: 'Buy One, Get One Free'. In very small print, this is explained as only applying to a particular brand of refrigerator. The advertisement also claims that purchases will be delivered free, but the small print again qualifies the claim by limiting it to pensioners. Although the small print is legible, nothing is done to draw the attention of a reader to its presence.

Consider whether these facts give rise to the offence of misleading pricing.

15. The MegaSave Emporium carries on its shelves tins of peas labelled as 'MegaSave produce'. An asterisk carries a reference to a note at the foot of the label which states that: 'This product was made and packaged on behalf of the MegaSave Emporium by Village Enterprises'. A purchaser of a tin of peas is made ill because of an impurity in the food. To what extent are the supermarket and the producer liable to the consumer? Would your answer differ in any way if the tin were not labelled as 'MegaSave produce', but if the product were imported by the supermarket from Sweden?

16. Examine the scope of the Consumer Protection Act 1987 with particular reference to property damage and the categories of excluded goods.

17. A drug is placed on the market after years of testing and the obtaining of Government approval. The drug company conducted an exhaustive range of tests on the product, on both volunteers and animals. In addition, their research staff kept a close watch on all medical and legal journals to see if the drug was in a category which had led to any problems. None was ever revealed. After the drug has been on the market for six years, it becomes clear that it is responsible for certain highly unpleasant and occasionally fatal side-effects.

How far is the drug company liable for these defects and what defences could be available?

18. The Our Baby Shop supplies a high chair which can be used as a simple chair or which, when fully assembled, can be used as a high chair. It is perfectly safe when used as an ordinary chair but, when assembled as a high chair, it tilts dangerously and both baby and food are placed in peril.

The chair is of a type for which no relevant safety regulations or standards exist. The parents become exasperated with their purchase and one day go to a local jumble sale. There they discover a high chair, which can be used as an ordinary chair, but which has been made by a parent for the purposes of the sale. They buy this, but it, too, turns out to be unsafe.

Consider the implications of these facts for both Our Baby Shop and the local parent with regard to the general safety requirement.

19. Give an account of the powers which are open to the Secretary of State for Trade and Industry and local enforcement officers with regard to banning and destroying unsafe goods.

20. A bun sold by Gourmand Foods is found to contain a dead beetle. It is found as a fact that the insect's presence in no way affects the safety of the food.

To what extent has an offence been committed by the seller?

21. Compare the food safety requirement with the general safety requirement.

22. Give an account of the powers available to local enforcement officers and the Minister of Agriculture, Fisheries and Food in relation to food and food premises which pose a health risk.

23. In what circumstances can an agreement giving rise to an otherwise binding agreement be cancelled by a consumer with no liability on his part?

Competition Law

A number of enactments regulate the way in which businesses are regulated in relation to their conduct of that business, specifically in regard to whether that conduct is anti-competitive. These enactments are concerned both with agreements between businesses, and the individual conduct of a business when not acting with another. It will be seen later in the chapter, that this is an area where the UK's membership of the EC is of considerable importance.

Restrictive Trade Practices Act 1976

1. Restrictive trading agreements

The Restrictive Trade Practices Act 1976 provides for the registration of restrictive trade agreements. An agreement is subject to registration with the Office of Fair Trading if the parties carry on business within the UK and the agreement is one under which restrictions are accepted by two or more parties in respect of such matters as the prices to be charged, the terms and conditions of supply, or the persons to or for whom, or the areas or places in which the goods or services are to be supplied.

Similarly, recommendations made by a trade association or a service supply association to its members which specify action to be taken in respect of any matters which would be registrable if the subject of a restrictive agreement between the parties, are themselves registrable. So, for example, a recommendation from an association as to the terms and conditions to be used by the membership would be registrable with the Office of Fair Trading.

2. Information agreements

The Act also applies to information agreements. These are agreements under which obligations are accepted by parties to exchange information about their selling prices or the terms and conditions of supply. Certain categories of agreement are excluded from the requirement of registration. These include agreements under which the sole restrictions relate exclusively to the supply of goods or services outside the UK, most sole agency agreements and most bilateral contracts of sale. Agreements under which the only restrictions relate to the supply of a professional service are also excluded, the most important being those where the information furnished has already been published in a manner making it readily available to customers.

3. Particulars of a registrable agreement

Particulars of a registrable agreement must be furnished to the OFT before the restrictions are to take effect, or, if the operation of the restrictions is postponed for more than three months after the agreement is made, within three months of the making of the agreement. If the time requirements are not complied with, then the agreement is void in respect of the restrictions and it is unlawful for any party who carries on business within the UK to give effect to, or to enforce them.

It is not a criminal offence to give effect to a void restriction, but the Director General of Fair Trading may apply to the Restrictive Practices Court for a restraining order. In addition, any person who has suffered loss as a result of the unlawful operation of a void restriction may bring civil proceedings for the recovery of damages for breach of the statutory duty owed to him.

4. Following registration

An agreement continues to have effect after registration, but the Director General of Fair Trading has a duty to refer it to the Restrictive Practices Court for it to determine whether or not the restrictions are contrary to the public interest. However, where he has made a representation to the Secretary of State for Trade and Industry, the DGFT may receive a direction discharging him from taking proceedings on the ground that the restrictions are not of such significance as to call for their investigation by the RPC.

A restriction is generally considered of significance if it

appears capable of causing detriment of which the RPC would be likely to take account if the agreement containing the restriction came before it.

5.   The gateways

Where an agreement is referred to the RPC, it is for it to decide on the basis of criteria laid down in the 1976 Act (generally referred to as the 'gateways') whether each restriction in the agreement is contrary to the public interest. A restriction is deemed to be contrary to the public interest unless the parties satisfy the RPC that it meets at least one of the eight criteria specified in the Act. In addition, the parties must prove that it is not unreasonable, having regard to the balance between the matters established in connection with a gateway and any detriment to the public or to persons not party to the agreement resulting from the operation of the restriction. This further requirement is generally referred to as the 'tailpiece'.

Where any restriction is found by the RPC to be contrary to the public interest, the RPC may make an order to restrain the parties from giving effect to the agreement.

6.   The Treaty of Rome

Article 85 of the Treaty of Rome provides that agreements between undertakings are banned, as are decisions of associations of undertakings and concerted practices, if they may affect trade between EC countries and which have as their object or effect the prevention, restriction or distortion of competition within the Common Market. The Article specifies a number of practices, including:

(a) those which directly or indirectly fix purchase or selling prices or any other trading conditions;
(b) those which limit or control production, markets, technical development, or investment;
(c) those which share markets or sources of supply.

Fines may be imposed for infringement of the Treaty provisions.

The EC Commission has the power to exempt agreements from the restriction imposed by Article 85, and has also issued block exemptions covering certain categories of agreement (covering, for example, agreements relating to turnover level; agreements relating to exclusive purchasing and supply; certain know-how agreements, etc.).

Resale Prices Act 1976

7. Resale price maintenance

The Resale Prices Act 1976 provides for the prohibition of minimum resale prices maintained by contract or agreement. Any term seeking to impose such a price is void. There is, however, nothing to restrict the notification or publication by the supplier of prices recommended as appropriate for the resale of the goods.

The Act also bans minimum resale prices maintained by a supplier outside any contract or agreement. Thus, it is unlawful for a supplier to withhold supplies on the ground that the dealer sells below the resale price. However, the Act does allow a supplier to take protective action to prevent the use of his goods as 'loss leaders'. Goods are loss leaders if they are sold by a dealer, not for the purpose of making a profit, but for the purpose of attracting customers likely to purchase other goods, or otherwise for the purpose of advertising the dealer's business. Supplies can be withheld from a dealer if the supplier has reasonable cause to believe that, within the previous twelve months, the dealer used any goods of the same or similar description as loss leaders.

Exempted goods

With the leave of the RPC, application may be made to it for a declaration that particular goods shall be exempted from the restrictions on resale price maintenance. An exemption order may be made if the RPC thinks that, without resale price maintenance:

(a) the quality or varieties of the goods available for sale would be substantially reduced;

(b) the number of outlets would be substantially reduced; *or*

(c) the retail prices of the goods would in general and in the long run be increased; *or*

(d) the goods would be sold by retail under conditions likely to cause danger to health in consequence of their misuse by consumers; *or*

(e) services provided in connection with or after the retail sale of the goods would cease or be substantially reduced.

The RPC must also be satisfied that in any of these cases the resultant detriment to the public outweighs any detriment resulting to them from the maintenance of minimum resale prices. Exemptions apply in relation to medicaments and to books subject to the net book agreement.

8. Not all resale price agreements are illegal

The RPA provides that individual resale price maintenance continues to be lawful where goods are sold by the supplier, subject to a condition which is not unlawful as to the price at which the goods may be resold. In relation to medicaments and books within the net book agreement (*see* **7** above) minimum resale prices can be lawfully maintained and enforced. Maximum resale prices can always be specified and lawfully enforced.

There are no criminal sanctions for any contravention of the provisions prohibiting minimum resale price maintenance. Compliance with those provisions is enforceable by civil proceedings on behalf of the Crown for injunction or any other appropriate relief. Civil proceedings may also be brought by any person affected by an infringement of the provisions for damages for breach of the statutory duty owed to him.

9. Free movement of goods

Article 30 of the Treaty of Rome provides that the Member States cannot as between themselves erect barriers to trade or measures which have equivalent effect. It is not often that Member States establish direct and intended barriers to trade, so that the majority of cases to go before the European Court of Justice relate to measures which have equivalent effect.

In the *Cassis de Dijon* case (1978) West Germany banned the import of a liqueur which was lawfully made in France because it did not comply with local law as to product descriptions. The European Court ruled that West German law was a measure having equivalent effect to a barrier to trade, since, under Article 30, once a product has been lawfully made and marketed in one Member State, it must be given access to all the markets of the other Member States, even if unlawful in the State to which the product is exported.

Following this decision, the UK was forced to drop its ban on the import of UHT milk and on fowl coming from regions where fowl pest was not treated by slaughter. It was ruled that the health measures put forward by the UK as reasons for the import bans were merely ways of imposing an unjustified ban on imports. However, Article 36 does permit barriers to trade if justified on grounds of protection of public health; and the European Court has accepted that consumer protection is a good reason for a barrier to trade so long as the measures adopted by the importing State are not out of all proportion to what is necessary in the circumstances of the case. The Court frequently holds that a complete ban is disproportionate if a simple relabelling of the product could convey to consumers sufficient information about the product.

Competition Act 1980

10. Domestic competition law

The Competition Act 1980 allows the Office of Fair Trading to investigate any trade practice which restricts, distorts or prevents competition. If the OFT concludes that such a practice has this effect, it can negotiate a settlement with the business concerned or it can refer the matter to the Monopolies and Mergers Commission (MMC) for it to decide if the public interest is adversely affected. If the MMC makes an adverse decision, the business must agree to make the appropriate changes in its practice. If it fails to do so, the Secretary of State for Trade and Industry can make an appropriate order.

The Secretary of State for Trade and Industry is also empowered under the Act to make what are generally called 'efficiency references' to the MMC of a particular business. No formal action need be taken on a report from the MMC in such a case, but the particular business will usually take up some or all of the recommendations made. There are also powers to investigate prices of 'major public concern'.

The Monopolies and Mergers Commission

11. Monopolies

Under the provisions of the Fair Trading Act and the Competition Act, the Monopolies and Mergers Commission has to report on any question referred to it in relation to:

(a) the existence of a monopoly situation (*see* below);
(b) the transfer of a newspaper or newspaper assets under the provisions of Part V of the Fair Trading Act;
(c) the creation of a merger situation qualifying for investigation under Part V.

In reporting, the MMC is required to take account of the desirability of:

(a) maintaining and promoting effective competition between UK suppliers of goods and services;
(b) promoting the interests of consumers, purchasers and other users of goods and services in the UK as regards price, quality and variety;
(c) promoting, through competition, the reduction of costs and the development of new techniques and products, and of facilitating the entry of new competition in existing markets;
(d) maintaining and promoting the balanced distribution of industry and employment in the UK;
(e) maintaining and promoting competitive activity in export markets.

A monopoly situation is determined with regard to whether one-quarter of the supply of goods or services is supplied by one person or an inter-connected group of persons or bodies corporate. A monopoly situation in relation to exports exists if these same criteria are fulfilled.

12. Mergers

The provision of the Fair Trading Act empower the Secretary of State for Trade and Industry to order that a merger should not proceed. The duty to keep mergers under review is that of the Director General of Fair Trading. It is open to him to recommend to the Secretary of State that a merger should be referred to the

Monopolies and Mergers Commission. The EC Commission has also jurisdiction in relation to certain mergers.

13. EC competition law

Article 86 of the Treaty also prohibits the abuse of a dominant position by an enterprise such that intra-Community trade might be affected. The Treaty gives the following as examples of abuse of a dominant position:

(a) the direct or indirect imposition of any purchase or selling price or any other trading conditions which are inequitable;
(b) the limitation of production, markets or technological development to the prejudice of consumers;
(c) the application of unequal conditions to parties undertaking equivalent engagements in commercial transactions, thereby placing them at a competitive disadvantage;
(d) making the conclusion of a contract subject to the acceptance by the other party to the contract of additional obligations which, by their nature, or according to commercial usage, have no connection with the subject of such a contract. The Commission can fine defaulting companies up to 10 per cent of turnover.

Specimen questions

1. Explain the functions and powers of the Monopolies and Mergers Commission and state what is meant by a 'monopoly situation'.

2. What agreements must be registered under the Restrictive Trade Practices Act 1976, and in what circumstances will such agreements be upheld?

3. The XYZ Co. manufacture and supply camera equipment to the retail trade. The camera trade is particularly aggressive and a great deal of price-cutting takes place. The manufacturers dislike this as it lowers their image and because it enables retailers to demand lower prices from the manufacturer. Accordingly, the manufacturers send a letter to all retailers who take their products stating that, while they are entitled to set such retail prices as they wish, preferential credit terms will be withdrawn if sales are executed below a stipulated minimum price.

Advise the recipients of such letters as to their rights.

4. Consider the implications of the following. A company in the UK markets cutlery in accordance with the prevailing legislation in that country. It then seeks to export its products to Belgium. However, an action is taken under Belgian law to prevent the export of the cutlery to that country on the grounds that the goods do not bear an indication of origin as required by Belgian law. It is confirmed by Belgian lawyers that, once the cutlery is marked 'Made in the UK', it will be given free access to the Belgian market.

5. The ABC Co. hires out office equipment throughout the Midlands and the south of England. It stipulates as part of its contractual arrangements that any repairs or maintenance must be done through its own engineers or from officially approved franchises. A number of office managers complain that this cuts them off from cheaper alternatives.

Advise the managers both with regard to Community and domestic law.

6. Company A, based in the Netherlands, and company B, based in Italy, have a big market, individually and collectively, in the market for over-the-counter drugs. Each has a dominant position in its own country. They come to an agreement between themselves not to compete in the other's country. In addition, they each agree not to supply third parties who would then supply outlets in the other's country.

Comment on the legality of such manoeuvres in relation to the Treaty of Rome.

Progress test 6

Consumer protection and fair trading

1. What descriptions constitute trade descriptions for the purposes of the Trade Descriptions Act 1968? **(17: 1)**

2. Explain how it can be possible to disclaim liability under the Trade Descriptions Act. (17: **1**)

3. Explain what is meant by saying that liability under s. 1 of the Trade Descriptions Act 1968 is an offence of strict liability and state how this can be mitigated by the 'due diligence' defence. (17: **2**)

4. To what extent does the Trade Descriptions Act 1968 cover statements made in relation to services, accommodation and facilities? In what ways does s. 14 of the Act differ from s. 1? (17: **3**)

5. In certain circumstances, the person whose act or default led to the commission of an offence under the Trade Descriptions Act 1968 can be charged with the commission of the offence. What are these circumstances? (17: **4**)

6. Give an account of the duties imposed on those who issue trading stamps and the rights of customers who collect them. (17: **5–6**)

7. Give an account of the functions of the Consumer Protection Advisory Committee. (17: **7**)

8. Explain the procedure by which written assurances can be obtained from traders who break the law. (17: **7**)

9. The Fair Trading Act 1973 provides for codes of practice and also sets out to control pyramid selling. Give an account of both of these aspects to the Act. (17: **7, 8**)

10. Explain the powers of the Director General of Fair Trading to ban estate agents. (17: **9**)

11. What are the duties of an estate agent in relation to client funds? (17: **9**)

12. What duties are laid on an estate agent before an estate agency contract is made? (17: **10**)

13. What rules apply where an estate agent has or may have a personal interest in relevant land? (17: **11**)

14. Give an account of the defence applicable in relation to offences under the Estate Agents Act. (17: **12**)

15. Give an account of the licensing provisions imposed by the Consumer Credit Act 1974, and explain the consequences of unlicensed trading. (9: **75, 77, 91**; 17: **13, 15**)

16. To what extent are there rules relating to the form of agreements falling within the Consumer Credit Act 1974? (9: **78, 79**; 17: **14**)

17. Explain when an agreement for credit or hire may be cancelled. (9: **81**; 17: **14**)

18. What are the rules as to how prices must be indicated? (17: **16**)

19. Give an account of how the law controls misleading indications as to price and explain the operation of the Code of Practice for Traders on Price Indications. (17: **16–17**)

20. What liability is imposed, and on whom, by Part I of the Consumer Protection Act 1987, in relation to damage caused by defective products? (17: **21**)

21. To what extent is agricultural produce within Part I of the Consumer Protection Act 1987? (17: **22**)

22. A person's property is damaged because of a defective product he has bought. To what extent does the amount of damage done determine whether a claim can be brought? (17: **22**)

23. What defences are available to a person sued under Part I of the Consumer Protection Act 1987? (17: **23**)

24. What is the 'general safety requirement' and to what goods does it apply?   (17: **24**)

25. To what extent can it be said that the general safety requirement does not impose 'absolute' liability?   (17: **25**)

26. Explain what is meant by safety regulations and state what goods can be subject to such regulations.   (17: **26**)

27. The Secretary of State for Trade and Industry, and local enforcement authorities, have certain powers in relation to unsafe goods. What are these powers?   (17: **27–29**)

28. It is an offence under the Food Safety Act 1990 to supply any food not of the 'nature or substance or quality' demanded by the purchase. Explain what this means.   (17: **30**)

29. What are the penalties for an offence as described in Question 28 above and what defences are available?   (17: **30**)

30. What is the 'food safety requirement': what penalties and defences are available?   (17: **31**)

31. Under what circumstances can food be seized and condemned?   (17: **31**)

32. When can improvement notices and prohibition orders be made against the proprietor of a food business?   (17: **32, 33**)

33. (*a*) What actions can be taken in relation to food emergencies? (*b*) What penalties and defences are available in relation to orders which might be made?   (17: **33**)

34. What rules apply with regard to the registration and licensing of food premises?   (17: **34**)

35. State briefly the controls applied to the marketing of medicines.   (17: **35**)

36. Give an account of those circumstances where an agreement can be cancelled. (17: **35–38**)

Competition law

1. Explain the nature of a registrable agreement under the Restrictive Trade Practices Act 1976, saying what particulars have to be furnished to the Office of Fair Trading and when, and what happens when a registrable agreement is not registered. (18: **1–3**)

2. Give an account of the procedure following registration. Say what is meant by the 'gateways' and the 'tailpiece'. (18: **4–5**)

3. To what extent does the Treaty of Rome also cover restrictive agreements between parties? (18: **6**)

4. To what extent is the establishment of a minimum resale price prohibited? (18: **7**)

5. Give an account of those circumstances in which it will be lawful to maintain prices, whether minimum or maximum. (18: **7–8**)

6. To what extent are barriers to trade, direct or indirect, between member States of the EC banned? (18: **9**)

7. Set out the main features of the Competition Act 1980. (18: **10**)

8. Explain the functions and powers of the Monopolies and Mergers Commission and say what is meant by a 'monopoly situation'. (18: **10–12**)

9. What is meant by a 'monopoly situation' and set out the powers which exist in relation to the control of monopolies and mergers. (18: **11–12**)

10. What control is exercised by the Treaty of Rome in relation to the abuse of a dominant position? (18: **13**)

Part seven

Bankruptcy

Bankruptcy

The whole of the law of bankruptcy has been substantially rewritten by the Insolvency Act 1986 which came into force in December 1987.

1. Introduction

While the Act legislates also for corporate insolvency (receiverships and liquidations), personal bankruptcy is dealt with in ss. 252–358 and in Schedules 5, 6 and 9.

The Bankruptcy Act 1914 is repealed, but the general intentions of the new law remain much the same:

(a) to identify cases of individuals' insolvency;

(b) to ascertain if the debtor's own proposals for a voluntary arrangement with his creditors are workable and acceptable; *and/or*

(c) to freeze debtor assets, and control them by the appointment of an even-handed caretaker;

(d) to pay to creditors what reasonably and realistically can be paid; *and*

(e) to rehabilitate the bankrupt.

Commencement of proceedings

2. Insolvency practitioners

The Act introduces a licensing procedure to ensure the professional competence, integrity and independence of practitioners in view of their considerable responsibilities to their parties. A person who holds office as: trustee in bankruptcy, liquidator, administrator or administrative receiver, or supervisor

under the new voluntary arrangement procedures is required to
be authorised.

3. Voluntary arrangements

The new voluntary arrangement procedure is available to any
debtor whether or not he is bankrupt. The purpose of the interim
order is to allow time for the formulation of proposals. The main
effects of the order are that during the period for which it is in
force, no bankruptcy petition relating to the debtor may be
presented or proceeded with, and no other proceedings or
execution or other legal process may be commenced or continued
against the debtor's person or property except with the leave of
the court. The individual concerned must intend to make a
proposal to a 'nominee' for a satisfaction of his debts or a scheme
of arrangement of his affairs.

4. Report by nominee

The nominee must form a professional judgment of the terms
of the proposal which the debtor is intending to put to his creditors.
Only if the nominee concludes that it would be worthwhile to put
the debtor's proposals to a meeting of creditors, and if he duly
reports to the court in those terms, will the court give the necessary
direction which has the effect of prolonging the duration of the
interim order pending the convening of a creditors' meeting.
Unless the nominee applies successfully for an extension to the
order, it lapses at the end of 14 days, from the date when it was
made, or at the end of the period which may be expressly given in
the order.

5. Creditors' meeting

Once a report has been made, a meeting of the creditors shall
be summoned unless the court orders otherwise. If the creditors
do not approve of the debtor's proposals, the court may discharge
the interim order, and the protection enjoyed by the debtor since
the order is discharged. If the proposal is approved, the
composition or scheme binds every person who has notice of and
was entitled to vote at the meeting, regardless of whether he in
fact attended or was represented at it, and regardless of whether
he voted for or against the proposal.

6. Implementation of approved composition or scheme

The person responsible for implementing an approved composition or scheme is known as the 'supervisor' who will either be the original nominee, or someone who was substituted for him, either by the court or the creditors.

7. Bankruptcy orders

Many aspects of the previous law and procedure regarding the commencement of bankruptcy proceedings have been completely eliminated. In particular, the whole concept of an 'act of bankruptcy' has been abolished, as has the preliminary species of order formerly known as the 'receiving order'.

(a) *Creditor's petition.* This introduced, in place of the former requirements relating to acts of bankruptcy, the new single concept of the debtor's apparent inability to pay the debt on which the petition is founded (or, in the case of a petition founded on a debt which is not immediately payable, if the debtor appears to have no reasonable prospect of paying the debt). The bankruptcy level is £750. The court has a duty to satisfy itself that the petitioning creditor's debt is either one that has become due and has in no sense been satisfied, or one which though not presently due for payment is a debt which the debtor has no reasonable prospect of being able to pay when it does fall due. The Act also effectively requires the creditor whose petition is based on a debt payable at a future time to show that circumstances have materially altered since he allowed the debtor to incur the debt, and that there was at the time a reasonable prospect, which has subsequently ceased to be operative, that the debt would be paid on time. The principle is retained from the earlier law that a debtor should not be adjudicated bankrupt if he is able to pay all his debts. The novel requirement is that the debtor must also have made an offer to secure or compound for the petitioning creditor's debt under circumstances where acceptance of that offer would have required the dismissal of the petition, and that offer has been unreasonably refused.

(b) *Debtor's petition.* The court is now required to give active consideration to the circumstances of each debtor presenting his own petition in order to establish whether the possibility exists for the conclusion of a voluntary arrangement between the debtor and his creditors. Even if this alternative to the making of a bankruptcy order is not undertaken, the court must still have regard to the appropriateness of invoking the summary administration procedure through the issue of a summary administration certificate. The aggregate amount of the unsecured bankruptcy debts must not be less than the small bankruptcies level, which will be determined in the Insolvency Rules.

8. Duration of bankruptcy

Persons who are adjudicated bankrupt for the first time will obtain an automatic discharge after three years from the commencement of bankruptcy, and in the case where the summary administration procedure is employed, that period is shortened to two years. Where a person has been previously adjudicated bankrupt, and had the status of undischarged bankrupt at any time in the period of 15 years prior to the date of commencement of his subsequent bankruptcy, it will be necessary for him to apply for discharge by order of the court, as it also will where a person is adjudged bankrupt on a petition based on a criminal bankruptcy order. A criminal bankruptcy order may be made under the Powers of Criminal Courts Act 1973. The procedure is designed to facilitate the recovery of the proceeds of criminal activity, or of compensation for the victims of such activities. Where an undischarged bankrupt who is eligible for automatic discharge after two or three years, as the case may be, is reported to the Official Receiver as failing or as having failed to comply with the obligations to which, as an undischarged bankrupt, he is subject for the time being, the court may make an order which suspends the running of the time up to automatic discharge.

9. Effect of discharge

The essential principle is that discharge releases the bankrupt from all those debts known as the 'bankruptcy debts'. These are any debt or liability to which the bankrupt is subject at the beginning of the bankruptcy or which, though the bankrupt did not become subject to them after the commencement of the bankruptcy (or even until after his discharge), arise from an obligation incurred before the commencement of the bankruptcy. The term 'bankruptcy debt' also includes any amount specified in a criminal bankruptcy order made against the debtor before the commencement of bankruptcy.

Discharge from bankruptcy does not release a bankrupt from any debt incurred by means of fraud or fraudulent breach of trust to which he was a party; from a fine, except with the consent of the Treasury; from other prescribed bankruptcy debts which are not debts provable in the bankruptcy; or from a bankruptcy debt which consists in a liability to pay damages for negligence, nuisance or breach of any duty, being damages in relation to personal injuries or from any order made in family or domestic proceedings, except to such extent as a court may order. Discharge from bankruptcy shall not affect the right of any secured creditor of the bankrupt to enforce his security for the payment of a debt from which the bankrupt is released.

10. Definition of bankrupt's estate

All property belonging to or vested in the bankrupt at the commencement of the bankruptcy is deemed to be part of his estate. This does not apply to such tools, books, vehicles and other items of equipment as are necessary to the bankrupt for use personally by him in his employment, business or vocation, or to such clothing, bedding, furniture, household equipment and provisions as are necessary for satisfying the basic domestic needs of the bankrupt and his family. A notable change in the rule regarding the vesting of the bankrupt's available estate in his trustee in bankruptcy is the abolition of the doctrine of 'relation back'. Another notable change in the law is the abolition of the doctrine of 'reputed ownership'.

11. Restrictions on dispositions of property

The making of a bankruptcy order has the effect of rendering void any disposition of property made by the bankrupt between the time of the presentation of the petition for the bankruptcy order which is subsequently made against him and the time when the estate vests in his trustee in bankruptcy, except to the extent that the disposition was made with the consent of the court or is or has been subsequently ratified by the court. A person is, however, protected from this particular provision if he either received the property in good faith before the day on which the order was made, for value, and without notice that the petition has already been presented, or if he is a person who derived his title from any such person. A special provision gives protection to bankers among others, who, after the commencement of the bankruptcy, honour a cheque drawn by the bankrupt before the commencement date in effecting a payment which is rendered void. The debt incurred by the bankrupt would, but for this particular provision, be provable in the bankruptcy because it was incurred after the commencement of the bankruptcy. However, provided that the banker did not have notice of the bankruptcy before the debt was incurred by, in this case, the banker's honouring the cheque, and provided also that it was not reasonably practicable for the amount of the payment to be recovered from the party by whom or on whose behalf payment was collected, the payment is deemed to have been made before the commencement of bankruptcy, with the effect that it will count as a provable debt in the bankruptcy.

12. Restrictions on proceedings and remedies

The Act provides for a moratorium under the control of the court in respect of all kinds of action and legal process against the person or property of a debtor or bankrupt, with effect from the moment of the presentation of a bankruptcy petition. The Act also provides that there is an exemption from the moratorium in respect of any creditors whose debts would not be provable in the bankruptcy; such creditors remain free to commence or continue any legal proceedings against the debtor pertaining to claims of that character. There is also a saving in respect of the right of a secured creditor to enforce his security notwithstanding the bankruptcy and the general terms of the moratorium imposed by the Act.

13. Interim receiver

The Act empowers the court, after presentation of a bankruptcy petition and before a bankruptcy order is made, to appoint the Official Receiver to be interim receiver of the debtor's estate where this is shown to be necessary for the protection of the debtor's property. This replaces the former provisions as to receiving orders. In most cases there will be an interval between the making of the bankruptcy order and the appointment of the trustee in bankruptcy in whom the bankrupt's estate will then automatically vest. During that period the Official Receiver is to be the receiver and manager of the bankrupt's estate, with the same powers as a receiver or manager appointed by the High Court. Immunity is granted to the Official Receiver when acting in the bona fide and reasonable belief that property which he is seizing or of which he is disposing is part of that which he is entitled to seize or of which he is entitled to dispose.

Proceedings after receiving order

14. Statement of affairs

The period of time allowed for the preparation and submission by the bankrupt of his statement of affairs is 21 days from the date of the bankruptcy order, and can be extended by the Official Receiver at his discretion. The Official Receiver also has the power to release the bankrupt from the duty to submit such a statement. It is intended that the Official Receiver should exercise his discretion under this provision to release a bankrupt who is too ill to lodge a statement of affairs, but in such cases the rules will provide that the Official Receiver will be subject to a duty to send out a report to all creditors explaining why no statement has been obtained.

15. Investigatory duties of Official Receiver

The Official Receiver is placed under a duty to investigate the conduct and affairs of every bankrupt and to report to the court if he considers it appropriate. Where the bankrupt applies for discharge, the Official Receiver must report to the court.

16. Public examination of the bankrupt

The holding of a public examination will only take place if the Official Receiver makes an application to the court for this to be done, and the court agrees. This reverses the previous law. It is also made possible for the creditors, or at least as many of them as represent one-half of the value of the bankrupt's debts, to serve notice on the Official Receiver requiring him to apply to the court for a direction that a public examination be held.

The trustee in bankruptcy

17. Summoning of meeting to appoint first trustee

The Official Receiver must decide within twelve weeks of the day on which the bankruptcy order is made whether to call a meeting of creditors for the purpose of appointing a trustee in bankruptcy. If he decides not to convene such a meeting, he is required to notify the court and all the creditors of the bankrupt and will be required at the same time to send the creditors a summary of the statement of affairs and a report thereon. Where no meeting of creditors has been summoned, or where the Official Receiver has decided not to summon a meeting, one-quarter or more in value of the creditors may require the Official Receiver to call a meeting. Where a general meeting of creditors is convened, but no appointment of a trustee in bankruptcy results, the Official Receiver must decide whether or not to refer the matter to the Secretary of State. If this is done, the Secretary of State may at his discretion appoint a qualified person to be the trustee in bankruptcy. If the Official Receiver decides not to refer the matter to the Secretary of State, or if the latter declines to make an appointment, the Official Receiver shall be the trustee in bankruptcy with effect from the date of his giving the requisite notice. The Act also gives the Official Receiver the general permission to apply to the Secretary of State for the appointment of a person as trustee in bankruptcy in place of the Official Receiver himself. The general rule is that the trustee may be removed from office only by an order of the court or by a general meeting summoned specially for that purpose.

18. Control of trustee

The Act empowers the creditors at a general meeting to appoint a committee to function for the purposes of the Act. A general meeting for this purpose may be convened by the trustee of his own initiative. If he elects not to convene a committee for this purpose, he can be compelled to do so if at least one-tenth in value of the creditors concur in formally requesting him to summon one. No meeting of creditors may establish a committee at any time when the Official Receiver is trustee, except where this happens in conjunction with the appointment by such a meeting of a person to replace him as trustee. However, the Act also provides for the functions which would otherwise be vested in a committee of creditors to be vested in the Secretary of State during any period when the Official Receiver is the trustee in bankruptcy, and to be likewise vested in the Secretary of State at any time when a person other than the Official Receiver is the trustee in bankruptcy but no committee of creditors has been established. The Act restates the former provisions of the Bankruptcy Act establishing a general principle that the trustee's actions are ultimately subject to control by the court at the instance of any properly interested party.

19. Liability of trustee

The Act establishes a summary procedure against the trustee in respect of loss to the estate caused by his misapplication or retention of property, or by his misfeasance or breach of duty.

20. Vesting of bankrupt's estate

The Act provides for the vesting of the bankrupt's estate in the trustee in bankruptcy immediately upon the latter's appointment taking effect. In the case where the Official Receiver becomes trustee, the vesting occurs simultaneously with his becoming trustee. All vesting of property by virtue of these provisions occurs automatically by operation of law, without the need for any conveyance, assignment or transfer.

21. After-acquired property

The Act establishes a procedure whereby any property acquired by the bankrupt after the date of the bankruptcy order may be vested in the trustee upon the latter's intervention to claim it. After-acquired property does not vest automatically in the trustee. Where notice has been served, and either before or afterwards a person acquires property in good faith for value and without notice of the bankruptcy, or a banker enters into a transaction in good faith and without such notice, the trustee shall not in respect of that property or transaction be entitled to any remedy against that person or banker, or any person whose title to any property derives from that person or banker.

22. Vesting in trustee of tools, clothes, etc.

Under the procedure established by the Act, the trustee may

claim by means of a notice in writing any item of the bankrupt's exempted property (*see* **10** above) which appears to have a higher intrinsic value than the cost of providing a reasonable replacement for the bankrupt or his family to use. The cost of providing a replacement is a first charge on the funds comprised in the bankrupt's estate.

23. Income payment orders

The court is enabled on the application of the trustee to make an income payment order whereby a proportion of the income of the bankrupt is claimed for his estate available for distribution to his creditors. The principle is laid down that any income of an undischarged bankrupt constitutes after-acquired property, so that the proper approach should be to ascertain by investigation what proportion of income can be regarded as 'necessary' for meeting the reasonable domestic needs of the bankrupt and his family.

24. Acquisition by trustee of control

The trustee is required to take control of the bankrupt's estate and of all his papers and records relating thereto. For this purpose, he is clothed with the power and rights enjoyed by a receiver of property appointed by the High Court, and may invoke any appropriate remedies for the purpose of invoking his rights of acquisition and retention. The bankrupt is required to surrender control of his property, papers and records to the trustee. Special provision is made with respect to the bankrupt's interest in a dwelling-house occupied by the bankrupt, his spouse or former spouse.

25. General powers of trustee

The Act gives extensive powers to the trustee and indicates which of them are exercisable on his own initiative without permission and which are exercisable with the permission of the creditors' committee if there is one. The former requirement that the trustee must obtain permission from the creditors' committee before employing a solicitor has been replaced by the requirement that where a trustee other than the Official Receiver employs a solicitor in the exercise of his powers, he must give notice of that fact to the creditors' committee if there is one in being at the time.

Where the trustee disposes of the property of a bankrupt to an associate of the bankrupt, he must inform the creditors' committee if there is one. The onus then rests with the committee to determine whether the transaction was abusive or not. It is also possible for the trustee to be challenged retrospectively on account of any transaction not initially received to be abusive and detrimental to the creditors' interests. The trustee is empowered to disclaim onerous property which is comprised in the bankrupt's estate. The Act also allows for the court to make a vesting order on the application of any person who has an interest in, or is subject to, a continuing liability in respect of any property disclaimed by the trustee.

26. Proof of debts

The proof of all bankruptcy debts by all categories of creditor is to take place in accordance with provisions to be contained in the rules. Interest is provable as part of a debt for any period up to the date of the making of the bankruptcy order. Payments in respect of any interest due for the period since the commencement of the bankruptcy will only be made if any surplus remains after payment in full of the preferential and ordinary debts.

27. Mutual credit and set off

The provisions as to mutual credit and set off apply where, before the commencement of the bankruptcy, there have been mutual credits, mutual debts or other mutual dealings between the bankrupt and any creditor of the bankrupt proving or claiming to prove a bankruptcy debt. An account is to be taken of what is due from each party to the other in respect of the mutual dealings and the sums due from one party shall be set off against the sums due from the other. Sums due from the bankrupt to another party shall not be included in the account taken if that other party had notice at the time they became due that a bankruptcy petition was pending. Only the balance, if any, of the account shall be provable as a bankrupt's debt or be paid to the trustee as part of the bankrupt's estate.

28. Manner of distribution of estate

When the trustee has sufficient funds for the purpose he is required, subject to the retention of such sums as may be necessary for the expenses of the bankruptcy, to declare and distribute dividends among the creditors in respect of the bankruptcy debts which they have respectively provided. The relevant provisions essentially re-enact the provisions of the Bankruptcy Act. However, there is no longer any provision requiring the trustee to distribute dividends at specified intervals of time. The following are the preferential debts: debts due to the Inland Revenue; debts due to Customs and Excise; social security contributions; contributions to occupational pension schemes, etc. and remuneration of employees. These debts shall be paid in full, unless there are insufficient funds available in which case they shall all be abated in equal proportions. Debts which are not preferential debts are subject to the same rules as to distribution. Bankruptcy debts owed in respect of credit provided by a person who was a bankrupt's spouse at the commencement of the bankruptcy rank after other non-preferential debts. The Act provides for the final distribution of dividend, or alternatively that no dividend, or no further dividend, will be declared. The Act also provides for the convening of a final meeting of creditors when the administration of the bankrupt's estate is complete. No such requirement is imposed in cases where the Official Receiver is acting as trustee, which is likely to be the case when the assets available for distribution are small. The purposes of the meeting are that the trustee should report on his administration of the estate and that the creditors should determine whether the trustee is to have his release. If the meeting resolves against release, he must apply to the Secretary of State to determine when his release becomes effective. If the final meeting does not resolve against his release, it is effective from the time he vacates office. There is no provision requiring the trustee to report on the outcome of the final meeting, but on his giving notice to the court that the final meeting has been held, together with a report of decisions there taken, the trustee is to vacate office.

29. Right of occupation, etc. of bankrupt's spouse

The Matrimonial Homes Act 1983 confers on a spouse without any beneficial interest in the matrimonial home rights of occupation as against the other spouse. Hitherto, where the spouse with a beneficial estate became bankrupt, the spouse without any such interest lost his or her rights of occupation against the trustee in bankruptcy. The Insolvency Act reverses that former position so that the spouse who has no beneficial interest in the property is placed in a similar position to a spouse with a beneficial interest. In the case of a spouse who already has a beneficial interest in the home, the trustee must make an application to the court before being able to sell the property concerned. The court's discretion is to make such orders as it thinks 'just and reasonable'.

Miscellaneous matters

30. Transactions at an undervalue and preferences

The general rule is that, where an individual is adjudged bankrupt and he has at any relevant time entered into a transaction with any person at an undervalue or given a preference to any person, the court may, on an application from the trustee, restore the position before the transaction or preference. A transaction is at an undervalue if: a gift is made to a person or the bankrupt otherwise enters into a transaction with that person which provides for him to receive no consideration; he enters into a transaction with that person in consideration of marriage; or he enters into a transaction with that person for a consideration the value of which, in money or money's worth, is significantly less than the value, in money or money's worth, of the consideration provided by the bankrupt. An individual gives a preference to a person if that person is one of his creditors or a surety or a guarantor for any of his debts or other liabilities, and the individual does anything or suffers anything to be done which has the effect of putting that person into a position which, in the event of the individual's bankruptcy, will be better than the position he would have been in if that thing had not been done.

31. Extortionate credit transactions

The court, on an application by the trustee, may vary or set aside any extortionate credit transaction between the bankrupt and the creditor. The Act provides that no application may be made by the trustee nor an undischarged bankrupt under the provisions of the Consumer Credit Act 1974 allowing for the reopening of extortionate credit agreements.

32. Contracts to which the bankrupt is a party

The court is empowered to discharge a contract between the bankrupt and another person, on the latter's application, on such terms as the court considers equitable.

33. Distress

The Act regulates the levying of distress by a landlord and by other persons on the property of the bankrupt. It generally restates the law formerly contained in the Bankruptcy Act.

34. Deeds of arrangement

A creditor who has not assented to a deed of composition is not bound by it, and can sometimes use it as grounds for filing a petition in bankruptcy against the debtor. The upheavals in bankruptcy law caused by the insolvency legislation have left the law on deeds of arrangement virtually untouched.

Progress test 7

Bankruptcy

1.   In what way are insolvency practitioners now subject to statutory control?   (19: **2**)

2.   Explain what is meant by a creditor's petition and by a debtor's petition.   (19: **7**)

3.   What is the duration of bankruptcy and what is the effect of discharge?   (19: **8, 9**)

4.   What are the powers of the trustee in bankruptcy?   (19: **25**)

5.   Explain how a bankrupt's estate is distributed.   (19: **28**)

Specimen questions

1.   Explain what is meant by bankruptcy petitions, bankruptcy orders and the commencement and duration of bankruptcy.

2. What is the effect of bankruptcy on rights of occupation of the family home?

3. Explain the position of a trustee in bankruptcy in connection with the following matters:

    (*a*) a lease held by the bankrupt;

    (*b*) a claim by a bankrupt for damages arising out of a collision between a Post Office van and the bankrupt's car while driven by him;

    (*c*) securities held by the bankrupt under a settlement created by his uncle.

Appendix
Examination technique

Questions in Business Law are of two types: (*a*) textbook questions — asking the student to expound or discuss a topic, e.g. 'What is specific performance and in what conditions will it not be granted?'; (*b*) problems — in which the facts of a case are given and the student is asked to apply the various appropriate rules of law and discuss the situation (or advise one of the parties), e.g. 'P's agent, A, exceeds his authority in contracting with C, and does not tell C that he is acting merely as an agent. Discuss'. (Or 'Advise C.')

These two types of question require slightly different approaches, but the following general points should always be borne in mind:

(a) First read the question carefully, to make sure you understand precisely what is involved. (If in doubt, underline *key-words*, or note the points you think are involved on a separate piece of paper.)

(b) Read the question a second time, noting down any points which may be involved but are not actually mentioned in the question. For instance in the problem on agency stated above: 'breach of warranty,' 'ratification,' 'agency by estoppel,' etc.

(c) Shuffle the points you have noted into a logical sequence. Thus in the agency problem above: (1) Agency; (2) Exceeding authority; (3) Breach of warranty of authority — damages; (4) Estoppel and Ostensible authority; (5) Undisclosed principal.

Time spent on these preliminary stages is not wasted. It helps you to put your answer into logical order, saves you time in writing, and — most important — shows the examiner that you have taken the trouble to plan your answer instead of leaping into the question without preparation. It will also make your answer easier to mark, and go some way towards endearing you to the examiner.

> NOTE: Citation of cases, etc. In studying law you should first learn the facts and names of leading cases; secondly, the facts of other cases; thirdly, the names of all. If in an examination you cannot remember the name of a case but can remember the facts, cite the facts on their own. If you cannot remember either name or facts it is permissible to invent facts of your own to illustrate an argument, providing you make it clear that they are your own invention. As to the method of incorporating cases in an answer, note the method used in the model answers below. (Remember always to underline case names and references to statutes; this is a legal tradition, and it also helps attract the examiner's attention.)

Textbook questions.
These test: **(a)** your memory of your textbook and notes; **(b)** your ability to organise your information. Therefore, before answering you should assemble your information carefully, and then write it down in a logical sequence. Use short sentences; long sentences tend to confuse you if you are in a hurry (and are also harder for an examiner to read).

In Business Law, textbook questions do not usually require a very detailed knowledge, but they do require that the information sought should be known precisely.

Example
'Summarise (or 'state briefly' or 'state' or 'describe,' etc.) the conditions and warranties implied in contracts for the sale of goods, and explain how these terms may be excluded.'

Model answer
Under the Sale of Goods Act 1979, the following conditions and warranties are implied in every contract covered by the Act (unless excluded by express agreement):

1. A condition that the seller has or will have the legal right to sell the goods at the time the property is to pass: s. 12(1).

2. A condition, in sales by sample, that bulk shall correspond with sample and that the buyer shall have reasonable opportunity to examine and compare, and that the goods shall be free of any

defect not likely to be apparent on reasonable examination: s. 15(2).

3. A condition in sales by description (where the buyer merely describes what he wants and leaves it to the seller to select the goods) that the goods shall correspond with the description: s. 13.

4. A condition or warranty as to quality or fitness is only implied in the following cases.

(a) Where the seller is a dealer in the goods sold, and the purchaser makes clear that he relies on the seller's skill and judgment, a condition is implied that the goods shall be reasonably fit for the purpose intended: s. 14(3).

(b) Where the seller is a dealer in the goods sold, there is an implied condition that they shall be of merchantable quality, i.e. of a quality generally acceptable: s. 14(2).

5. A warranty that the buyer shall enjoy quiet possession: s. 12(1).

Any condition (main term) or warranty (subordinate term) implied by the Act can be excluded by express agreement: s. 55(1). But exclusionary clauses are construed strictly against the party inserting them and certain clauses are in any case void against consumers: s. 55(3) and (4). The seller cannot avail himself of an exclusionary clause if he broke the contract in some other way: *Karsales Ltd* v. *Wallis* (1956). Thus where printed conditions of sale excluded liability for misdescriptions, it was held that the express and written exclusion was cancelled by an express oral representation: *Couchman* v. *Hill* (1947).

Problems
This type of question tests: **(a)** your understanding of the application of basic rules of law to an unfamiliar situation; **(b)** your ability to present a rational argument.

Conseqently you should (*i*) state the points of law involved in the problem, (*ii*) decide whether they are in fact applicable to the particular circumstances, and (*iii*) state your decision as to who is liable (if asked), etc. The most important parts of this answer are (*i*) and (*ii*). You can still get a good mark on a problem question, even if you fail to reach a decision on point (*iii*) or reach a wrong decision.
Example

'A is P's agent for the purchase of certain goods, and is authorised to pay up to £100. In fact he buys the goods from X at a price of £120. Can X enforce the contract against A and/or P? Would it make any difference to your answer if A had concealed the fact that he was merely acting as agent for P?'

Model answer
This question appears to involve two main points, namely (*i*) excess of authority by an agent, and (*ii*) the doctrine of the undisclosed principal.

Where an agent exceeds his authority, his principal incurs no liability to the third party, but the agent is liable for damages for breach of his implied warranty of authority: *Collen* v. *Wright* (1857).

The principal may however incur liability where:

(a) he ratifies the agent's transaction, in which case the agent ceases to be liable. Ratification is only possible where:
  (*i*) the principal had capacity to make the particular contract at the time the agent contracted, and at the time of ratification;
  (*ii*) the agent contracted expressly as agent for the principal, naming him;
  (*iii*) the principal was in possession of all material information or agreed to dispense with it;
(b) he is estopped from denying the agent's authority to make the contract in question, e.g.:
  (*i*) where the principal has held out the agent as having authority to make the contract in question (for instance where the agent has in the past made such contracts with the principal's concurrence); *or*
  (*ii*) where the agent's ostensible authority covers the transaction in question, even though he has exceeded his actual authority (for instance where the agent occupies a position which normally carries with it authority to make such contracts, and the principal has imposed restrictions on that authority which are unknown to X).

Thus a factor has implied authority to sell goods in his possession, and can give a good title to a purchaser even though he was instructed not to sell the particular goods: Factors Act 1889, s. 2.

The doctrine of the undisclosed principal would be applicable to the problem stated if A had concealed the fact of his agency. The doctrine is that in such a case the third party (here X) can enforce the contract against the agent, and on discovering the identity and existence of the principal has an alternative right of action against the principal.

In the problem therefore it is submitted that:

(a) X has a right of action against A for breach of his warranty of authority, and is entitled to damages whether the breach was innocent or fraudulent;

(b) X has no right of action against P, unless P ratifies the transaction or is estopped from denying A's authority.

Index

acceptance,
  bills of exchange, 251, 254–5,
    258–60, 263–6, 277
  sale of goods, 165, 167, 170–2
accident insurance, 210–11
accommodation party, 260
accord and satisfaction, 75–6
acknowledgements, 33, 78–9
Acts of God, 189, 191, 198–9, 210
affreightment *see* bills of lading;
  charterparties
agency, 34, 53, 74, 107–24, 197–8,
  327
  authority of agent, 116–18, 197–8
  bills of exchange, 254, 257
  definition and formation, 107–10
  duties of principal and agent,
    112–15, 122–3
  implied, 108, 128–9
  kinds, 107–8
  of necessity, 42, 110, 113
  partnerships, 128–30
  principals, named and
    undisclosed, 117–18
  sale and supply of goods and
    services, 169–71, 173, 180
  special classes, 118–19
agents *see* auctioneers; bankers;
  brokers; commercial agents; *del
  credere* agency; estate agents;
  factors; wives as agents
agreements (not contracts), 3–4
agriculture, 149, 329, 331–2
air, carriage by, 193–4
aliens, contracts by, 41
allonge, 257
American share certificates, 279
ancillary credit business, 182

anticipatory breach, 82
arbitration, 129, 226–36
  agreements, 227–30
  proceedings, 230–4
arrangement, deeds of, 372
assignment, 33, 92–4, 215, 229, 296
  legal and equitable, 93–4, 208, 296
  life insurance, 207–8
Athens Convention 1974, 197
auction sales, 172–5
auctioneers, 107, 126, 139, 173–5
average loss, 196, 214–15
awards, 55, 229, 231–2, 234–5

bailment, 22–3, 37, 218–24, 297–8
  definition, 218
  duties, bailees and bailors, 218–20
  innkeepers, 223–4
  involuntary bailees, 219–20
  power of sale, 221–2, 224
  types, 222–3
bank notes, 246, 277–8, 279
bankers, 119–20, 127, 268–76, 305
  bankruptcy, 275, 364
  collecting and paying, 273–4
  guarantees, 305
  negotiable instruments, 265,
    268–79
  securities, 297, 301
bankers' drafts, 278
bankers' liens, 301
bankruptcy, 359–72
  agency, 111
  arbitration, 229–30
  creditors' meetings, 360
  discharge, 77, 362–3, 372
  insolvency practitioners, 359–60
  married women, 42

negotiable instruments, 265, 275
nominees and supervisors, 359–61
partnerships, 126, 129, 134, 140
petitions, 361–2
proceedings and remedies, 359–65
property and estate, 360, 363–5, 367–70
public examination, 365
sale and supply of goods, 170
securities, 306–7, 311
statement of affairs, 365
trustees, 275, 359, 364–71
undervalue and preferences, 371
voluntary arrangements, 359–60
bankruptcy orders, 361–2, 368
barratry, 199, 214
barter, 150
bearer bills, 250, 253
bearer debentures, 246
bidding rings, 174–5
bills of exchange, 33, 61–2, 246–80
　address to drawee 248
　agency and partnership, 117, 129
　conditional payment, 253
　consideration and capacity, 249
　dates, 249, 252, 264, 269–70
　definition, characteristics, kinds, 247–53, 278–9
　illegality, 61–2
　inchoate bills, 251
　inland and foreign, 250–1
　lost or overdue bills, 252–3
　material alterations, 76, 251–2, 271–2
　order and bearer bills, 250
　parties and liability, 248, 258–64
　payment, 249–50, 253, 265–6, 270
　referee, 260
　sets, 251
　signature, delivery, indorsement, 129, 253–8
　sum payable, 249–50
　unconditional order bills, 248
　see also acceptance; bills of lading;
　　cheques; dishonoured negotiable
　　instruments; holders of bills;
　　payments, negotiable
　　instruments

Bills of Exchange Act 1882, 33, 247–53, 255
　cheques, 268–9, 273–6, 278
　partnerships, 129
　possessory lien, 301
bills of lading, 159, 166, 194–9, 246, 278–9
bills of sale, 296–7
breaches of contract and regulations, 7, 21–3, 35–7, 48, 57, 63
　agency and partnership, 110, 134–5, 325
　banker's authority, 275
　carriage of goods, 189
　competition law, 343
　condition, 25–6, 57, 72–3, 82–3, 151–2, 173, 200
　　quantum meruit, 11, 72, 86–7
　consumer protection and fair trading, 321–6, 331–2, 334–5
　discharge, 73, 77–8, 82–9, 363
　guarantees, 311
　insurance, 208
　sale and supply of goods, 164–5, 171–3, 180–1
　securities, 291, 298
　warranty, 25–6, 57, 73, 82–3, 116–17, 152, 173
　　carriage of goods, 190, 194, 197–200
British Rail, 187, 191–3
brokers, 118–19, 126, 215–16, 327
burglary insurance, 210
business names, 63, 127, 139
'by-pass' provision, 321

cancellation, 179, 326, 335–6
canvassing agents, 122
capacity, contractual, 8, 34, 41–5, 151, 249, 265
　guarantees, 305
　partnerships, 125
cargo, full and complete, 200
carriage of goods, 110, 166–7, 170–1, 187–201
　arbitration agreements, 236
　common carriers, 187–91

catalogues, 322

caveat emptor, 48, 52

charterparties, 171, 194, 198–201

chattels, 149, 222, 291, 296–7, 299–300

cheques, 251–3, 263, 268–76, 278–80

  agencies, 117, 120

  alterations, 271–2

  bankers, 272–5

  crossed, 251, 253, 270–3, 278

  customers' duties, 275–6

  definition, 268–9

  discharge of contracts, 74–5

  illegality, 61–2

  stale and overdue, 269

  undated and post-dated, 269–70

  see also dishonoured negotiable instruments; indorsements; payments, negotiable instruments

choses in action, 93–4, 296

choses in possession, 93

CIF (cost, insurance, freight), 166–7

clauses,

  arbitration, 227–30, 236

  average, 209

  cesser and lien, 200–1

  deviation, 195

  exclusion, 21–3, 154–8, 156–7, 173, 176–7, 189–90, 218–21

  'excepted perils', 196, 199, 210

  indemnity, 23

  meaningless, 24

  paramount, 199

  retention of title, 168

  suicide, 206

coercion, 8, 39, 58–9, 263

commercial agents, 110, 113, 119, 122–4

common law liens, 300–1

Common Market, 122–4, 193, 328–30, 344–7, 349

competition, 342–49

conditional orders, 278

conditional sale agreements, 150, 177, 180

conditions, 25, 48, 57, 151–3, 173, 296–7, 349

carriage of goods, 191–2, 198–201

  kinds, 25–6

  negotiable instruments, 253, 265, 278

  see also breaches of contracts and regulations, condition

confirming houses, 122

conflict of laws, 29–31

consensus ad idem, 3, 8

consideration, 4, 7–8, 43, 59, 64, 91

  bills of exchange, 249, 262

  bills of sale, 297

  executed and executory, 36–7

  guarantees, 303, 310–11

  real or past, 39–40

  rules relating to, 37–41

  valuable, 8, 36–7, 75–6, 262

Consumer Credit Act 1974, 22, 33, 62–3

  bailment, 222

  consumer protection, 303, 326–7, 336

  extortionate credit transactions, 371

  implied agency, 108

  negotiable instruments, 279–80

  sale and supply of goods and services, 177, 180–2

  securities, 293–4, 298

consumer credit agreements, 33, 63, 171–80, 326

  see also hire agreements; hire-purchase agreements

consumer protection, 173, 319–37

Consumer Protection Act 1987, 77, 173, 327–32

  game and agricultural produce, 239

Consumer Protection Advisory Committee, 323–4

continuing guarantees, 130, 302, 310–11

contra proferentem rule, 22, 28

contracts, 3–94, 302–12, 342–7

  agency and partnership, 58, 116–18, 325

  bailment, 218–21

  bankruptcy, 372

carriage of goods,   189, 194,
    197–9, 201
collateral,   28–9, 151, 180
common law illegality,   60–71
conflict of laws,   29–31
definition, classification,
    formation,   3–31
disabilities,   62–5
duress and undue influence,   58–60
executory and executed,   36–7,
    75–6
form,   19–21, 32–6, 151, 178
insurance,   203–6, 209–11
investment,   63–4
misrepresentation and fraud,
    52–8, 66, 153
necessaries for,   43–4
of record,   6
privity, doctrine of,   90–2, 107
restraint of trade,   67–71
sale and supply of goods and
    services,   149–80, 194–5, 220,
    326, 335–6
simple (parol),   7–8, 35, 37, 75
specialty,   6–7, 36, 76–7, 79
standard form,   19–21
substitution,   76, 129
transfer and assignment,   92–4
unenforceable,   8–9, 22, 35, 76, 181
variation of,   76
void *see* void contracts
voidable,   8, 26, 37, 42–3, 46, 52–60
work and materials,   150, 175
see also acceptance; breaches
    of contract and regulations;
    cancellation; discharge; capacity,
    contractual; consideration;
    clauses; mistakes; termination;
    terms
copyright,   33, 44
corporations,   42–3, 229
court orders,   134–5, 178, 182,
    226–9, 275, 324–5

damages,   25–6, 35, 37, 77–8, 82–6,
    343
  agency,   113, 116–7

carriage of goods,   188–90
consumer protection,   329
discharge from bankruptcy,   363
lapses of time,   77–8
liquidated,   85–6
misrepresentation,   54–6
release of debtor,   311
sale and supply, goods and
    services,   152–3, 170–4
dangerous goods,   188, 190, 195,
    331–2
dates, bills of exchange,   249, 252,
    264, 269–70
death,   14, 48, 76–8, 80
  agency and partnership,   111, 129,
      134–5, 140
  arbitration and awards,   229–30
  carriage of goods,   193–5
  guarantees,   306, 311
  insurance,   208
  negotiable instruments,   265, 274,
      277
  suicide and murder,   206–7
deceit *see* fraud
deeds,   6–8, 33, 75–6, 129, 297
defective products,   328–30
deferred creditors,   126
del credere agency,   108, 122
delivery,   31, 159, 163–8, 170–2, 296
  negotiable instruments,   253, 256
demurrage,   199, 201
deposit receipts,   278
deposits,   222, 325
deviation, route,   191–2, 195, 200,
    215
diplomatic immunity,   41–2
Directives, EC,   122–4, 328–9
directory entries,   133
disability,   62–5, 78
discharge,   40, 46, 72–89, 111, 215
  bankruptcy,   77, 362–3, 372
  breach of contract and remedies,
      73, 77–8, 82–9, 363
  by agreement,   75–6
  by performance,   72–5
  frustration,   79–82
  guarantor,   309–12
  insurance,   209, 215

negotiable instruments, 252, 265, 266, 268
operation of law, 76–9
statutory assignments, 93
disclaimers, 320
disclosure, 53–4, 58, 153
agency, 112–13, 117–18, 120, 325
insurance, 204–5, 208, 212
securities, 303–4
dishonoured negotiable instruments, 74, 253–4, 258–68
dispatch money, 199
distress, 372
dividends, 278
dock warrants, 279
domiciling a bill, 265
double insurance, 205–6
drunkards, 42, 151
due diligence defence, 320–1, 326, 328, 331–5, 337
duress, 58–9

employment, 33, 44, 69–70, 236
enemy nations, 66, 189, 199
equitable assignment, 94, 208, 296
equitable interests and mortgages, 295
equitable liens, 300–1
equity, mistakes in, 51–2
estate agents, 121–2, 126, 324–6
estoppel, 7, 109, 130, 160–1, 259–60
European Community, 122–4, 193, 328–30, 344–7, 349
evidence, 8, 34–6, 130, 197, 231–2, 235
ex post facto, 26, 82–3, 152, 173
ex turpi causa non oritur actio, 62
exchequer bills, 246
express appointment, 108, 113, 115
express terms and undertakings, 24–5, 27, 113, 115
extortionate credit bargains, 182

fact, mistakes of, 47
factors, 118–19, 122
fair trading, 323–37
families, 58–60, 125, 363

married women, 42, 109, 305
spouses, 3–4, 42, 44, 109–10, 126, 305, 370–1
see also marriage; minors; widows; wives as agents
fictitious/non-existing person, 260–1, 265–6
fire, 195, 198, 214, 222
insurance, 209–10
firm names, 63, 127, 139
fitness, 156–7, 175, 190, 220, 319
floating policies, 212
FOB (free on board), 166
food premises, 335
food safety, 328–35
Foreign Arbitral Awards, New York Convention on Recognition of, 227
foreign bills, 250–1, 301
forfeiture orders, 332
forgery, 120, 254–6, 273, 275
fraud, 8, 55–6, 78, 275
agents, 117, 324
arbitration and awards, 228, 230
bankruptcy, 363
bidding rings, 174
guarantees, 304
securities, 297
freight, 166, 195–6, 199–200
frustration, 79–82, 111

gaming contracts, 64–5
'gateways', 344
general average loss, 196, 214–15
good faith, 58, 61–2, 113, 117, 262–3, 363
goods,
on approval, 159
future, 150, 159
meaning of, 149–50
protected, 182
specific, ascertained, unascertained, 158–60
see also sale of goods; selling methods
goodwill, 135, 137–8
gratuitous bailment, 37
gratuitous services, 37

Green Card system, 211
guarantees, 23, 33–5, 45, 129–30,
    302–12
  continuing, 130, 302, 310–11
  specific, 302
guarantors, 34, 259, 266–7, 302–3,
    306–12, 371
Hague Rules, international, 197
hire contracts, 175–80, 220, 222, 326
hire-purchase, 27, 108, 175–83, 222,
    293–4
  liability, 180–1
  statutory rights, 179–80
holders of bills, 64, 197, 253,
    259–65, 279–80, 301
  for value, 263–4
  presumption in favour of, 263
holding out, 130

illegality, 8, 37, 60–71, 263
  common law, 65–7
  partnerships, 127–8, 134
  restraint of trade, 67–71
illness, 80, 210, 236
implied agency, 108, 128–9
implied terms and undertakings,
    7–8, 24–5, 27, 48, 113, 175
  agency, 113, 115–16
  carriage of goods, 194, 199–200
  Sale of Goods Act 1979, 151–8
  warranties, 116, 213–14
improvement notices, 334
inchoate bills, 251
income payment orders, 368
indemnities, 23, 34, 114, 213, 305,
    308
indorsements, 94, 253–8, 260–3,
    272–3
information agreements, 343
information, right to, 181
inherent vice, 189
injunctions, 88–9
injury, personal, 5, 78, 173, 193–5,
    211
inland bills, 250
innkeepers, 222–4, 300
innocent misrepresentation, 54–5,
    153

insanity *see* mental incapacity
insolvency *see* bankruptcy
insolvency practitioners, 359–60
insurance, 31, 44, 57–8, 64–5,
    203–16
  arbitration agreements, 236
  carriage and delivery of goods,
    166, 188
  double, 204–5
  insurable interest, 212
  kinds of policy, 212
  state supervision, 215–16
interest warrants, 278
interests, legal and equitable, 294–5
investment contracts, 63–4
involuntary bailees, 219–20
IOUs, 246, 279

joint and several liability, 74, 128,
    130, 180–1, 277–8
  guarantees, 306, 311

land,
  agency and partnerships, 126, 325
  arbitration agreements, 229, 236
  growing crops and attachments to,
    149, 331–2
  mortgages, 294
  restrictive covenants, 92
Land Charges Registry, 92
law, mistakes of, 47
lay days, 199
legal assignment, 93–4, 208, 296
legal interests and mortgages, 294–5
liabilities, acquisition of, 92
libel, 275
licences, 63, 178, 326, 335, 359
liens,
  agencies, 114, 119–20
  bailment, 222, 224
  carriage of goods, 191–2, 201
  sale and supply of goods and
    services, 159, 169–71, 173–4,
    188
  securities, 293, 299–301
life insurance, 48, 206–8
limitation of actions, 7, 77–9, 312
limited partnerships, 138–40

Lloyd's brokers, 215
London Clearing Docks, Committee, 272
London Transport Executive, 187
luggage, 192, 222–4
lunacy *see* mental incapacity

Manpower and Mergers Commission, 347
marine insurance, 211–15
maritime liens, 300
market overt, 162–3
marriage, 65–6, 371
  see also families; widows; wives of agents
medical conditions, 236
medicinal products, 331, 335
mental incapacity, 42, 78, 108, 111, 134, 140, 275
merchantable quality, 155–7, 175, 220
merger, contracts by deed 7, 76
mergers, 348–9
minors, 32, 42–5, 78, 126, 249, 307
misconduct, 60, 135, 192, 214, 230–1, 235
misleading conduct, 53
misrepresentation, 39, 52–9, 108, 136, 153, 180–1
mistakes, 8, 46–52, 78, 232, 320
  credit reference agency files, 327
  mutual and unilateral, 49–51
mixed policies, 212
mock auctions, 175
moneylenders, 59, 62, 297
Monopolies and Mergers Commission, 347–9
mortgages, 150–1, 177–8, 307
  insurance, 207–8, 215
  legal and equitable, 208, 295
  personalty, 295–6
  securities, 292–6
Motor Insurer's Bureau, 211

named principal, 117–8
National Freight Corporation, 187
necessity, agency of, 42, 110, 113
negligence, 21, 23, 37, 53, 77–8, 153

agency, 115, 120
arbitration awards, 231, 233
bailment, 220, 222–3
carriage of goods, 188–9, 191–5, 198
holder of bills in due course, 263
insurance, 209–11
liability for defective products, 328
pledges, 298
negotiability, 245–7
negotiable instruments, 53, 61–2, 94, 167, 245–80
  miscellaneous banking instruments, 278–9
  see also bills of exchange; cheques
novation, 76, 129

offers, 12–16
Office of Fair Trading, 63, 178, 298, 323–6, 342–3, 347–8
open cover, 212
operation of law, 76–9, 134
operative mistakes, 46–70
options, 15–16
order bills, 250, 253, 257
overdue cheques, 269
ownership, 158–60, 175, 176, 291–2, 295

partnership, 58, 63, 125–40
  agency, 128–9
  change of partners, 129–30, 132
  dealings with outsiders, 128–30
  dissolution, 133–8, 140
  formation, 125–7
  illegal associations, 127–8
  rights and duties in, 131–3
  tests for establishing, 126–7
passengers, 192–3
pawnbrokers, 294, 297–8
pawns, 218, 222, 293, 295–9
payments, 31, 73–5, 81–2, 93–4, 126, 167
  appropriation, 75
  instalments, 126, 183
  negotiable instruments, 53, 249–50, 253, 265–6, 270, 273–4
  part, 78–9

rules, 74–5
smaller sums, 40–1
penalties, 85–6, 328, 334, 337
performance, 21, 26, 31, 36–7, 87–8, 163–7, 172
 agency, 112–13, 115, 121
 discharge, 72–5
 impossibility of, 79–80
 partial, 36, 72
 sale and supply of goods and services, 163–7, 172
 specific, 51, 83, 87–8, 172, 229
 substantial, 73
perjury, 232
personal services, 76–7
personalty, mortgages of, 295–6
pledges, 218, 222, 293, 295–300
Policyholders' Protection Board, 216
possessory liens, 300–1
Post Office orders, 246
post-dated cheques, 269–70
power of attorney, 108, 111, 117, 129, 279, 305
power of sale, 221–22, 224
premiums,
 insurance, 208, 214
 partnerships, 135
prices
 competition law, 345–7
 indications, 327–8
privity, doctrine of, 90–2, 107
prohibition notices, 331–2, 334
promissory notes, 246, 276–8, 301
property, 8, 21, 44, 47, 60–1, 172, 236
 arbitration and awards, 236
 bankruptcy, 360, 363–5, 367–70
 consumer protection, 329
 estate agents, 121–2
 insurance, 208–11
 partnerships, 126, 132–3
 real and personal, 291–2
 recovery of transferred, 62
 sale, 121–2, 158–60, 167–9, 172–3
 securities, 291–5
pyramid selling, 324

quantum meruit, 11, 72, 86–7

quasi-contracts, 9–11
quasi-negotiable instruments, 278–9
Queen's enemies, 66, 189, 199

rail, carriage by, 191–3
ratification of agency, 109–10
rebates, 182
receipts, 74, 197, 246, 297–8
records, contracts of, 6
rectification, 51–2
referee, bills of exchange, 260
registration,
 agreements, 342–3
 bills of sale, 297
 business names, 63, 139
 companies, 33, 125
 partnerships, 139
re-insurance, 212
release, deed of, 75
representation, 152–3
resale price maintenance, 345–6
Resale Prices Act, 345–7
rescission, 54–8, 56–7, 60, 76
restitution, doctrine of, 44
restraint of princes, 199
restraint of trade, 67–71
restrictions, 21–2, 92, 263, 342–5, 363–4
Restrictive Practices Court, 343–6
revocation of offers, 14–15
risk, 159–60, 166, 191–2, 210, 214
road, carriage by, 190–1, 193
Royal Charter, 42

safety, 173, 194–5, 323, 328, 330–5
 emergency action, 334
sale of business, 70–1
sale of goods, 121–2, 149–75, 343
 acceptance, 165, 167, 170–2
 bailment, 221–3
 consumer credit, 177–83
 consumer protection, 319–24
 contracts, 149–60, 163–7, 171–3
 delivery, 163–7
 implied conditions, 151–3
 nemo dat quod non habet, 160–3
 passing of ownership and risk, 158–60

stoppage in transit, 169–70
under voidable title, 162
unpaid sellers, 167–71
warranties, 151–2
work and materials, 150
writs of execution, 161–2
see also auction sales; selling methods
Sale of Goods Act 1979, 24, 26–7,
149–61, 173, 179
common law lien, 300
lunatics, drunkards and minors, 42
trading stamps, 322–3
sea, carriage by, 194–201
secret profit, 113
securities, 61–2, 150–1, 208, 222,
253, 291–301
seller's lien, 169
selling methods,
by description, 154–5
by sample, 157
by sheriff, 161–2
goods on approval, 159
sale or return, 159
services, 31, 44, 120, 149–50, 175–7
gratuitous, 37
personal, 76–7
sets of bills, 251
several liability *see* joint and several
liability
severance, doctrine of, 61
sexual immorality, 65
share warrants, 246
sheriff, sale by, 161–2
shipowners, 194–200
signatures, 7, 19–20, 34–5, 46–7
agencies and partnerships, 117,
129
guarantees, 305
negotiable instruments, 249, 251,
253–8, 264
registration of business names, 63
simple contracts, 7–8, 35, 37, 75
specialty contracts, 6–7, 36, 76–7, 79
specific guarantees, 302
stale cheques, 269
standard form contracts, 19–21
statute-barred debts, 33
statutory assignments, 93–4, 208

stoppage in transit, 169–71
strict liability 320–1
subject-matter, mistakes of, 47
subrogation, 209–10
substantial performance, 73
substitution, 76, 129
'sum payable', 249–50
Sunday trading, 62–3
sureties *see* guarantees
suspension notices, 332

'tailpiece', 344
tenders, 18, 73–4
termination, 86–7, 151–8, 180–1, 326
agency, 110–12
bailment, 222
terms, 8–9, 23–5, 28, 34–5, 199,
152–3
certainty of, 23–4
ignorance of, 47
'innominate terms', 152
representation, 57
setting aside agreement, 51–2
see also breach of contracts and
regulations, conditions;
conditions; express terms and
undertakings; implied terms and
undertakings
theft, 189, 210, 298
third parties, 56, 61–2, 64, 74
agency, 107, 109–11, 113, 117–18,
123–4
sale and supply of goods and
services, 151, 180
time factors, 73–4, 77–8, 112, 163,
171, 229, 233–4
time policies, 212
timeshares, 336
trade barriers, 346–7
Trade Descriptions Act 1968,
319–21, 326–7, 336
'by-pass' provision, 321
trading stamps, 321–3
transfers, 32–3, 36, 44, 61–2, 92–4,
291–2
transit, meaning of, 170
Treaty of Rome, 344–7, 349
trust accounts, 275

uberrimae fidei, 54–5, 57–8, 204–5, 212, 303–4
ultra vires doctrine, 42–3
unconditional orders, 248
undated cheques, 269–70
undisclosed principal, 118
undue influence, 58–60
unenforceable contracts, 8–9, 22, 35, 76, 181
Unfair Contract Terms Act 1977, 5, 21–3, 154–8, 175–7, 220
   arbitration and awards, 226, 236
   carriage of goods, 189–90, 193
unpaid sellers, 167–71
unvalued policies, 212

valuable consideration, 8, 36–7, 262
valued policies, 212
vicarious liability, 114–15
void contracts, 8, 14, 22, 26, 32, 37, 46–52
   competition law, 343, 345
   corporations, 42–3

frustration, 79
illegality and restraint of trade, 60–71
presumption in favour of validity, 61
voidable contracts, 8, 26, 37, 42–3, 46, 52–60
voidable title, 162
voyage policy, 212

wagers, 64–5, 203
warranties, 12, 22, 25–6, 57, 152, 174
   agencies, 116–17
   carriage of goods, 190, 194
   consumer protection, 322–3
   implied, 151–4, 156, 213–14
   marine insurance, 213–14
widows, 44, 126
withdrawal, right of, 179
witnesses, 7, 229, 232, 297
wives as agents, 42, 109–10
writs of execution, 162